MW00835202

NATURE'S RETURN

NATURE'S

An Environmental
History of Congaree
National Park

RETURN

Mark Kinzer  THE UNIVERSITY OF SOUTH CAROLINA PRESS

© 2017 University of South Carolina

Published by the University of South Carolina Press
Columbia, South Carolina 29208

www.sc.edu/uscpress

Manufactured in the United States of America

25 24 23 22 21 20 19 18 17 10 9 8 7 6 5 4 3 2 1

Library of Congress Cataloging-in-Publication Data
can be found at http://catalog.loc.gov/.

ISBN: 978-1-61117-766-4 (hardcover)
ISBN: 978-1-61117-767-1 (ebook)

This book was printed on a recycled paper with 30 percent
postconsumer waste content.

To Nancy, Emily, and Ben
and
to the memory of my father,
James R. Kinzer,
who indulged my love of nature from an early age.

Nature is always ready to retake what we abandon and pursue tranquilly her ordinary course, serene and beautiful and timeless, which, when observed with loving understanding, has the power to confer some of that beauty and some of that serenity on the receptive heart.

Archibald Rutledge, *Santee Paradise*, 1956

Contents

List of Illustrations   *ix*

Acknowledgments   *xi*

Chronology   *xiii*

Introduction   *1*

1 | Managing the Presettlement Landscape   *7*

2 | First Settlement, Land Clearing, and the Open Range   *28*

3 | The Rise of Plantation Agriculture   *47*

4 | Early Park Plantations   *69*

5 | Reclaiming the Floodplain   *87*

6 | The Location and Extent of Historic Clearing   *101*

7 | Industrial Logging: First Inroads, 1870–1918   *125*

8 | Logging after 1920   *161*

Conclusion: The Impact of Human Disturbance   *182*

Appendix A: Selected Floodplain Cultural Features   *195*

Appendix B: Biographical Sketches   *205*

Notes   *219*

Bibliography   *267*

Index   *291*

List of Illustrations

Figures

1   Floodplain Microtopography and Associated Forest Cover Types   *12*

2   Joel Adams Sr.   *33*

3   Major General Charles Cotesworth Pinckney   *43*

4   Edward Rutledge   *43*

5   Brigadier General Isaac Huger   *55*

6   Colonel William Thomson   *56*

7   Detail from Marmaduke Coate's *Survey of Richland District, 1820*   *65*

8   Plat Showing Spigener's Fields, 1839   *89*

9   Relation of Soil Types to Topography at Congaree National Park   *111*

10   A Large Sweet Gum, Richland County, ca. 1904   *120*

11   Dense Canebrake, South Carolina, ca. 1904   *121*

12   Tupelo Gum Slough, Congaree River, ca. 1904   *121*

13   A Cypress Slough in the Dry Season, ca. 1904   *122*

14   A Large Cottonwood, Richland County, ca. 1904   *122*

15   Second-Growth Sweet Gum, Ash, Cottonwood, and Sycamore, on Hardwood Bottomland, ca. 1904   *123*

16   Francis Beidler   *133*

17   Hardwood Bottomland Recently Logged, Richland County, ca. 1904   *152*

18   Peeled Sweet Gum Logs Seasoning in the Woods, ca. 1904   *154*

Maps

1   Congaree National Park, Showing the Beidler Tract   *xiv*

2   Congaree National Park, Parcel and Tract Numbers   *xv*

3   Congaree National Park, Boardwalk and Trail System   *xvi*

4   Partial Route of the Hernando de Soto Expedition (1540)   *19*

5   Route of the Juan Pardo Expeditions (1566–67, 1567–68)   *21*

6 | Known Plantations in the Park ca. 1785   *71*

7 | Known Plantations in the Park ca. 1850   *93*

8 | Vegetation Associations Linked to Possible Past Agricultural Activity   *106*

9 | Known Sites of Land Disturbance, Eighteenth through Early Twentieth Centuries   *108*

10 | Logging in the Beidler Tract and Vicinity, 1969–1978   *166*

11 | Park Cultural Features Described in Appendix A   *195*

Tables

1 | Recognized Periods of Human Occupation in South Carolina prior to European Settlement   *8*

2 | Corn Production in 1860, Beidler Tract Landowners   *64*

3 | Slave Ownership in Richland District (Excluding Columbia), 1790–1840   *66*

4 | Selected Entries from Ledger Book for Plantations Owned by C. C. Pinckney and E. Rutledge, 1784–1787   *74*

5 | Assets of Congaree Lumber and Veneer Company, July 1890   *130*

6 | Timber Shipments on the Congaree River, 1894–1897   *132*

7 | Acquisition Data, Beidler Tract Parcels   *137*

8 | Beidler Tract and Vicinity: Timber Deeds/Timber Leases, 1896–1907   *140*

9 | Average Cost to Log Bottomland Sites in 1914   *148*

10 | Profitability of Various Bottomland Species in 1914   *154*

Acknowledgments

Not a time goes by when walking the trails at Congaree National Park that I don't find myself thanking the men and women whose efforts led to the protection of this magnificent forest. I feel privileged and grateful that two of these individuals, John Cely and Richard Watkins, have encouraged me in the writing of this book. Without their wise counsel and deep knowledge of local history, this book could never have been written. John's beautifully drawn maps, in particular, are not only arresting works of art but essential resources in understanding the natural and cultural history of the park. Dick Watkins is legendary for his wealth of knowledge about the history of the park and the lower Congaree valley generally. Dick's unwavering commitment to getting details absolutely right has set a standard I have attempted to live up to in my own work.

I have had the pleasure of consulting a number of very knowledgeable people during the writing of this book. For discussing their research and responding to questions, I would like to thank Bruce Allen, Gavin Blosser, Tom Fetters, L. L. Gaddy, Paul Gagnon, Robert Jones, John Kupfer, Kimberly Meitzen, Matthew Ricker, David Shelley, Rebecca Sharitz, and Gail E. Wagner. Special thanks go to Rebecca Sharitz of the Savannah River Ecology Laboratory for responding so generously years ago to a novice posing questions about bottomland hardwood forests. In a very real sense, that response and her team's research at the park led to the writing of this book. For supplying details about their family history, I would like to thank John McKenzie and Reggie Seay. Additional information about the park and its history was provided by Martha Bogle, Charles Broadwell, Jim Elder, Claire and David Schuetrum, Dr. Robert Taylor, Jackie Whitmore, and John, Rhonda, and Caroline Grego. Naturally, any errors of fact or interpretation in the book are entirely my own.

Staff members of the South Carolina Department of Archives and History have been unfailingly helpful in responding to my many inquiries, as has the staff at the South Caroliniana Library of the University of South Carolina and the Richland County Public Library. My colleagues in the National Park Service, both in the Southeast Regional Office and at Congaree National Park, have been quick to provide information and assistance whenever asked. I take great pride in working with them to further "America's best idea." It should be noted that the views expressed in this book are entirely my own and do not necessarily represent the views of the United States government, including the National Park Service.

I gratefully extend recognition to John B. Harmon for permission to publish his recollection of logging near Kingville in the 1940s. Quotations from the William Fishburne Papers and the Henry Savage Jr. Papers are courtesy of the South Caroliniana Library, University of South Carolina, Columbia. The quotation from the Joshua Evans diary and autobiography is courtesy of the Southern Historical Collection at the Wilson Library, University of North Carolina at Chapel Hill.

Lynne Parker prepared the maps and figures for the book. Her patience and forbearance through numerous revisions is greatly appreciated. I also gratefully acknowledge comments received from two anonymous reviewers for the University of South Carolina Press.

Finally, my children have never known a time when their father was not working on this book. At times it must have seemed that way to my wife, Nancy, as well. It is for their love and support that I offer my deepest thanks.

Chronology

1540	Spanish explorer Hernando de Soto traverses uplands to north of what is now Congaree National Park.
1566–1567 & 1567–1568	Spanish explorer Juan Pardo crosses park on two exploratory expeditions from coast.
1750s–1770s	British Crown issues majority of original land grants in park.
1756	John McCord operates private ferry on present-day Bates Old River (ferry is made public in 1766).
1786	Brigadier General Isaac Huger begins construction of ferry and approach road in park, about six miles upstream from McCord's Ferry.
1830s (?)	James Adams Sr. commences major dike project at western end of park.
1842	Railroad completed from Branchville to Columbia, crossing park.
1890s	Large-scale commercial logging begins in park.
1899–1907	Santee River Cypress Lumber Company acquires land and timber rights in park; begins selective logging ca. 1899.
Ca. 1914	Logging operations cease on Santee lands.
1969	Renewed logging on former Santee lands sparks campaign to preserve Congaree Swamp.
1976	Congress establishes Congaree Swamp National Monument.
2003	Congress redesignates monument Congaree National Park.

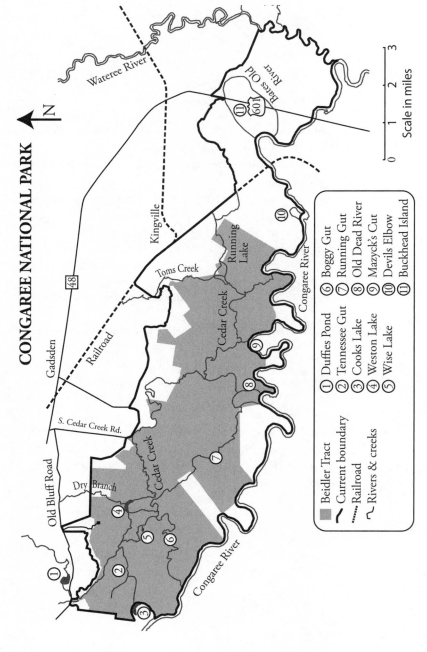

CONGAREE NATIONAL PARK

N

Gadsden

Kingville

Railroad

48

Wateree River

Bates Old River

109

Toms Creek

Running Lake

Cedar Creek

Congaree River

S. Cedar Creek Rd.

Old Bluff Road

Dry Branch

Cedar Creek

Congaree River

① ② ③ ④ ⑤ ⑥ ⑦ ⑧ ⑨ ⑩ ⑪

Beidler Tract
Current boundary
Railroad
Rivers & creeks

① Duffies Pond
② Tennessee Gut
③ Cooks Lake
④ Weston Lake
⑤ Wise Lake
⑥ Boggy Gut
⑦ Running Gut
⑧ Old Dead River
⑨ Mazyck's Cut
⑩ Devils Elbow
⑪ Buckhead Island

Scale in miles
0 1 2 3

Map 1. Congaree National Park, Showing the Beidler Tract. Map by Lynne Parker.

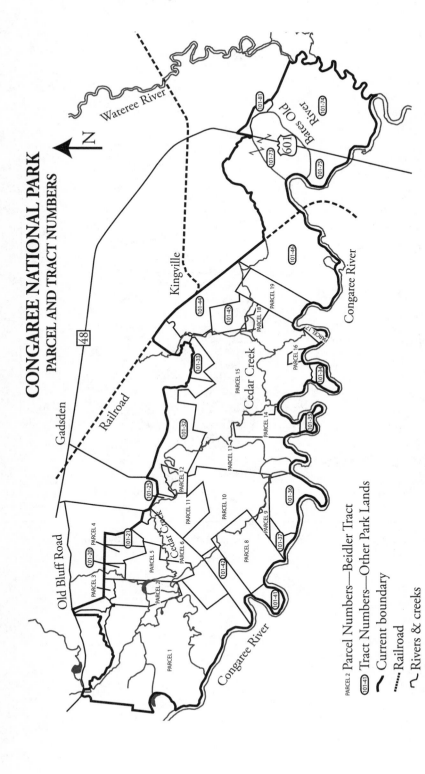

Map 2. Congaree National Park, Parcel and Tract Numbers. Map by Lynne Parker.

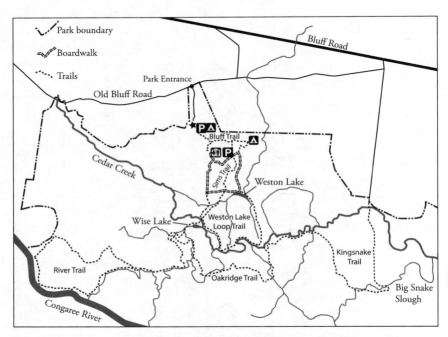

Map 3. Congaree National Park, Boardwalk and Trail System. Map by Lynne Parker.

Introduction

Actually the Congaree Swamp forest is a little bit on the young side even though it is a primitive or virgin stand.

James T. Tanner to Gary Soucie, 1975

CONGAREE, IT HAS BEEN SAID, is not everyone's idea of a national park. Small in size, it lacks the awe-inspiring natural wonders of a Yellowstone, Yosemite, or Grand Canyon. Congaree is a different kind of park, of a later era, meant less to preserve natural "wonders" and scenic grandeur than to protect an intact remnant of a major ecosystem. In this it resembles Everglades National Park, its principal forerunner in the national park system. But where Marjory Stoneman Douglas could confidently proclaim that "there are no other Everglades in the world," the same could hardly be said of the floodplain forests of central South Carolina. Bottomland hardwood forest once covered more than 24 million acres of river swamp from Maryland to Texas. More than 1 million of those acres occurred in South Carolina alone. Even today, this ecosystem remains widespread along the region's major rivers, albeit thoroughly cut over and much diminished in extent. What sets Congaree apart is not the ecosystem itself but the park's comparatively undisturbed core area. Within this core lies the largest surviving expanse of old-growth bottomland hardwood forest in the nation. Parts of this area appear never to have been significantly disturbed by humans. Others were last logged or cleared one hundred years ago or more.

Of course, not every important natural area makes it into the National Park System. For that to happen, an area needs advocates—and luck. The road to Congaree's designation as a national park took many twists and turns, but it started with a very rare bird, the ivory-billed woodpecker, and the decimation of that bird's bottomland habitat.

By the mid-1930s, the ivory-billed woodpecker was confirmed to exist in only one location, an eighty-thousand-acre tract of river swamp straddling the Tensas River in northeast Louisiana. Known as the Singer Tract (after its owner, the Singer Sewing Machine Company), the tract was said to be over 80 percent "virgin timber," the largest such tract in the country. Biologist James T. Tanner studied ivory-bills on the Singer Tract between 1937 and 1939, paying particular attention to the bird's dietary requirements and feeding habits. Tanner ultimately concluded that only old-growth bottomland hardwood forests like those on the Singer Tract provided the conditions necessary for the ivory-bill to escape extinction.

Largely as a result of this finding, Tanner and the National Audubon Society launched a campaign in 1941 to make the Singer Tract a national park. Almost immediately they found themselves opposed by the holder of logging rights to the tract, the Chicago Mill and Lumber Company. The officers of Chicago Mill and Lumber adamantly refused to relinquish these rights, mostly because of the wartime demand for lumber. Had it not been for the self-admitted "money grubbers" of Chicago Mill and Lumber, there might well have been a Tensas National Park today rather than a park at Congaree.[1]

Employing local labor and even German prisoners of war, Chicago Mill and Lumber hacked its way through the Singer Tract, the timber going to support the war effort in the form of PT boats, pallets, trucks, fuel tanks, and so on. Some was even used to make crates for shipping tea to the English army. In the meantime, the area that would become Congaree National Park somehow managed to escape the wartime ax. The old growth at Congaree was less extensive than the Singer Tract forest and had no documented sightings of ivory-bills, but its quality was such that veterans of the Singer Tract fight would one day push for its permanent protection and for essentially the same reason: within its borders lay an old-growth remnant of an otherwise common ecosystem, its age and scarcity making it critically important for those species requiring old-growth bottomland habitat.[2]

Early efforts by local conservationist Harry R. E. Hampton and others to protect the old-growth forest at Congaree failed to bear fruit. Hampton and Richard H. Pough (a cofounder of The Nature Conservancy) did manage to convince the National Park Service (NPS) to do a study of the area, and NPS study teams visited the swamp in 1959 and 1961. The NPS even published a report in 1963 recommending that "Congaree Swamp be favorably considered for addition to the National Park System as a National Monument."[3] However, a lack of public support and active opposition by the hunt club that leased the critical tract effectively nullified this recommendation. Interest in the proposal languished for almost a decade until the onset of logging in 1969 prompted renewed calls for a national park. A statewide citizen-action campaign ensued under the leadership of Jim Elder, a high school biology teacher from Columbia. The campaign demonstrated widespread public support for preservation of the swamp and managed to attract significant attention from the national press. After some initial reluctance, the state's congressional delegation came on board, clearing the way for legislation in 1976 that established Congaree Swamp National Monument.

In creating the monument, Congress sought to preserve and protect "an outstanding example of a near-virgin southern hardwood forest situated in the Congaree River floodplain in Richland County, South Carolina."[4] The "example" in question was the Beidler Tract, a 15,138-acre tract of mature and old-growth forest owned by the Beidler family of Chicago (map 1). The tract had been assembled at the turn of the twentieth century by the Santee River Cypress Lumber Company and its controlling officers, Chicago lumbermen Francis Beidler and B. F. Ferguson. For Beidler and Ferguson, the principal attraction of the lower Congaree was its extensive stands of virgin bald cypress *(Taxodium distichum)*, which filled the floodplain's myriad sloughs and swampy depressions. Santee logged old-growth timber on the tract from 1899 until around 1914, when marginal profitability (if that) and a glut in the cypress market convinced Beidler to cease operations. Thereafter Beidler's descendants turned their attention elsewhere, leaving the Beidler Tract uncut and largely untouched for the next half century.

In 1969 fiduciary obligations and rising timber prices led the family to resume logging on the tract. When cutting ceased in 1976, around 10,000 acres of old-growth bottomland hardwood forest still remained. Subsequent park expansions served to augment and buffer the Beidler Tract, resulting in an authorized boundary of approximately 26,640 acres. The monument was redesignated Congaree National Park in 2003.

At the time the monument was established, many observers believed that the Beidler Tract had been largely unaffected by historic land-disturbing activities, apart from a few small diked areas, a handful of "cattle mounds," and some abandoned agricultural fields along the river. Park advocates acknowledged that most of the large cypress trees on the tract had been cut decades before by the Santee River Cypress Lumber Company. However, they argued that the bulk of the tract had escaped the large-scale logging that decimated the South's bottomland forests in the late nineteenth and early twentieth centuries. Some advocates went further, asserting that, apart from the logging of old-growth cypress, no major human disturbance had ever taken place in the floodplain prior to the resumption of commercial logging operations in 1969. The view of many at the time was that Congaree was that rarest of ecosystems, a surviving remnant of the presettlement forest. Today, it is still often said that the old-growth portion of Congaree National Park is pristine and largely untouched—that to walk its trails is to experience a southern floodplain forest as it would have looked hundreds or even thousands of years ago. But whether this forest is truly pristine and whether it really resembles the forest of centuries past are questions that have only begun to be investigated.

One thing is clear: the size of the park's trees is no guarantee that the Beidler Tract is untouched by human activity. Recent tree ring data show that some species at Congaree tend to grow much more rapidly than has often been supposed, making the forest appear older in places than it actually is.[5] In fact, parts of today's forest may have experienced periods of hyper-growth in the past because of the mass wasting of Piedmont soils in the nineteenth and early twentieth centuries. Rivers that ran clear in the early eighteenth century have run red for the past two hundred years, depositing rich loads of nutrients as they hit the flatter gradients of the inner coastal plain.[6] Added to these nutrient loads were fertilizers that saw increasing use across the piedmont after the Civil War. As a result, the size of Congaree's trees may not tell all that much about the history of this forest. Given the rapid regrowth of floodplain vegetation, today's old-growth forest could very well mask extensive land-disturbing activities during the eighteenth and nineteenth centuries.

Even if the Beidler Tract did manage to escape large-scale human disturbance, it does not necessarily follow that today's forest provides a window into the distant past. Ecologists have increasingly called into question the whole notion of an ideal, static "climax" toward which a forest inevitably trends via ecological succession. Today, forests are widely believed to be essentially dynamic within a range of variation. Differing disturbances trigger slightly different successional responses, depending on (a) the nature of the disturbance, (b) the types of plants and animals present at the time of disturbance, and (c) the relative abilities of those species to capitalize on new conditions and out-compete their neighbors for nutrients and living space. The concept of more or less stable vegetation communities is especially problematic in southern floodplains, where stream migration, flood scouring, sediment deposition, and tip-up mounds create constantly shifting substrates, forcing species to colonize land forms that are continuously changing in shape and elevation. In the Congaree floodplain this diversity of physical gradients is attended by frequent wind disturbance, including the occasional hurricane. To a far greater extent than on the adjoining uplands, the Congaree floodplain is a constantly changing mosaic of disturbed patches, each patch varying by age and species concentrations.[7]

This point should not be pressed too hard, however. Despite the essentially dynamic nature of this forest, it is still likely that the Beidler Tract resembles in many respects the forest that has existed along the Congaree for thousands of years. The southern bottomland hardwood forest is a relatively young ecosystem and has never known a time without disturbance of one sort or another, including human disturbance. Its range of vegetative communities is determined in large part by a fluctuating hydrologic regime that perhaps only dates to around 18,000 years ago, the point in the late Pleistocene when the shift toward today's pronounced seasonal climates began. Modern vegetation communities are more recent still, having developed across the Southeast only within the last several thousand years. Paleoecological studies at Congaree and elsewhere suggest that hardwoods typical of the present-day Southeast did not begin to achieve dominance until after 8,500 Y.B.P. (years before present). And it was not until after 5,000–3,000 Y.B.P. that a cypress-gum community existed throughout the Atlantic Coastal Plain. By that point, humans had inhabited the Southeast for at least 8,000 years and perhaps significantly longer.[8]

Witness-tree data from the original Beidler Tract land grants suggest that the principal species of the eighteenth-century floodplain were identical to those growing in the park today. Farther back in time the situation was the same. Spanish conquistadors exploring the Wateree bottomlands encountered "forests of walnuts and oak, pines, evergreen oaks and groves of sweetgum, and many cedars [cypress (?)]." What is not so clear is whether the relative abundance and distribution of plant species at Congaree are the same now as they were at the time of first contact with Europeans. To begin to answer this question, it is necessary to understand as much as possible about the nature and extent of disturbance, including human disturbance, this forest has experienced over time. Regarding human disturbance, there is the archaeological and historical record to provide guidance. And what this record shows is that people have been active in the Congaree floodplain for hundreds of years, especially along the riverbank and the higher floodplain ridges. First with fire and then with agriculture, human inhabitants have actively and extensively modified the floodplain environment to create conditions that would help ensure their survival.[9]

In managing the floodplain environment to meet their needs, residents of the lower Congaree valley behaved no differently from people living along the region's other major rivers. Evidence from the park can therefore help illuminate patterns of resource extraction and settlement along rivers throughout the South Atlantic Coastal Plain. It can also point to the specific cultural practices that allowed humans to adapt and subsist in this resource-rich but unpredictable environment. The Beidler Tract is especially valuable on this score because its relative lack of modern human disturbance means that early signs of manipulation and adaptation have not been thoroughly obscured by the effects of industrial-scale agricultural and logging. At the same time, the age of the Beidler Tract forest makes it easier to gauge the impact of long-ago human disturbance on the composition of modern-day vegetative communities. This is not to say that the entire Beidler Tract has experienced human disturbance—indeed, one task of this book is to attempt an assessment of just how much of the tract may have been affected by historic clearing and logging activities. But it is clear that parts of the Beidler Tract have been manipulated by humans, some areas more than others.

This study explores in detail the interplay of human disturbance and forest dynamics at the park over the past three thousand years. Particular emphasis is placed on the old-growth and maturing forests of the Beidler Tract, but other parts of the park are addressed as well, especially as they reflect the more intense human disturbance typical of the twentieth century. The general approach throughout is to synthesize information from disparate sources and disciplines to create a more detailed picture of historic human impacts to the park than has hitherto been available. A review of materials such as property and census records, studies of forest succession, tree-ring analyses, slave narratives, aerial photographs, and historic news accounts shows that the human impact at Congaree is greater than has commonly been supposed.

The intent here is not to call into question the grounds upon which the park was created. Whether "near virgin" or not, the Beidler Tract remains one of the most intact, and important, natural areas in eastern North America. Rather, the aim is to provide a more complete picture of the nature and extent of historic human disturbance in the park over time. Doing so reveals patterns of human activity along the lower Congaree River going back hundreds of years. It also gives some idea of how and where activities such as farming, grazing, and logging have altered the vegetative cover of the park. With this information in hand, it will be possible to draw some preliminary conclusions regarding the effect of historic human disturbance on the old-growth and second-growth forest in the park today.

1

Managing the Presettlement Landscape

This day the Governor arrived with some on horseback (although few) at the town [on the Congaree] that is called Himahi, and the army remained two leagues back, the horses being tired. He found in this town a barbacoa of corn and more than two and a half cahices of prepared pinol, which is toasted corn. And the next day the army arrived, and they gave out rations of corn and pinol.

Roderigo Rangel, *Account of the Northern Conquest and Discovery of Hernando de Soto,* post-1540

HUMANS HAVE BEEN MODIFYING THE LANDSCAPE of the American Southeast for thousands of years. In the lower Congaree Valley the first evidence of human occupation dates back to the Paleoindian period—that is, from 12,000 B.C.E. (before Common Era) to 8000 B.C.E. Evidence of occupation continues through and beyond the first arrival of Europeans, confirming that indigenous people occupied the lower Congaree during the Archaic (8000–1000 B.C.E.), Woodland (1000 B.C.E.–900 C.E.), and Mississippian (900–1520 C.E.) periods.[1] Throughout much of this time, human impacts to the land stemmed principally from the use of fire to drive game and improve habitat for preferred food species. Eventually people across the region began to supplement traditional hunting and gathering with the cultivation of domesticated plants on cleared ground. As populations grew, community reliance on agriculture steadily increased, and the imprint of human activities on the landscape became more and more pronounced.

At first, agriculture was associated with temporary camps and villages, where people grew crops in small garden plots concentrated in alluvial bottoms and mountain coves. As time passed, people lived increasingly in stationary settlements near major streams, supported by ever more expansive bottomland agriculture. By the height of the Mississippian period, American Indian impacts were concentrated along the corridors of most major southeastern rivers, as well as many intermediate-size streams. For Mississippian people, survival itself depended on maintaining extensive agricultural fields near their villages and towns.[2]

Although archaeological studies have shown that humans occupied the Congaree valley at various times from the Paleoindian through the Woodland and Mississippian periods, the timing and extent of cultivation along the Congaree River has yet to be investigated in any detail. Most of the prehistoric settlements identified to date on the Congaree were concentrated just below the fall line near Columbia or on high ground south of the river. A particularly good example of the latter is the state Congaree Bluffs Heritage Preserve, located across the river from the park in Calhoun County. Situated on a high, north-facing bluff just upstream from Devil's Elbow (map 1), the preserve has sites with archaeological components dating from 8000 B.C.E. to 6000 B.C.E., 200 B.C.E., 500 C.E., and the Mississippian period. In later years the preserve may have been the location of one or more long-term Indian settlements. The impact of any of these occupations on the local environment is not known.[3]

Very little in the way of serious archaeological investigation has been done on the lands that now make up Congaree National Park. As a result, it is not possible to describe with any confidence the land-disturbing activities that may have taken place in the floodplain before European settlement. The discussion that follows therefore relies heavily on studies conducted at nearby sites, particularly sites along the Broad and Wateree Rivers. The attempt here is to draw reasonable inferences about land use in the Congaree floodplain based on both the available archaeological evidence and the findings from similar sites in South Carolina's inner coastal plain.

Table 1 Recognized Periods of Human Occupation in South Carolina prior to European Settlement

PERIOD	YEARS
Paleoindian	12,000–8000 B.C.E.
Archaic	8000–1000 B.C.E.
Woodland	1000 B.C.E.–900 C.E.
Mississippian	900–1520 C.E.

Land Use in the Woodland Period

Apart from using fire to drive game or modify habitat, it is unlikely that humans engaged in significant land-disturbing activities in the Congaree floodplain until sometime toward the middle or end of the Woodland period (500 B.C.E.–900

C.E.). Little clearing would have occurred during the earlier, Archaic period (8000–1000 B.C.E.) because this was primarily a time of nomadic hunting and gathering. In contrast, the Woodland period was characterized in many areas by a gradual shift from a nomadic existence to a more settled existence in permanent or semipermanent villages.

In the Early Woodland period (1000–500 B.C.E.), the people of South Carolina's inner coastal plain were starting to become more sedentary, but they still migrated to base camps to gather specific resources. Settlements were located primarily in inter-riverine areas, with base camps sited along streams and rivers to facilitate resource gathering. In the Congaree River valley, Early Woodland occupations often consisted of resource extraction sites or upland settlements occupied by single-family units. Campsites apparently conforming to this pattern have recently been found above the north arm of Bates Old River in the U.S. 601 corridor. However, these sites have not been intensively studied or even dated to a particular phase of the Woodland period. Little is yet known about the nature of these sites or the uses their inhabitants made of the surrounding landscape. Somewhat more is known about the Fork Swamp area to the south, in the far eastern end of the park. Archaeological investigations at Fork Swamp in 2007 and 2014 found a high frequency of Late Archaic and Early Woodland ceramics in an ancient sand ridge known as Sampson Island. The age and distribution of these artifacts suggests that Sampson Island saw prolonged stretches of seasonal occupation during the Late Archaic and Early Woodland periods.[4]

In the Middle Woodland period (500 B.C.E.–500 C.E.), subsistence patterns generally followed those of the Early Woodland. People of the inner coastal plain gravitated increasingly to riverine areas at this time, establishing seasonal camps on terraces above the river swamps, where they could exploit the great variety of resources offered by the floodplain environment.[5] By the end of the Middle Woodland, many of the seasonal camps located on major rivers had developed into more permanent villages, and one or more Middle Woodland villages likely existed along the Congaree. One such village may have been located south of the river on the bluffs overlooking the Fork Swamp area. The investigation at Fork Swamp in 2007 found a number of decorated sherds at Sampson Island consistent with styles from the Early and Middle Woodland periods (1000 B.C.E.–500 C.E.). However, no evidence of a settlement has yet been found on the sand ridge, so the presence of decorated pottery, which has also been recovered from other sand ridge interments in the Congaree valley, raises the possibility that the ridge was a ceremonial burial ground associated with a seasonally occupied village on the bluff across the river.[6]

The Middle Woodland period is especially noteworthy for an intensification of regional and interregional trade in exotic goods. Much of the trade in the Southeast during the Middle Woodland period took place with people of the

Hopewellian tradition, a dispersed set of related populations centered on the Ohio River valley. Often associated with the construction of earthen mounds and related structures, the Hopewellian tradition may have influenced the construction of oval- or dome-shaped mounds in South Carolina during this period, including one or more in the Congaree floodplain. A Woodland period mound ("Congaree Swamp Woodland Mound" 38RD327) has been identified in the park about midway between the Norfolk Southern railroad track and U.S. Highway 601. The oval-shaped mound is approximately 40 feet (12 meters) wide and 270 feet (83 meters) long, and rises about 5 feet (1.5 meters) above the surrounding floodplain. Initial archaeological work has placed the mound site in the Early to Middle Woodland period. Other Woodland period mounds may also exist in the park, including Starling's Mound and one or more of the so-called "cattle mounds" typically attributed to eighteenth- and nineteenth-century landowners and their slaves. Some of the latter may actually be Indian mounds that were adapted or augmented at a later date to provide cattle a place of refuge from floods.[7]

The purpose of Middle Woodland–period mounds is uncertain. Many mounds and mound sites appear to have been used on a recurring rather than continuous basis, which may indicate that they were intended to exert some type of control over the supernatural world. Clearly, mounds could only have been built in areas cleared of woody vegetation; but Middle Woodland mounds were not necessarily associated with areas of significant habitation, and the presence of a mound does not in and of itself denote the site of a large village or extensive fields. The people of the Middle Woodland period still relied primarily on game animals and gathered plants, and the archaeological evidence they left behind differs little from that found at Archaic sites. Thus, to the extent that Middle Woodland mounds exist in the park, their presence is not necessarily evidence of extensive land disturbance in the precincts surrounding the mounds.[8]

Unlike the more concentrated settlement patterns of the Middle Woodland period, settlement in the Late Woodland (500 C.E.–900 C.E.) was more dispersed. People lived in smaller but more numerous village sites, reflecting an overall growth in population. As populations increased, competition for resources may have become more pronounced, increasing the pressure to supplement game and gathered plants with cultivated foods. Indeed, throughout the Late Woodland period a more systematic, though by no means uniform, approach to horticulture was evolving in parts of the eastern and midwestern United States. Intensive pre-maize-dominated agriculture was concentrated primarily in the Midwest and Midsouth—specifically, north of the lower Mississippi valley and west of the Appalachians.[9] Archaeological work in South Carolina has turned up very little in the way of seed remains from this period, suggesting that intensive pre-maize agriculture was not practiced in the midlands during most of the Late Woodland period. Even at this relatively late date, subsistence practices in the inner coastal plan appear to have been essentially a continuation of Archaic ways. Why this should be so is not entirely clear, but it has been hypothesized that the area's mild climate and long growing season may have limited the need to rely on stored food.[10]

Much is still being learned about the transition from the Late Woodland to the Early Mississippian period in central South Carolina. During this time new groups from the Mississippian cultural tradition may have migrated into the area from the west, bringing with them new cultural beliefs and practices, as well as a dependence on the cultivation of maize. A complementary possibility is that Mississippian cultural and agricultural practices spread into the major drainages of South Carolina as a result of trade or other cultural interactions with Mississippian settlements to the west. Throughout this transitional period—and in some places much longer—people of both cultural traditions lived side by side while continuing to practice their respective customs. Mound building appears to have increased at this time among some Late Woodland people, with mounds being used both as burial centers and as areas for food preparation and the production and display of ritual objects.[11]

Toward the end of this period, Late Woodland and Early Mississippian communities may have responded to the continued growth in population by increasing the scope and intensity of pre-maize agriculture. Evidence from the Belmont Neck site on the Wateree River indicates that Early Mississippian people were clearing fields below the fall line as early as 950 C.E., growing maygrass *(Phalaris caroliniana)*, chenopod *(Chenopodium* sp.), maize *(Zea mays)*, and tobacco *(Nicotiana* sp.).[12] If the Congaree valley was likewise inhabited at this time, it is conceivable that clearing was taking place there as well. In any event, it seems likely that by the beginning of the Mississippian period (ca. 900 C.E.) agriculture was gradually increasing in importance as a source of sustenance for native people in central South Carolina, with maize poised to assume an ever-greater role in cultural and economic life.

Development of Mississippian Culture

Mississippian culture emerged when people of the Southeast began to cultivate maize for a substantial portion of their diet. In time the production of maize led to a significant increase in population, causing people to become increasingly dependent on it and other cultivated crops for survival. The result was that cultural practices in many parts of the Southeast evolved to facilitate the production of maize on a large scale. These changes transformed the egalitarian, tribal societies of earlier periods into what many have interpreted as the hierarchical chiefdoms of the Mississippian period. The elites of these chiefdoms maintained dominance over others in large part via their control of the flat-topped pyramidal mounds that lay at the center of Mississippian religious life.[13]

The chiefdoms of the Mississippian period were not dispersed randomly across the landscape but were concentrated near the scarce soils most suitable for growing maize. Maize is a demanding plant that requires rich soils and large amounts of labor to generate high yields. The best areas for prehistoric maize production were the rich soils of alluvial bottomlands, especially the elevated natural levees along the region's major rivers. Not only were these light soils particularly fertile, but they were also conducive to tilling with the hoe and hence could be made more productive than those in adjacent upland areas. These soils had the added advantage of being periodically enriched by overbank flooding, making it possible for floodplain fields to withstand repeated cultivation.[14]

Natural levees are the product of sediment deposited during periodic flooding events. During a flood, as a river top its banks, the heaviest sands and silt particles drop out first, forming levees parallel to the active river channel. Over

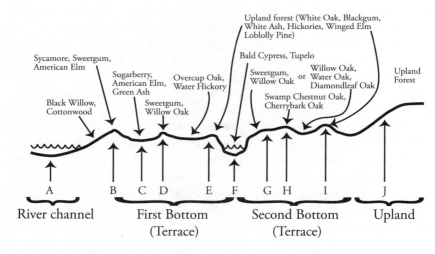

Figure 1. Floodplain Microtopography and Associated Forest Cover Types. Soil type and elevation help dictate the plant communities of the floodplain environment. Even slight changes in elevation affect soil type and the frequency and duration of flooding. These factors in turn affect the types of plants that can grow in a particular location. Legend: A = river channel; B = natural levee; C = backswamp or first terrace flat; D = low first terrace ridge; E = high first terrace ridge; F = oxbow lake; G = second terrace flat; H = low second terrace ridge; I = high second terrace ridge; J = upland. Vertical scale is exaggerated. Figure adapted by Lynne Parker from Figure 21 in Wharton et al., *The Ecology of Bottomland Hardwood Swamps of the Southeast* (1982).

thousands of years, as the river migrates across its floodplain, once-active channels become sloughs, and old levees become ridges.[15] Early farmers naturally gravitated to active and relict natural levees, where better-drained soils and less frequent flooding increased the chances for growing a successful crop (figure 1).

Typical Indian agricultural practice consisted of girdling trees with a hatchet, burning off the understory, and then planting beans, maize and squash together under the dead snags. In many, if not most instances, fields were intended to be more or less permanent and consequently were the focus of careful husbandry. Having nothing to use but stone tools, the Indians would have found clearing heavily forested bottomlands to be particularly arduous, and it was simply not feasible to move from place to place every few years to engage in slash-and-burn, swidden agriculture. Accordingly, fields were used continuously, and many Indians took pains to remove stumps and roots over time, fallowing the fields for only short periods. To save work, the larger trees were often left standing. English explorer William Hilton observed these clearing practices firsthand in 1663 while traveling along the Cape Fear River in North Carolina. As he later wrote, "We saw several plats of Ground cleared by the *Indians* after their weak manner, compassed round with great Timber-Trees; which they are no ways able to fall, and so keep the Sun from their Corn-fields very much; yet neverthelesse [*sic*] we saw as large Corn-stalks or bigger, than we have seen any where else." In time, soils would be depleted or stocks of fuel wood exhausted, and settlements would be forced to move.[16]

Settlement in the inner coastal plain tended to be highly localized during the Mississippian period, as it had been since the Middle Woodland. Compared to the hardwood forests of large river floodplains, the longleaf pine (*Pinus palustris*) forest that dominated inter-riverine areas in the coastal plain lacked the resources to support large human populations, and settlements thus tended to be concentrated on terraces adjacent to the floodplains of major rivers and their tributaries. Rivers also facilitated movement across the landscape, as well as commerce among and within groups. A range of characteristic Mississippian sites has been identified, including mound centers, villages, hamlets, and individual farmsteads. Hunting activity in the coastal plain appears to have been concentrated relatively close to settlement centers, with more extensive hunting areas located in the piedmont, where game was more evenly distributed.[17]

Mississippian culture began to appear in South Carolina sometime before the tenth century c.e. As noted above, Mississippian people were already living at the Belmont Neck site on the Wateree River by around 900 c.e. This site, the earliest known single-mound town in central South Carolina, appears to have given rise over time to a series of twelve mound towns strung out along the Catawba and Wateree Rivers. These towns formed the basis of an extended polity known as Cofitachequi, the easternmost expression of Mississippi society in the southeastern United States. Archaeological evidence suggests that work on the platform mound at Belmont Neck may have started around 1200 C.E. Construction of some other known mounds along the Wateree probably began at about this same time, as did construction of the Fort Watson Mound on the Santee, near present-day Lake Marion. During this same period, Mississippian people appear to have been living in adjacent areas to the west, particularly along the Broad River in Fairfield and Chester Counties.[18]

Maize agriculture was well established by 1200–1300 C.E., but its overall contribution to diet during this period is open to doubt. What is not in doubt, however, is that by this time Indians were, and had been, actively managing floodplain vegetation to suit their needs for food, building materials, and fuel. The preponderance of pine, oak, and cane pollen in the archaeological record suggests that Indians may have engaged in significant burning in and around the upper Wateree floodplain from at least 900 C.E. onward. Because many floodplain vegetation communities do not support either lightning-ignited ground fires or the spread of fire from adjacent savannas, it is likely that Indians intentionally increased the flammability of floodplains by encouraging the growth of pyrophytic vegetation. Setting fire to cane (*Arundinaria* spp.) would produce fires hot enough to kill many hardwoods and also create substantial openings, where loblolly pine and still more cane could generate or spread into new areas. These species, in turn, were essential to meeting the Indians' needs for fuel, food, and shelter.[19]

As of around 1300 C.E., a series of established Mississippian societies existed throughout the Southeast, with principal towns scattered along the fall line at the Flint, Ocmulgee, Oconee, Savannah, Catawba-Wateree, and Pee Dee Rivers. Population increased steadily during this period and with it the rate of clearing, causing forests to become increasingly fragmented. By about the twelfth to fourteenth centuries C.E., escalating competition for limited resources resulted in ever more frequent periods of warfare. In the fifteenth century, Indian populations in many areas began to concentrate in large, fortified towns, a cultural response to increasing competition among powerful chiefdoms.[20]

Cofitachequi was among the most important of the Middle to Late Mississippian polities in the Southeast. Its principal town of "Cofitachequi," or "Canos," was located on the east bank of the Wateree River, well north of the present-day park. The actual location of this town has yet to be confirmed, but the leading candidate is the Mulberry mound site near present-day Camden, South Carolina.[21] For many years Cofitachequi constituted both a simple chiefdom, taking in the area around its principal town, and a "paramount chiefdom," encompassing people of several cultures or archaeological phases, who spoke languages from at least two, and possibly as many as four, language families. The paramount chiefdom of Cofitachequi covered an area extending eastward from the Wateree to the Great Pee Dee River and northward to the North Carolina state line and possibly beyond.[22] While its major towns lay along the eastern bank of the Wateree, one or more outlying settlements appear to have been located along the lower Congaree. Of these, the only one about which any specific knowledge exists is Hymahi (or "Himahi," later known as "Guiomae"), a small but possibly significant village that appears to have been located north of the Congaree River just west of its confluence with the Wateree.

Mississippian Land Use before Contact

Little is presently known about the nature and extent of anthropogenic disturbance to forests in the Congaree floodplain during the Mississippian period. No Mississippian mound centers appear to have been located along the Congaree River during the major mound-building era in central South Carolina (ca. 1200–1450 C.E.), which may indicate that the area lay outside the principal Mississippian population centers. In fact, it has been suggested that throughout the period 1000–1600 C.E., the Congaree floodplain lay at the eastern edge of an extensive buffer zone. This largely vacant area was visited mostly by Indian hunting and extraction parties, and its width varied over time. The zone was not entirely unoccupied, however. Archaeological evidence confirms that at one time or another Mississippian people lived in the Congaree River valley on a more or less permanent basis. Intrusive Mississippian burial urns have been found at Green Hill Mound (38RD4) and Mullers Barn Ridge (38CL18), two sand ridges located within the Congaree Swamp bottomlands but outside the park boundary.[23]

Artifacts suggest that Mississippian people also occupied sites in the park during this period, although the extent of these occupations is unknown. Archaeologist James Michie argued that the Congaree and Tawcaw soils that constitute much of the park are not conducive to intensive agricultural activities in the absence of drainage systems and dikes. He concluded that human occupation of the majority of the floodplain was probably limited to seasonal hunting parties scouting the area for deer and other game. However, Mississippian artifacts have been identified at various sites on the bluffs south of the Congaree River (including the Buyck's Bluff, High Creek Plantation, and Congaree Bluffs sites south of the park), and it is possible that some or all of these communities farmed the rich levee soils on the river's north bank, as was common elsewhere in the Southeast. Given the lack of detailed investigations to date, it is not clear precisely when or where such agricultural activities might have taken place. It is worth noting, though, that Michie discovered three Lamar period (1350–1600 C.E.) sand-tempered sherds (complicated stamped) while conducting an archaeological survey of the park in the late 1970s. (Michie did not identify these sherds to particular phases in the Lamar archaeological sequence.) These large, heavy sherds were found on a sandbar near the western boundary of the park. Subsequent testing has failed to locate an occupation site on the adjacent riverbank, and it is possible that the sherds came to rest on the sandbar from a Lamar-period occupation a short distance west of the park.[24]

In recent years, a number of Lamar pots and pottery sherds (Pee Dee phase) have been discovered along both sides of the Congaree River. The Pee Dee phase has been variously dated, with one authority putting it at 1300–1500 C.E. and another placing it in the period 1400–1550 C.E.[25] In 2004 a Belmont Neck phase sherd (1200–1250 C.E.) was discovered on the same sandbar where the Lamar period sherds had been discovered years earlier. The presence of Pee Dee and Belmont Neck ceramics appears to suggest that Mississippian people occupied the lower Congaree valley at least sporadically, and perhaps continuously, during the general period 1200–1550 C.E. Pee Dee–phase pottery has also been found in the earliest stages of the Mulberry site mounds near Camden, as well as at the Fort Watson mound on the Santee. Assuming that intensive agricultural practices in South Carolina date from about 1400 C.E., the presence of Pee Dee–phase pottery in the Congaree valley opens up the possibility that Mississippian people cleared and farmed fields along the Congaree River during the period 1400–1550 C.E., if not before.[26]

The chroniclers of sixteenth-century expeditions by Hernando de Soto and Juan Pardo provide the first written descriptions of the interior Southeast, including descriptions of agriculture. The De Soto chronicles are particularly noteworthy for highlighting the extent to which different parts of the region varied in their suitability for human occupation. Describing the terrain of what is now west Florida and southwest Georgia, one De Soto chronicler noted that it is "a lean land, and most of it covered with rough pine groves, low and very swampy, and in places having lofty dense forests, where the hostile Indians wandered so that no one could find them nor could the horses enter there—which was annoying to the Christians because of the provisions which had been carried off and the trouble experienced by them in looking for the Indians to guide them." Far different was the area in present-day Georgia roughly between Montezuma and Greensboro. This area the chronicler described as being "a rich land, beautiful, fertile, well watered, and with fine fields along the rivers." Similarly, the land along what has been interpreted to be the Wateree River was said to be "very pleasing and fertile, and had excellent fields along the rivers, the forest being clear and having many walnuts and mulberries." This "clear" forest was presumably quite different from the thick forest growing along the Wateree today. The walnut and mulberry trees were likely grown in intentionally managed orchards, similar to ones known from other locations in the eastern United States. The presence of such orchards on the Wateree is a sign of the length of time humans had been living in this area.[27]

The De Soto chroniclers make clear that parts of the inner coastal plain were highly conducive to long-term occupation by Mississippian people. And, as noted previously, there is ample archaeological evidence that people lived and died along the Congaree River during the Mississippian period. This does not necessarily mean, however, that the Congaree was the site of widespread land disturbance, particularly the kind brought on by intensive maize agriculture. Settlement along the Congaree appears to have been intermittent rather than continuous and not spread uniformly across the landscape. A 2004 archaeological survey in the U.S. Highway 601 corridor failed to turn up any Mississippian artifacts, even though a complicated-stamped, Pee Dee–style vessel had been discovered some years before on the Bates Old River levee. Likewise, the investigation of Sampson Island in 2007 failed to reveal any clear evidence of prehistoric occupation after the Middle Woodland period, despite the presumed proximity of this area to the Late Mississippian village of Hymahi. A number of untyped, simple-stamped sherds collected at the site may reflect a Late Woodland to Middle Mississippian decorative style, but this identification is only tentative. Archaeological work at the nearby Congaree Bluffs Heritage Preserve tends to indicate periodic Mississippian occupation, but like Sampson Island this site appears to have been unoccupied at the time of contact. (Additional study of the site's distinctive ceramics may affect the latter conclusion.)[28]

A number of factors could have limited settlement and cultivation along the lower Congaree. Key among them are the relatively narrow levees that characterize the area and the year-round threat of flooding. These two constraints may have impeded Mississippian agriculture in significant parts of the upper Atlantic coastal plain, limiting settlement to sporadic or seasonal occupations along many river stretches. The natural levees of rivers in the South Atlantic Coastal Plain tend to narrow and low, making them subject to rapid inundation whenever there is heavy rainfall in the Piedmont portion of the watershed.[29] While the levees drain relatively quickly—on the order of two to three days—the lower backswamps may stay flooded considerably longer. Moreover, unlike the bottomlands of the lower Mississippi River valley, rivers in the South Atlantic Coastal Plain are subject to unpredictable overbank flooding at all times of the year, including the critical summer months, when the watershed receives much of its rain. The nature of the threat is such that extended settlement along coastal plain rivers was restricted in many areas to relatively dry climatic periods, when growing-season flooding posed less of a hazard.[30] Assuming these conditions obtained along the Congaree, dispersed cultivation would have taken place primarily during extended periods of comparatively low rainfall, being restricted at most other times to the higher levees and floodplain ridges.

The extent to which environmental factors actually limited settlement and cultivation along the Congaree is not known. Elsewhere in the Southeast,

Mississippian people were able to live quite successfully on the margins of coastal plain rivers—or even within the floodplain itself.[31] Regardless, there is reason to believe that much of the Congaree floodplain was abandoned before the onset of intensive maize agriculture in the Late Mississippian period. By that point the majority of people in central South Carolina lived along the Wateree River, concentrated in villages and mound centers near the fall line. The Congaree, on the other hand, appears to have been something of an outlier, lying around thirty miles south of the town of Cofitachequi and flanked on the west by a vast buffer zone. The park was most likely the site of seasonal extraction camps, farmsteads, and small villages rather than major settlements.

The reason for the relative neglect of the Congaree floodplain during the later Mississippian period is not entirely clear, but it may be due in part to inter-tribal conflict. Recent scholarship suggests that the period 1300–1500 C.E. was a time of upheaval in the South Atlantic Coastal Plain, characterized by major shifts in population throughout eastern Georgia and western and central South Carolina. Around the beginning of this period, chiefdoms in the lower Savannah River basin below the fall line began to experience significant decline. Conditions became sufficiently dire in the early to mid-fifteenth century that most of the towns and territory in this area were abandoned more or less suddenly in about 1450. The Broad and Saluda Rivers were likewise abandoned around this same time. By about 1500 all of the mound centers to the south and west of the Wateree valley had been abandoned, including the Fort Watson site on the upper Santee River. The reason for these multiple abandonments is not known, but the most likely explanation may be twofold: a preponderance of bad crop years over a span of decades and a long, bitter war between the paramount chiefdom of Ocute (centered on the Oconee River in Georgia) and the paramount chiefdom of Cofitachequi.[32] The result was the vast buffer zone that the De Soto chroniclers referred to as the "Wilderness of Ocute" (map 4). This expansive area, virtually unoccupied at the time of European contact, was widest at the fall line and extended over 130 miles from side to side. The people of Ocute told De Soto that they had long been at war with the people of Cofitachequi and were constantly on guard against attack when hunting and traveling in the buffer zone. Based on certain details in the De Soto chronicles, it appears that the eastern edge of the Wilderness of Ocute—that is, the western boundary of Cofitachequi—was the Broad-Congaree river system.[33]

The chroniclers relate that De Soto and his party of around six hundred armed men experienced severe hardship while crossing the Wilderness of Ocute from Georgia. It was not until they reached the confluence of the Congaree and Wateree Rivers in April 1540 that they again encountered a settlement of any size and adequate food. According to a reconstructed route of the De Soto expedition established by Charles Hudson and colleagues, De Soto and

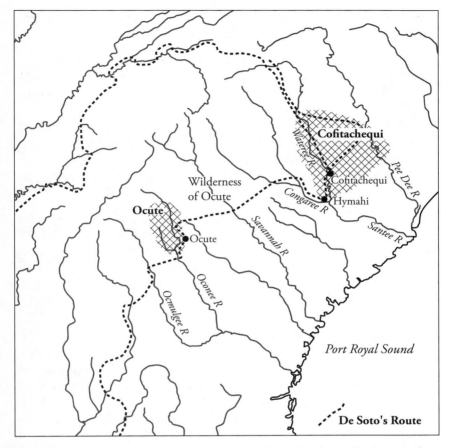

Map 4: Partial Route of the Hernando de Soto Expedition (1540). Map by Lynne Parker, adapted from Charles Hudson, *Knights of Spain, Warriors of the Sun: Hernando de Soto and the South's Ancient Chiefdoms*, ©University of Georgia Press, 1997, and Chester B. DePratter, "Cofitachequi: Ethnohistorical and Archaeological Evidence," 1989. Reprinted by permission of University of Georgia Press, Chester DePratter, and the South Carolina Institute of Archaeology and Anthropology.

his straggling army arrived at the town of Hymahi over the course of April 26 and 27, 1540. Hymahi appears to have been a more or less permanent settlement, supported by the cultivation of maize and other crops.[34] Because it lay within the paramount chiefdom of Cofitachequi, the village may have been free of much of the conflict endemic to the buffer zone.

Hymahi was described by two of the four De Soto chroniclers as having a relatively large supply of corn—more than would have been expected for a village of its small size.[35] Rodrigo Rangel, the most reliable of the De Soto chroniclers, described the landscape surrounding the settlement as having

> infinite mulberries, because there were many mulberry trees and they were in season: this was a great help. And also they found in the savannahs some *morotes* like those that grow in Italy on some plants and next to the ground, which are like delicious and very fragrant strawberries, and even in Galicia there are many of these. In the kingdom of Naples they call this fruit *fraoles*, and it is a delicate and exquisite thing, and they esteem it. And apart from this, they found there by the fields infinite roses, and native ones like those of Spain; and although not of so many petals through being wild, they are not of less fragrance, but rather more delicate and mellow.

Garcilaso de la Vega, a less reliable source, provided additional details, noting that "after having seen [the corn that] was in the houses, [the Spaniards] went [down] into the [lower] ones and discovered that, from there on [down] the river, the land was dotted with many pueblos, large and small, with many cultivated fields on all sides."[36] Estimates of the amount of corn stored at Hymahi ranged from three to five thousand pounds. Garcilaso gave the amount as more than fifty thousand pounds, but here as so often he was prone to exaggeration.[37]

Hymahi was still located near the confluence of the Congaree and Wateree Rivers in 1566–1568, the years Juan Pardo undertook his two expeditions to western North Carolina from the coastal settlement of Santa Elena (present-day Parris Island; see map 5). Referred to by Pardo's chronicler as "Guiomae," the village continued to maintain its own storage buildings for corn. The Indians told Pardo that cured corn was delivered to the storage areas at Guiomae by canoe, indicating that the village's corn was grown in bottomland fields strung out along the Congaree, Wateree, and Santee Rivers. Elsewhere in the South, Mississippian fields and farms were typically dispersed along river bottoms to utilize the most fertile and workable soils. The ready availability of canoes meant that fields could be established up and down the river as needed without having to move the village those fields supported.[38]

Hudson has suggested that the fields serving Guiomae may have been located downriver on the Santee, near the mound later known as Fort Watson. However, upstream soils closer to the fall line were more convenient and less flood-prone, making it likely that some of the town's fields were located in what is now the park. Assuming they were, and that Hymahi also grew food for other villages and towns, the potential for clearing was not insubstantial, as one to two acres of cropland were needed to sustain a single person.[39]

The needs of the village itself were compounded by the demands of the Spanish invaders. In September 1567 Pardo informed the "cacique" (headman) of Guiomae "that he should gather a certain amount of maize and have a house

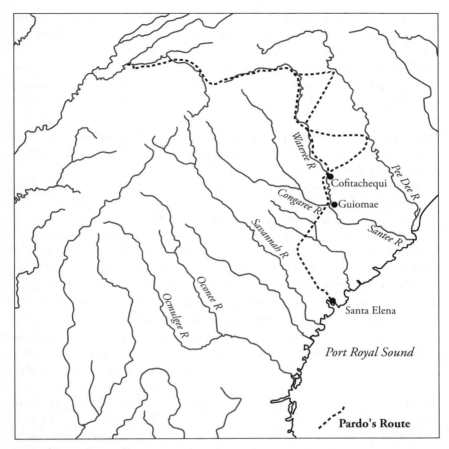

Map 5. Route of the Juan Pardo Expeditions (1566–67, 1567–68). Map by Lynne Parker, adapted from Chester B. DePratter, "Cofitachequi: Ethnohistorical and Archaeological Evidence," 1989. Reprinted by permission of Chester DePratter and the South Carolina Institute of Archaeology and Anthropology.

built where it might be put, to which maize he should not come except with permission from His Majesty or of one who has the authority which . . . captain [Pardo] had." In response, the cacique, EmaE Orata, declared that "as for having the maize gathered and brought and having the house to hold it built, that he has already gathered the maize and that when the maize is cured he will make the house which is to hold it, and from it neither he nor any other for him will take out any amount except with said permission."[40]

In February 1568 Pardo sent word to the Indians at Guiomae and elsewhere encouraging them to "sow a large quantity of maize because by all of this they would serve Our Lord and His Majesty very much." This corn was to be made available for soldiers garrisoned at Guiomae and also serve as a reserve for Santa Elena on the coast. The import of this request was all too evident to the Indians, as Pardo had previously expropriated much of the prior year's harvest from Canos and Guiomae to alleviate food shortages at Santa Elena. If the Indians chose to comply with Pardo's request, they may have been forced to clear substantially more land to support both themselves and the ravenous Spanish. Santa Elena experienced additional food shortages between 1568 and 1570, leading the Spanish to make continued and increasing demands on the local Indians and possibly those farther inland as well.[41]

It seems virtually certain, therefore, that Indians were cultivating fields in the natural levee complex of the park at the time of contact. Some may have reached their fields by boat from Hymahi/Guiomae, while others may have crossed over the Congaree from homes on the high southern bluffs, much as white settlers were to do in later years. The size and extent of these Indian fields is not known, but the levee zone itself can be fairly large, extending in places nearly thirty-three hundred feet (one thousand meters) or more into the floodplain. Finding cultivatable land in the park would not have been a problem.[42] However, it is an open question how much of this land the Indians actually had under cultivation in the mid-sixteenth century. As noted above, few late Mississippian artifacts have been found in the Fork Swamp area of the park, and it is possible that summer flooding and the operation of buffer zones worked to limit the extent of settlement and cultivation on the lower reaches of the river. If so, then the park may have experienced far fewer impacts from late Mississippian agriculture than was the case at population centers farther east and north on the Wateree. Nevertheless, impacts from clearing likely occurred in a number of locations in the park and may have extended into the Beidler Tract. (The reader may notice that terms such as "the park" and "the Beidler Tract" are sometimes used in discussions of past events that occurred before such designations actually came into use. This is to avoid excessive repetition of phrases such as "the future park," "what would later become the park," "the present-day Beidler Tract," and so on.)

It should be noted that the Indians' impact on the landscape was not limited to clearing fields and cultivating crops. As they had done throughout the period before contact, local Indians actively managed the lands radiating out from their homes to enhance their physical and spiritual well-being. By setting fires, collecting firewood, nurturing favored species, maintaining clear lines of sight, and so on, the Indians not only worked to meet their physical needs, they also imposed structure on the surrounding landscape.[43] The impacts of these activities would have become less and less evident the farther one went into the buffer zone, but they likely reached into all or much of the park.

Post-Contact Land Use

At the time De Soto visited Cofitachequi in 1540, a number of towns in the chiefdom had recently been abandoned. Why is not clear, but the Spaniards came to believe, perhaps erroneously, that the people had been ravaged by an epidemic. By the time of the Juan Pardo expeditions (1566–1568), this paramount chiefdom may well have been sliding into decline, although this conclusion has been disputed.[44]

In decline or not, Indian health as a whole appears to have been deteriorating in the centuries leading up to first contact with Europeans, largely as a result of the shift from hunting and gathering to agriculture and urban living. Demographic concentration rendered indigenous peoples particularly vulnerable to introduced diseases when the first Spanish explorers reached the interior Southeast. According to one estimate, diseases spread by Hernando de Soto and others caused Indian populations to decline by as much as 85 percent in the Southeast. Disease and the ravages of slave raiding caused entire chiefdoms to collapse, with many peoples disappearing outright or being absorbed into other tribes. By 1700 tribes such as the Congaree and Wateree were in severe decline. These tribes and others would soon be absorbed by the Catawba, which was emerging as the dominant tribe in an area that centered on the Catawba/Wateree River valley and extended west to the Broad River.[45]

For a time, and despite overall declines in population, the distribution of population centers in the Congaree and Wateree River valleys continued to correspond roughly with what had existed two centuries before. When English explorer John Lawson made his famous trek through the Carolinas in 1701, the major population centers in the area were located along the Catawba Path on the east bank of the Santee and Wateree Rivers. It was here that Lawson encountered the remnants of the Santee, Congaree, and Wateree tribes. In contrast, the "Forks of the River" area between the Congaree and Wateree Rivers appears to have been a largely vacant no-man's-land for most of the seventeenth and early eighteenth centuries. Other than a brief period when the Congarees occupied a site near present-day Columbia, the "Forks" constituted a buffer between the Catawba (and their allies) and the Cherokee.[46]

In the century or so before it came to be settled by Europeans, the Forks appears to have been used primarily as a game preserve and hunting area, with some Indians reportedly coming from as far away as Canada to hunt game. Historian Robert Meriwether suggested that the "Catawbas or Waterees" probably continued to hunt in the bottomlands south of Mill Creek even after the establishment of Saxe Gotha Township in 1733. But by that time the Catawba were down to fewer than 570 warriors. The great majority of them resided near the confluence of the Catawba River and Sugar Creek, just east of present-day Rock Hill, South Carolina.[47]

Evidence of Indian Agricultural Practices: Canebrakes and Old Fields

The decimation of human populations in the post-contact period led to the decline of the Mississippian agricultural system across the South. Many Indian fields were subsequently invaded by giant cane *(Arundinaria gigantea)*, resulting in extensive canebrakes. (Most, if not all, of the cane seen at Congaree today is switch cane *[Arundinaria tecta]*, a separate species that is considerably shorter than giant cane.) Traveling through South Carolina in the 1720s, naturalist Mark Catesby observed that in "places on the banks of [the larger] rivers extend vast thickets of cane . . . between twenty and thirty feet high, growing so close, that they are hardly penetrable but by bears, panthers, wild cats, and the like." Historic descriptions such as this, coupled with references to canebrakes in early land records, provide important clues to the possible location of areas used for agriculture prior to the arrival of Europeans.[48]

Cane thickets have existed in parts of the Southeast since at least 7500 B.C.E., including the higher portions of the region's floodplains. The relative antiquity of the canebrake ecosystem is pointed up by the bodily adaptations of the Bachman's warbler *(Vermivora bachmanii)*, a critically endangered species whose bill morphology and apparent reliance on cane suggest that it evolved in conjunction with its canebrake habitat. At the same time, this ecosystem is young enough that its perpetuation and spread may have owed as much to human burning and agricultural practices as it did to natural disturbance.[49]

A series of studies by Paul Gagnon and others has clarified the disturbance regime that may have facilitated the formation and spread of extensive canebrakes. Cane is clonal by nature and thrives in the presence of light. It will persist on higher floodplain elevations, even under old-growth forest, given periodic disturbance. It also burns readily. Around six thousand years ago, as climate patterns in the Deep South became more like modern ones, storm activity rose, lightning strikes became common, and fire frequency likely increased at the landscape level.[50] With increased disturbance came larger gaps in the forest canopy, allowing cane stands in the understory to increase in density and spread outward along ridges and natural levees. Once filled with pyrophytic cane, these gaps were susceptible to lightning-ignited fires. Bottomland cane fires were often intense, burning hot enough to kill surrounding trees and make individual gaps larger. Cane thrived in the wake of such fires, not only persisting, but increasing in density. In time, assuming conditions remained favorable, individual cane stands would have merged to form brakes. The size of these brakes, once established, made them that much more susceptible to lightning strikes, giving them the potential to perpetuate themselves and spread farther through the landscape. Intentional burning by Indians likely accelerated this process, helping establish and maintain large monospecific canebrakes as a feature of the presettlement landscape.[51] Absent continued disturbance, however, cane stands would eventually decline. Trees would gradually overtop and suppress cane, reducing brakes to scattered stands under the forest canopy.[52]

By burning cane every seven to ten years, Indians were able to both drive the game animals that sustained them and maintain the canebrake ecosystem. John Lawson saw this practice firsthand in 1701 while traveling up from the mouth of the Santee: "As we went up the River, we heard a great Noise, as if two Parties were engag'd against each other, seeming exactly like small Shot. When we approach'd nearer the Place, we found it to be some *Sewee Indians* firing the Canes Swamps, which drives out the Game, then taking their particular Stands, kill great Quantities of both Bear, Deer, Turkies, and what wild Creatures the Parts afford." Even after Indian populations crashed in the sixteenth and seventeenth centuries, native peoples continued to burn canebrakes, including those that began to invade abandoned agricultural fields. Indian burning appears to have increased significantly during the first half of the eighteenth century to meet the intense European demand for deerskins. Indians augmented past burning patterns to drive more game and as a consequence may have facilitated the spread of cane to new areas.[53]

Vast brakes of giant cane persisted well into the nineteenth century in South Carolina and throughout the Southeast. Canebrakes appear to have been particularly common along riverbanks, but canebrakes were also found on ridges well back in the floodplain. President Theodore Roosevelt wrote at some length about such canebrakes in his account of a bear-hunting trip to the Tensas Bayou country of northeast Louisiana: "The canebrakes stretch along the slight rises of ground, often extending for miles, forming one of the most striking and interesting features of the country. They choke out other growths, the feathery, graceful canes standing in ranks, tall, slender, serried, each but a few inches from his brother, and springing to a height of fifteen or twenty feet. They look like bamboos; they are well-nigh impenetrable to a man on horseback; even on foot they make difficult walking unless free use is made of the heavy bush-knife."[54]

Unfortunately, canebrakes like those that existed two and three hundred years ago have virtually disappeared in modern times, obscuring the extent of anthropogenic influence on the presettlement landscape. Yet as recently as 1906, dense canebrakes had been "common" along the Congaree, with culms reaching a height of twenty feet. During the Civil War, canebrakes stood out along the banks of the Congaree and Santee, a fact confirmed by the recollections of William Calkins, one of a group of escaped Union soldiers who floated down these rivers to freedom late in the war. On the night of December 2, 1864, Calkins and the other escaping soldiers encountered three fugitive slaves living in a cane-brake on the banks of the Congaree, where they had been hiding unmolested for two years. (This canebrake was said to be three miles upstream from the South Carolina Railroad bridge, which would place it either inside the park, or on the opposite shore.) The following morning, while camped some miles below the confluence of the Congaree and Wateree, Calkins observed that "around us in every direction were immense cane brakes, which grew very thick and tall, and were well calculated to hide us from unwelcome visitors." [55]

Evidence that canebrakes were once common on the Congaree extends as far back as colonial times. Several prerevolutionary plats from the Beidler Tract contain notations indicating that either the parcel itself or adjacent land was dominated by cane. One, a plat certified in 1757 for Elizabeth Mercier, shows a 440-acre riverside tract said to be "all a cane swamp." Others show "cane swamp" and "impassable cane swamp" along Cedar Creek in the vicinity of to-day's Weston Lake Loop Trail and Kingsnake Trail (see map 3 for trails).[56] These references to cane are likely a sign that indigenous peoples had previously culti-vated some of the higher ground along the river and interior waterways or, alter-natively, had perpetuated existing canebrakes by periodically burning them.[57] While it is possible that flood scour, windthrow, and lightning fires combined to maintain canebrakes on the scale suggested by the early plats, other hints in the record suggest that disturbance by Indians played a major role.[58]

Local historian William F. Medlin noted that many early plats for land along the Congaree and Wateree Rivers depict prehistoric farming areas as "Indian fields." No such notations exist for lands within the Beidler Tract, but a few eighteenth- and nineteenth-century documents make reference to "old fields" within or immediately adjacent to the Beidler Tract. Specific references include an "Old field" in Beidler Tract Parcel 11, Lightwood's Old Field in Beidler Tract Parcel 15, McJacob's Old Field in Beidler Tract Parcel 19, and Hooker's Old Field in the southwest corner of Tract 101-46, on the river (see map 2 for location of Beidler Tract parcels). The origin of the term "[——'s] Old Field" is somewhat obscure, but originally it may have referred to agricultural plots abandoned by Indians and taken up by settlers of European descent. Writing in 1761, James Glen noted, "There are dispersed up and down the Country several large Indian old Fields, which are Lands that have been cleared by the Indians, and now re-main just as they left them." Hooker's Old field, for example, dates from at least 1760, the time when lower Richland was first being settled in significant num-bers. Settlers selecting land in the backcountry typically showed a preference for "Indian old fields," not only because they were already cleared but because it was assumed that these areas had better soil and would be more productive. Allusions to "old fields" in local wills and plats may thus constitute some of the best evidence available of presettlement cultivation in the Beidler Tract.[59]

Any Indian old fields in the Beidler Tract have long since disappeared, as have the brakes of giant cane that once lined the river and interior ridges. However, the fact that loblolly pine (Pinus taeda) persists to this day in the floodplain may be due in part to the agricultural activities of indigenous peoples. Loblolly pine was no doubt present in the floodplain long before the advent of agriculture, primarily in small groups or as scattered individuals. As a shade-intolerant species, it would have been perpetuated by windthrow, drought, and fire. Yet for hundreds of years it also regenerated in patches created by the agricultural and burning activities of pre-European cultures. The presence of loblolly pine in prehistoric times is confirmed by witness tree data collected by naturalist and historian John Cely. These data indicate that at least four loblolly pines, all in the Congaree floodplain, served as witness trees in the original land grants for the Beidler Tract. Three of these pines were located near the western boundary, and one was located east of the park's elevated (eastern) boardwalk.[60]

The Indian Legacy

The crash of indigenous populations after contact had a profound impact on the landscape of South Carolina. By the early 1750s, when the first land grants were being awarded in the park, major floodplains across the colony had largely been reclaimed by canebrakes and old-growth forest. This was true even in the heart of the former paramount chiefdom of Cofitachequi. In 1809 historian David Ramsay remarked, "The Wateree Swamp . . . is almost in a state of nature. It produces canes and forest trees of a prodigious size. Of the latter the white and red oak, the sweet gum, the cotton tree and sycamore are the most remarkable."[61] Thus to the first European settlers, the canebrakes, forests, and big trees of the Beidler Tract would have seemed ancient and pristine, largely untouched by humans except for the occasional Indian old field. Yet on the Congaree as in much of the Southeast, the mix and concentration of species was partly the legacy of landscape manipulation by native peoples.[62]

Future studies may give a better idea of the extent of Indian horticulture and burning regimes in the park. They may also illuminate the extent to which these activities were complemented or subsumed by natural disturbance. Until then, the extent of prehistoric human impacts to the Congaree floodplain will remain a subject of conjecture. What seems clear, though, is that prehistoric people had less of an impact on the lower Congaree than they did on lands along other major southern rivers. The Wateree, Oconee, and Ocmulgee each had much larger human populations than the Congaree, with higher human impacts on vegetation and biological communities. It would not be until the late eighteenth century that the Congaree would begin to see comparable levels of human disturbance.

First Settlement, Land Clearing, and the Open Range

The richest soil in [Carolina] lies on the banks of those larger rivers, that have their sources in the mountains, from whence in a series of time has been accumulated by inundations such a depth of prolific matter, that the vast burden of mighty trees it bears, and all other productions, demonstrates it to be the deepest and most fertile of any in the country.

Mark Catesby, "An Account of Carolina, and the Bahama Islands," 1743

FOLLOWING TWO DECADES OF TROUBLED OCCUPATION, the Spanish permanently abandoned the settlement of Santa Elena in the summer of 1587. Thereafter and for the next hundred-plus years, few Europeans other than hunters and Indian traders entered the South Carolina interior. Things began to change in the early eighteenth century, when livestock herders started moving inland from the coast. The inexorable spread of rice and indigo plantations across the lowcountry was fundamentally incompatible with the running of large herds of free-ranging cattle and swine, and stockmen soon found themselves pushed into the inner coastal plain in search of fresh forage for their animals. The canebrakes along the Congaree and its tributaries would have been particularly attractive to stockmen: cane was the highest yielding native pasture in the South, and it provided the bulk of forage consumed by cattle wherever it was plentiful.[1]

In time the stockmen were followed by more or less permanent settlers, people intent on farming the area's rich soils. They, too, would have been attracted to tall brakes of giant cane, as these were known to be an indicator of the most productive soil. Between them, stockmen and farmers reduced the extent of canebrakes through a combination of overgrazing, clearing, and grubbing. In the process, they effected an early and important alteration to the presettlement landscape.[2]

The first known European settlement in what is today Richland County occurred in the early 1740s in an area known as "the Congarees." Encompassing land on both sides of the Congaree River just below the fall line, the Congarees was dominated by the township of Saxe Gotha, a new community that stretched along the river's west bank in modern-day Lexington County. It was here during the 1730s that most of the initial settlement of the Congarees took place. Although some early tracts were laid out east of the river as early as 1732, so far as is known the first actual resident east of the Congaree River did not arrive until the early 1740s. This was also about the time that settlement was starting to take place on the west bank of the Wateree, several miles upstream from the future Congaree National Park.[3]

Saxe Gotha Township (under its original name "Congaree Township") had been established in 1733 by order of the royal governor and council of South Carolina. Saxe Gotha was one of eleven new townships established by the colonial government for the purpose of encouraging white settlement in the backcountry. The hope was that settlement in the townships would buffer the coast from Indian attacks while helping offset the colony's growing racial imbalance. Accordingly, the majority of the townships were laid out along key waterways south and east of the fall line. To bolster the fledgling townships, the authorities actively recruited new residents from abroad and offered to pay their way to the colony. A number of the original settlers at Saxe Gotha immigrated from Germany and Switzerland, their passage paid for by the Royal Council. East of the Congaree, settlement proceeded more slowly, with many of the new residents arriving from Virginia and North Carolina. After an initial surge in population between 1740 and 1750, growth lagged east of the river for the next ten or so years. This was especially true for the vast swamps south of Mill Creek, where Indian hunting parties continued to roam in the early years after settlement of Saxe Gotha Township.[4]

Upon arriving in the area, most settlers chose to settle on land near the Congaree River or along its major tributaries and creeks. By the 1740s settlers along the upper river were concentrated primarily near Gills Creek, Mill Creek, and Green Hill, while settlers lower down were concentrated at the fork of the Congaree and Wateree Rivers. Areas in the vicinity of the Beidler Tract were bypassed at first because they were not convenient to the Cherokee Path, an ancient Indian trail that passed south of the Congaree River through present-day St. Matthews and served as a principal overland travel route between the backcountry and the coast. By 1740 the trail had been converted to a wagon road.[5]

Among the inducements drawing early residents to the lower Congaree was the colony's generous land-grant policy, which reserved 60 percent of the land in each county for commoners. Under the "headright" system, a settler was entitled to fifty acres for himself and each person in his household, slave or free.

(After 1755, the head of a family was entitled to one hundred acres.) Settlers typically chose land based on its agricultural productivity, preferring accessible land along rivers and streams. Demand for river frontage was so great that colonial officials acted to restrict the size of such holdings to ensure denser settlement patterns and an adequate supply of land along waterways. Beginning in 1730, the maximum width of each grant fronting on a navigable waterway was one-fourth of the tract's depth.[6]

The demand for riverfront land was much in evidence during the 1740s among settlers on the west banks of the Congaree and Wateree Rivers. The east side of the Congaree, with its wider floodplain, was more prone to serious flooding, and as a result the most sought-after lands here were located on a terrace of silt loam at the edge of the bottom, about two miles from the river. Nevertheless, settlers on the east side still chose the river bank whenever feasible. By 1747 over fifty plats had been surveyed along the Congaree River north of the mouth of Mill Creek. South of Mill Creek, little settlement took place for the next fifteen years.[7]

In the vicinity of today's park, land remained mostly unsettled until the end of the Anglo-Cherokee War in 1761. Impediments to settlement came both from fear of Indian hunting parties and the size of the floodplain itself. At two to three miles wide, the floodplain precluded ready access to the river and downstream markets. Settlement was further inhibited by the tree-choked condition of Cedar Creek. This stream is rarely mentioned in early records, so it may have been even less navigable in the 1740s and 1750s than it is today.[8]

Most of the original tracts platted along the upper Congaree River were small and had a high percentage of swampland. Riverbank and swampland tracts were highly sought after by eighteenth-century settlers because crop yields were considerably higher on these sites than on the adjacent uplands. With no ready access to fertilizers, settlers appreciated swampland for its fertility, and they were willing to tolerate the risk of flooding and the hard labor of clearing for the chance to obtain higher yields. The swamps in the upper Congaree valley were more highly sought after than most, being well known throughout the state for their productivity. For the next several decades, it was not unusual for people to place advertisements claiming that a particular tract of swampland was the equal of, or superior to, the best lands on the Congaree.[9]

Swamps and bottomlands were critical to other aspects of subsistence in the South Carolina backcountry. Not only did they provide critical opportunities for hunting and fishing, but they also afforded optimal forage for free-ranging cattle and hogs, especially in the winter months. Feral pigs *(Sus scrofa)* thrived on the abundant mast of the bottomland forests, providing settlers with an inexpensive source of much-needed protein.[10] Above all else, the rich resources of the bottomlands made it possible for settlers to survive as they slowly cleared their lands for cultivation. In some cases the bottomlands even allowed individuals to accumulate wealth. Settlers fortunate enough to build up large herds of cattle and hogs could export excess animals to Charleston and the coast, where the meat was needed to feed a growing slave population. Others supplemented the profits from selling surplus stock and crops with income from such activities as milling grain, trading goods, and surveying. The capital accumulated in this way permitted industrious settlers to acquire slaves and additional land, which they could then pass on to their descendants. By the beginning of the nineteenth century, the area below Mill Creek was the home of a number of individuals who had acquired enough slaves to be considered planters. These included, among others, members of the Howell, Goodwyn, Scott, Tucker, Adams, and Weston families. Each of these families would own land in the park at one time or another.[11]

Colonial and Antebellum Logging Activities

Before crops could be grown in the bottomlands, fields had to be created by girdling or felling trees. Oftentimes trees were viewed as nothing more than an impediment to cultivation and were cut and burned. However, where a commercial outlet was available, timber could constitute a valuable commodity, whether produced as a byproduct of clearing or cut to meet a particular market need.[12]

A commercial market for wood products developed early on in South Carolina, both in the backcountry and on the coast. According to Harry Hammond, son of the famed South Carolina governor and U.S. senator James Henry Hammond, lumber had been rafted to Charlestown during the colonial period, together with wood to supply the city's insatiable demand for fuel. A strong demand for wood products also existed in the British West Indies, where forest cover had long since been stripped for plantations. Pine boards, barrel staves, cypress shingles, and red oak bark (for Charlestown's tanneries) were among the wood products produced by the colony. The market for these items only grew in importance after the Revolution.[13]

Hammond did not say whether commercial logging took place on the Congaree River, but it is apparent from other sources that it did. The water-powered sawmill had been introduced to the Carolinas by the early to mid-1700s, and wood was being cut far up the Savannah River before the Revolution and sent to market on the coast.[14] In 1774 Dr. Benjamin Farrar informed readers of the *South Carolina Gazette and Country Journal* that his new sawmill at Saxe Gotha would "supply any person with LUMBER, to be delivered on the river back at the Congarees, or at any landing on Santee river; also, PLANK for ship building, of any length, not exceeding 45 feet. Any person taking a quantity either for Charles-Town or the West-Indies, and can send a vessel, shall have it considerably under the market price."[15]

Sawmills were doubtless operating elsewhere in lower Richland from an early date. Of particular interest is the millpond known today as Duffies Pond, which was in use by the time of the Revolution (see map 1). Located just above the northwest corner of the Beidler Tract, Duffies Pond could have been used to power a sawmill, a gristmill, or possibly both.[16] Robert Mills reported in 1826 that the principal staples being produced in Richland District at the time were cotton and lumber, and elsewhere in the state commercial logging was occurring far inland along many waterways.[17]

Very little specific information has been found about early commercial logging in the Congaree valley, but it is clear that local landowners sought to send timber and lumber to market to the extent they could. Around 1835 residents of Lexington District petitioned the state senate asking that Congaree Creek be "opened, so as to make it navigable for rafts of lumber." The petitioners asserted, "There is a great and constant demand for lumber in Columbia, Charleston and on the river between those places. As there are no saw mills on the River below Columbia this demand must increase, unless the purpose of your petitioners can be effected."[18]

The absence of sawmills alleged by the petitioners is somewhat belied by petitions submitted in 1828 on behalf of stockman and planter Joel Adams Sr. (1750–1830). By the 1820s Adams owned much of the western fourth of what would one day become Congaree National Park. Adams complained that construction of Barber's Cutoff in 1819 had deprived him of the use of his landing on the Congaree River, which he used to ship "produce, lumber and other articles intended for the Charleston or Columbia market" (see entries 1 and 2 in appendix A). Located on the north shore of what is today Cooks Lake, the landing was relatively close to Duffies Pond, where Adams was operating a sawmill by at least 1820 and probably much earlier (see map 1 and figure 2). Adams considered the landing to be a "great convenience" because it was situated "not more than one mile" from higher ground, with ready access to the agricultural and timber lands beyond.[19] Prior to construction of the cutoff, Adams's sons had put into service the first steamboat on the Congaree, the *James Adams*, which the family used for a time to ship products to market and bring back plantation supplies.[20]

Adams almost certainly logged and milled longleaf pine from the uplands on his plantation, but whether and to what extent he logged hardwoods in the floodplain are not known. One has to assume that the more valuable species lining the route to the landing were cut at one time or another, as there was a market for cypress, oak, and other hardwoods on the coast and beyond.[21] It also seems likely that valuable trees elsewhere in the floodplain were cut and sent to the plantation sawmill whenever it was profitable to do so or else rafted directly to market. Species of particular value may also have been segregated and sold, rather than burned, whenever new fields were cleared. Not enough information

Figure 2. Joel Adams Sr.
From Wiki Commons.

has survived, however, to estimate the extent of floodplain logging by Adams, Dr. William Weston III, and other antebellum owners of the Beidler Tract.

Some have asserted that extensive commercial timber cutting occurred throughout the Congaree floodplain during both the colonial and antebellum eras, opening up fairly sizable areas for both row crops and pasturage. In October 1975 Joy Buyck Carpenter testified about these activities at a hearing held on whether the state should urge establishment of a national park unit in the Congaree Swamp. A descendant of one of the oldest families in Calhoun County, Carpenter sought to keep her land from being included in any park by emphasizing that the floodplain was not "virgin timber." According to Carpenter, "These swamps have been logged for over 200 years. In my grandfather's and great grandfather's time [that is, David D. Buyck (1861–1920) and Peter A. Buyck (1804–1879)], the logs were cut, allowed to dry for a year in the swamps, and then they were bound into rafts, which were manned and floated down the river to the sawmills in Charleston. I am talking about the Beidler Tract as well as my own. The cutover land was then used for grazing cattle until the forest grew again. You can incidentally still see the outlines of the old cattle corrals in the swamps."[22]

It has to be said that much of this claim appears to be true, at least in broad outline. However, Carpenter may have somewhat overstated the extent of disturbance to the swamp to bolster her case against the preserve. For one thing, her mention of trees being cut and allowed to dry in the swamps appears to describe the logging of old-growth bald cypress, not the forest as a whole (see chapter 7). In the Beidler Tract, logging of old-growth cypress did not begin on a large scale until the 1890s, and most of the cut logs were rafted to Ferguson, South Carolina, not Charleston. As for bottomland hardwoods, widespread commercial harvesting of these species did not begin in South Carolina until the first decades of the twentieth century. Until the circular saw came into general use in the 1880s and the band saw in subsequent decades, the technology for milling lumber on an industrial scale simply did not exist in South Carolina.[23]

Nevertheless, Joy Carpenter was quite correct in her assertion that the sites of old cattle corrals are present in the floodplain. The presence of these corrals may point to small-scale commercial logging operations that had been going on since the time of the Revolution and before. Throughout the South the more valuable hardwood species (for example, oaks and hickories) had been selectively cut for personal and commercial use from the days of the first settlements. Planters who directed their slaves to cut timber during the idle winter months did more than just obtain the wood needed for housing, fencing, and fuel on the plantation; they also secured a potential source of income between harvests. A number of valuable tree species were present in the Congaree Swamp, including cypress, ash, and several species of oak. The rot-resistant qualities of bald cypress made it an especially valuable species, and advertisements of the period routinely touted the commercial prospects of cypress on those tracts where it was found. An 1802 advertisement for a large tract on the lower Congaree near McCord's Ferry (see entry 30 in appendix A) specifically noted that the property "abounds with great quantities of the largest cypress trees."[24]

Landowners having good timber near a major waterway were well situated to supplement their income by floating logs downstream to a sawmill.[25] Considerable floating of pine timber occurred on the Congaree during the eighteenth and nineteenth centuries, but it is unclear how many hardwoods from the park made it to the coast in this way. Around 1820 a petition to move the McCord's Ferry approach road on Buckhead Neck noted, "From the scarcity of timber, it is impossible to keep the Causeways in order."[26] However, the lack of trees in this part of the park was not necessarily the result of commercial logging. Sweet gum *(Liquidambar styraciflua)*, the most common hardwood in the floodplain, floats fairly well if allowed to dry first in the woods, but little sweet gum was logged during this period because it lacks strength and warps badly when drying. Shunned in the market until the early twentieth century, sweet gum was routinely left standing in the woods after logging, a point noted by the U.S. Bureau of Forestry in a 1906 report:

[Sweet gum] grows in mixture with ash, cottonwood, and oak throughout the hardwood bottomlands of the South. These rich, alluvial bottoms are among the best natural farming lands of the region. In the past the gum, having no marketable value, has been left standing after logging, or, where the land has been cleared for farming, has been girdled and allowed to rot, and then felled and burned as trash. Not only were the trees a total loss to the farmer, but from their size and the labor required to handle them, they were so serious an obstruction as often to preclude the clearing of valuable land.

Other hardwoods in the park were in much greater demand than sweet gum, but large-scale water drives of these species were not feasible because many became waterlogged easily and sank. The only practical way to float hardwoods to the mill was via raft. Rivermen assembled rafts by alternating lighter "floater" logs such as cypress, ash, or cottonwood with logs of heavier, poorly floating species such as oak, sugarberry, maple, sycamore, and hickory. Since heavy species make up most of the hardwoods found in the park, the need to use floater logs no doubt limited the number of hardwood logs that could be sent downstream in rafts.[27]

Logistics were another impediment to commercial logging. The best time for rafting in shallow coastal plain rivers like the Congaree was during high water, when rafts were able to clear snags and fast currents, allowing more logs to reach the mill before becoming waterlogged. In this environment regular large-scale rafting operations were most feasible during those years when the river was being actively cleared of obstructions. On the Congaree this meant the period from around 1820 to the 1840s, and after 1885. Even with the arrival of the railroad in the early 1840s, finding an economical way to get bottomland hardwoods to distant markets was an ever-present problem. As late as 1876, the U.S. Department of Agriculture (USDA) noted that "oak, ash, gum, hickory etc., abound in the swamps [along the Santee River]; but, in order to make the timber of much value, machinery must come to the material and skilled labor must be imported."[28] Thus, most rafts on the Congaree were likely made up of longleaf pine, a high-value, upland species commonly floated elsewhere in South Carolina.[29]

Only eighteen active sawmills are listed for Richland District in the census of 1850 (as compared to thirty-six for Orangeburg) and each of these is shown as producing "pine plank." The USDA's 1876 report describes the timber output of Richland County solely in terms of pine production and makes no mention of bottomland hardwoods: "In *Richland,* the forests are pine, yielding 50 cords per acre or yielding 40 to 50 gallons of turpentine per acre. Delivered at the railroad wood is worth $2 per cord; lumber, $10 per M." A few years later, the census of 1880 reported, "The most accessible hard-wood timber has been cut from the forests of the middle districts [of South Carolina], although vast quantities still remain remote from railroads or protected in deep river swamps, inaccessible except during a few months of summer." The relatively limited extent of commercial logging in South Carolina during the early to mid- nineteenth century is pointed up by an 1867 report issued by the state Immigration Commission. The report noted that only about 23 percent of the state's land area had been cleared as of that time, the remainder being still virgin forest. Although the rate of cutting began to increase thereafter, and shot up dramatically in the 1890s, the principal species being cut at the end of the century were pine and, to a far lesser extent, bald cypress.[30]

The extent to which logistics limited hardwood logging along the Congaree is made clear by an 1893 letter from W. J. Murray, president of the Columbia Board of Trade, to the U.S. Army Corps of Engineers. In the letter Murray noted, "From Columbia to the mouth of the Congaree . . . there are thousands of acres of original forests containing oak, hickory, beech, ash, cypress, etc.; large saw mills and shingle mills would doubtless be put up and operated could they get means of transportation to Columbia by steamers where they would reach the railroads centering at Columbia to distribute their output." When large-scale commercial logging of cypress at last began in the 1890s, it did so in part because regular clearing and snagging of the river had begun in 1886, allowing logs to be rafted more easily to downstream sawmills. Before that, commercial logging in the park had been conducted on a relatively limited scale, restricted to select, high-value species in areas with easiest access to the river, the railroad, or the northern bluff. Trees cut elsewhere in the swamp were typically burned or left to rot. It was precisely because a substantial portion of the Beidler Tract's hardwoods had escaped logging during the nineteenth and early twentieth centuries that Harry Hampton and others were able to seek protection of the area as a national park.[31]

Cord Wood: Fuel for Farms, Steamboats, and the Railroad

Large trees were not the only type of timber with economic value for riverside landowners. In a time before electricity, when the nation was heated and powered almost entirely by wood, cordwood was a valuable commodity. Smaller trees that could be easily cut, split, and transported made the best fuel. Hardwoods were generally preferred for domestic use in the South because they burn cleaner than yellow pine and have a heat value almost as high. The need for fuel wood to heat homes, fire steamboats, and power railroad engines was so great that huge quantities of wood were cut throughout the eighteenth and nineteenth centuries to satisfy the demand. The census of 1880 estimated that the annual consumption of cordwood was approximately three cords per person.[32]

The trade in fuel was for the most part local in nature and went largely unrecorded, so it is easy to lose sight of cordwood when reckoning the impacts of logging on the postsettlement forest. Yet all over America, and especially in the South, the amount of wood consumed for heat and power continued to grow in absolute terms well into the twentieth century, even as wood's contribution to overall fuel consumption decreased.

It is not known what impact the cutting of cordwood may have had on the Beidler Tract over the course of decades, but it must be assumed that such cutting occurred. A May 11, 1797, advertisement in the *Charleston City Gazette* is one of many suggesting that the Congaree valley was a source of fuel wood for the city. The advertisement offered for sale a "Congaree Boat" that would carry about twelve cords of wood.[33] (Twelve cords is equivalent to a stack of wood measuring four by four by ninety-six feet.) Two decades later, an advertisement in the same publication offered for sale "a Congaree BOAT, with anchor, cable, sails, &c. will carry 20 to 25 cords of wood." In places the impacts from cutting cordwood must have been considerable, especially on trees in the smaller size classes. Impacts would not have been uniform across species, however, as some species, most notably sweet gum, had only slight value as cordwood.[34]

The resinous yellow pines were the preferred fuel wood in much of the South. Although they produced an oily black smoke, they also grew widely and had a high heat value. However, hardwoods such as ash and oak were also avidly sought by steamboats and railroads. Wooding stations for steamboats appeared at frequent intervals along the banks of major rivers, as boats seldom carried more than a twenty-four-hour supply of wood. Such wooding stations are known to have existed along the Savannah River in 1841 and probably much later. In his diary, James Henry Hammond noted that he supplemented the income from his plantation by selling cordwood to steamboats on the Savannah River. Similar arrangements must have been developed to serve the steamboats that traveled the Congaree because efficient travel would have been impossible without them. In 1820, while making its maiden voyage from Charleston to Columbia, the steamboat *South Carolina* "experienced a detention of three or four days in the upper part of the river, for want of fuel."[35]

It is not possible to calculate at this remove how much timber was cut on the Beidler Tract to provide fuel for steamboat traffic on the Congaree. There is reason to believe, however, that the rate of cutting was not as great as on other rivers. Commercial traffic on the Congaree was always depressed and erratic because of the unpredictable nature of the river—too low during the autumn dry season, too dangerous during the floods of late winter and early spring.[36]

To encourage commerce on the Congaree, the state spent considerable sums in 1818 and 1819 to clear the river of snags and obstructions. These expenditures complemented the much larger sums appropriated to begin construction of a three-mile canal around the rapids at Columbia, where the Broad and Saluda Rivers combined to form the Congaree. Investors immediately rushed to take advantage of these efforts, chartering at least five steamboat lines between 1817 and 1824. The canal was successfully completed in 1824 and two steamboats transported cotton on the river throughout the mid-1820s. Although these early ventures soon failed, service was revived in 1834, and by 1836 no fewer than four steamboats were running the river, giving rise to what was perhaps the heyday of steam travel on the Congaree.[37]

The revival of the 1830s was impossible to sustain. Traffic on the Columbia Canal largely ceased after the mid-1830s because of unreliable water levels and maintenance issues, and the state withdrew its support for the canal after 1840. A further blow came in 1842 when the Louisville, Cincinnati and Charleston Railroad reached Columbia via a route that crossed the Congaree floodplain just east of the Beidler Tract (see entry 28 in appendix A).[38] From then on, the railroad increasingly displaced steamboats as a means of transporting cotton and people.[39] The mid-1840s saw operations cease for the *James Boatwright,* a side-wheel steamer that had run between Columbia and Charleston since 1835. Another side-wheeler, the *John Adams,* likewise terminated its Columbia-to-Charleston run at this same time. Other steamboats made the Charleston-to-Columbia run in the 1850s, but conditions in the river were such that navigation was difficult, especially for large vessels.[40]

Despite the fall-off in steamboat traffic after the 1840s, it is unlikely that tree cutting along the Congaree came to a complete halt. The completion of the railroad may simply have shifted cutting to those portions of the floodplain traversed by the rail line. For adjacent landowners, the advent of the railroad presented a double opportunity to profit from their standing timber. Not only could they ship their wood or lumber by train, they could also derive extra income by staging cordwood along the tracks for fuel. Given its location at the junction of the Columbia and Camden rail lines, Kingville would conceivably have made a logical wooding station, yet eyewitness accounts suggest that the floodplain forest below Kingville remained largely intact in the decades after completion of the railroad. In a piece from 1854 called "Memories of Home Travels," a correspondent for the *Southern Literary Messenger* recalled that "not far from Columbia the [rail]road crosses, upon a wooden causeway, the Congaree swamp. On each side is the dark, sluggish water, in which cypress trees are growing, with trunks so black and bare, that they seem to have life only at their tops. The fantastic protuberances from the roots, and numberless decaying logs complete the picture of desolation. Water here is no longer emblematical of purity, and the whole scene calls up visions of Stygian floods."[41]

This area was still forested in 1869, almost thirty years after completion of the rail line. In September of that year, a tree three feet in diameter—"one of the largest in the swamp"—fell across the line, severing the track and causing a horrific night-time accident. According to the *Charleston Daily News*, "the trees in the swamp also took fire," and there was concern that "the conflagration would become general." The fact that the swamp was still forested at this relatively late date may indicate that pine, and not hardwood, was the preferred fuel for locomotives along this route as long as pine remained readily available. In time, some swamp hardwoods may have been cut for fuel, but the amounts may have been relatively small, at least as compared to the large-scale commercial logging operations that began in this part of the swamp in the 1890s (see chapter 7).[42]

After the Civil War the river channel became so obstructed by fallen timber and overhanging limbs that eventually few steamboats were able to run. Further limiting traffic was the low railroad bridge at Fort Motte, which appears to have lacked a usable draw beginning sometime in the 1870s or 1880s. Thus situated, the bridge constituted a major impediment to navigation for a number of years. It was not until a new drawbridge was completed in 1889 that outbound shipments of cotton, naval stores, and other products at last began to increase. Also assisting travel after 1885 was a series of appropriations from Congress to clear the river of snags and obstructions.[43]

Even after operations resumed, steamboat traffic was often seasonal at best, and low water, accidents, and delays rendered service irregular and unpredictable. These factors, plus the increasing reliance on coal at the turn of the twentieth century, suggest that the rate of clearing for fuel wood was probably substantially lower on the Congaree than along other rivers. Even so, some clearing must have continued for as long as wood-burning steamboats ran on the river, and a wood-burner was still operating on the Congaree in 1904.[44]

From what has been said, it seems reasonable to conclude that a substantial amount of timber in the levee zone of the park had been cut for fuel and raw material by around 1890, leaving much of the interior floodplain relatively intact. This process may have facilitated agriculture along the river, which in turn may have generated additional clearing. But it would be wrong to picture the banks of the Congaree as devoid of trees at the turn of the twentieth century. In 1896 a reporter taking part in an excursion on the snag boat *Great Pee Dee* was struck by the amount of tree cover between Columbia and "Lovers Leap" near Fort Motte: "The banks were for the most part heavily wooded—dense masses of foliage coming down to the water's edge—but here and there a great river plantation or a sweeping white sandbar added variety to the scene."[45] The effort and expense needed to clear the river of snags in the 1880s and 1890s points clearly to the remaining tree cover along its banks.

Running Stock in the Bottomlands

Throughout the colonial period, the running of feral and semiferal stock remained one of the dominant agricultural activities over much of the Congaree floodplain, as reflected in such place names as "Horsepen Gut."[46] (A "gut" is a drainage artery in the floodplain.) Management of free-ranging stock was governed by the conventions of the open range, conventions that originated in South Carolina and Georgia. As Thad Sitton has noted, "Rather quickly, a tradition of stock raising developed based on using the woods as unfenced open range. The common-law doctrine that confined livestock to one's property did not apply in the Old South. There, the traditional practice required the farmer to fence *in* his crops and fence *out* foraging stock. The burden of fencing was on the farmer, not the stockmen, and landowners were liable for damage to stock when their properties were not properly fenced."[47] Even after stockmen gave way to planters along the lower Congaree, the vastness of the swamp meant that large numbers of cattle could continue to range freely through the woods for the benefit of nearby plantations. Major landowners such as the Adams and Weston families relied on free-ranging livestock to provide much or all of their meat supply, and the Congaree floodplain would have provided ideal conditions for maintaining their stock.[48]

Cattle and hogs were tended in the swamps by slave "cattle hunters," who in many respects were the forerunners of the western cowboy. Each fall the cows and hogs were rounded up by slaves and driven to markets in Charleston or other cities. These roundups supplied a reliable source of income to local planters, whose other products were more susceptible to the vicissitudes of the weather. Between roundups, stock could be managed at little cost to the planters other than the expense of housing a few slaves too old or too young to do other work. Joel Adams Sr., for example, is said to have settled slaves along the river for the purpose of minding cattle in the western part of the park.[49]

Free-ranging cattle were a much tougher lot than the pasture cows of today, but they were still vulnerable to floods. After 1906 lower Richland stockmen had access to the U.S. Weather Bureau's flood signal service, which alerted them in time to drive their stock out of the swamp to high ground. Here their animals could be provided with food until the floodwaters receded. In earlier times, however, cattle and hogs were extremely vulnerable to the twin threats of drowning and exposure. To increase the odds of survival, some stockmen used "cattle mounds" as points of refuge from flood waters. One wonders how many cattle were actually saved by a handful of small mounds widely scattered through the swamp, but stockmen used the tools they had to hand—tools that were not always up to the task. After the flood of May 1886, the *Orangeburg Times and Democrat* reported that the "mounds provided in the swamp for safety of stock during high water were entirely covered, in many cases high enough to swim the stock, consequently the loss was heavy."[50]

Approximately eight cattle mounds have been identified in the park, at least three of which show signs of usage into the twentieth century. The origin of these mounds is not entirely clear. According to archaeologist Meredith Hardy, some may actually be old Indian mounds that were kept clear of vegetation for use by stock.[51] Judging from the ceramics recently found there, Starling's Mound may fit into this category (see entry 14 in appendix A). An article on the 1886 flood in the *Columbia Register* appears to refer to this mound when reporting that a "telegram received by Captain W. D. Starling yesterday from his manager reports the loss of all his cattle, about one hundred head, many of them thoroughbred and grade Jerseys, one fine mare and two colts. The water was several feet over the 'Mount,' the highest point on the plantation, which has never been covered before, and was at least three feet higher than the greatest freshet of 1852."[52] Starling's Mound likely received continuous usage until well into the twentieth century.[53] Another putative Indian mound in the park may have been modified to enhance its utility as a cattle mound. The squared-off shape of Cooner's Mound appears to indicate an Indian origin, but the borrow pits at its base look to be from a later time, suggesting that a preexisting mound had been expanded to serve as a cattle mound in the postsettlement era (see entry 10 in appendix A).[54] The expansion may have occurred around 1840, the date often given for the construction of this mound.

Other mounds, such as Braddy's Mound and Mitchell's Mound, were purposely built to protect cattle from floods (see entries 9 and 26 in appendix A).[55] Mitchell's Mound is unique in having a long gentle slope on its south side, presumably to allow cattle ease of access to the top. Braddy's Mound is thought to have been built around 1900, but purpose-built cattle mounds may go back to the first decades of the nineteenth century or even earlier. The spread of agriculture during these years gradually stripped the Congaree watershed of much of its tree cover, producing more frequent and intense "freshets." Building cattle mounds was one measure downstream residents could take to protect their valuable free ranging livestock.

To manage semiwild stock in the bottomlands, it would have been necessary to build "cowpens" at strategic points across the landscape. In addition to being used for periodic roundups, cowpens could be used throughout the year to protect the youngest and most valuable cattle and thus enhance the size and quality of the herd. In many cases, young calves were kept in the cowpen overnight for protection against nocturnal predators. Their presence at the cowpen would prompt the cows to return every evening to suckle their young before returning to the forest to graze. This behavior was observed firsthand by former slave Charles Ball at a Congaree plantation a short distance below Columbia.[56]

On the whole, cowpens on the South Carolina frontier were relatively small compared to operations closer to the coast. To take but one example, the Catherine Brown cowpen near the Savannah River covered an area measuring just eighty by one hundred feet. This area contained a dwelling, outbuildings, and a livestock enclosure. Another colonial-era cowpen, this one about six miles upstream from the Beidler Tract, may have been constructed on a similar scale. Known as the Thomas Howell site, this cowpen was located on Mill Creek and appears to have been occupied from the 1740s until the 1820s. Thomas Howell was involved in a number of economic activities in the Mill Creek area during 1740s and 1750s, but he was primarily a planter and stock raiser. At the time of his death around 1760, he owned 35 horses, 111 neat cattle, and 9 sheep.[57]

Thomas Howell's brother William also seems to have been a stock raiser. The inventory of William's estate (1757) lists 52 horses, 185 hogs, and 36 sheep. Among William's real estate holdings were tracts in lower Richland and a cowpen that he and his wife Martha reportedly owned in the southwest part of present-day Fairfield County. Like Thomas, William Howell engaged in a variety of enterprises in lower Richland, including running a trading post and cultivating indigo.[58]

William and Martha Howell were among the first persons to apply for grants of land in the Beidler Tract. William died before the grants were finalized, but by late 1758 Martha was the owner of two grants totaling almost 350 acres in the western end of the park. It is not known what use, if any, William or Martha made of these lands. Both tracts consisted of relatively high ground fronting on the river, so they were probably intended for cultivation rather than stock raising. However, it is possible that neither William nor Martha made any improvements to these lands. They did not live in the immediate vicinity of the future park, but made their home about six miles to the west on a tract adjacent to Thomas Howell's property.[59]

No specific information appears to have survived regarding cowpens in the park. Of the various "old fields" in the floodplain, the one most likely to have been used as a cowpen was arguably Joseph Martin's large field near the middle of the Beidler Tract. A plat of the Martin tract prepared between 1789 and 1802 places this field just to the north of a waterway identified as "Cowpen Gut."[60] Martin started assembling this tract around 1770 and held it for a number of years before selling it to Charles Cotesworth Pinckney and Edward Rutledge, prominent planters and politicians from the coast (map 6). A rough estimate places the size of the field at approximately seventy acres, certainly large enough to have been a substantial cowpen. The field appears to have been located north of today's Big Snake Slough and east of the Kingsnake Trail (see map 3 for the location of the slough and trail).[61]

Figure 3. "Major General Charles Cotesworth Pinckney" by James Earl, about 1795–96. Oil on canvas. Worcester Art Museum (Mass.), Museum Purchase, 1921.86. Image © Worcester Art Museum.

Figure 4. Edward Rutledge. Courtesy of State Archives of Florida.

It is not known which of the Joseph Martins living in Richland County in the late eighteenth century was the owner of the tract. Perhaps the most likely candidate is Joseph Martin Sr., who named Joel Adams Sr. and Isaac Tucker as executors of his estate. At the time of his death around the end of 1804, Joseph Martin Sr. appears to have been a farmer rather than a stockman, as the inventory of his estate included, among other items, seven slaves, one lot of corn, one lot of cotton, a quantity of indigo seed, and only ten head of cattle.[62] Nevertheless, it is entirely possible that the field on the Joseph Martin tract had been used as a cowpen throughout the 1770s and 1780s. This field may even have been the feature that induced Pinckney and Rutledge to acquire the tract.

By the late antebellum period, most of the Beidler Tract was owned by wealthy planters, some or all of whom may have established large cowpens in the floodplain. If the cowpens at Congaree ever reached the size of colonial-era cowpens described in various Charleston newspapers, they would have consisted of one-hundred- to four-hundred-acre clearings with a large enclosure for cattle, as well as smaller enclosures for horses and hogs. They also could have included dwellings and other buildings for the manager and hands, together with a garden tract for food.[63]

Stock raising remained an important activity in the park during the one hundred years or so after initial settlement, but the number of cowpens and pastures in the floodplain may have declined for a time after the Civil War. By all accounts, the number of stock animals in the postwar South declined rather precipitously from prewar levels. This pattern is reflected in the census data from Richland County, where the decline in farm animals was part of a long-term trend stretching back to the 1850s. By 1880 the number of farm animals in the county was still less than it had been in 1860, despite a 56 percent growth in population and a tremendous increase in the number of farms (2,246, as compared to 225 in 1860).[64]

Among the various causes of this trend, two stand out. First, many animals had been slaughtered during the war to feed local families and support the war effort; still more had been taken to feed the Union army as it moved through Columbia and lower Richland in early 1865. Second, the "open" range was gradually becoming less open. As large estates were broken up into smaller tracts and as more intensive agricultural practices like sharecropping took hold, people had less incentive to engage in stock raising as an independent activity.[65]

One result of these changes was the implementation of a stock law in lower Richland County. This law, which required stock to be fenced rather than crops, had long been advocated by the larger landowners in lower Richland, but only in the late 1870s had conditions changed to the point where the resistance of smaller landowners could be overcome. The new law did not cover all of Lower Township; it specifically excepted from the fencing requirement all "lands lying below [the] high water mark in Congaree Swamp." Accordingly, many people in the area continued to treat the Congaree Swamp as open range, just as they always had.[66] When John Mitchell sold land just east of the Beidler Tract in 1884, he reserved for life the right "to pasture cattle and stock in the swamp on said land and the right to cultivate so much of said land as he will and does keep under a good durable and lawful fence." Similarly, David D. Buyck was at pains to formalize his grazing privileges when he sold Parcel 13 of the Beidler Tract to the Santee River Cypress Lumber Company in 1918. The deed of conveyance reserved to Buyck the exclusive right to graze stock on the conveyed lands during his life and the life of his children.[67]

By the turn of the twentieth century, cattle numbers in the floodplain appear to have been on the rise, and a fairly significant amount of land in the swamp was devoted to pastures. It was during these years that much of the land north of the former Mitchell tract was known as the Silver Lake Stock Farm. Other "stock farms" were located closer to the river, especially in the western half of the Beidler Tract. The amount of even-age forest along the river today suggests that fairly large areas were in pasture and fields in the late nineteenth and early twentieth centuries.[68]

Indeed, it is possible that the number of cattle run in the Congaree bottomlands in the late decades of the nineteenth century defied an overall trend away from stock raising in the state as a whole. By 1906 not less than ten thousand head of cattle roamed the Congaree and Wateree swamps, with a reported value of around $250,000. Moreover, stock raising continued long after the Santee River Cypress Lumber Company assembled and logged the Beidler Tract. Old riverside fields are still evident in aerial photos of the Beidler Tract from the 1940s, and Santee reportedly derived substantial value from grazing leases in the first part of the century.[69] By 1950, however, the fields were already starting to succeed to tree cover (see entry 14 in appendix A). Ten years later, when the National Park Service first studied the area for possible inclusion in the National Park System, only small-scale cattle grazing was still taking place in the tract.[70]

When cowpens and pastures were abandoned, as they increasingly were in the twentieth century, they reverted to early successional woody species such as loblolly pine or sweet gum, depending on the availability of seed sources. But the impacts of grazing were not limited to areas that had been cleared for pastures and cowpens. Grazing itself had impacts to floodplain successional patterns, although opinions differed in the early twentieth century as to whether these impacts were significant. Forester Alfred Chittenden had occasion to observe grazing in the Beidler Tract firsthand in the early 1900s. He felt that cattle had comparatively little impact on tree growth in floodplains. Others, however, contended that free-ranging cattle trampled undergrowth and stripped forests of regenerating seedlings. At the very least, cattle consumed other types of understory plants besides switch cane, and grazing probably created a much more open forest than exists at present.[71]

A number of observers from the nineteenth and early twentieth centuries describe people of the period riding easily through some bottomland forests on horseback.[72] Thomas Philip Weston recalled that his grandfather, Dr. William Weston III, although an extremely sober man, "was very much addicted to the sport of hunting . . . and used to take [my father, Isaac T. Weston,] when he was eight or ten years old behind him on the horse into the [Congaree] swamp to shoot ducks as they would fly to their roosting grounds in the afternoon." Well over a century later, John Cely observed a distinct browse line at a hunt club he belonged to a few miles above the park. He concluded that the open understory in that part of the swamp was created by free-ranging cattle.[73]

In addition to its impact on trees and shrubs, grazing hit canebrakes particularly hard. Not only was cane grazed heavily for its nutritional value, bottomland canebrakes were often burned during the summer or winter to improve forage for cattle. In many localities such burning took place annually or biennially—much more frequently than the seven- to ten-year cycle the Indians had favored—with attendant impacts to floodplain vegetation. Frequent burns weaken cane, and the intensive burning regime initiated by stockmen caused canebrakes in many parts of the South to decline and eventually die out.[74]

The extent to which frequent burns may have affected canebrakes in the Beidler Tract is not known. Scientific studies conducted in the park to date are inconclusive regarding the historic frequency of fire in the Congaree floodplain. A study led by Neil Pederson found no fire scars on sampled loblolly pines and no charcoal in the top ten centimeters of sampled soils.[75] Furthermore, no obvious evidence of butt rot is apparent in old-growth sweet gum on the tract. The absence of fire scars and charcoal may indicate that intentional burning ceased soon after settlement. If so, then most of the pines observed by the Pederson team sprouted in parts of the floodplain that have not had a history of fire over the past two-hundred-plus years. An alternate possibility is that intentional burning in the floodplain fell out of favor over time and was largely discontinued after the Civil War. Either way, the result was the same: a decline in pure brakes of giant cane. And however it occurred, a reduction in the burning regime would have had other, corresponding impacts on species composition and forest structure in the park. The impact to giant cane would have been just one among many.

3

The Rise of
Plantation Agriculture

Me glad it rain; it raise de water in Cong[a]ree river; den boats come down, bring corn; corn very scarce, very dear; den more plenty.

Unidentified Lowcountry slave, quoted in diary of Joshua Evans, February 10, 1797

THE FIRST PRIORITY OF PERSONS SETTLING in the backcountry was to erect a shelter and get a crop in the ground. Where possible, new arrivals would settle near an old Indian field, but otherwise the heavily wooded land would have to be cleared or the trees girdled. Settlers typically cut all of the trees in a space of five to ten acres and used the wood to construct a dwelling for the family. Additional trees could be girdled in the Indian manner to expand the original "field," but some settlers preferred to cut all trees in a chosen area and let the trunks rot on the ground.[1]

The Germans who settled south of the Congaree generally came with the intent of staying for the long term and hence were more likely to clear stumps from their fields, nurture the soil, and rotate their crops. North of the river, the English settlers were more transient in outlook. They favored girdling over clearing, and cultivated plants that could thrive among dead snags and downed trunks and limbs. Because it could take several years for roots and stumps to decay in these new fields, the plow was of necessity bypassed in favor of the hoe. Shallow planting was not a problem for quickly maturing plants such as pumpkins, corn, and beans, and plenty of room remained among the stumps, felled trees, and girdled trunks to raise enough food for a family and its stock. Limbs from felled trees even made a ready source of fencing to protect crops from marauding cattle and pigs.[2]

With the end of the Anglo-Cherokee War in 1761, the population of what became lower Richland County began to increase dramatically. Between 1750 and 1790, the population of the area grew from around 500–700 people in the early years, to 3,930, including 1,437 slaves. As settlement progressed, the farming economy on the Congaree gradually began to change, with small subsistence farms gradually giving way to larger river plantations supported by slaves. Historian S. Max Edelson succinctly distilled the human cost of this change, observing that "in practical terms, a plantation was less a physical place than it was a process of settling slaves on the land and forcing them to develop it."[3]

By the 1790s the cultivation of indigo, corn, and provision crops was occurring over significant parts of the Congaree floodplain. Cultivation took place at various points along the river but was concentrated in the upper part of the floodplain between Columbia and Mill Creek, an area of roughly fifteen thousand acres. Prominent landowners in this area included Colonel Thomas Taylor, Wade Hampton I, Pierce Butler, and Governor Charles Pinckney. By the time of the Civil War, thousands of acres of swampland had been opened in this area and were in cultivation.[4]

Generally speaking, the soils above Mill Creek contain a sizeable amount of sand and mica and thus are less sticky or boggy than the more clayey soils farther downriver. Being comparatively well-drained, these soils were better suited to growing lucrative crops of indigo and green-seed cotton than the soils of the lower ground downstream. The quality of these bottomlands was such that noted architect and geographer Robert Mills described the Congaree as being "bordered with a rich alluvial soil, of unknown depth, inexhaustible, and productive in the highest degree."[5]

The productivity of riverfront and floodplain land was reflected in its valuation for tax purposes. In lower Richland, "high river swamp, or low grounds, cultivated and uncultivated, including such as are commonly called second low grounds," were assessed as follows after 1784: first quality, three pounds per acre; second quality, two pounds; third quality, one pound. Lands lying so low as to be "clearly proved to the assessors to be incapable of immediate cultivation" were rated at five shillings. Less valuable than high swamp or low ground were "oak and hickory high lands," which were assessed at fifteen shillings per acre. These same relative valuations, expressed in dollars, remained in place through the Civil War.[6]

It is important to note, however, that this rating system reflects land values as they existed near the end of the eighteenth century—that is, before cotton became the state's principal staple crop. Once cotton production spread across the uplands, the state's oak and hickory highlands became significantly undervalued for tax purposes and remained so throughout the entire antebellum period.[7] The high valuation initially placed on bottomlands for tax purposes reflects the fact that they were in the forefront of the state's agricultural production in the late eighteenth and early nineteenth centuries. According to Colonel

Abram Blanding, by 1817 "more than two thirds of the market crops of the state [were] raised within five miles of a stream capable of being made navigable."[8]

Poorer soils did not stop planters downriver from cultivating parts of the floodplain. Although not as desirable as lands closer to the fall line, virtually all the land in the Beidler Tract had been laid out to local farmers and absentee landowners by the end of the eighteenth century. Then as now, though, location was key, and lands in the park did not always measure up. In 1821, lowcountry planter Richard H. Fishburne accepted a price of $8.37 per acre for a pineland tract north of the park but rejected an offer of $2.00 an acre for a six-hundred-acre tract of "first quality Swamp Land" near the center of the Beidler Tract. (This tract comprised most of the swamp portion of the Joseph Martin tract plus two hundred acres to the south originally granted to Francis Goodwyn (map 6).) Fishburne declared this offer—the only one he received for the swamp tract—"to[o] insignificant to reply to." Working against Fishburne was the fact that the swamp tract, previously put together by his father, Major General William H. Fishburne Jr., was actually situated in one of the wetter parts of the floodplain: in 1799 it had been assessed at $4.00 per acre, being "3d quality second low grounds." By 1832 the family's local agent felt justified in asserting that "the tract in the swamp is absolutely unsaleable." Whether all parts of the tract were uniformly unattractive is not known; remnant old-growth loblolly pines suggest that at least parts of the tract may have been cultivated at some point or used for cowpens. What can be said for sure is that the Fishburne family still owned the southern part of the tract in 1850 (map 7).[9]

More than seventy-eight plats were certified in the Beidler Tract and adjoining lowlands between 1749 and 1806, covering tracts ranging in size from twenty-two to one thousand acres. The majority of the surviving original plats (fifty-two of seventy-eight, or 67 percent) were prepared in the decade 1756–1766. Just over half of the tracts (forty-one of seventy-eight, or 53 percent) abutted the Congaree River or were immediately adjacent to the river in the levee zone. Tracts located along the river tended to be smaller than those located in the heart of the floodplain.[10] Typically, each of the tracts laid out in the Beidler Tract would have been granted either to the person commissioning the plat or to a third party who purchased the survey and completed the process for obtaining a grant.

Care should be taken not to read too much into the number and size of the original Beidler Tract land grants. Just because a tract was surveyed and granted does not necessarily mean it was occupied and improved. Some grantees neglected to improve their land if it was too wet or otherwise failed to meet their needs. Land also remained vacant because of speculation, which, despite efforts to prevent it, was pervasive throughout the colony. Numerous individuals across the fall line obtained grants to far more land than they could ever hope to plant on their own. Without the slaves to work it, raw land was just an underperforming asset, and many grantees held their land for only a short time before selling to third parties.[11]

Speculators were certainly active along the lower Congaree, especially in the years leading up to and following the Revolutionary War. Some grantees of land in the park lived at a considerable remove from the area, making it questionable whether they had any immediate intention of improving their land. James McKelvie, for example, was a planter residing at Eutaw in St. Johns Parish. His fellow grantee John Cook operated Cook's Ferry on the Broad River. Cook was a substantial landowner in the Beidler Tract, with two grants totaling 750 acres and other property besides. Other grantees lived well upstream of the park at the Congarees. These included individuals such as Elizabeth Mercier, who operated a trading post at Saxe Gotha, and her future (third) husband, David Webb. Still others owning land in the park were business people living in and around Charleston. Among the latter were William Creighton, an "Innholder," Michael Muckenfuss, a blacksmith and tavern keeper, and Michael Sullivan, the owner of a brickmaking business.[12] Creighton and Sullivan were small-time speculators who flipped their grants soon after acquiring them. But others—men like physician and deputy surveyor Benjamin Farrar of the Congarees and John Mitchell, a deputy surveyor from St. Matthews Parish—dealt on a far larger scale. Farrar, in particular, bought and sold land extensively in the lower Congaree valley during the 1760s and 1770s.[13]

Between 1760 and 1772, parcels in the Beidler Tract totaling more than forty-five hundred acres changed hands within a short time of being granted. Some were sold just days or months after the original grant. Others were held somewhat longer but ended up being bought and sold multiple times in the five years after the grant.[14] The pattern is illustrated by the dealings of William Mazyck of Charleston. Mazyck was the son of Isaac Mazyck, a wealthy Huguenot trader and landowner.[15] Over the course of his brief lifetime, William Mazyck acquired almost ten thousand acres in grants throughout the colony, including a nine-hundred-acre grant that consisted mostly of land in the western end of today's park. In August 1764, two months after obtaining the Congaree grant, Mazyck turned around and sold it to Dr. Benjamin Farrar. Farrar himself only held onto the full grant until 1769, when he sold over two hundred acres to Martha (Howell) Goodwyn (widow of William Howell). By 1775 Farrar had sold most, if not all, of the remainder of the tract to other buyers.[16]

Throughout the colonial period and up until around 1820–30, when the frequency and intensity of flooding noticeably increased, it was possible to plant the higher bottoms with manageable risk. The fact that some features of the Beidler Tract have names dating from the mid-1700s suggests that parts of the swamp were cleared, fenced, and cultivated from the earliest days.[17] In his *Statistics of South Carolina,* Robert Mills described in some detail the opportunities available to planters in the less flood-prone portions of the Richland District bottomlands:

> The land immediately on the river . . . is literally a sand bed . . . and is a complete natural barrier against ordinary floods. I scarcely know a place where the river breaks over this natural embankment. Our low lands are partially subject to inundation, but in these cases the river finds its way invariably through our creeks or inlets. This natural fortification has lulled the planter into listless security. The risk of loss by freshets has not been deemed sufficiently great to justify a resort to embankments in a solitary instance. The excess of sand in the soil immediately on the river renders it unproductive. It is best adapted to the growth of Indian corn and pease.
>
> The soil of the swamp land, which is in most cases alluvial, (being subject to occasional inundation,) evinces a total absence of sand. . . . This land, when drained, is well calculated to produce either corn or cotton, and would be invaluable for rice, particularly where it can be rendered subject to irrigation. The land composing the immediate space between the swamp and the sand bed on the river is of a proper consistence of sand and vegetable substance . . . and is known to be well adapted to the various products of the country, particularly corn, cotton, and wheat.

The lands described by Mills were probably the more heavily cultivated bottomlands just below Columbia, and these lands, especially the plantations of John Taylor and Wade Hampton I, were "among the few that are situated so high up the river as to have been accustomed, to a great extent at least, free from the hazard of freshets." Farther down, the risks of flooding increased substantially. In an 1810 advertisement, Governor Charles Pinckney (second cousin of Charles Cotesworth Pinckney) was at pains to assure potential purchasers that his plantation near Granby was "on the very safest part of the whole Congaree River . . . all the Lands three or four miles below being hazardous, and increasingly so as you go down." But even lower down it was possible to cultivate the highest parts of the floodplain without diking.[18] In St. Stephen's Parish (Berkeley County), significant portions of the Santee Swamp had been successfully cultivated without dikes during the second half of the eighteenth century. Touring Major Samuel Porcher's Mexico plantation in 1843, agricultural reformer Edmund Ruffin observed,

> The swamp land was not, as I had previously inferred, incapable of being tilled before being embanked. [During the colonial period, at those times when] the river was at ordinary heights, the higher parts of the land was

enough above the water to be worked; & hazardous as was the business, because of liability to freshes of frequent, but uncertain occurrence, & of irregular height & duration, still this land was annually cropped, & in indigo while that was the great staple & general crop of this country. And often as the crops were damaged or totally lost, the estates of the former proprietors of the adjacent high lands, were accumulated by making indigo in these swamp lands.

By the 1840s, indigo had been largely abandoned as a cash crop, but the practice of cultivating the more elevated parts of floodplains endured.[19]

The process of clearing the bottomlands was well described by former slave Jacob Stroyer, who grew up on Matthew Singleton's Headquarters Plantation, about five miles north of the park. Sometime in the mid-1850s, Stroyer was sent to help a group of men and women clear a patch of ground on the Wateree. "A few days after my last whipping the slaves were ordered down into the swamp across the river to clear up new grounds, while the already cleared lands were too wet from rain that had fallen that night. Of course I was among them to do my part; that is, while the men quartered up dry trees, which had been already felled in the winter, and rolled the logs together, the women, boys and girls piled the brushes on the logs and burned them." Clearing of the type described by Stroyer also took place in the swamps of the Congaree. As Robert Mills noted in 1826, the "rich low grounds [along the Congaree] are owned by gentlemen whose agricultural skill and exertions are, perhaps, not exceeded by any in the southern states." Mills may have had in mind men like Wade Hampton I when writing these words, but miles downstream Joel Adams Sr. and others were also planting land in the floodplain, including areas now inside the park.[20]

For landowners such as Matthew Singleton, the potential returns from cultivating rich bottomland soils clearly outweighed the risks. However, even those who chose not to plant their floodplain holdings may have had slaves who did. Across the South it was common for planters to set aside land where slaves could grow provisions on their own time, or even staples for the market. Thomas B. Clarkson of lower Richland followed this practice in the early 1850s—possibly in bottomlands, based on hints in his correspondence—and it seems likely that other slaveholders in the area did so as well.[21] At any rate, whether by planters, their slaves, or both, bottomlands in the park were planted in a variety of crops in the decades after settlement. Principal among them were indigo, corn, rice, and cotton.

Indigo

Indigo was the preferred cash crop for many inland planters in colonial and early postcolonial South Carolina. Although it was hard on the land and could exhaust some soils within a few years, indigo was attractive to planters because it tolerated a variety of soils and the dye was of sufficiently high value to justify the cost of transporting it by wagon to the coast. Indigo did well on both drier, well-drained uplands and rich, fertile bottomlands, being very well suited to the "high river swamp" of the midlands. Among the many attractions of the crop was a bounty of six pence per pound paid by England. This bounty, first offered in 1749, was granted in part to encourage indigo production in the back-country. Over time, as ever larger quantities of indigo were grown to meet for-eign demand, the production of indigo contributed to the spread of plantation agriculture and slavery into the interior of the state. For the most part, only wealthier farmers and planters could engage in indigo production, since the crop required a large capital outlay in the form of vats, equipment, and sheds for producing dye, not to mention slaves for doing the work. However, the capital requirements for a budding indigo producer were much lower than those for a lowcountry rice planter, and individuals who could afford the startup costs could reasonably expect handsome returns on their investment.[22]

Indigo seeds were typically sowed in staggered plantings beginning in mid-to late April and lasting into May. With favorable weather, a grower on the Con-garee might expect two cuttings per year.[23] Writing of the benefits of indigo, Governor James Glen observed that "an Acre of good Land may produce about Eighty Pounds weight of good *Indigo;* and one Slave may manage two Acres and upwards, and raise Provisions besides, and have all the Winter Months to saw *Lumber* and be otherwise employed in . . . . As to the Charge of Labour, both *Indigo* and *Rice* may be managed by the same Persons; for the Labour at-tending *Indigo* being over in the Summer Months, those who were employed in it may afterwards manufacture *Rice,* in the ensuing Part of the Year, when it becomes most laborious." For inland landowners, indigo was particularly ap-pealing because the output of an entire acre or more could be compressed into a single eighty-pound cask, making transport to market relatively easy. When the high returns made possible by the bounty were factored in, the incentives to grow indigo were difficult to resist. Indigo made possible large profits for inland landowners, allowing more than a few middling farmers to become substantial planters.[24]

Indigo was first grown in South Carolina during the days of the Lords Pro-prietors, but had been abandoned in favor of rice by the end of the seventeenth century. Credit for successfully reintroducing indigo in South Carolina is tra-ditionally given to Eliza Lucas, whose son Charles Cotesworth Pinckney would one day cultivate indigo in the future park with Edward Rutledge. But Eliza Lucas was by no means the first, or only, person in the colony to experiment with indigo production. Lucas's real contribution was in making fellow planters aware of indigo's possibilities as an alternate staple to rice.[25]

Lucas began experimenting with the crop while still a young teenager. After a series of setbacks, she finally succeeded in producing seventeen pounds of dye in 1744. Her neighbors took notice, and a brief uptick in indigo production followed in the late 1740s. It was not until the French and Indian War (1754–63), however, that the conditions finally developed for indigo to come into its own as a staple crop. The resulting interruption in the supply of French and Spanish indigo gave South Carolina growers an advantage in the English market, one they quickly exploited. It may be more than coincidental that this is roughly the same time that the majority of the original Beidler Tract plats were recorded. Regardless, contemporary sources indicate that indigo was grown along both the Congaree and Wateree Rivers by the late 1750s. Local tradition is to the same effect, holding that European settlers cleared fields for indigo and corn along the Congaree throughout the last half of the eighteenth century.[26]

It is unlikely that indigo fields on the lower Congaree were very large, even on the more substantial plantations. Backcountry planters tended to own fewer slaves than their lowcountry counterparts, and they needed them to accomplish multiple tasks throughout the year. Even plantations with a larger numbers of slaves needed to devote substantial effort to growing provision crops for sustenance. As a result, few if any plantations in the backcountry were devoted exclusively to indigo production; most also produced crops such as corn, rice, wheat, peas, and potatoes. Constraints on indigo production were most acute in the years immediately after the Revolution. Although the full brunt of the war did not hit South Carolina until 1780–81, when it did, many slaves managed to escape, and others were captured or killed.[27]

The acreage devoted to indigo along the lower Congaree is unknown, but its cultivation appears to have been largely split between local planters and non-resident landowners from the coast. Among the few local indigo planters about whom information has survived is William Howell, who lived about six miles upstream from the park. As noted in chapter 2, Howell started the process of acquiring land in the Beidler Tract in 1756, the year before his death. Backcountry residents sometimes began to clear and plant land before applying for a warrant, so it is possible that Howell had started to cultivate portions of his Beidler Tract parcels before he died. However, Howell owned too few slaves to fully exploit the four hundred acres of his home plantation, let alone the various other tracts he owned. At the time of his death, only six of the twelve slaves listed in the inventory of his estate were adults. This may not have been enough to cultivate large amounts of land, but it was more than sufficient to provide Howell with considerable income from indigo. In 1757 Howell's estate was owed over £739 for indigo, an amount almost three times the value of his best male slave.[28]

Statewide, indigo plantings for small slaveholders ranged from a few to up to thirty acres. By 1790 the majority of slave owners in Richland and northern

Orangeburgh Districts still held well less than 40 slaves, so it seems likely, based on data collected from around the backcountry, that plantings by local landowners averaged around eighteen acres throughout the second half of the eighteenth century. For planters owning more than 40 slaves, indigo plantings appear to have averaged about fifty-eight acres. Into the latter category fell several lowcountry planters with satellite plantations on the lower Congaree, including Major General Charles Cotesworth Pinckney and Edward Rutledge, who together had 50 slaves on the Congaree in 1790, and Brigadier General Isaac Huger, who had 44 slaves. Huger's downstream neighbor Colonel William Thomson had 154 slaves in 1790, a very large number for a backcountry planter at the time.[29]

The size of fields was constrained not only by the limited availability of labor, but also by the amount of work involved in tending the fields and generating dye. Swamp fields were prepared by being "well cleared, drained, and thoroughly broken up and pulverized; after all apprehension of frost was over, the fields were laid off in drills about an inch deep, and from twelve to fifteen inches apart from each other." Slaves had to be "always at the hoe" to keep the growing plants from being choked by weeds.[30] Without constant attention whole crops could be destroyed by caterpillars and grasshoppers. Yet even in the face of these demands, a group of slaves could grow far more indigo than it could actually process for market. According to planter Charles Woodmason, fifteen hands could plant fifty acres in indigo, "but to work the *Indigo* plants raised on it (if a full crop) will require 25, and those very able ones."[31]

Figure 5. Brigadier General Isaac Huger, about 1789. Emmet Collection, Miriam and Ira D. Wallach Division of Art, Prints and Photographs, The New York Public Library, Astor, Lenox and Tilden Foundations.

Figure 6. "Colonel William Thomson" by Edward Savage, about 1790. Watercolor on ivory. ©Image courtesy of the Gibbes Museum of Art/Carolina Art Association.

Landowners in the Beidler Tract most likely cultivated indigo in small- to medium-sized fields throughout the period 1760–95. This was the time when indigo became a commercial staple in South Carolina second only to rice. Local historian Edwin L. Green noted, "Before the Revolution a large acreage, especially in the Congaree Swamp, was devoted to [the] production [of indigo], and for some years after the struggle it continued to be raised. . . . For many years traces of the old indigo fields and of the vats were to be seen." Much of this indigo was probably grown on the higher, sandier soils west of Mill Creek, but indigo was also grown in various locations inside the park.[32]

One part of today's park that may have seen significant indigo cultivation is the area traversed by the elevated (eastern) boardwalk. For much of its length this leg of the boardwalk passes through an expansive alluvial fan, which radiates outward from the point where Dry Branch enters the floodplain (map 1). Given the number of old-growth loblolly pines present on the fan, it is probable that much of this area was cultivated during the colonial and early national periods. The sandy soil that characterizes the fan drains more quickly than adjacent mucks and clays, making it potentially conducive to indigo cultivation. In this regard, an 1839 plat covering the western end of the park shows a stream called "Indigo Branch" running just north of the alluvial fan and the park boundary.[33]

Any obvious traces of indigo fields have long since disappeared from the park, but references to indigo cultivation still survive in the written record. The most explicit such reference occurs in a map drawn around 1791 covering the lower reach of the Congaree River. The map shows a set of "William R. Thomson's Indigo Vattes" on the riverbank just east of the Beidler Tract. The operator of the vats, William Russell Thomson, was the son of Colonel William Thomson. A substantial planter in his own right, William Russell Thomson was the owner of fifty-three slaves in 1790. Assuming that at least thirty of these slaves were of working age, Thomson had the wherewithal to cultivate well over sixty acres of indigo on his various lands.[34]

The physical location of Thomson's vats is consistent with what is known about the mechanics of indigo production in the late-eighteenth-century back-country. Processing took place using a series of three vats, which required access to a large volume of fresh water. Clear, soft water was thought to be ideal. Charles Woodmason claimed that the "quiet running water of the river will not answer; pond or stagnated water is the softest and best; and the longer it has been exposed to the sun-beams, the better for accelerating the fermentation." Indigo had to be processed as soon after cutting as possible but with minimal damage to the cut plants. The ideal processing site was therefore a waterside location as near to the fields as practicable. Where topography allowed, guts and sloughs could be dammed to ensure an adequate supply of water, particularly in times of drought. An 1803 plat showing a drain called to "Indigo Vat Gut" (today's Tennessee Gut) confirms that guts in the Beidler Tract were used for processing indigo. This gut flowed into Cedar Creek in the northwestern part of the park (map 1). Miles to the east, about halfway between the modern rail line and U.S. Highway 601, a long dam across Running Lake Slough may also have been used for indigo (or rice) production.[35]

In a life of endless toil, one of the worst tasks a slave could be assigned was to assist with the making of indigo. Producing dye from the cut "weed" was a notoriously unpleasant and laborious task. The process began with slaves pumping clear water into the first of a series of elevated vats made of thick cypress planks. The first vat, elevated above the rest, was known as the "steeper." Plants cut earlier in the day were carried immediately to the steeper and placed under the water, where they fermented until dye from the leaves and stems had become thoroughly dissolved. When "the weed [had] yielded all its valuable qualities," the liquor was discharged into the adjoining "beater" vat.[36] Here the solution was violently agitated, often by bottomless buckets attached to rods. The agitation continued until the indigo had precipitated out of solution and thickened grains settled to the bottom part of the vat. South Carolina planters differed from their counterparts in the French West Indies in that they often used lime-water in the beater to hasten the separation process.

Just before agitation caused the precipitate to begin dissolving back into solution, the clear water on top was drawn off and the blue liquid below was diverted to a third vat. Here the solids were given additional time to settle. The resulting "mud" was strained through cloth bags and set out in shallow boxes or molds to harden and dry. A drying shed was used for this part of the process because the indigo would lose its color and much of its value if exposed to direct sunlight while drying. When dry, the indigo was cut into bricks or lumps and packed in casks for shipment.[37]

The fermentation part of the process generated such noxious odors and attracted such swarms of flies that planters made every effort to locate the vats at least a quarter mile from the main plantation house. It was the lot of slaves both to endure the awful stench and to keep flies from laying eggs in the bricks of final product, as the bricks would rot if eggs were allowed to hatch. But noisome though it was, managing the flow of product through the vats required a high level of expertise to produce acceptable dye. Not infrequently, that expertise was supplied by slaves.[38]

The international demand for indigo collapsed after 1795 because of overproduction in the Americas and East Indies. But by that point the adoption of improved processing methods by foreign growers had already cut into South Carolina exports. Middle country growers would continue to produce indigo into the 1840s but on a much smaller scale than before and primarily for consumption in the local and national markets.[39]

Rice

Like indigo, rice had been grown in the Congaree River valley since the colonial period. By 1850 production had spread widely in lower Richland, although the amounts cultivated were mostly small. Rice was also cultivated along the Wateree River from the mid–eighteenth century until the time of the Civil War. Because rice is an extremely heavy crop, most planters growing rice for market sought to locate their fields near navigable waterways, where they would have ready access to cheap transportation.[40]

On the whole, there is little evidence to indicate that rice was ever a significant commercial crop in lower Richland. Daniel Huger II's Goodwill Plantation on the Wateree River and John Hopkins's Back Swamp Plantation west of Myers Creek were among the few that may have grown rice for the market.[41] The paucity of commercial rice acreage in the district had mostly to do with geography and the timing of local settlement. By the time most planters started to take up land along the lower Congaree, commercial rice cultivation, previously concentrated in the inland swamps above Charleston, had already started to shift to the tidewater region, where daily tidal movements of freshwater guaranteed a dependable water supply and significantly higher yields per slave. This shift was largely complete by the end of the eighteenth century. In 1802 John Drayton reported that rice was "sometimes grown in the middle country; but of small quantity, more for the use of its inhabitants, than for the purposes of sale." Census data suggests that the growth of rice for local consumption continued in lower Richland into the early 1850s.[42]

Like indigo, rice was probably cultivated most intensively in those parts of the swamp northwest of the park, closer to Columbia. River access was easier there because the floodplain was narrower. Also, since this area had been settled since the 1740s, more time had elapsed for residents to accumulate the capital necessary to support the expense of cultivating rice in a floodplain environment. Nevertheless, it is possible that the Beidler Tract was the site of some rice cultivation. National Park Service ranger Guy Taylor believed that the Old Dead River Dike system constituted the remnants of an old rice plantation, and he speculated that the Adams Pond Dike (also known as the Southwest Boundary Dike) may have been associated with rice cultivation as well (see entries 4 and 18 in appendix A).[43]

Data from the 1850 census reveals that two Beidler Tract landowners—Joel Adams Jr. and Lieuellan Woodward—produced a total of one thousand and forty-five hundred pounds of rice, respectively, from their various properties in lower Richland. The same census indicates that James H. Seay produced nine thousand pounds of rice on his land holdings near Kingville, parts of which were located in the park southwest of the railroad. These outputs, it should be noted, are quite small. Assuming a conservative output of around 1,000 pounds (almost twenty-three bushels) per acre, Seay's crop would have required less than ten acres to produce, Woodward's less than five, and Adams's around one. Moreover, Adams and Woodward were both major landowners in lower Richland, and their rice could have been grown in any number of locations, including high land, where rice was cultivated "somewhat like corn." Seay's plantation consisted of around twenty-five hundred acres in various tracts, the largest of which contained a substantial amount of upland. Only six hundred acres of Seay's plantation were "improved"—that is, cleared and utilized for grazing or crop production, and it is not possible to say how much, if any, of this improved acreage lay in what is now the park.[44]

Stronger evidence that rice was cultivated in the park is provided by Jack Brady (formerly "Braddy"), whose family owned land within the present park boundary for at least 150 years. Citing information conveyed by his grandfather, Brady maintained that rice had been grown in or near the Beidler Tract at some point in the past. Brady did not point to any specific locations, but suitable sites would have existed throughout the park, especially in areas having a high groundwater table or moisture-retaining soils.[45] As Bernard Romans observed in 1776, "rice will grow in any soil though it loves watery ones best." One place where rice may have been cultivated is the part of the floodplain between Weston Lake and the toe of the northern bluff. The prevalence of old-growth loblolly pine in this area is a strong indicator that it was once cleared for crops or pasture. If cultivated, the high-water table and saturated soils in much of this area would appear to have favored rice in particular. Rice could also have been grown on the better-drained soils of the Dry Branch alluvial fan, located immediately to the east. However, as noted above, planters may have opted to use the latter area for growing indigo, as well as other crops preferring somewhat drier soils.[46]

By far the best evidence of rice cultivation in the general vicinity of the park comes from an eyewitness account by Charles Ball, a former slave whose description of his life in bondage was first published in 1837.[47] From about 1805 to late 1806, Ball lived as a slave on a large plantation in lower Richland, where his wealthy owner planted cotton, rice, indigo, corn, and potatoes. According to Ball, his master lived about two miles "from C[on]garee river; which bordered his estate on one side, and in the swamps of which were his rice fields. The country hereabout is very flat; the banks of the river are low; and in wet seasons large tracts of country are flooded by the superabundant water of the river." Ball stated in his narrative that the plantation had about five hundred acres in cotton, one hundred acres in corn, ten acres in indigo, and ten to twelve acres in sweet potatoes. Ball never identifies his master, but certain details in his story suggest that his owner was Wade Hampton I (1754–1835), one of the wealthiest planters in the state and the owner of a very large plantation on Gills Creek, about eleven miles northwest of the park. Hampton had previously owned property in what is now the park as well.[48]

Ball's master had just acquired some new acreage in the Congaree floodplain when he purchased Ball at a slave sale in Columbia. These new lands "adjoined the river for more than a mile in extent, along its margin." Before long, Ball's owner "had cleared the highest parts of this morass, or swamp, and had here made his rice fields," which eventually covered about fifty acres. The growing and harvesting of the rice crop was arduous and debilitating work, which Ball described at some length:

> At the time of which I now speak, the rice was ripe, and ready to be gathered. On Monday morning . . . the overseer took the whole of us to the rice field, to enter upon the harvest of this crop. The field lay in a piece of low ground, near the river, and in such a position that it could be flooded by the water of the stream, in wet seasons. The rice is planted in drills, or rows, and grows more like oats than any of the other grain, known in the north.
>
> The water is sometimes let in to the rice fields, and drawn off again, several times, according to the state of the weather. Watering and weeding the rice is considered one of the most unhealthy occupations on a southern

plantation, as the people are obliged to live for several weeks in the mud and water, subject to all the unwholesome vapours that arise from stagnant pools, under the rays of a summer sun, as well as the chilly autumnal dews of night. At the time we came to cut this rice, the field was quite dry; and after we had reaped and bound it, we hauled it upon wagons, to a piece of hard ground where we made a threshing floor, and threshed it. . . . After getting in the rice, we were occupied for some time in clearing and ditching swampy land, preparatory to a more extended culture of rice, the next year.

If rice was grown in the Beidler Tract, some of it may have been cultivated in the way that Ball described. However, no infrastructure survives on the tract that can clearly be linked with rice cultivation.[49]

Corn

For most settlers putting down stakes in the backcountry, existence was precarious until they were able to clear land and plant a corn crop. The same went for slaves carving out plantations for absentee masters on the coast. Early records indicate that settlers in Saxe Gotha Township planted corn in conjunction with other "provision" crops, including rice, sweet potatoes, peas, pumpkins, beans, wheat, barley, oats, and rye. One hundred years later, descendants of the first settlers were still growing these same crops. Wheat was an especially important crop to the first settlers—so much so that the Commons House of Assembly provided a grant of twenty-two pounds to complete construction of a water-powered grist mill in the township. By 1820, however, most wheat in lower Richland was being grown for domestic use.[50]

A number of planters grew corn and other provision crops on their Beidler Tract lands. Corn was the principal food source for most of the area's early inhabitants, and it remained the most widely planted inland crop in South Carolina throughout the colonial period. Corn was one of South Carolina's major commercial crops as well. In 1792 the state produced 99,985 bushels for export to overseas markets. Corn continued to be grown in large quantities during the ensuing years, resulting in a glut by around 1807. Oversupply drove down the price, which in turn made transporting corn over long distances unprofitable. Things improved after about 1826, when increased demand led to higher prices. By the end of the antebellum period, corn had gone from being an item of home consumption to a staple crop in many parts of the state. Some planters in the southern half of the state grew corn for the market, but many planted corn primarily to support the production of cotton.[51]

That corn was cultivated in the park during the colonial and antebellum years is clear, but information on the actual amount cultivated is lacking. Some comments by John Drayton in 1802 hint at the extent of early corn cultivation near the fall line, and these comments appear to fit the lands along the Congaree. Drayton remarked that many of the rice plantations in the lowcountry planted little in the way of food crops but were provisioned in large part by "Indian corn, brought down the rivers from the middle parts of the state." Regarding the middle country, he observed, "Whenever large rivers penetrate through these lands [that is, the sand hills], there the adjacent soil is of excellent quality, favoring the growth of the heaviest timber; and is capable of producing from fifty to seventy bushels of Indian corn, and twelve hundred weight or more, of cotton in the seed, to each acre." Drayton emphasized that fields yielding fifty to seventy bushels of corn per acre were "only spoken of, as relating to the high river swamp lands in the middle parts of the state."[52] These yields still obtained during the antebellum period, a point confirmed by Robert Mills. Writing a quarter century after Drayton, Mills observed that the swamplands of Richland District would produce forty to eighty bushels of corn per acre, a yield far greater than the best pine lands, which produced only ten to fifteen bushels per acre.[53]

Quite apart from comments like these, one can infer that a substantial amount of corn was grown in the Beidler Tract from simple logistics—the typical large plantation of lower Richland was a diversified operation, growing a number of different crops and drawing upon the various resources of its land base to achieve a high degree of self-sufficiency. This was achieved, in part, by setting aside land on the plantation to grow corn and other crops such as rice, oats, peas, beans, and sweet potatoes. Corn's short growing season complemented the longer growing season of cotton, making it possible—in theory at least—to meet the subsistence needs of the plantation while concentrating on the production of cotton. Corn was typically planted in March, with cotton following some weeks later in April. If corn was postponed until June, as often happened, the crop could be left in the field until after the first cotton of the year was picked in August and September. The two crops complemented each other in their soil moisture requirements as well. River bottomlands too low to grow good cotton would still grow corn.[54]

In practice, many planters in the major cotton-growing regions neglected their corn in the field to focus on cotton. Some planted just enough corn to get by, if that. Others deliberately planted less corn than they needed to maximize the acreage devoted to cotton, counting on buying corn from others when the time came. Planters on the lower Congaree were well situated to adopt the latter strategy if they chose, as they could readily supplement their corn crop with surplus foodstuffs produced upstream or, in later years, brought in by rail. As state geologist Oscar M. Lieber observed in 1859, a line drawn through the state more or less at the fall line "would exhibit, above it, the region in which corn is produced for export, and below it, that in which the entire corn crop is consumed at home."[55]

The incentive for lower Richland planters to neglect corn in favor of cotton would have been particularly strong between 1794 and 1819, South Carolina's first cotton boom. At times during these years, cotton prices were as high as they would ever be before the Civil War. By the late 1830s and into the 1840s the incentives were reversed, the result of an agricultural depression brought on by the Panic of 1837. Conditions were made even worse by overproduction in 1839 and a severe drought in 1845. Low cotton prices during this period pushed many planters to grow more corn and strive for a greater degree of self-sufficiency than they had in years past. Then came the state's second great cotton boom (1848–60), and conditions changed again. By 1860 corn production in Richland District had declined to about half of what it had been in 1850. Some portion of this reduction may have been due to the outmigration of numerous large and small landowners from the district during the preceding decade, but a more important factor appears to have been planters reducing the amount of land devoted to corn.[56]

It is not clear to what extent corn production in what is now the park mirrored trends in the district as a whole. The amount of land planted in corn doubtless varied over time, but judging from the experience of the 1850s, corn production in parts of the floodplain may have remained fairly substantial throughout the period from the Revolution to emancipation. By 1860 only a few planters owning land in the Beidler Tract had materially reduced corn production from 1850 levels, and others actually increased their output. Even those who did scale back were still growing enough corn in 1860 to feed their field slaves.[57] The typical corn ration for an adult slave was around one peck of cornmeal per week, or thirteen bushels per year.[58] By this measure, most of the Beidler Tract landowners for whom information is available were growing enough corn in 1860 to meet all of their agricultural and domestic needs. Many were actually producing a considerable surplus (see table 2 below).

All the planters listed in table 2 were substantial landowners, and each could have grown corn on land outside the Beidler Tract.[59] However, many probably grew at least part of their corn inside the tract, particularly those who owned land on the natural levee along the river.

Corn is known or presumed to have been grown at several locations along the natural levee in the park. In his cultural survey of the Beidler Tract, Michie lists corn as the crop most likely to have been grown within the Old Dead River Dike, a suggestion that seems reasonable, not only because of corn's importance to the plantation economy but also because corn was grown immediately upstream on the plantation of Charles Cotesworth Pinckney and Edward Rutledge. Joel Adams Sr. also grew corn in the park, some of it perhaps destined for

Table 2 Corn Production in 1860, Beidler Tract Landowners

LANDOWNER	PART OF BEIDLER TRACT OWNED	CORN PRODUCED PER SLAVE TEN YEARS OF AGE AND OLDER (TOTAL, FROM ALL LANDS OWNED)
Mary G. Adams	Parcel 1 (⅔ interest)	34 bushels
Grace W. Adams Davis	Parcel 1 (¼ interest)	38 bushels
James U. Adams	Parcels 1 (⅙ interest) and 6	30 bushels
Isaac T. Weston	Parcels 2–5	14 bushels
Daniel Zeigler	Parcels 8, 9, and part of 10	71 bushels
Alfred M. Hunt	Parcel 13	88 bushels
Paul Spigener	Parcel 14	50 bushels
Lieuellan Woodward	Parcel 15	14 bushels
James H. Seay	Parcel 18 (portion of)	34 bushels
Daniel McKenzie	Parcel 19	60 bushels

Source: 1860 Manuscript Census Returns, Agriculture and Slave Schedules, Richland and Orangeburgh Districts, SCDAH.

shipment to market. At his death in 1830, Adams had on hand $2,250.00 worth of corn "at [the] swamp place," considerably more than would have been required to feed the one hundred slaves he then owned. The inventory of Adams's estate does not state precisely where on the plantation the corn was grown, but the most likely spot was near "Adams' Quarter" on the riverbank in the western end of the park (figure 7). Adams' Quarter appears to have been the hub of a substantial operation. In 1831 Adams's estate paid $126.00 for "bricks for [the] swamp plantation." That same year the estate paid Washington Nixon $173.34 for "overseeing [the] swamp place" in 1830.[60]

Traces of old agricultural fields may indicate other locations where corn was grown in the park. In the early 1980s ranger Guy Taylor discovered "old rows, five feet apart" on a site east of the Sims Trail, as well as in an area adjacent to Toms Creek. Considering the erosive power of floods and the effects of sedimentation, these features were probably of relatively recent origin at the time. Nevertheless, if the spacing observed by Taylor reflects longstanding agricultural practice, these rows may indicate places where corn was grown in the past. John Drayton noted in 1802 that "[if corn is planted] with the plough, a furrow is run across the field at every five feet, intersected by others, at right angles; and corn is sown at the intersections: If with the hoe the land is drawn up into beds, at the same distance; and the corn is planted along the bed in holes at every four or five feet." The rows discovered by Taylor appear to approximate this spacing.

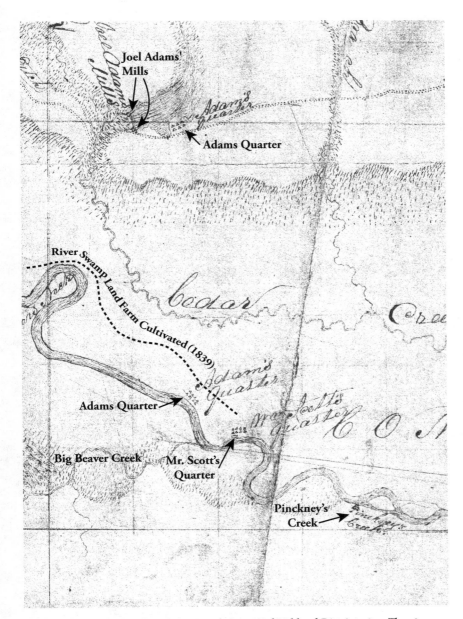

Figure 7. Detail from Marmaduke Coate's *Survey of Richland District, 1820*. The 1839 cultivation line superimposed on the map is taken from an 1839 plat of the Adams swamp plantation, now lost, reproduced by Tomlinson Engineering in 1936. Detail of Coate *Survey* courtesy of South Carolina Department of Archives and History, adapted by Lynne Parker.

But again, this physical evidence has to be approached with caution. On higher sites, such spacing could also be indicative of cotton, which was sometimes planted in five-foot rows on high (or drained) land capable of generating large yields.[61]

Cotton

When the market for indigo collapsed in the mid-1790s, inland planters found themselves in a decidedly vulnerable position. Without an export staple to provide return on investment, growers turned to wheat, corn, and tobacco, but with lackluster results. Soon, however, the success of the cotton gin showed planters and small farmers alike that salvation lay to hand in the form of green seed cotton. Inland planters found themselves doubly favored in that the lands formerly used to produce indigo were, in the words of John Drayton, "fortunately well adapted to the cultivation of cotton." From this point on, the number of slaves in the district would grow to keep pace with demand for the new staple (see table 3 below).[62]

As cotton began its rise to ascendancy in the 1790s, Wade Hampton I of lower Richland was among the first to plant the new staple in large quantities. Drayton noted in 1802 that "in the middle country . . . the *high swamp* lands, produce the *green seed,* in great abundance." In 1826 Robert Mills reported that the swamplands of Richland District would produce "from 3 to 400 pounds of clean cotton" per acre, four times as much as the best pine lands. Twenty

Table 3 Slave Ownership in Richland District (Excluding Columbia), 1790–1840

YEAR	TOTAL HOUSE- HOLDS	TOTAL SLAVE OWNERS	NUMBER OF HOUSEHOLDS OWNING:							
			1–9 SLAVES	10–19	20–29	30–39	40–49	50–99	100–199	200+
1790	483	154	99	28	15	7	1	3	1	—
1800	*	*	*	*	*	*	*	*	*	*
1810	613	268	155	61	16	11	5	16	3	1
1820	557	273	129	64	29	7	10	22	9	3
1830	727	334	172	59	32	18	10	29	10	4
1840	680	322	149	62	34	13	19	26	16	3

Source: US Census Bureau, manuscript population schedules, 1790, 1810–40, South Carolina, Richland District, SCDAH.

*The 1800 census returns for Richland District are lost.

years later, R. L. Allen observed that an "average cotton crop on good uplands in South Carolina, is from 600 to 1,000 lbs.; and on bottom lands, 800 to 1,600 lbs. per acre." But while yields on the district's bottomlands were greater than those on the uplands, moister soils meant that the cotton tended to be a little less white and hence not as valuable.[63]

The Beidler Tract must have seen its share of cotton cultivation during the early national and antebellum periods, although probably not nearly as much as the higher-quality lands just below Columbia.[64] Where cotton was concerned, the principal shortcoming of the present-day park area was clayey soils, which predominated even in the levee zone. Cotton requires well-drained soils for optimal growth. In the absence of effective drainage, plants grown on clays tended to "run to weed"—that is, they continued growing throughout the growing season but failed to ripen before the first frost. Furthermore, a labor-intensive plant like cotton was a very risky crop to grow in bottomland fields, especially ones that had not been diked. Unlike indigo, which could be replanted after a late spring flood, or corn, which could be left standing for free-ranging hogs, flood-damaged cotton was a total loss.[65]

Confirmation that cotton was grown in the park dates from the late 1840s, when Revolutionary War historian Benson Lossing saw cotton being cultivated on reclaimed portions of Buckhead Neck about five miles downstream from the Beidler Tract. Cotton was surely grown elsewhere in the park during this period as well, although documentary evidence has yet to come to light. The best areas for growing cotton would have been the higher riverside areas in the central and western parts of the park, including the lands owned by Joel Adams Sr. and William Scott Jr. (see figure 7 and appendix A). Decades later, the James O'Hanlon plantation immediately west of the park was said to embrace "some of as productive lands, both for corn and cotton, as are on the Congaree River." In the park itself the proportion of productive high ground was considerably less than that on the O'Hanlon place, and planters faced greater limits on their ability to cultivate cotton in large quantities.[66]

Even on diked fields, however, cotton was a gamble. Major Samuel Porcher grew only corn and oats on his floodplain lands at Mexico Plantation, despite having constructed one of the largest and most celebrated embankments in the state to keep the Santee at bay. Cotton had been cultivated on these lands at one time, but as Edmund Ruffin noted, "Cotton is a precareous [sic] crop on this land, & is not now [in 1843] planted on it." [67]

With Porcher's example in mind, a modern observer might question the extent to which landowners in the area of today's park would have assumed the risk and expense of growing cotton in the floodplain. In the late 1840s Governor Whitemarsh Seabrook complained that too many South Carolina planters took the path of least resistance, growing cotton only on readily worked upland areas rather than making the effort to cultivate the state's fertile swamplands. This could well have been the case in the park, as many of the principal landowners, including the Adams, Weston, and Woodward families, owned large tracts of prime farmland north of the present park boundary. However, economic conditions of the antebellum period were such that landowners in the park would have had to at least consider growing more cotton in the floodplain. Senator and renowned orator Daniel Webster saw the problems facing planters firsthand in 1847, when he toured the plantation of Wade Hampton II outside Columbia. Webster noted that "the cotton lands, except the bottoms, are very much worn out and exhausted. Many planters having large numbers of slaves, now buy new lands in the Southwest, and send some of their slaves there."[68]

Beginning in the 1820s, western cotton grew in volume, driving down prices and making it increasingly difficult for South Carolina planters to compete in the market. By 1848 William Elliott was suggesting that South Carolinians plant cotton only on "such bodies of land as approach in fertility the rich alluvium of the West."[69] The result in many instances was an intensification of efforts to grow cotton in river swamps. Some growers, having little choice, played the odds each year with respect to flooding. Others, being more prosperous, took a different tack. For them, dikes were the way to minimize their losses from flooding.

4 ❧ Early Park Plantations

While there remain[s] one acre of swamp-land uncleared of South Carolina, I would raise my voice against restricting the importation of negroes.

Charles Cotesworth Pinckney, statement supporting adoption
of the Federal constitution, 1788

THROUGHOUT THE LAST HALF of the eighteenth century, most landowners in lower Richland, even the more prosperous ones, remained stock raisers and small farmers. They either owned no slaves at all or held a relatively small number, which limited the extent of their clearing activities. Over time, however, this situation began to change, and by the census of 1790 at least eighteen individuals in the lower Congaree valley owned twenty or more slaves. This figure may actually understate the number of well-to-do growers in the area, since some may have lost slaves in the war. But with a few notable exceptions, local planters did not begin to acquire truly large numbers of slaves (fifty or more) until the start of the cotton boom in the early nineteenth century (see table 3 above).[1]

Plantation agriculture soon came to be the predominant form of cultivation in floodplains below the fall line. The risk of flooding made occupation of family farmsteads impractical over the long term, favoring instead the aggregation of large tracts worked by slaves. As a result, the last half of the eighteenth century saw inland planters vying with wealthy planters from the coast to obtain the most desirable river-bottom tracts for planting.[2] Along the Wateree, lowcountry planters were acquiring tracts of five hundred or a thousand acres as early as the 1750s. Some of these tracts extended for two or three miles and lay entirely in the swamp. In the same way, wealthy planters and merchants from the coast were increasingly drawn to the fertile floodplain soils of lower

Richland. As S. Max Edelson has noted, eighteenth-century planting in South Carolina was often "an activity that was initiated from the city and enacted in the countryside. . . . Even the most remote outpost was connected—by coasting schooners, wagons, and flatboats—to direct communication with the colony's dominant Atlantic port."[3]

For a coastal planter of the mid- to late eighteenth century, having a back-country "supply" plantation could be both profitable in itself and an important source of provisions for his lands in the tidewater. The soils on backcountry rivers and creeks produced both indigo and provision crops (principally corn) in large quantities. On the lower Congaree, growers typically shipped their crops to the coast by road until the advent of steamboats and the railroad eventually provided other options. Not only were the roads between Charleston and Columbia shorter than the water route (110 miles versus 500 miles), the water route was so hazardous that shippers in the first two decades of the nineteenth century preferred to send their cotton to market via wagon even though it cost twice as much per ton shipped.[4]

One cannot help but be struck by the number of wealthy lowcountry planters, many related by blood or marriage, who owned or had ties to working plantations on the lower Congaree. Prominent individuals such as Alexander Gillon, Charles Cotesworth Pinckney, Isaac Huger, Lieutenant Governor William Bull Jr., Lieutenant Colonel Barnard Elliott, and Miles Brewton each owned land on the high bluffs south of river, with adjoining acreage in the swamps to the north (map 6). Since most, if not all, of these individuals derived substantial income from their Congaree plantations, it is likely that each cultivated land in what is now the park. The actual cultivating would have been done by slaves, of course, supervised by local overseers. For Gillon and Huger, control was sometimes exercised at closer quarters, as each resided for a time at his Congaree plantation. The same went for Rebecca Brewton Motte, sister of the wealthy slave trader and merchant Miles Brewton, who inherited her brother's Mount Joseph Plantation after his death in 1775. The Motte home, fortified by the British and known as Fort Motte, would be the site of a celebrated patriot siege in May 1781 (see entry 30 in appendix A and "Rebecca Brewton Motte" in appendix B). [5]

A major factor drawing lowcountry planters to the Congaree was the surge in demand for indigo brought on by the French and Indian War. Demand for indigo increased steadily in Britain after the war, and total exports from South Carolina more than doubled between the early 1750s and early 1770s. Lowcountry planters responded by setting up no fewer than seven plantations in the park. Major Samuel Wise, a former Charleston merchant turned backcountry planter, had acquired 1,250 acres on Cedar Creek and Wise Lake by the time of his death in 1779 (map 6). In addition to his acreage in the park, Wise had extensive land holdings in the Cheraws District, with additional real estate elsewhere

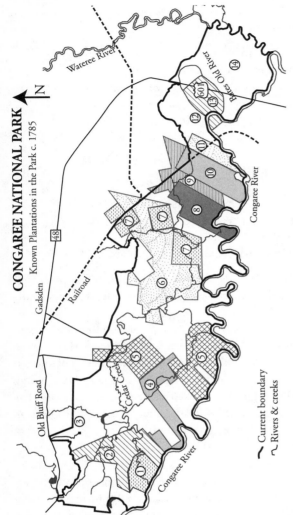

CONGAREE NATIONAL PARK

Known Plantations in the Park c. 1785

N

Old Bluff Road

Gadsden

Railroad

48

Wateree River

Bates Old River

Cedar Creek

Congaree River

Congaree River

Map 6. Known Plantations in the Park, ca. 1785. Owners of known plantations are listed below, together with plantation names where available. See appendix B for details on owners and plantations. Note: Plantation boundaries are approximate. Boundaries are based principally on Kinzer, *A Partial Chain of Title Covering the Principal Floodplain Tracts within Congaree National Park* (2016), and Cely, *Map of Original Land Grants, Congaree Swamp National Monument* (2001) and *Map of Early Land Grants, Congaree National Park, East and Vicinity* (2014). Map by Lynne Parker.

LANDOWNERS:

* Boundary of ownership not known.

1. Joel Adams Sr.
2. Estate of Samuel Wise
3. William Weston II*
4. Francis Goodwyn
5. Charles Cotesworth Pinckney and Edward Rutledge (Precipice Plantation) [two compartments, including Joseph Martin tract on north]
6. Peter Mazyck
7. Edward Lightwood [three compartments]

8. Isaac Huger
9. William Bull Jr.
10. Barnard Elliott
11. Rebecca Brewton Motte (Mount Joseph Plantation)
12. William Thomson (Belleville Plantation)*
13. Mary Brewton Motte (Buckhead Plantation)
14. William Thomson (Belleville Plantation),* Sophianisba McCord,* others*

~ Current boundary
⌐ Rivers & creeks

in the state. Hints about the nature of his Congaree operation are found in an advertisement placed by his executors in 1783:

> To be SOLD,
> ON TUESDAY the 23d of December instant; at
> HOWELL'S FERRY, on the Congaree River;
> Twenty-two Valuable NEGROES,
> Horses, Hogs, Indigo Seed,
> Cattle, Corn, Plantation Tools,
> Sheep, Blades, &c, &c.
> Belonging to the Estate of Major SAMUEL WISE,
> deceased. . . .
> Likewise, at the same Time and Place, will be Sold,
> A NEGRO-WOMAN and her TWO CHILDREN,
> the property of Miss Jane Ann Wise.
> Thomas Boak, [Executor and] Guardian

The Congaree plantation remained in Major Wise's estate for many years after his death, apparently worked by his executors to help pay off debts. It was finally advertised for judicial sale in 1806.[6]

One of the largest eighteenth-century plantations on the lower Congaree was assembled by wealthy lowcountry landowner and politician Henry Middleton (1717–1784). Middleton had acquired much of the land in this plantation by late 1772.[7] At the time he sold the plantation in 1783, "those valuable Indigo lands of Henry Middleton's Esq" appear to have constituted between twenty-five hundred and twenty-nine hundred acres of upland and swamp, split roughly in half by the "Santee" River (as the Congaree was often called in the early days of settlement).[8] The part of the plantation within the park included what is today Old Dead River and lands to the west.

Middleton actively managed the plantation during his tenure, both in person and through his local site manager, Colonel William Thomson. Thomson was a prominent figure in the local area who would soon earn renown as a hero of the Revolution. He owned various tracts on the river's lower reaches, including several in the eastern end of the park. He also managed the plantations of various absentee landowners, including those of Middleton, Lieutenant Governor William Bull Jr., and possibly Miles Brewton. Thomson made his home south of the river at Belleville, a large plantation located just downstream from Rebecca Motte's Mount Joseph. There he was an important grower of indigo before switching to cotton in the mid-1790s.[9] It is not known how much land Thomson may have cultivated in the park on his own behalf or while acting as land manager for Middleton and others. Yet it is virtually certain that he and his son William Russell Thomson were active in the floodplain north of the river. As noted earlier, a map of the lower Congaree valley from around 1791[10] specifically identifies the location of a set of William R. Thomson's indigo vats, showing them on the north bank of the river just east of the Beidler Tract.[11]

Middleton held on to the Congaree plantation for a relatively short time before deciding to sell. Sufficiently impressed with the quality of the plantation, Colonel Thomson and a partner offered to buy it for the considerable sum of six thousand guineas. Middleton, however, declined the offer, choosing instead to sell to two of his sons-in-law, Charles Cotesworth Pinckney and Edward Rutledge. He sold the plantation to them "cheap— & purely on family consideration." At the time Pinckney and Rutledge were thirty-seven and thirty-three years old, respectively, each looking to restore his fortunes after many years of service in the Revolution. The two long-time friends went in together as law and business partners, jointly acquiring the Middleton plantation and relying on income from legal fees to meet their initial debt payments. It took years, though, for this and other partnership investments to begin to produce appreciable income. For Pinckney, a succession of bad crop years and heavy borrowing forced him to spend ten years concentrating on his law practice to avoid financial ruin. In 1791 he declined an appointment from President Washington to the United States Supreme Court, citing the need to attend to his private affairs. Edward Rutledge declined the same appointment for similar reasons.[12]

Pinckney and Rutledge closed on the plantation in early 1783, relying (they later said) on representations that it contained "prime" swampland for cultivation. Some years later, the two partners acquired the 693-acre Joseph Martin tract, two-thirds of which was in the floodplain northwest of the main plantation. (The Joseph Martin tract included the large area of swampland later owned by the Fishburne family and found to be "unsaleable" in the 1820s and 1830s.) All told, the Pinckney and Rutledge holdings in the park included the area surrounded by Old Dead River, plus an additional 1,800 acres of swamp to the west and north (map 6).[13]

Pinckney and Rutledge needed someone to serve as their local agent and overseer at the plantation, and they soon hired Joel Adams Sr. for the job. Apparently a cattleman in his early years, Adams arrived in lower Richland from North Carolina about 1768, when he would have been eighteen years old. He married Grace Weston in 1773 and obtained a tract of 565 acres east of Cedar Creek, about four and a half miles north of the park. This land, which included the present-day site of St. John's Episcopal Church, Congaree, would serve as his home plantation, which he called "Homestead." By 1777 Adams also owned "Half of Four Hundred & fifty Acres of Swamp Land" that he cultivated in partnership with Isaac Rivers. The location of this tract is not known.[14]

After the war Adams followed the track blazed by William Thomson, working at least part of his time for others on the way to amassing a fortune of his own. As the *American Gazetteer* observed in 1804, "for 40 or 50 miles back [from the South Carolina coast], and on the rivers much farther, the cultivators are all slaves. No white man, to speak generally, ever thinks of settling a farm, and improving it for himself, without negroes; if he has no negroes, he hires himself as overseer to some rich planter, till he can purchase for himself." In time Adams would come to own at least 119 slaves and acquire land enough to be known as "Joel of All" by his peers. In fact, over the course of his life Adams is reputed to have acquired more than twenty-five thousand acres in the fork of the Congaree and Wateree Rivers. These lands included much of the Cedar Creek watershed and about one-third of what would one day become the Beidler Tract. All that lay far in the future, however, when Pinckney and Rutledge hired him as overseer in late 1783 or early 1784. Once hired, Adams immediately set to work purchasing livestock, indigo seed, and other necessities. He also arranged for slaves to be transported to the plantation. An indeterminate number of slaves was carried to the plantation in 1784 and "23 new Negroes" in 1785.[15]

Some of Adams's activities are detailed in Pinckney's ledger book for the period 1784–91. This small notebook records cash outlays for various plantations that Pinckney and Rutledge jointly owned during the last two decades of the eighteenth century. Relevant portions of the ledger, reproduced in table 4 below, give a glimpse into the workings of the Congaree plantation in the mid-1780s.

Table 4 Selected Entries from the Ledger Book for Plantations Owned by C. C. Pinckney and E. Rutledge, 1784–87

CASH PAID BY C. C. PINCKNEY FOR PLANTATION EXPENSES		
1784		
March 24th	To cash sent by Col Taylor[16] to Mr. Adams to purchase Horses &c. 50 Guineas	£54=7=6
May 6th	To Mr. Joel Adams to purchase stock &c. 100 Guineas	108=15= —
June 10th	To 3 bushels clean rice to send with Negroes seven dollars—Pipes of Tobacco 1 dollar	1=17=4
10th	To Melchior Smith for carrying Negroes and Iron &c. to Congarees. 4 Guineas	4=7= —
June 26th	To John McWilliams 26 Dollars – 6 for carrying the negroes, the rest for spike nails— Overseer's Hat, provisions and rum for Negroes—	6=1=4
1785		
Jan. 1th [*sic*]	To Joel Adams on Account	70=1=4
14th	To W. Weston[17] for Corn & Indigo seed and Hogs	53=15=8
Feb. 22.d	To Mr. Joel Adams in favor of Mr. George Banks for Indigo seed £22=18=10. Also sent Mr. Adams by	22=18=10

Mr. Barch twenty one Guineas given me by Mr. E. Rutledge to put him in Cash for Indigo seed

April 20th	To Droine & Zeigler for Carriage for Bacon from the Congarees 23 Dollars	5=7=4
May 11th	To cash sent to Mr. Joel Adams by Mr. Ford Fifty five Guineas English and 5 french Guineas on Account/one half of this paid by Mr. E. Rutledge.	32=11=5
	To Mr. Daniel Ford 34 dollars & ½ for Killingsworth a Waggoner to carry 23 new Negroes to the Congarees, & one Guinea for Mr. Ford's own trouble	9=0=5
	To Mr. Ford 3 half [Johannes] to buy provisions for Negroes	5=12= —
June	To Col. Wade Hampton for Indigo Plants	27=0= —
July	To cash paid Taylor for Provisions, stock &c. 50 half [Johannes]	93=6=8
August 10th	To 6 Bushells of Salt for Congaree—Barrel casking & Coopering	0=18=10
August 24th	To Mr. Charles Butler for carrying salt & Coffee to the Congarees 9 Dollars	2=2= —
Dec. 16	To Milos Jackson for carrying sundry Articles to the Congarees 12 Dollars & ½	2=18=4
	To Milos Jackson for bringing Indigo to Town 18 Dollars & ½ paid [the] 14th of this Month	4=6=4
15th	Paid Joel Adams Ov. Account of Plantation Expense	21=14= —
2d	To James Boykin for Cattle, Hogs & Indigo seed –	19=6=3
	To Jos. Martin for carrying 4 Negroes to the Congarees Omitted in Sept. 1784 as pd. receipt	1=12=8
1786		
June 29	Paid order of Joel Adams in favor of Mr. Greenwood £21-6-8 this being part of ballance due Adams by us—	
Sept. 14	Paid Mr. Adams order in favour of Boykin £23-10-0 -	
1787		
Jan. 30	Paid Joel Adams Ballance of old Account—24-8-6 ½—	24-8-6 ½

Source: Gen. Charles Cotesworth Pinckney Account Book, 1784–91, in C. C. Pinckney Family Papers, Library of Congress.

The Congaree plantation was one of at least three that Pinckney and Rutledge acquired as partners during the hopeful and speculative years just after the Revolution. Pinckney and Rutledge went into significant debt to acquire their plantations, and they needed and expected these lands to generate income to pay back loans and enhance their wealth. Thus, when it turned out that the

Congaree plantation contained much less "prime" swamp than the partners had expected, the economic fallout led to considerable discord within the family. Pinckney and Rutledge appear to have submitted a claim against some members of the Middleton family, asserting that the now-dead Henry Middleton had misrepresented the quality of the plantation's swampland. Thomas Middleton responded that, to his knowledge, his father had never claimed the plantation contained "prime" swampland, only that it had one thousand acres of "good plantable swamp. —not too low or too much broken for Indigo or Corn." That was all the same to Pinckney and Rutledge, who had seen more than a few indigo and corn crops washed out by floodwaters. In July 1793 Pinckney informed his brother Thomas that "at the Congarees the freshes have destroyed both Corn & Indigo, we have already planted three times & at this late season are attempting a fourth time." It is not known how the dispute with the Middletons was ultimately resolved. The fact that it came to a head in the mid-1790s—over ten years after the plantation had originally been acquired—suggests that Pinckney and Rutledge had long been trying to make a go of things at Congaree but without notable success.[18]

Edward Rutledge died in 1800. To wind up the partnership's affairs, Pinckney put its assets up for sale, including all its property along the Congaree River. A major selling point of the Congaree plantation was its suitability for growing green seed cotton and other crops, as indicated in the 1802 notice of sale:

Public Auction.
Two hundred and thirty prime Negroes, and Cotton and Rice Plantations, for sale. In order to close the Partnership Concerns of CHARLES COTESWORTH PINCKNEY and the late EDWARD RUTLEDGE, deceased, there will be sold without reserve. . . .

[A 700-acre tract, "composed mostly of Congaree swamp, and known by the name of MARTIN'S TRACT."]

[Also, near the above,] a PLANTATION on both sides of Congaree river, formerly belonging to the hon. Henry Middleton, esq. and known by the name of the PRECIPICE, containing by the original surveys 2910 acres of land, through which the Congaree river flows; of which 1392 acres, according to the original plats, should be swamp. Green seed cotton, hemp and corn may be cultivated to advantage on this plantation.

Regarding the amount of cotton that may have been grown at the Precipice, it is not possible to give a precise answer. The cotton gin had only been invented in 1793, less than ten years before the date of Pinckney's advertisement. On the other hand, Colonel William Thomson had begun planting short-staple cotton at Belleville in 1794, and Wade Hampton I and Governor Charles Pinckney were experimenting with its production on the upper Congaree at about this same time. Hampton is generally credited with being among the first in the state to produce short-staple cotton on a large scale. In 1799 he raised over six hundred bags of cotton on six hundred acres in Richland County, worth $75,000 (over $1.4 million in 2015 dollars). Soon thereafter, Governor Pinckney sent his own sizable shipments to Charleston from his lands in Richland and Orangeburgh Districts. South Carolina went from exporting 94,000 pounds of cotton in 1794, almost all of it the Sea Island variety, to 20 million pounds in 1800, most of it short staple. It seems likely, therefore, that Rutledge and Charles Cotesworth Pinckney had planted some part of the Precipice in cotton before 1802, especially since Rutledge had become caught up in the fever for cotton planting by 1798.[19]

Pinckney managed to sell the Martin tract in 1802, but he still owned large tracts on both sides of the river at his death in 1825. He thus would have had ample opportunity to plant cotton on the Congaree in his later years if he so chose. However, neither the census of 1810 nor 1820 lists any slaves for Charles Cotesworth Pinckney in Orangeburgh District, so it is possible that Pinckney leased his Congaree plantation to others in the early nineteenth century. Administering such leases would have been the responsibility of Joel Adams Sr., who, in addition to now being one of the largest cotton planters in lower Richland, was still acting as agent for Pinckney's lands on the Congaree. Alternatively, Pinckney may have worked the plantation himself by periodically dispatching hands to the "Congarees" from his plantation on Pinckney Island (Beaufort District), where he lived for much of the year beginning around 1800.[20]

The Precipice was hardly the largest plantation on the lower Congaree. Quite a bit larger was "Gillon's Retreat," an upstream plantation owned by Commodore Alexander Gillon. Gillon was a prominent Charleston businessman, politician, and naval officer, whose friends included Charles Cotesworth Pinckney, Pierce Butler, and Isaac Huger. His plantation covered about five thousand acres on the south side of the river, stretching three miles or more from Big Beaver Creek on the west (see figure 7) to a point near the future village of Totness. Until 1777 almost six hundred acres of the plantation were located north of the river in the western part of the park.[21] Parts of this acreage would end up being farmed and grazed for much of the nineteenth and twentieth centuries (see entry 8 in appendix A). Whether these same areas were cultivated as far back as the 1770s is not known, but an advertisement from 1793 suggests that, at the very least, indigo and corn were cultivated in the bottomlands nearby. The advertisement offered for private sale a "very valuable plantation on Congaree river, adjoining commodore Gillon's, containing 610 acres of prime swamp, equal to most on that river, for the culture of indigo and corn, and 1052 acres of high land."[22]

Not far downstream from the Precipice was another large tract, this one assembled by John Mitchell, a deputy surveyor from St. Matthews Parish. Totaling some twenty-five hundred acres, the Mitchell tract, like the Precipice, consisted of large expanses on both sides of the river. When Mitchell put the tract up for sale in December 1769, he touted the economic potential of both its swamp and upland areas, claiming that "the Mill-Seat on said Tract . . . abounds with good Pine and Cypress Timber contiguous [and] there is so much good River Swamp, as to render it a most complete Hemp or Indico Plantation." In a follow-up advertisement from October 1770, Mitchell went into quite a bit more detail, providing a good example of backcountry land speculation in action:

FOR SALE

THE FOLLOWING VALUABLE

TRACTS OF LAND, viz.

Two Thousand Five Hundred Acres on *Santee*-River, near Colonel *Thomson's*, above the Fork of *Wateree* and *Santee*, on the Foot of a Creek called *Cedar-Creek*, on the North Side of the River, and a Creek called *High-Hill Creek*, on the South Side; lying on both Sides of the Said River; and hath a very extensive Front, capable of being divided into four or five smaller Tracts, each very commodious for Settlements. —The greatest Part of the said Tract is high rich Beach, Oak, Gum, and Cane Swamp: The high Land (which is very commodious for a Settlement for the Swamp) includes, from the River upwards, near a Mile of the said *High-Hill-Creek;* which (being a constant Stream, and always having Plenty of Water, sufficient to drive three Saws) renders it a very commodious Place for a Saw-Mill, and might be much improved if converted to that Use, by running out the Pine Land contiguous thereto, of which there is great Plenty, and well-timbered. The said Tract is noted for one of the best Places for a Saw-Mill of any on *Santee* River, which adds much to the Value thereof, having a double Advantage, for it is as good Land for the Culture of Hemp, Indico, Rice, Corn, or any Thing else, as any on *Santee*.

· ·

For further Particulars enquire of Colonel William Thomson, in St. *Matthew's* Parish, or of John Fisher, Merchant, in *Orangeburgh* . . . or of

JOHN MITCHELL.[23]

From other sources it appears that the portion of the tract north of the river comprised the original grants to James McKelvie, Phillipina Hoofman, and Michael Sullivan, which together covered 850 acres. Not long after the second ad appeared, Mitchell sold these tracts to Peter Mazyck, a wealthy young merchant from Charleston (and William Mazyck's older brother). Peter Mazyck's plantation soon grew to encompass 3,150 acres in the floodplain, together with a separate 500-acre tract on the low bluff to the north. At its southern end the plantation spanned the area where Mazyck's Cut now flows into the Congaree River (map 6).[24]

Peter Mazyck had little time to develop his new plantation; he died unmarried in 1772, just thirty-four years old. In his will Peter devised his lands north of the river to his nephew Isaac, and a 780-acre plantation south of the Santee to another nephew, William. Given that Isaac and William were both less than ten years old at the time of Peter's death, the will essentially established a trust arrangement, with their father, William Mazyck Sr., acting as trustee. William Mazyck Sr. himself died three years later. Since Isaac and William Jr. were then still well below the age of majority, the Congaree and Santee properties were probably managed as part of William Sr.'s estate.

Surviving land records suggest that the estate of William Mazyck Sr. still controlled all or some portion of the Congaree plantation in 1786. By then it is likely that parts of the property had been under cultivation for a number of years. Peter's will had expressly directed that the lands devised to Isaac and William "be carefully improved from time to time & planted in Common And the plantation Slaves be employed thereon as usual & to the utmost advantage for their Joint use & benefit & my said Nephews maintained & Liberally Educated & all taxes & other Charges on the said lands & Negroes paid out of the Issues & profits arising & accruing therefrom."[25]

In 1790 Isaac and William Mazyck owned thirty-four slaves in Orangeburgh District. Neither brother lived in the area at the time, so these slaves must have worked under the supervision of one or more local managers. William still owned the Santee plantation in 1790, but it is not known whether Isaac continued to hold his plantation on the Congaree. If he did, the two plantations may have been planted in common, as in previous years. At some point, however, the Mazyck brothers decided to quit the area. William put the Santee plantation up for sale in 1791, and by 1800 neither brother owned any slaves in Orangeburgh District.[26]

Lying east and south of the large Mazyck tract was a 1,164-acre plantation, mostly floodplain, owned by Edward Lightwood, a Charleston slave dealer and merchant. The plantation consisted of six partly contiguous tracts near Toms Creek that Lightwood acquired between 1771 and 1778. The largest of these tracts eventually came to be known as "Lightwood's Old Field." An advertisement published in the summer of 1783 claimed that Lightwood had cultivated "a great part" of these lands:

On WEDNESDAY the 23d of July,
Will be SOLD by Public Auction,
Before the Exchange,
Mr. EDWARD LIGHTWOOD'S
PLANTATION
In the forks of *Congaree* and *Wateree Rivers,*

Containing 1144 [*sic*] acres, more or less, chiefly river swamp, a great part
of which has been cleared and lately planted; it adjoins General Huger's: It
is a tract well known, and needs no farther description. . . . The purchasers
may be accommodated with a small stock of Cattle, Hogs and Poultry on
the spot, and Provisions for the next year. —This Plantation is within four
miles of [Col. William Thomson's] *Belville,* the proposed seat
of Government.

COLCOCK & GIBBONS

The part of the plantation later referred to as Lightwood's Old Field was a 500-acre tract straddling Cedar Creek near the eastern end of the Beidler Tract.
Whatever the origin of the "old field" on the tract—whether attributable to Indians, as the name may indicate, or the product of slave labor—Lightwood presumably kept it open and planted it. The "old field" tract was bordered on the
south and northeast by two of Lightwood's other tracts, containing 114 and 300
acres respectively.[27]

It is hard to know how literally to take the assertion that "a great part" of
Lightwood's plantation had been "cleared and lately planted." The idea that
Lightwood cultivated hundreds of acres of what was mostly interior floodplain
seems hard to credit. Yet the wording of the advertisement strongly implies that
Lightwood planted staple crops on parts of the plantation, while also running
stock and growing provisions. There is physical evidence of clearing, too; today,
old-growth pines can still be found in the northeast corner of the "Old Field"
tract. Furthermore, large portions of the Lightwood plantation appear to have
been ideal for giant cane, a plant that grows best on rich soils that are only intermittently flooded. John Cely's detailed map of the park shows "cane" and "heavy
cane (short)" occurring in the southern part of the Lightwood's Old Field tract,
and the original plat for the three-hundred-acre tract shows it being bordered
on the north and west by "impassable cane swamp."[28]

It thus seems plausible that Lightwood operated a plantation of some substance here, comparable to those of his neighbors along the river. Among its
likely outputs were indigo, corn, and hemp for the commercial market, as well
as provisions for Lightwood's plantation on the coast. A post-1786 plat of what
appears to be the Lightwood plantation shows a house on the low bluff east

of Toms Creek, with a cornfield descending toward the floodplain. This spot, assuming it was the location of dwellings on the plantation, may have been the "Lightwoods," South Carolina from which Colonel William Washington wrote Major General Nathanael Greene in late July 1781 regarding British troop movements in the Orangeburg area.[29]

Despite the 1783 notice of sale, Lightwood retained ownership of the plantation until his death in 1797.[30] While it is conceivable that he continued to plant here in later years, it seems more likely that he leased what portions of the plantation he could to others and concentrated his efforts on his lowcountry lands. In 1790, seven years after the advertisement, Lightwood owned a total of seventy-three slaves, split between his main plantation on James Island and the city of Charleston, with none on the Congaree. If Lightwood ever sent gangs upriver to work the Congaree plantation, the amount of land cultivated was probably not large, especially if the crop being grown was indigo.[31]

Just to the east of Lightwood's land was the plantation of Brigadier General Isaac Huger, a commander of patriot troops at the battles of Stono Ferry and Guilford's Courthouse, among others. Like many of the large plantations on the river's lower reaches, Huger's plantation combined swampland north of the river with drier, sandier upland on the southern bluff. The ten tracts making up the plantation totaled around two thousand acres, including almost nine hundred acres in the park.[32] It can be assumed that Huger, like his neighbors, devoted the plantation to farming, grazing, and timber cutting. However, in one important respect, Huger's Congaree plantation stood apart. For a period of about five years or perhaps somewhat longer, the plantation formed a significant link in the state's nascent transportation network.

By the mid-1780s there were enough farms and plantations in lower Richland and sufficient commercial activity in the region at large for residents to petition the legislature for a new public ferry over the Congaree River. The charter to McCord's Ferry had lapsed during the war, but rather than seek its reauthorization, a number of local residents petitioned the General Assembly to establish a new public road "to General Huger's Plantation on Congaree River, and there to Establish a Ferry about Six Miles above McCord's Ferry, Which will by many Miles shorten the Road to Charleston, and be of other Public utility." After studying the matter, the General Assembly established the new ferry in 1786. To connect the ferry to existing roads, the legislature appointed commissions on either side of the river to build approach roads leading to General Huger's plantation. The resulting road system was part of a larger, concerted effort in the years immediately after the Revolution to facilitate settlement and assist commerce by improving transportation in the state.[33]

General Huger bowed to the legislative will despite having personal objections to the project. Soon he had constructed an approach road on the Richland side of the river through what is today the eastern end of the Beidler Tract. This road, traces of which can still be seen today, was sited along a narrow floodplain ridge through generally swampy terrain (see entry 25 in appendix A). Construction of the road was a hardship for Huger, who petitioned the legislature for restitution, complaining that

> your Petitioner has been under the necessity at his own expense of open-
> ing all the Roads leading [to the ferry] for a considerable distance and thro
> a large difficult Swamp over which with great Labour and Charges he has
> made a Cause[wa]y and Bridges in the accomplishment [of] which the
> work of [a] great part of his Negroes was lost to his planting Interest for
> Two Years as the Commissioners have never sent a Single Negro to work
> on said Road since the Establishment of said Ferry. That in Consequence of
> the Establishment of said Ferry your Petitioner's Plantation has been much
> Injured and your Petitioner in some measure obliged to purchase another
> place for Negroes to plant on which he did at the Expence of upward of
> Two Thousand pounds Sterling.

Old-growth loblolly pines grow in places along the route of Huger's road, suggesting that these parts of the swamp may once have been cleared to grow crops or provide pasture for livestock. The discovery some years ago of a foot adze along the route, at a spot near Running Lake, is evidence that structures may have been built here as well. The adze is now housed in the park's museum collection.[34]

Huger reportedly "resided for some years" at his Congaree plantation, but by the time the ferry was established in 1786 he was living on the coast and serving as sheriff of Charleston District. In 1787 he decided to put the plantation up for sale. The decision to sell was prompted in large part by the chance to plant recently acquired rice lands on the Santee River—possibly the "[other] place for Negroes to plant on" mentioned in his petition to the General Assembly. However, his decision may also have been influenced by the perceived "injury" to the Congaree plantation caused by the road and ferry.[35]

Huger put the plantation on the market in September 1787. His notice announcing the sale gives a tantalizing glimpse of late-eighteenth-century life along the lower Congaree:

A Valuable Plantation,
for Sale.

The SUBSCRIBER having purchased a tract of Rice Land on Santee, which he wishes to cultivate, induces him to offer for sale his well known valuable Plantation on the Congaree, three miles above Colonel Thomson's, containing 1750 acres, more or less, 1000 of which is rich river swamp, equal to any within ten miles above or below; it has the whole width of the tract on each side of the river, over which has lately been established a ferry, and the road leading through the swamp, on each side put in good order, by which the communication opens by Camden, Waxhaws, Charlotte, Columbia, Winnsborough, and the New Acquisition [York County]:—this must inevitably occasion a great concourse of travelers, wagons, carriages, &c. to pass the ferry, be productive of great profit, and afford a ready market on the spot for all kinds of grain and forage, which the fertility of the soil when cultivated, produces in the greatest plenty. —On the upland (which is suitable for the culture of indigo and provisions) are two of the most beautiful spots for a settlement, and the situation of the tract is such as to afford two separate compact plantations. —On one of the settlements is a comfortable dwelling-house, kitchen, barn, negro houses, and a spring of the purest water at a convenient distance, issuing from the side of a hill; and through the tract runs a stream sufficiently copious for supplying a tub-mill and other machinery, and its direction such, as to be equally convenient for either settlement. —In fine, few tracts of so fertile a quality, and with so many advantages, both from nature and art, have been offered for sale in this country.

For further information and terms of disposal, apply to James Kennedy, Esq. in Charleston, or to the subscriber.

Isaac Huger.

Of particular note here is Huger's contention that the "the fertility of the soil when cultivated, produces in the greatest plenty." This wording appears to imply that some portion of Huger's lands north of the river had been planted in "grain and forage" sometime between 1771, when he originally acquired the ferry tract, and 1787, when the plantation as a whole went up for sale. It is also possible that rice and indigo were being planted on these lands. An advertisement in the *City Gazette* the following year offered for sale "as fine a rice and indigo plantation as any in the state, on Congaree river, on which there is erected a ferry worth from 6 to 800 l. per year." While the property in this advertisement cannot definitely be identified as Huger's, the advertisement appeared at the same time Huger was actively marketing his plantation.[36]

An important factor limiting cultivation of Huger's plantation was the high percentage of saturated ground on the part lying north of the river. By Huger's own admission, the ferry portion of the plantation (six hundred acres, later to form Beidler Tract Parcel 19) contained "a large difficult Swamp." Today, this area is known for having the largest concentration of old-growth bald cypress in the park. The prevalence of low swamp north of the river may have been one reason the plantation as a whole was slow to sell, despite Huger's efforts to paint it in glowing terms. The ferry tract languished until 1797, when it was finally acquired at auction by Samuel Brailsford, a prominent Charleston merchant who had made his fortune in the slave trade. A contiguous tract to the west took even longer to sell.[37]

Huger's neighbor to the east was William Bull Jr., for many years the royal lieutenant governor of South Carolina and the last to serve in that capacity before the Revolution. A committed Loyalist, Bull was a major landowner at the time of the war and the holder of 284 slaves. Among his many properties was a 1,750-acre plantation "at the Congarees[,] some high land mostly River Swamp improved." The plantation took in land on both sides of the river, including land now in the Congaree Bluffs Heritage Preserve and over a thousand acres of swampland to the north. It is not known when Bull began acquiring the properties that made up this plantation, but he had obtained land bordering the Beidler Tract by 1771. The plantation consisted of a large tract of around 1,170 acres, together with a 576-acre tract north of the river bounded in part by lands of "Brigadier General Huger." There were 52 slaves on the 1,170-acre parcel in 1777.[38]

Bull resided most of the year in the lowcountry and may have paid only the occasional visit to his Congaree plantation. To oversee the site's day-to-day management, he retained the services of his downstream neighbor William Thomson, from whom he purchased the 576-acre tract around 1778. The Congaree plantation was among Bull's largest sources of income, being only just surpassed by his 3,300-acre plantation on St. Helena Island. According to John Hopton, who visited the plantation in 1780, Bull had "above 400 Acres in Crop at that time . . . chiefly in Corn and Indigo." Considering the number of slaves living there after the war, Bull's plantation was probably one of the most intensively developed on the lower Congaree. There were ninety-two slaves on the plantation in 1790, well more than the fifty stationed at the Precipice or the forty-four at General Huger's.[39]

With a substantial portion of its total area in cultivation, Bull's plantation would have produced large harvests in good years. Bull had a full forty-three hundred bushels of corn on hand when Brigadier General Thomas Sumter conducted a wartime raid of the plantation in May 1781. The loss of this corn figured prominently in a Loyalist claim Bull later submitted to the Crown. Also part of the claim was a detailed itemization of slaves, equipment, and livestock lost at the "Congarees."[40]

Bull's claim reflected the many changes that had occurred along the lower Congaree since the days of first settlement. In less than fifty years, a combination of local landowners and wealthy planters from the coast had established a series of substantial farms and plantations up and down the river. These had been settled, in large part, to supply staple commodities to Charleston and world markets. Other plantations in the area, including the downstream plantations of

Rebecca Brewton Motte, William Thomson, and Sophianisba McCord, were part of the same network. Each contained large areas of swampland in areas that are now part of the park.

The proliferation of swamp plantations on the Congaree was part of a larger pattern across much of the Santee basin. Writing in 1858, planter Samuel Dubose reminisced that the Santee Swamp of St. Stephens Parish (Berkeley County) "was once a second Egypt. A breadth of three or four miles of swamp as fertile as the slime of the Nile could have made it, was safe for cultivation." In Dubose's telling, there were "upwards of five thousand" slaves in the Santee Swamp before the Revolution, "there being no settlements out of its limits."[41]

All that changed beginning in 1784. Increased flooding on the Santee rendered large swathes of its bottomland almost worthless. One year soon after the Revolution, planter Peter Gaillard lost his entire crop save for a few baskets of unmatured corn. To support his family, "credit had to be obtained from the more fortunate who planted on the Wateree or Congaree." But by 1794 even those lands were vulnerable. Reporting on the flooding of that year, the *City Gazette* noted that "one [remark by our correspondent] appears of a very serious nature indeed, as it respects the whole of the swamplands situated on the Wateree, from Statesburgh or the High Hills, and on the Congaree from Howell's ferry until these rivers join the Santee, and from thence down the Santee until within a very few miles of the sea. The loss on these rivers this year has been almost total, and has extended nearly to the lowest tide plantations on Santee, and by that means lands which were supposed among the safest in the state have lost their crops."[42]

Planters James and Peter Sinkler of St. Stephen's Parish experimented with a series of dikes to protect their crops from flooding along the lower Santee, but as flooding grew worse in the closing years of the century, James Sinkler moved the center of his operations to the higher ground of St. John's Parish. Historian David Ramsay observed in 1809 that "there are at present many waste old fields both on the high-lands along the edge of the river swamp and in the swamp, which 30 years ago were in the highest state of cultivation, and produced luxuriant crops of corn, indigo, and rice."[43]

Assuming the Congaree watershed was similarly affected by unusually high rainfall between 1784 and 1796, a corresponding pattern of abandonment and reentry may have played out within the park. The difficulties of Charles Cotesworth Pinckney and Edward Rutledge have already been noted. Joel Adams Sr. may also have been affected by high water. In September 1792 he sought to acquire two upland tracts in lower Richland from William H. Fishburne Jr. of Round O, South Carolina, possibly because of summer floods in the bottomlands. Adams informed Fishburne that "my Crop is but short this year Occasioned by the bad seasons we have had. . . . the shortness of my Crop puts in my power to begin to work in the pine Land sooner than I expected. . . . if I Do not get yours I must fix myself otherwise; as I do not intend to remain where I am no longer than I can fix a place of my own." It appears that Fishburne declined to sell Adams the two tracts, as they and a large swamp tract were offered for sale by Fishburne's son and coexecutor, Richard, in 1821. (See discussion in chapter 3.)[44]

In time the rains abated and cultivation began to rebound. Flooding on the Santee diminished in frequency and height after 1796, encouraging some planters to reenter the swamp to plant corn and rice, and engage in the culture of cotton. As Ramsay noted, "The ground is found to answer for the latter, and extraordinary crops have been lately made." Yet even as rainfall patterns returned to normal, other forces were at work blunting the impetus to reenter the floodplain. One was the collapse in demand for South Carolina indigo after 1795. Another was the overproduction of foodstuffs in the South Carolina midlands and lowcountry starting around 1807. The latter meant that, after about 1806, and apart from a spike in demand during the War of 1812, growers of corn in lower Richland faced a glut in Charleston and other lowcountry markets.[45]

Thus, by the early part of the nineteenth century, the demand for the park's principal floodplain crops had fallen considerably and with it the incentive to clear ever larger amounts of swampland. While cotton would eventually take the place of indigo in the middle and upper parts of the state, cotton's need for well-drained soils meant that its cultivation in the park would generally be restricted to the levee zone and the highest floodplain ridges.[46] As South Carolina entered the antebellum period, corn and other provision crops would continue to be grown in the park to sustain plantation operations, and cotton would increasingly be raised in those parts of the floodplain where suitable soils were present. But over time, as more and more land in the piedmont was stripped of its cover, losses from flooding would multiply. Some planters would respond by concentrating their efforts on their upland holdings, while others would continue to roll the dice each year in the bottoms. Still others, if they had the resources, would double down, building embankments to keep the "freshes" out of their floodplain fields.

5

Reclaiming
the Floodplain

*It is on such lands as the Santee, Congaree, Wateree and Pedee, that the only exten-
sive and successful trials have been made to reclaim swamps . . . . [However,] each of
the enterprising proprietor[s] acts solely in reference to his own land, and frequently
in error as to that.*

Governor Whitemarsh Seabrook, "Reclamation of the Swamps," 1848

THE DECADE OR SO FOLLOWING THE END of the Revolution was one of great hardship for many South Carolina planters. Thousands of slaves fled or died during
the conflict, making it impossible for many planters to achieve prewar production levels without going into debt to obtain additional labor. Compounding
these difficulties was a collapse in the international demand for South Carolina
indigo. Overproduction in the Americas, Indonesia, and the East Indies, together with a tide of inexpensive, high-quality indigo from India, effectively
eliminated the state from the world market after 1795. As if these problems were
not bad enough, the disastrous floods of the 1780s and 1790s wiped out whole
crops in the Santee drainage and elsewhere across the state.[1]

The "Great Yazoo Freshet" of January 1796 was the most damaging, taking
with it much of the agricultural infrastructure in the Congaree floodplain. The
Charleston City Gazette reported that the "freshes in the Congaree and Wateree
rivers have risen five feet higher than they were ever before known; the damage
done by them is immense. At Granby, the ware-house was swept away, with 150
hogsheads of tobacco in it; col. Hampton's bridge is entirely destroyed. Below
Granby, dwelling houses, corn houses, cattle, horses, &c. have been all carried
down the stream. . . . On the Santee, the dist[r]ess is equally great. . . . We have
not heard that any lives are lost, though it is supposed many negroes have per-
ished at their settlements in the swamps."[2]

Flooding became especially pronounced after 1820, when large parts of the piedmont were stripped of vegetation to grow cotton. On the Congaree, major floods occurred in 1823, 1824, 1829, 1831, 1833, 1840, 1841, 1845, and 1852. These years saw the most extensive flooding in the Congaree valley since the great floods of the 1790s. The massive flood of 1852 was said to be six feet above the flood of 1840 and about seven and a half feet higher than the Great Yazoo Freshet. So intense was the 1852 flood that the river at last broke through the base of Buckhead Neck, leaving behind Bates Old River, the largest oxbow lake on the Congaree River and one of the largest oxbows in South Carolina.[3]

Despite the risk of flooding, many South Carolina planters continued to plant without embankments in the early national and antebellum periods, knowing full well that in any given year floods could wipe out their bottomland crops. On the Savannah River, James Henry Hammond managed to plant his "island field" in corn and pumpkins for twenty-three years without major losses. Only the crop of 1852 was seriously damaged by flooding in the years between 1838 and 1860. Within the park, some planters may have had similar success, as there is evidence to suggest that the highest areas flooded an average of once per year or less. A 370-acre tract granted to Paul Spigener in 1839 contained two cleared fields in the levee zone by the river, and Spigener (d. 1867) evidently cultivated this tract for the rest of his life (figure 8). About 60 acres of the tract were said to be "cleared" in 1869, and in 1886 a major flood on what appears to have been this same property caused the loss of up to $1,800 worth of "stock and grain crops."[4]

Owners of lower ground were often not so lucky. Along the Savannah River, Edmund Ruffin observed that "the lands on both sides of the river for 12 miles [below J. H. Hammond's Silver Bluff Plantation] are low. The higher (which is at Silver Bluff,) 20 to more than 30 feet above the present low level of the river, & that not always & entirely free from the injury of highest freshes. More generally, the cultivated lands are 10 to 15 feet above, & more or less endangered. On the lower cultivated lands, is estimated that only one crop in three is made & saved."[5] Thus, position in the floodplain played a critical role in the risk associated with cultivating a given site. Higher sites and sites closer to the fall line tended to be less flood prone, but lower sites could be, and often were, cultivated by those willing to take their chances. Planters not in a position to weather losses would have felt pressure to abandon their more flood-prone lands.

Regardless of the potential losses from flooding, some clearing probably continued to occur in the park right up until the Civil War, as the land was simply too fertile to leave idle. According to Harry Hammond, the river swamps of South Carolina's inner coastal plain "were being rapidly cleared and cultivated anterior to the war," producing high yields of cotton and corn if carefully managed. In the 1850s—the years of the state's second great cotton boom—prices approached levels not seen since the mid-1830s. It was during these years that

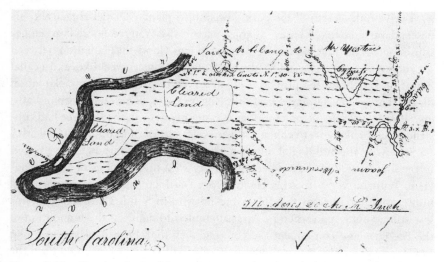

Figure 8. Plat Showing the Paul Spigener Regrant (1839), Including Spigener's Fields. The Spigener regrant consisted of today's Beidler Tract Parcel 14 and NPS Tract 101-35. Courtesy of South Carolina Department of Archives and History.

Jacob Stroyer had been ordered into the Wateree Swamp to clear up new ground with his fellow slaves. It is questionable, however, whether major clearing occurred in the park at this time, at least for cotton. Relatively little reclamation work was ever actually completed within the park, and damaging floods made growing cotton in unreclaimed fields an increasingly chancy undertaking in the years before the war.[6]

Early Reclamation Efforts

As incidents of damaging floods increased in the late eighteenth century, some planters in the fork of the Congaree and Wateree Rivers began to enclose their bottomland fields behind earthen embankments. Properly drained and diked, river swamplands could be devoted to a wide range of staple and provision crops, including indigo, corn, rice, oats, rye, wheat, potatoes, pumpkins, peas, and cotton.[7]

Advertisements from the mid-1790s give some idea of the scale of the first embankments in the area. In 1793 a plantation about six miles from McCord's Ferry on the Wateree River was advertised as containing 1,536 acres of river swamp, 270 of which were "cleared and under good banks, the soil equal to any in that neighborhood for the culture of indigo and corn, and . . . scarcely ever affected by the freshes." Three years later W. Clarkson advised potential buyers that 240 acres of his 2,000-acre tract in the Wateree Swamp were "cleared and under compleat Dams and Fences, free from all but the highest Freshes."[8]

Twelve miles north of the park, lowcountry planter Daniel Huger and his descendants embanked an even larger part of the Wateree floodplain. Huger consolidated the bulk of what became known as Goodwill Plantation between 1779 and 1795. By 1820 he and his descendants had constructed dikes and a canal irrigation system on the property, which served in part as a supply plantation for the family's lowcountry operations. Huger's example may have inspired others, since by the mid-1820s a number of other planters on the Wateree had constructed embankments to enhance the productivity of their bottomland fields.[9]

Statewide, the building of dikes on a truly large scale appears to have begun in the first decade of the nineteenth century with the activities of David Rogerson Williams (1776–1830), a planter from Darlington District who regarded himself as the father of floodplain reclamation in South Carolina. Williams was still a young man when he "first attempted to dam out the inundation of the Pee Dee, and consequent thereon, had well nigh been deprived of a seat in Congress, because it was thought any man who believed he could keep the freshets from the low grounds was too big a fool to go to Congress. Now there is nearly as much swamp land reclaimed from the freshets in South Carolina as in Mississippi." Williams was a forward-thinking planter, who wished to substitute efficient, scientific agriculture for the traditional but wasteful approach to floodplain cultivation, which he described as "[first] cut down and fence the land, to grow on them a few years, annually decreasing crops, then . . . give them up to weeds and briers, and finally . . . abandon them in quest of new settlements."[10] From around 1800 to 1808 Williams constructed a dike about five miles in length along the Great Pee Dee River in Darlington District. Behind this dike, which averaged seven or eight feet in height, he produced corn, oats, cotton, and other crops, using improved agricultural methods to resuscitate old fields and keep them in continuous production. His example was widely followed, and by 1825 some twenty thousand acres of river swamp in Darlington District were estimated to lie within embankments. On the Santee, the loss of eight crops in succession prompted Samuel Porcher to begin constructing his massive embankment at Mexico Plantation in 1817.[11]

Some of the most impressive embankments in the state were located along the Congaree River just below Columbia. The large plantations of John Singleton and Wade Hampton II, in particular, used an elaborate system of levees to protect extensive floodplain fields.[12] It was probably on one of these plantations (most likely that of Wade Hampton II) that English social activist Harriet Martineau observed floodplain cultivation during her tour of the eastern United States in the mid-1830s:

When the traveller observes the quality of some of the land now under cultivation [in the South], he wonders how other estates could have been rendered so unprofitable as they are. The rich Congaree bottoms, in South Carolina, look inexhaustible; but some estates, once as fine, now lie barren and deserted. I went over a plantation, near Columbia, South Carolina, where there were four thousand acres within one fence, each acre worth fifteen hundred dollars. This land has been cropped yearly with cotton since 1794, and is now becoming less productive; but it is still very fine. The cotton seed is occasionally returned to the soil; and this is the only means of renovation used. Four hundred negroes work this estate. We saw the field trenched, ready for sowing. The sowing is done by hand, thick, and afterwards thinned.[13]

Almost a decade later, Edmund Ruffin made his way to the Hampton plantation to see for himself the "neatness & perfection of all the processes of Col. Hampton's management [that] are noted throughout this country." He recorded his impressions in his diary:

[I] went out to breakfast at Millwood, the residence of Col. Wade Hampton, 5 miles from Columbia, & to see the large & splendid plantation. . . . The chief value & beauty of his wide domain is the embanked low grounds of the Congaree. The quantity of this land is 5000 acres in one body, all more or less subject to freshes, & to guard against which the whole is surrounded & protected by an excellent embankment, which is about 8 miles in length. As most of the land is high, & barely exposed to the highest freshes known, its embankment is comparatively low. But everywhere the embankment is kept 4 feet higher than the highest fresh known. Where the land is lowest, the embankment, to be up to this general level, is 22 feet high & of 90 feet base. This however is but a short stretch.[14]

Shortly thereafter, R. L. Allen observed additional details of Hampton's dike system, noting specifically that "numerous ditches drained off all stagnant water, and an extensive embankment (underneath which, an aqueduct, carefully protected by gates, led off the surface water) effectually guarded the lowest of the land from the overflowing of the floods." According to Allen, Hampton's dike system allowed him to cultivate cowpeas and pumpkins in the bottomlands, as well as "800 acres of corn and 1,600 acres of cotton . . . in a single field."[15]

Downstream from Millwood the Congaree was subject to deeper, more damaging floods, but this did not stop a number of landowners from diking their lands to reclaim the floodplain for cultivation. W. Peter Buyck Sr. described these efforts to a committee of the South Carolina House of Representatives in 1975: "The area from Columbia down as far as Fort Motte was diked and planted in indigo and corn before the Civil War. There are lots of the old dams criss-crossing the entire area. In fact, I have been using some of them along with newly constructed dams to keep the high waters out of my fields that I plant in corn or beans. The old dams are an integrated part of the new ones."[16] At the time of this statement, Buyck was the owner of a 710-acre tract on Bates Mill Creek (formerly High Hill Creek), directly across the river from Tract 101-35 of the future national park. Given the location of this tract, it is possible that one of the dams adapted by Buyck was the historic Frederick Cooner dam, originally constructed sometime before 1856. The Cooner dam was built, in the words of the *Charleston Mercury,* "on the Orangeburg side of the Congaree river, one mile and a quarter long, for the purpose of guarding against overflows and thereby reclaiming some very rich and valuable swamp land, which otherwise was utterly worthless."[17]

Reclamation in the Park

The only person known with certainty to have attempted large-scale reclamation in the Beidler Tract is James Adams Sr. (1776–ca. 1840), the oldest son of Joel Adams Sr., who was said to have been "a silent, resolute man, as stern as a Roman Patriot." Although lacking the college education of his brothers, he was a very successful planter, raising cotton "on almost a princely scale." The entire Adams family was among the wealthiest families in Richland District, with various family members collectively owning 27,904 acres of land and 1,142 slaves in 1850.[18] Adams himself had extensive landholdings in the district, including over 4,000 acres in the Beidler Tract that he and his brothers Joel and Robert had inherited from their father (map 7).[19] When James undertook to reclaim these lands, he began a project that, had it been completed, would have dwarfed other reclamation efforts in the park.

The provisions of Adams's will suggest that sometime in the 1830s, or perhaps earlier, he had started to embank the western end of the Beidler Tract. The will, signed in 1840, states that Adams had "commenced" embanking his swamplands some time before but does not say precisely when. Adams's use of the word "commenced" may indicate that he had begun embanking his land in the mid- to late 1830s. Alternatively, this wording may simply refer to the fact that he had not yet completed the dike at the time of his death. One factor militating against a late 1830s start date is the construction of the Branchville-to-Columbia rail line during this period. From roughly 1838 through 1841, many planters in lower Richland District hired out slaves to construct the roadbed for the new line. Adams may have been one of them. In 1846 James's son Joel R. Adams would lease eight slaves to the railroad for a work detail near Gadsden, north of the park.[20]

The principal remnant of Adams's reclamation project is the so-called Northwest Boundary Dike on the western edge of the park. Adams may also be responsible for the Adams Pond Dike and two smaller dikes nearby (see map

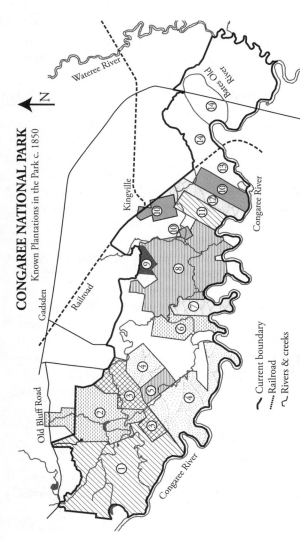

CONGAREE NATIONAL PARK

Known Plantations in the Park c. 1850

Map 7. Known Plantations in the Park, ca. 1850. Owners of known plantations are listed below, together with plantation names where available. See appendix B for details on owners and plantations. (Note: Plantation boundaries are approximate. Not all ownerships extending beyond park boundary are shown. Boundaries are based principally on Kinzer [2016] and Cely [2001, 2014]). Map by Lynne Parker.

LANDOWNERS:

* Boundary of ownership not known due to missing/destroyed land records.
† Ownership extends beyond park boundary
** All or part of this property belonged to Frederick Cooner by June 1851

1. Joel Adams Jr., Robert Adams, and heirs of James Adams Sr. (James U. Adams et al.) (Adams swamp and bluff plantations)†
2. Estate of Dr. William Weston III (Gum Tree Plantation)
3. James U. Adams (Pea Ridge Plantation)†
4. Daniel Zeigler [two compartments]
5. Estate of William H. Fishburne Jr.**
6. Estate of Dr. William Weston III
7. Paul Spigener
8. Lieuellan Woodward
9. James H. Adams†
10. James H. Seay [three compartments]
11. Daniel McKenzie
12. Washington Mitchell†
13. Charles Neuffer*
14. John Bates*†, others*

Legend:
- Current boundary
- Railroad
- Rivers & creeks

Map labels: Wateree River, Bates Old River, Congaree River, Kingville, Gadsden, Railroad, Old Bluff Road, N

9 and entries 3 and 4 in appendix A). Whether Adams initiated embankment with the intention of growing corn, cotton, or other crops is impossible to say. Also unknown are the specific factors that drove Adams to begin embanking the floodplain in the first place. Michie suggests that he may have been forced into the floodplain in search of more productive soils. The soil in the vicinity of the Northwest Boundary Dike is the only significant area of nonhydric soil in the floodplain portion of the park, apart from a much smaller area on the river opposite the mouth of Bates Mill Creek.[21]

As for the particulars of Adams's motivation, an almost contemporaneous reclamation proposal by James Henry Hammond may provide some insights. Writing in his diary in 1841, the fourth year of a serious downturn in the price of cotton, Hammond contemplated the potential benefits of reclaiming a portion of his lands along the Savannah River: "[The recent flood was] rather high. . . . Yet it wanted 3 feet of being on my river swamp land behind the Marsh. I am sure I could make cotton there 4 out [of] 5 perhaps 7 out of 8 years without a dam, and with a dam of five feet I could not lose a crop once in 30 years. I think I have 500 acres of this land that lies convenient and perhaps there may be 700, and, I believe, it will yield me at least 350 lbs of clean cotton pr. acre for 20 years. . . . Five Hundred acres of such land will keep me here. I can then make five hundred bales of cotton and some 500,000 bushels of corn to sell with my present force."[22] Hammond hoped that utilizing his swampland could compensate for the disappointing crops on his "poor pine lands at Silver Bluff" and allow him to stay in South Carolina rather than have to emigrate west. James Adams Sr. may have felt similar pressures.[23]

Surviving documents indicate that substantial clearing had already taken place on the Adams swamp plantation by the time it was regranted to Adams and his brothers in 1839. Marmaduke Coate's *Survey of Richland District* (1820) shows two parallel rows of slave houses along the river in "Adams' Quarter," clear evidence that substantial parts of the natural levee were being cultivated in corn, and possibly cotton, at that time. In addition, an 1839 plat of the Adams regrant, now lost, drew a line parallel to the river extending from around the top of Cooks Lake to the eastern boundary of the plantation. Above the line appeared the legend "River Swamp Land Farm Cultivated" (see figure 7). These riverside fields would have been directly threatened by the increased overbank flooding of the period, and Adams's ultimate goal may have been to embank these lands to minimize flood damage to his crops.[24]

Work on the Adams embankment seems to have started at the northern bluff and proceeded southward in the direction of the river. Based on historic plats and surviving ditch work, it appears that Adams meant to extend this leg of the dike all the way to the river. Ultimately, however, only about two-thirds of this distance was ever completed, with the part above Cooks Lake being ditched but not diked (map 9). Why the project was never finished is a mystery, but it may be that major flooding in 1840 and 1841 was a factor. The flood of May 1840 was said to have been the worst since the Great Yazoo Freshet of 1796. According to one account, the 1840 flood was so powerful that it even destroyed the "immense dams" on the upstream plantations of Wade Hampton II and John Singleton.[25]

The three other dikes—which, again, may or may not have been built by James Adams Sr.—are much smaller structures built on the natural levee of the Congaree River. Each is a single straight embankment lying on the north bank of a small stream, or "gut," that feeds into the river (see map 9). None of these dikes is squared off, and it may be that none was ever completed as designed. If finished, their likely purpose was to break the current of floodwaters from adjoining guts. The fact that one of the dikes runs perpendicular to the river would seem to support this interpretation.[26]

However ambitious his plans may have been, Adams's reclamation efforts appear to have had poor prospects, for work on the dike system apparently ceased soon after his death around the end of 1840. At the time Adams prepared his will in July 1840—less than two months after the great flood of that year—he seems to have anticipated that his children would want to abandon the project. The will expressly gave his children the option of selling their interests in the swamp plantation should they "become unwilling to continue embanking the swamp lands as I have commenced." In the event, the plantation remained in the family, but the dike was never finished. Even James U. Adams, possibly the most driven of Adams's children and in time a very wealthy man, must have decided that his father's project was not worth the effort and cost.[27]

It is not known how much clearing accompanied construction of the Northwest Boundary Dike. Considering the immense amount of labor required just to build the dike itself, the project may have been intended primarily to reclaim existing fields rather than add new ones. Aerial photos from 1955 show a large concentration of loblolly pine in the northwest part of the park just east of the dike. Corings from a number of these trees show that they started growing in the 1830s and early 1840s. Similarly, researchers counting tree rings in the mid-1970s identified a loblolly pine not far from the dike that had 143 rings (see note 6 of chapter 6). This tree sprouted about 1832, approximately eight years before James Adams Sr. included the language in his will about embanking his swamplands. The age and location of these trees may be evidence that the dike was built, at least in part, to protect existing fields that had lain fallow for a time and were starting to grow up in pines. However, if construction did entail the clearing of new fields, the presence of old-growth pines may indicate that these fields, like the others, were abandoned around the time that work on the embankment ceased.[28]

Possible allusions to the Adams dike(s) and fields can be found in the published works of Edward Clarkson Leverett Adams (1876–1946), a direct descendant of James Adams Sr. In 1912 E. C. L. Adams acquired a large tract of land about seven miles southeast of Columbia. A large number of African Americans lived on this land, and their stories formed the basis of most of Adams's literary output. (Judging from the place names mentioned by his characters, a number of Adams's tales are set farther downriver near the ancestral family lands around Gadsden.) In the foreword to his second book of Congaree tales, Adams states that his stories show "the influence of slavery, the . . . terror created by the canebrakes and jungles of the Congaree, with its lakes, streams, guts, mysterious shadows, and yellow waters, *with its old fields and dikes, relics of slave days*" (emphasis supplied). The tale "Goose Pond," for example, centers on the character Cap'n Bob and his memories of the swamp around Goose Pond, including "ole time slavery folks, . . . [and] mens an' womens dat nuse to work in de swamp fields." Another tale, entitled "The Rat," involves a bizarre chase scene in the swamp, "back on Lykes's plantation in de ole field by de river."[29]

Apart from James Adams Sr., the only other planter of the period to have attempted significant reclamation in the park appears to have been Dr. William Weston III (1795–1848). Weston was the grandson of William Weston I (ca. 1716–ca. 1771), who moved to lower Richland from Edenton, North Carolina around 1769. William Weston I established Brite Savannah Plantation on Dry Branch and adjoining lands to the west. He reportedly built his home near the future railroad stop of Weston, about three miles northeast of today's park visitor center. Here he became a successful planter of indigo. His son William Weston II (ca. 1750–1821) established Gum Tree Plantation some distance to the south, below Old Bluff Road. When William Weston II died in 1821, both plantations passed to his sole male heir, Dr. William Weston III. Dr. Weston lived at Brite Savannah until around 1840, at which point he moved to his uncle Robert Weston's former plantation about two and a half miles to the northeast. The main house on the plantation, known as Grovewood, still stands today just south of the McEntire Air National Guard base.[30]

The Weston family's holdings in the Beidler Tract came to rival and eventually exceed those of the Adams family. According to Edwin L. Green, "the Weston family cultivated indigo extensively" in the eighteenth century, and it is virtually certain that William Weston II cultivated indigo in what is now the park. Weston obtained a state grant in 1785 for service in the Revolutionary War, and this grant may have formed part of Gum Tree Plantation. By the time of his death, William II owned "a thousand acres or more of Congaree River swamp lands," and Gum Tree appears to have extended south past Weston Lake and Cedar Creek (see map 7).[31] William II's uncle Malachi may also have cultivated indigo in the park, as a person by that name obtained a plat for a three-hundred-acre tract on the Wateree River (Fork Swamp area) in 1765.[32]

By the mid–nineteenth century Dr. William Weston III owned a sizable portion of what would later become the Beidler Tract. His holdings included not only Gum Tree Plantation but also a large parcel east of Old Dead River containing the Old Dead River Dike (map 7).[33] This dike was a long, angled structure on the north bank of the Congaree River just upstream from the historic dams referred to in the testimony of W. Peter Buyck Sr. It is not known for certain who constructed the dike or when. Possible candidates include the Reverend Isaac Tucker, who owned the underlying property during the early part of the nineteenth century, and William Weston III himself, who married Tucker's daughter Christian Grace Tucker in 1818. William Weston III is arguably the most likely person to have constructed the dike, as he may have controlled the dike property from 1818, the year of his marriage, until his death in 1848.[34] Weston was said to have been an excellent businessman who "improved and built up the large estate left him by his father. . . . He was exceedingly methodical and neat in everything he did, and . . . all of his plantations were cultivated like gardens."[35] Another possibility is Paul Spigener of Orangeburg District. Spigener was granted the adjacent tract to the east in 1839, and he could have acquired or leased the dike property around this same time. Yet another, less likely possibility is Alfred M. Hunt, a Columbia hotelier and beginning planter. Hunt acquired the dike tract sometime in the 1850s, after the death of William Weston III.[36]

A 1909 study by U.S. drainage engineer D. G. Miller concluded that most of the dikes along the Congaree had been built before 1850, and the Old Dead River Dike is probably at least that old. Today the dike is significantly eroded and dissected, but when first built it was approximately seventy-five hundred feet long. Examining the dike in 1978, ranger Guy Taylor noted that it "is very well constructed apparently engineered by someone who knew his business. It is perfectly level making it as high as five feet above ground level in low places and not over a couple of feet on higher ground. It does not curve at all, but makes angular turns when bearings change. It is up to 6' wide on top sloping at approx. 30° to ground level. . . . This would have been a pretty big construction project with a dragline. The man hours with shovels was tremendous." Few planters in lower Richland would have been able to take on a project of this magnitude using only their own resources. Even William Weston III, a wealthy man by the 1840s, would have been hard pressed to do so in previous decades.[37]

Weston owned fifteen slaves in 1820 (forty-two if the slaves of his father [d. 1821] are included). By 1830 he had increased this number to eighty-six. While the latter was a large number by lower Richland standards (ranking him sixteenth out of 334 slaveholders outside Columbia), the hard labor of excavating and moving soil would have meant that he had access to no more than about thirty able-bodied men and women to construct the embankment, assuming he used only his own slaves. South Carolina planters did not recognize a strict division of labor between the sexes, and a crew of this size may have been sufficient to build the dike, especially if the project was extended over a number of years. However, strong males were typically preferred on major excavation projects, and in 1830 Weston owned just seven males between the ages of twenty-four and fifty-four (he owned thirteen additional males between the ages of ten and twenty-three). This figure is obviously quite low, and furthermore, it seems unlikely that Weston would have dedicated all able-bodied males to the dike project while work on his other land languished. Under the circumstances, Weston would appear to have had no choice but hire slaves from other planters or forego the project altogether.[38]

In later years Weston could easily have taken on the project using only (or mostly) his own forces. He owned 180 slaves in 1840 and had 220 at the time of his death in 1848. By way of comparison, David Rogerson Williams owned 165 slaves in 1810, the year after completing his five-mile dike project on the Great Pee Dee River.[39] Of the slaves Weston owned in 1840, fewer than 50 were males capable of heavy construction. It may never be known for certain who constructed the Old Dead River Dike, but Weston clearly had the ability to do so toward the end of his life. Moreover, the resources then available to him far exceeded those of most of his peers.[40]

Weston's Gum Tree property stretched over the west-central portion of the Beidler Tract, encompassing the present-day location of the Harry Hampton Visitor Center, the elevated and low boardwalks, and the Weston Lake Loop Trail. The area around the elevated boardwalk is particularly noteworthy for containing a large number of old-growth loblolly pines, many of which seeded in during the time that Weston and his descendants owned the property. After Weston's death, his sons Isaac T. Weston and Dr. William Weston IV continued to own property in the Beidler Tract for many years. (Isaac got Gum Tree from his father, and William Weston IV obtained an ownership interest in "Dr. Weston's Quarter" via his wife [see entry 23 in appendix A].) Some of these lands appear to have been grazed or cultivated, but there is no evidence that either man engaged in any reclamation activity.[41]

Downriver from the Old Dead River and Adams Dikes lie two other reclamation projects, one a semicircular embankment at the northern bluff line near Toms Creek, the other a set of dikes located somewhere on the Buckhead Neck peninsula. About the former virtually nothing is known except that its remnants are located on what was at one time the extreme southern end of Stoney Hill Plantation, owned by Governor James H. Adams (see map 7 and entry 24 in appendix A).[42] Regarding the latter, the only information currently available comes from an account of a visit to the peninsula by historian Benjamin Lossing. In 1849, three years before the river completed its cut through the peninsula, Lossing observed that "Buck's Head Neck is formed by a sweep of the Congaree, of nearly eight miles, when it approaches itself within a quarter of a mile. The swamp land of this neck has been reclaimed in many places, and now bears good cotton."[43] It is possible that portions of these dikes still exist on the part of the neck now surrounded by Bates Old River.

The design of dikes in the park mirrors the designs used by planters elsewhere in the Santee drainage. For example, the Toms Creek dike ties in with the bluff on either end of its length in a manner similar to the far more extensive dike system of Wade Hampton II below Columbia. According to Ruffin, Hampton's embankment was designed in such a way that it "takes in all the low ground, & connects it by his bank with the highland." But diking projects did not have to exclude all floodwaters from the floodplain to be successful. Ruffin's account of Major Porcher's embankment illustrates how such a dike system worked:

> The embankment does not exclude the water from the lower [that is, downstream] part [of the property], nor is it desired. There is a fall, supposed to be 18 inches the mile along the course of the river; & if the embankment secure, as it does, the land from the first approach of the river & along its course, the mere back water which will enter below is not regarded. Of course the land subject to this back water is more or less injured, & is not cultivated. The general slope of the swamp serves to drain all the upper & cultivated part into this lower part subject to back water, even during the continuance of freshes.

The Old Dead River Dike may have been intended to work in just this way. Assuming that the remains visible today are those of a completed structure, the dike was essentially three-sided, being mostly open on its downstream side.[44]

It is somewhat surprising that so few dikes were completed in the park given the degree to which prominent citizens advocated for the reclamation of the Congaree and Wateree bottomlands. Beginning as early as 1824, and continuing off and on into the early twentieth century, calls for individual and governmental support of reclamation came in from various quarters. The general tenor of these proposals was this: for a relatively modest expenditure (as compared to the potential return), the value of the state's bottomlands could be increased dramatically, with the investment paying for itself many times over in increased production and tax revenue.[45] In 1840 an anonymous Sumter District reader of the Carolina Planter lamented that so much of the area's bottomlands continued to lie idle, still covered, at this late date, "with heavy growth of timber, thick matted vines and cane brakes." The vast potential of these areas was just waiting to be tapped if only neighboring landowners would cooperate and make the necessary investments in embankments. In his view, the fact that past embankments had "been often made without success" was more the result of inadequate engineering than the inherent futility of the enterprise.[46] But the experience of Frederick Cooner, whose large dam was located across the river from the park, illustrates why coaxing was needed. In July 1856 the *Charleston Mercury* reported major damage to Cooner's dike system:

> We learn with great regret that the late freshet in the Congaree has been productive of much damage to all cultivation in the swamp, and has swept away a large portion of the extensive dam of Mr. F. Cooner. . . . It is to be hoped that the rumor has exaggerated the extent of the injury sustained. The energy and enterprise necessary for the accomplishment of works of improvement on so large a scale as that of Mr. Cooner, are too rarely exhibited among our agriculturalists, and we should regret not only the individual loss sustained by a destruction of the work, but also the discouragement from similar enterprises on the part of our people, which would result from it.[47]

Later that same year, in a belated attempt to promote floodplain agriculture, the General Assembly passed "An Act to Promote the Draining and Improvement of Inland Swamps." The act provided a mechanism whereby landowners could incorporate an embankment company when at least two-thirds of the landowners in a particular locality agreed to do so. However, beyond providing the benefits of incorporation and allowing embankment to proceed on the lands (and over the objections) of nonmember landowners, the law did nothing to address the problem of funding. Under the terms of the law, companies were to finance construction of new dike systems via assessments against their members. Ultimately, only one such company—the Wateree Embankment Company— was established before the beginning of the Civil War.[48]

Practice thus never caught up with theory. The cost of reclamation was too high and the risks too great for many landowners to venture their own capital. This was already true enough in the 1850s; it was all the more so after the economic devastation brought on by the Civil War. As the century wound down and the frequency and duration of flooding only increased, cultivating inland river swamps became riskier than ever. By the late 1890s growing corn on such lands was, in the words of the *State,* "a mere lottery."[49]

6

The Location and Extent of Historic Clearing

Then the big fish ate up all the little ones—so the great estates grew up here. I mean the large plantations. There are only two or three of such in every district: Williams's in Peedee country—Hamptons, Taylors, Adams on the Congaree. Singleton— Richardsons in Sumter.

Mary Boykin Chesnut, *Diary,* November 30, 1861

THE HISTORIC RECORD LEAVES NO DOUBT that cultivation and other forms of clearing took place in and around the Beidler Tract during the eighteenth and nineteenth centuries. The presence of cattle mounds and dikes demonstrates clearly enough that people sought to wrest a living from the floodplain. Slave narratives, land grants, wills, and other contemporary documents provide further evidence of clearing activities. Taken together, these documents suggest that the period 1750–1820 saw a gradual growth in floodplain cultivation, followed by a tapering off in the antebellum years, when increased flooding and the need to generate revenue from cotton caused resources to be concentrated on upland soils. While it can be assumed that parts of the Beidler Tract were cleared in the late antebellum period, tree-ring studies suggest that abandonment was well underway in parts of the tract by the 1840s and 1850s. In some places abandonment had begun one to two decades earlier. It appears likely that over time row crops gave way to stock raising as the dominant agricultural use of the floodplain, at least north of the levee zone.

It should come as no surprise that some of the park's old-growth forest obscures farms and pastures from long ago. The patterns of cultivation that existed in the Congaree floodplain were hardly unique to lower Richland. In Louisiana the Singer Tract experienced a similar history before being logged in the 1930s and 1940s. Although the Singer Tract's eighty thousand acres covered an area more than five times the size of the Beidler Tract, in many respects the tracts were similar. Maps from 1846 show a number of plantations lining the Tensas River, including one, the largest, that had about three thousand acres in cultivation.[1] James Tanner estimated that about sixteen thousand acres of the Singer Tract had been cultivated or otherwise disturbed in the antebellum period. Annual cotton production in Madison Parish reached around 110,000 bales by the time of the war, and the cotton grown on the Singer Tract plantations would have contributed significantly to this total. After the war, however, trees invaded the abandoned fields on the tract and grew quickly. By the 1930s evidence of human disturbance had become so obscure in the deeper woods that, according to Tanner, only an experienced eye could see the traces that had been made.[2] Today, it takes a comparably experienced eye to distinguish second growth from old growth in many parts of the Beidler Tract. In those parts of the floodplain where loblollies cluster in large numbers, the possibility of past clearing is quite evident, but in other areas the signs of human disturbance become more obscure with every passing year.

Unfortunately, the historical record is far more useful in confirming that human disturbance took place in the Beidler Tract than it is for estimating the extent of past clearing activities. No plantation logs, planter's diaries, or other firsthand accounts survive that describe the precise location of fields or the size of cleared areas. Some indication of clearing exists in various old plats, but these are few in number and do not always provide clear depictions of the amount of land cleared. The situation is not entirely hopeless, however. Owners of large tracts sometimes advertised them for sale in newspapers, occasionally including details of prior land use for the benefit of potential buyers. Moreover, vegetative patterns in parts of the park provide evidence of past land-disturbing activities. Enough of the latter evidence exists that it is possible to infer, in a general way, the extent of clearing in the tract.

Where Clearing Took Place

Any attempt to estimate the extent of historic clearing in the Beidler Tract must take into account the presence of old, yet even-aged stands of pine and sweet gum in the floodplain. These blocks of early successional species can provide important evidence of historic clearing.

One of the most noticeable features of Congaree National Park is the clumping of old-growth loblolly pine in the northern portion of the floodplain, particularly along Cedar Creek and other waterways. The frequent occurrence of this highly shade-intolerant species indicates that some fairly significant portion of the area's forest canopy was removed in the eighteenth and early to mid–nineteenth centuries. Canopy disturbance is often attributable to wind storm or fire, and loblolly pine has been observed to regenerate in obvious canopy gaps on the banks of Cedar Creek. However, loblolly regenerates best on exposed mineral soil, especially where there is minimal competition from hardwood rootstocks. This fact suggests that many of today's stands of old-growth loblolly may have grown up in areas that were once cultivated or converted to pasture.[3]

For most park visitors the most visible stand of loblolly pine is the one found between the elevated boardwalk and the old service road to Weston Lake (now known as the Sims Trail). The original land grant for this area dates to 1770. One witness-tree pine predates the grant, suggesting that the area had been affected by fire, storms, or clearing prior to European settlement. Coring studies reveal that the former state-record loblolly near Weston Lake began growing around 1765; another large pine—possibly from this same general area—had 320 rings when cut, indicating that it generated about 1645.[4] But aside from these very old stems, many of the loblolly pines on either side of the Sims Trail began growing between 1810 and 1870, with a large number generating during the ownership of Dr. William Weston III and his son Isaac Tucker Weston. The high concentration of loblolly pine in this area—more evident before Hurricane Hugo (1989) than it is today—is typical of what would be expected of abandoned agricultural fields. However, as noted previously, the soils in parts of this area tend to be wet for much of the growing season. Conditions in these locations may have precluded crops other than rice, absent artificial drainage measures.[5]

Researchers acknowledged early on the presence of even-aged forest in the Beidler Tract, which they took to be possible evidence of past human disturbance, especially in the levee zone and along floodplain ridges. In fact, the first intensive vegetative study of the tract pointed to the presence of approximately fifteen hundred acres of mature, even-aged forest in the floodplain. According to the authors of this study,

> Transect studies revealed large areas of seemingly undisturbed uneven-aged stands, along with smaller areas of even-aged stands. The even-aged stands apparently are former fields and pastures or the result of widespread natural disturbances. The even-aged stands along the river appeared younger than those found along the inner-floodplain ridges, based on the stem diameters of canopy trees, and evidence of former cultivation (rectangular corners, etc.). On the other hand, the even-aged stands inland were asymmetrical, covering the highest ground only. These could have originated from either fire or ridge pastures.[6]

Lead author L. L. Gaddy later elaborated on these findings, noting that areas of even-aged sweet gum are clearly visible from the air. In a helicopter flight over the floodplain, Gaddy observed that some of these areas are "squared off" and most likely constitute old fields in the floodplain. Other stands are irregular in shape and appear to snake along ridge tops.[7]

Gaddy's findings appear to corroborate the assertion of Joy Carpenter (see chapter 2) that parts of the floodplain were once logged and used for "corrals." Similarly, decades of exploring and mapping the floodplain have led John Cely to conclude that a number of possible cowpen sites exist in the floodplain. Among them are sites located northeast of Weston Lake, to the east of French-man's Gut, and around Cooner's Cattle Mound (see entries 6, 9, and 10 in appendix A). Another is the late-eighteenth-century "old field" north of Big Snake Slough, discussed above in chapter 2.[8]

The suggestion that scattered clearings once occurred in the swamp, particularly along floodplain ridges, is consistent with observations made by Edmund Ruffin about the Savannah River swamp in the 1840s. Describing a trip through the swamp to reach the river, Ruffin observed that "between the wide & miry river swamp, & the still wider Back Swamp, there is a narrow strip of higher land, partly in small plantations, & through the length of which runs the road we travelled today." Ruffin noted that only the higher portions of the Savannah floodplain were cultivated: "A [large] proportion is low swamp, which though now 6 or 8 feet above water, & appearing firm, is left undisturbed under its dense & tall forest growth. . . . [As for the Big Back Swamp, the] name would convey an erroneous idea of this wide body of wood land. Though subject to high freshes from the river, & truly a swamp of water or mud at some other times, the ground was now firm and dry. . . . Different from the usual very sandy soils, this body is very stiff, close, & also poor, so that very little is cleared or deemed worth cultivation. It seems in no quality to be like alluvial soil."[9]

Additional evidence of agricultural disturbance in the park came to light in the 1990s as a result of efforts to locate champion trees.[10] While searching old-growth areas of the floodplain, researcher Robert Jones saw occasional evidence of past agricultural activities, including drainage ditches, fence rows, and old road beds. He concluded that clearing for agriculture may have been important in some areas, including areas that are now old-growth forest: "Observations of current species composition and stem size class distribution suggest that approximately one half of the area mapped as 'bottomland hardwoods' but not mapped as clearcut or selectively cut forest by Gaddy (1979) . . . is even-aged forest derived from abandoned agricultural fields. Most of the obviously even-aged stands are within a kilometer of the river. Many are between 60 and 120 years old (reflecting time since abandonment of agricultural practices), but some are older."[11]

It is important to note that this conclusion may overstate the extent of agricultural disturbance in the levee zone and beyond. As discussed in chapter 7, far more timber harvesting took place in the levee zone at the turn of the twentieth century than has often been assumed. Nevertheless, agricultural disturbance was certainly an important component of disturbance near the river.[12]

The findings of Gaddy and Jones are corroborated by John Cely's map of the park. On this map Cely points out those parts of the floodplain dominated by loblolly pine, as well as areas containing substantial amounts of even-age timber, especially even-age sweet gum. The map notes that areas of pine and even-age sweet gum "are important indicators of previous openings or clearings in [the] swamp." This statement is based largely on biology—both loblolly pine and, to a lesser extent, sweet gum are classified as early successional, shade-intolerant species. However, personal observation and deduction also underlie this conclusion. In the early 1970s, just as commercial logging was resuming on the Beidler Tract, Cely and his colleague Jim Elder personally observed a large stand of even-age sweet gum in the western end of the tract near the river. This stand was located well within the area marked "River Swamp Land Farm Cultivated" on the old plat of the Adams family lands. Cely noted that this stand, later selectively cut, consisted almost entirely of even-aged sweet gum, with stems ranging from twenty-four to thirty inches in diameter at breast height (dbh). The age of these trees is not known, but a ring count from a large cherry-bark oak *(Quercus pagoda)* stump in the same general area showed that it had begun growing in the 1830s. Similarly, an age-dbh curve developed by Peter Minchin and Rebecca Sharitz suggests that the sweet gum stand described by Cely and Elder generated between 1800 and 1850.[13]

Cely's map is notable for revealing two fairly distinct but discontinuous bands of disturbance where land clearing activities in the park likely took place. The "patchier" of the two bands is located just below the northern bluff line and is characterized by areas of loblolly pine on floodplain ridges. Significantly, a number of these pine stands are found south of Cedar Creek—a natural firebreak—which strongly suggests that they arose from agriculture rather than fire. The more extensive band consists of areas of even-age timber adjacent to the river, primarily in the western third of the Beidler Tract. Cely identifies a large amount of even-age sweet gum in this band, some of which is even denoted "young even-age."[14]

Cely does not delineate the boundaries of individual patches within the two bands, but considering where they occur in the floodplain, it would appear that most of the patches fall within just two of the twenty-one vegetation associations identified in the park's vegetation map. These are: (1) the sweet gum–water oak–laurel oak/giant cane/thicket sedge forest,[15] and (2) the sugarberry–sweet gum–laurel oak/American hornbeam/giant cane/hop sedge forest.[16] The first of these associations occurs for the most part just below the northern bluff line. In places it includes a loblolly pine component. The second dominates the entire floodplain and comprises two phases—a main, green ash phase and a sweet gum phase.[17] The sweet gum phase encompasses much of the area where Cely's band of even-age timber is found (map 8). It lies principally along and

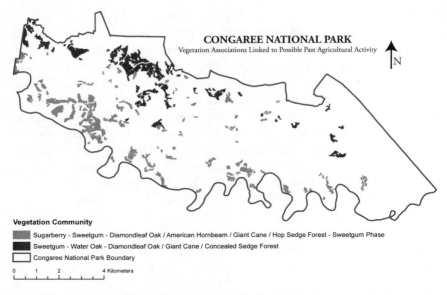

CONGAREE NATIONAL PARK
Vegetation Associations Linked to Possible Past Agricultural Activity

Vegetation Community

▨ Sugarberry - Sweetgum - Diamondleaf Oak / American Hornbeam / Giant Cane / Hop Sedge Forest - Sweetgum Phase

■ Sweetgum - Water Oak - Diamondleaf Oak / Giant Cane / Concealed Sedge Forest

☐ Congaree National Park Boundary

0   1   2   4 Kilometers

Map 8. Vegetation Associations Linked to Possible Past Agricultural Activity. National Park Service map, adapted by Lynne Parker.

just back of the river and is most prevalent in the western third of the Beidler Tract.

A particularly noteworthy aspect of the first association and the sweet gum phase of the second is that each includes areas known to have been cleared for crops or pasture in the relatively recent past. Just as important, neither community is found in areas where clear-cutting took place in the 1970s and 1980s. The latter point bears emphasizing because it may indicate that neither of these communities typically appears in the wake of heavy logging—at least in these particular locations. What this all suggests is that the park's vegetation map may turn out to be a helpful tool for approximating the extent of historic clearing (as opposed to logging) in the Beidler Tract. More study of this possibility remains to be done, but it may be that the park's vegetation map, when read in light of the visual observations in Cely's map, can be used to pinpoint many of the areas that were cleared for agriculture from the late eighteenth through the early twentieth centuries.

Two caveats are in order, however. First, it is unlikely that these two communities encompass every area cleared for agriculture in historic and prehistoric times. For example, an area just east of the Beidler Tract known as Mitchell's Quarter appears to have been used for pasture and crops in the 1880s, but it is shown on the vegetation map as being within the main (green ash) phase, rather than the sweet gum phase, of the Sugarberry–Sweet Gum–Laurel Oak association (see chapter 2 and entry 26 in appendix A).[18] Second, even though clearing is known to have occurred within both communities, it is probable that each includes areas that were never cleared for agriculture. In the sweet gum phase, specifically, the dominance of sweet gum may be due in some areas to oak blowdown during Hurricane Hugo rather than to sweet gum seeding into abandoned agricultural fields.[19]

Cely's map might well have depicted additional areas of even-age timber had it not been for the logging activities of the 1970s and 1980s. Buyers of veneer logs were frequently attracted to the sweet gum in even-age stands because the trunks were long and straight and harbored relatively few limb knots.[20] The stand observed by Cely and Elder was among the first to be cut along the river, and others soon followed. It is thus tempting to posit that much of the logging of the 1970s was concentrated in areas where even-age stands were common. The fact that the stands logged by the Beidlers tended to be in areas that were relatively dry and easy to reach is also salient. This combination of ready access and higher ground would have been just as attractive to antebellum planters as it was to the loggers who followed them. (It should be noted that the Beidlers' main logging road through the middle of the Beidler Tract [the "New Road"] lay quite close in places to the route of a late-eighteenth-century wagon road to the river. See entry 17 in appendix A.) All of this suggests that the areas logged in the 1970s—especially in the western part of the Beidler Tract—may be the same areas where fields and pastures were concentrated in the nineteenth century. Stated another way, it is possible that the timber cutting of the 1970s has obscured the full extent of historical clearing activities in the Beidler Tract. Careful study of areas that were only selectively logged by the Beidlers could possibly yield additional insight into past land use in these areas.

Perhaps the best way to appreciate the extent of human disturbance in the floodplain is to survey the cultural features that have been identified there to date. Map 9 shows a number of the places known to have been modified by human activity from the mid–eighteenth through early twentieth centuries. (Some of the more notable of these locations are described in appendix A.) Among the features identified to date are two slave quarters, at least thirty-five fields or pastures, sixteen primitive roads, eight bridges, three ferries, two logging camps, three sawmills (on or east of the rail line), and seven home sites. Remnant earthen structures include seven dikes of various lengths, at least five ditches, twelve Indian or cattle mounds, three sets of bridge abutments along the historic route to Huger's Ferry, and three "cutoffs" where water courses were shortened to facilitate the movement of vessels and timber. As can be seen from the map, human activities were spread across the entire park, with the highest concentration of individual sites occurring near the river.[21]

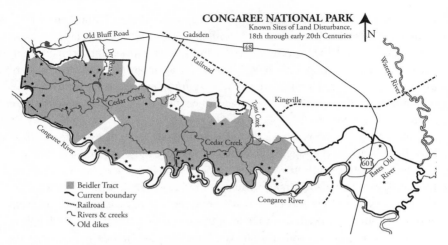

Map 9. Known Sites of Land Disturbance, Eighteenth through Early Twentieth Centuries. Map by Lynne Parker.

Factors Limiting Floodplain Clearing Activities

Given the large number of cultural features in the park, as well as the telltale concentrations of loblolly pine and even-age sweet gum scattered across the floodplain, it is tempting to conclude that intensive cultivation took place over large parts of the park between the mid–eighteenth and late nineteenth centuries. Certainly the Adams, Weston, and Woodward families—who collectively owned the majority of the Beidler Tract in the two decades before the Civil War—had the slaves, equipment, and capital assets to exploit their bottomland acreage.[22] Real estate controlled by James U. Adams, Mary G. Adams (widow of Joel Adams Jr.), Isaac T. Weston, and Lieuellan Woodward made up about 65 percent of the Beidler Tract in 1860. An idea of the wealth of these individuals can be gleaned from the number of slaves held by each at the outbreak of the Civil War:

James U. Adams	309
Mary G. Adams	273
Isaac T. Weston	154
Lieuellan Woodward	168

James U. Adams, Mary G. Adams, and Lieuellan Woodward were among the 10 largest slaveholders (out of around 600) in Richland District in 1860.[23]

Historian Chalmers Davidson maintained that the plantations in lower Richland and Sumter District "were no less prosperous [than those in the low-country] and the mansions even more imposing. In fact, here was the high tide of Cotton Kingdom prosperity in the State during the 1840's and 1850's." Still, not all the suitable land in lower Richland was in cultivation in the years leading up to the war. In 1825 a mere 25,000 acres (out of 403,200) were cultivated in all of Richland District (as calculated by Robert Mills). Of course, substantial clearing and cultivation occurred in subsequent decades, as planters in lower Richland continued to clear new fields to replace those exhausted by cotton production. But many plantations of this period, large ones in particular, still contained significant blocks of "unimproved" land (that is, woodland and old fields not producing crops or other products).[24]

During his 1850 tour of the midlands, agricultural journalist Solon Robinson complained that "the greatest drawback to improvement is the disposition of many persons to buy up all the land that joins them" and leave it unimproved. Census figures reveal that of the 325,121 acres in Richland District designated "farmland" in 1850, fully 235,695 acres (72 percent) were unimproved, while only 89,426 acres (28 percent) were improved. Much of the latter acreage was found in the plantation country of lower Richland, but the Forks still had its share of unimproved land, including both abandoned fields grown up to scrub and old-growth and second-growth forest. Free-ranging stock needed extensive areas of forest and pine savannah to survive, and this fact alone militated in favor of large plantations with substantial amounts of unimproved acreage.[25]

Not only did unimproved land remain available in the decades before the war, but people increasingly felt compelled to abandon lower Richland for richer and more profitable lands to the west. In the 1830s the combination of soil exhaustion from cotton cultivation and the effects of an economic downturn resulted in considerable outmigration from the area. Within the park, Thomas Seay (younger brother of James H. Seay) appears to have sold his land east of the railroad by the mid-1840s. At the end of the decade he was living in Murray County, Georgia. So many people left Richland District in the 1850s—predominantly large landowners and their slaves—that the total population of the district actually fell by the end of the decade: and this despite the fact that the 1850s were boom years in antebellum South Carolina.[26]

For many of those who stayed, the amount of land in production continued to decline. James H. Seay reported 600 improved acres in 1850 (out of a total of 2,500) but only 425 in 1860. Overall, the number of farms in Richland District declined from 632 in 1850 to 225 in 1860, and the production of rice fell by 89 percent to a mere 9,286 pounds. The census of 1860 shows that total reported farmland in the district was 269,075 acres, a reduction of 56,046 acres from 1850. Of this total, only 77,118 acres (29 percent) were improved, a reduction of 12,308 acres from 1850.[27]

In view of these trends, it is possible that some planters scaled back cultivation in the Beidler Tract during the decade before the war. District-wide, total cotton production declined by 1,419 bales between 1850 and 1860.[28] On the other hand, the census data reveal that the Adams, Weston, and Woodward families actually increased their production of cotton between 1850 and 1860, notwithstanding the overall decline in the district as a whole.[29] Whether this increase is in any way attributable to cultivation in the Beidler Tract is impossible to say. However, it seems unlikely that these or other planters would have attempted a dramatic increase in cotton production on the low ground of the park. The risk of loss in these years was substantial unless, like Wade Hampton II, John Singleton, and other wealthy planters, they had completed an elaborate system of dikes. The assistant marshal of Sumter District stated in 1850 that the alluvial swamps of the Wateree River valley, although having "amazing fertility," were subject to such extensive flooding that "comparatively little of it is cultivated."[30] The same may have been true of the Beidler Tract, where levees and impoundments were rare.

Hard data on the tract as a whole are hard to come by, but the case of Isaac T. Weston is illuminating. Weston was the owner of Pine Bluff Plantation (formerly Gum Tree Plantation), a large tract of upland and swamp extending roughly from Old Bluff Road on the north to just below Cedar Creek on the south. This plantation, which Weston inherited from his father, Dr. William Weston III, took in Weston Lake and the surrounding area.[31] According to the census of 1860, Weston's plantation consisted of 1,800 acres, of which 1,486 acres were unimproved. By 1870 the amount of unimproved land on the plantation had increased to 1,650 acres, including 1,400 acres of unimproved woodland. The latter figure is significant because it exceeds by over 100 acres the total amount of floodplain acreage on the plantation as a whole. A plat of the plantation dated January 1, 1873, shows approximately 1,250 acres lying in the floodplain, centered more or less on Weston Lake. The plat contains a descriptive legend stating that "most of the above tract is heavily timbered and some of the upland fine cotton land."[32]

With so much of his land having been unimproved in 1860 and 1870 and with most of it still "heavily timbered" in 1873, the strong likelihood is that much (or all) of Weston's swampland was unimproved throughout the late antebellum and immediate postwar period. Tellingly, an 1866 notice advertising the plantation for sale stated that the "portion of the plantation in the swamp contains a variety of Timber, comprising white oak, beach, ash, gum and cypress."[33] This is not to suggest that the swamp was untouched: there is evidence that the plantation may have had a sawmill in 1866, and one area just below the bluff line was kept open until the 1930s (see entry 6 in appendix A).[34] Clearly, though, most of the large bottomland fields once present on this plantation were growing up in trees by 1870.

The fact is, despite the continued efforts of bottomland growers to generate wealth from the swamp, a number of factors militated against widespread cultivation, with periodic flooding being only the most obvious. The cost of removing large trees with little commercial value (especially sweet gum) was a major factor that often precluded the clearing of new fields.[35] Other practical constraints included difficult terrain dissected by sloughs and guts and the persistent threat of disease in a malarial environment. But perhaps the most important factor limiting floodplain agriculture was the soil of the floodplain itself. Unless drained and diked, much of it was just not well suited to long-term cultivation.

Most of the floodplain in the park consists of Tawcaw silty clay loam, with numerous inclusions of Chastain silty clay loam (figure 9). Tawcaw soils are generally too wet to serve as either cropland or pasture unless drained. Other major soil types in the park include soils in the Congaree, Toccoa, and Chewacla series, found primarily along the banks of the Congaree and Wateree Rivers. Congaree loam, which dominates the levee zone of the Congaree, is well drained to moderately well drained. This soil has high potential for both pasture and the cultivation of corn and small grains. Historically, cotton was also grown on this soil in narrow inclusions of Congaree silt loam and Congaree sandy loam near the river. However, absent supplemental drainage, cotton tended to mature late on this soil, exposing boles to risk of loss from frost. Toccoa loam has properties similar to Congaree loam but is only moderately suited for pasture and field crops such as corn. Chewacla loam, which occurs principally along the west bank of the Wateree, is somewhat poorly drained and generally not well suited to cultivation unless artificially drained.[36]

It is significant that many of the cultural features indicated in map 9 are concentrated in those parts of the park having Congaree and Toccoa loam soils, the soils best suited for pasture or cropland. Moreover, the location of these features is consistent with evidence cited previously showing two bands of disturbance across the floodplain. However, the precise extent to which human activity is

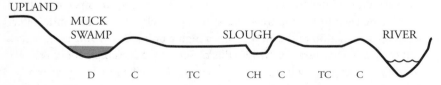

Figure 9. Relation of Soil Types to Topography at Congaree National Park. Soil classification in the floodplain, per Lawrence, *Soil Survey of Richland County* (1978): D = Dorovan muck; C = Congaree loam; TC = Taw caw silty clay loam; CH = Chastain silty clay loam. Figure adapted by Lynne Parker from Figure 16 in Wharton et al., *The Ecology of Bottomland Hardwood Swamps of the Southeast* (1982).

responsible for these two bands of disturbance is not known. Although many disturbed areas were no doubt produced by clearing land for fields and pastures, others may have been the result of natural disturbances such as floods and windstorms.

What seems clear is that care should be taken not to overstate the extent of cultivation in the Beidler Tract. The vegetation of South Carolina's lowlands was so thick in the decades before the war that runaway slaves were not only able to escape capture for long periods, but some were even able to set up small settlements back in the swamps. Along the Congaree, the floodplain remained so forested during these years that it was a perennial hiding place for fugitive slaves. Charles Ball encountered a manacled runaway in the swamp upstream of the park around 1806, and in the early 1820s a notorious escaped slave by the name of Joe—who called himself "Forester" for his ability to melt into river swamps—was able to travel undetected from his master's plantation near Toms Creek to the lower Santee region of the state. Hiding in "the most dense and impervious swamps," Joe was able to evade capture for over two years.[37] News accounts in the autumn of 1823 reported that Joe and several other escaped slaves had "for some time past secreted themselves in the fork of the Wateree and Congaree," as well as along the eastern banks of the Wateree and Santee, from Manchester to Nelson's Ferry. Joe was eventually killed at the Santee Canal, and his head stuck on a pole "as a solemn warning to vicious slaves."[38]

Twenty years later, the Congaree floodplain was still heavily forested. Traveling the south side of the river in 1843, Edmund Ruffin had occasion to view the floodplain from the high bluffs near Fort Motte:

> In passing to Dr. Stark's (Belville) on the Congaree, we passed by the site of Fort Motte, so noted in the revolutionary war. . . . The banks of the Santee at Fort Motte, & some distance below, are very high, & as precipitous as any can be not formed of rock wholly or in part. The views from the tops of these banks are magnificent, & would appear to be of mountain scenery. The crooked & narrow Congaree is seen in the distance as well as almost immediately under the observer. The bordering swamp, covered with a dense forest of tall trees, lies spread out below for many a mile, offering no obstruction to the view from so high a point, & showing an expanse of the richest verdure. The High Hills of Santee are seen high above & far distant, appearing like mountains compared to the low-lying swamp forest.[39]

From his vantage point near Fort Motte, Ruffin could see a part of the floodplain where William R. Thomson's indigo vats had stood some fifty years before. What he saw now, however, was not improved agricultural fields, but a dense forest of tall trees spreading to the far horizon.

Abandonment of Floodplain Agriculture

Some indication of the duration of cultivation in the park can be found in the history of two bottomland plantations owned by members of the Adams family. Both were located in the Beidler Tract, and both included areas that appear to have been intensively cultivated and then abandoned.

The larger of the two plantations, often referred to as the Adams "swamp plantation," was owned by multiple members of the extended Adams family. This plantation consisted of over 4,000 acres in the far western end of the park, including a 790-acre riverfront tract apportioned to a bankrupt James U. Adams after the war. The latter tract contained the old "Adams' Quarter" as well as one of the ancillary Adams dikes. When sold by the sheriff in 1870, the James U. Adams tract was described as "swamp, adapted to the cultivation of corn &c.—all heavily timbered."[40]

The description of the Adams tract as "all" heavily timbered is somewhat surprising. Just thirty years earlier Adams's father, James Adams Sr., appears to have cultivated a substantial portion of this very same tract. The men and women who did the actual cultivating likely lived in the riverside slave quarter originally built by James U.'s grandfather, Joel Adams Sr. (figure 7). Yet judging from the tenor of the advertisement—with no mention of cleared land, ongoing cultivation, or existing dwellings—by 1870 much if not all of the cleared land on the tract had begun to revert to forest. That in itself is noteworthy, but more interesting still is the fact that this pattern seems to have repeated itself at Adams's other bottomland plantation, Pea Ridge.

Pea Ridge Plantation was located near the middle of the Beidler Tract in an area traversed today by the Kingsnake Trail (map 7).[41] According to a plat of Pea Ridge prepared in 1886, the plantation consisted of both uplands and lands that "are situated in the Congaree River swamp and are heavily timbered lands."[42] Parts of the latter acreage are now dominated by old-growth loblolly pine, and it is possible that these areas were either cultivated or in pasture during the early nineteenth century. The actual timing of disturbance at Pea Ridge is not known, but tree-ring evidence suggests that the pines in this area began generating in the 1840s and 1850s. This was about the same time that pines were sprouting on the Adams swamp plantation east of the Northwest Boundary Dike. It was also soon after the time that Cooner's Mound is believed to have been constructed on a floodplain site just east of Pea Ridge.[43]

The apparent convergence of these events—namely, the abandonment of a major diking project, the construction of a large cattle mound, and the invasion of certain parts of the floodplain by loblolly pine—may only be coincidence. Then again, the timing of these developments could be emblematic of a general shifting away from planting in favor of grazing. Edmund Ruffin observed just such a shift in the 1840s at some parts of Mexico Plantation. There, after "nearly all culture [had been abandoned] because of the increasing freshes, the land became a rich pasture for cattle, & presented a scene of great beauty before it began again to grow up in trees."[44]

Tree-ring studies conducted in the park strongly suggest that many, if not most, cultivated areas in the northern portion of the floodplain had been abandoned by the late 1850s. One such study from the early 1990s found that about half of the pines measured below the northern bluff had sprouted between 1840 and 1865. Actual abandonment may have occurred well before that, as it can take decades for an abandoned agricultural field to succeed from the herb stage to one dominated by loblolly pine. Evidence of abandonment during the early national and antebellum periods comes from a 1906 U.S. Bureau of Forestry study, which dated an even-aged sweet gum stand in the park to around the 1820s. A few years later, drainage engineer D. G. Miller observed that practically all the historic dikes along the Congaree were covered with trees, underbrush, and cane, with some trees measuring twenty to thirty inches in diameter. Trees of that size may indicate abandonment in the antebellum years, as had occurred near the Northwest Boundary Dike.[45]

Additional evidence of early abandonment can be found in the observations of British researcher George Peterken. Studying cut stumps along park trails after Hurricane Hugo, Peterken concluded that many of the pines, oaks, and sweet gums he saw had sprouted between 1770 and 1830. He also noted that a younger age class, which included American elm *(Ulmus americana)*, green ash *(Fraxinus pennsylvanica)*, and bitternut hickory *(Carya cordiformis)*, originated between 1860 and 1900. Six of the trees studied by Peterken had grown slowly for fifteen to sixty years before being released, which he took to be the result of intense competition in regenerating thickets. Whether these stands originated in old fields or large blowdown areas is not known, but the presence of pine may be an indicator of abandoned agricultural fields. Moreover, the younger age class (1860–1900) corresponds to a period of known abandonment: the postwar years after emancipation. The older age class (1770–1830) could have been the product of abandonment as well, owing in large part to increased flooding during the early national period.[46]

Thus, there appears to have been a general turning away from cultivation in the Beidler Tract starting around the 1820s or 1830s. This trend increased dramatically after the war, when landowners throughout South Carolina largely abandoned the cultivation of corn in the state's river swamps. In the early 1880s Harry Hammond observed that the "upper pine belt" (inner coastal plain) contained a substantial amount of "corn lands whose culture has been . . . largely abandoned, but which are not yet entirely grown up." He saw great potential for corn to be grown profitably in these areas, noting that "under the system of agriculture, at present pursued, the chief attention is paid to the more easily tilled, but less fertile uplands. Nevertheless, there is in the upper pine belt a body of 600,000 acres of productive corn land, now almost wholly neglected, but once cultivated with great profit, when corn was worth only fifty to sixty cents a bushel, capable now of yielding fifty per cent. more than the present entire corn crop of the State."[47]

Among the factors speeding the abandonment of floodplain agriculture was the incredible loss of life, both black and white, during the war years. This, coupled with the widespread destruction of fences and other property, meant that the amount of land that could be kept in agricultural production dropped sharply. Also affecting production was a persistent shortage of circulating money after the war. The collapse of Confederate currency and bonds had wiped out the savings of many of the formerly well-to-do, leaving them with few resources to finance labor contracts and purchase supplies. As a result, many planters found it difficult to adjust to their new economic relation to their former slaves. Large numbers of freedmen wished to work independently for wages or to rent land of their choosing, where they could make their own decisions about which crops to grow.[48] Many planters in lower Richland seem to have balked at this push for autonomy, attempting to continue the old ways as much as possible.[49] More than a few signed freedmen to annual contracts for a share of the crop and then skimped on payment at the end of the year. Disgust with the contract system, together with recurring crop failures, drove many freedmen to leave lower Richland for other areas. The result was a chronic labor shortage that left fewer workers available to cultivate risky bottomland fields. In 1868 the shortage was sufficiently acute in lower Richland that Dr. William Weston IV and others formed "The Immigration Society of Richland Fork" to encourage the importation of German, Irish, and other foreign white workers.[50]

With money to pay wages scarce and access to capital limited, sharecropping took hold rather quickly as the dominant labor system across the cotton belt. Ideally, sharecropping accommodated the desire of freedmen to work more or less independently on rented, dispersed allotments, while freeing planters from the need to pay cash wages. Given the labor shortage in lower Richland, one might expect that few tenant farmers would want to gamble their livelihood, not to mention the lives of themselves and their families, by setting up in flood-prone lands. Some did so, however, especially on the best floodplain soils upstream from the park. But their numbers were small compared to the groups that had worked the swamp earlier in the century. The result was that many of the floodplain fields still in cultivation at the time of the war were abandoned in ensuing decades because of a lack of laborers to maintain them.[51]

The shortage of cash after the war meant that some planters lost their bottomland holdings altogether. The only hard asset many planters had left to offer as collateral was land, but land prices fell dramatically in the postwar era, both in Richland County and throughout the region. Low valuations were accompanied by high taxes, as the state's Reconstruction government attempted to motivate large landowners to work their land with hired labor or renters rather than leave it idle. It was hoped that high tax rates would, if nothing else, make it difficult for former planters to hold onto large unused tracts of land. On the latter score, at least, the policy seems often to have had the intended effect.

James U. Adams was reduced to relative poverty after the war and, unable to meet his obligations, filed for bankruptcy in 1868. By 1870 his neighbor Isaac T. Weston was likewise seriously in debt. Thomas Philip Weston would later recall that "after the war the situation of the family was critical. My father [Isaac T. Weston] was crippled [from a war wound] and the plantation was in the hands of Negroes as croppers. They would not or could not pay rent, and the family was almost in destitute circumstances." To address his debts, Weston was forced to divide Pine Bluff Plantation into fifteen lots and offer them for sale. (Only four of the lots sold; Weston's son William W. Weston bought the remaining lots [1,554 acres] out of foreclosure in 1881.) During this same time period, various members of the Zeigler family lost their floodplain lands near the center of the Beidler Tract, forfeiting them to the state for nonpayment of taxes (see entry 14 in appendix A).[52]

Cultivation may have declined in the park after the Civil War, but it did not come to a complete stop. In a period when fertilizers were still not widely used, floodplain soils would have remained ideal for demanding plants like corn and cotton. In the levee zone, particularly, cultivation continued into the postwar period and beyond. Newspaper descriptions of the flood of May 1886 make clear that a number of farmers continued to plant bottomland fields in the park despite the risks. For example, the *Columbia Register* reported that "Messrs. John Williams, John James, Joe Bates, Paul Joyner and most of the other planters of the Fork low lands, from Eastover to Gadsden, lost heavily in stock. As to the crops, everything has been submerged, and the entire cotton crop is regarded as lost as well as their stocks of seed corn and cotton, forage, &c."

The willingness of farmers to plant cotton in the floodplain may actually have increased for a time after Reconstruction because of the state's growing dependence on cotton as a cash crop. A fictionalized depiction of this practice can be found in the work of Pulitzer Prize–winning author Julia Mood Peterkin, whose Lang Syne Plantation overlooked the Congaree from a high bluff near Fort Motte. Her story "Ashes," published in 1924, begins with a description of what rather clearly is the confluence of the Congaree and Wateree Rivers below Lang Syne: "The two rivers commonly lie complacent, but on occasion they rouse and flood low places with furious, yellow water. They lunge and tear at the hillsides that hold the plantation above them until their violence is spent; then they creep back into their rightful channels, leaving other sodden acres desolate and covered with bent, ruined stalks that show where fields of cotton and corn were ripe and ready for harvest." This account and others confirm that some amount of cultivation persisted in the park decades after the war.[53]

Nevertheless, the general abandonment of the state's major floodplains continued throughout the postwar period and even accelerated at the turn of the century. No longer able to cultivate their lands as intensively as before and faced with the need to generate cash for supplies and other necessities, many of the region's large landowners devoted themselves to growing cotton on their upland acreage, expending less and less effort on corn and other food crops formerly grown in the bottomlands. Increasingly food was imported, allowing southern farmers to concentrate their efforts on cotton—the one crop that seemed certain to generate cash.[54]

Increased flooding was another factor pushing people to abandon their floodplain property. The widespread clearing of headwater forests in the late nineteenth century, combined with the elevated rainfall levels of the period, resulted in numerous damaging floods along the Congaree. Between 1891 and 1905, the number of floods reportedly increased by 94 percent and their duration by 113 percent.[55] In 1906 a representative of the U.S. Weather Bureau observed that flooding in the midlands was becoming more and more "flashy":

> The large acreage of abandoned bottom lands bears tribute to the fact that severe floods occur with greater frequency than in former years, and for this condition of affairs deforestation of the water-sheds is held to be responsible in great measure. It is an indisputable fact that that during the days of the forests there was plenty of water for purposes of navigation but comparatively few great floods, as the forests held the water, allowing it to flow out gradually. Now navigation on the Wateree, Congaree and Santee rivers is either difficult or impossible, while the floods have increased in frequency and suddenness.[56]

About this same time, the South Carolina Department of Agriculture confirmed that increased flooding was having an adverse impact on floodplain agriculture. It noted that "the frequent floods of recent years, due to the deforestation of the head waters of the streams is making agriculture upon bottom lands impossible, and many acres which once grew an abundance of corn are now abandoned to weeds and bushes. The damage caused by these floods amounts annually to several millions of dollars."[57]

Impacts from turn-of-the-century flooding were mostly felt in the fertile bottomlands just below Columbia. According to the Weather Bureau, the areas farther down were already considered "principally heavily wooded swamp land." What fields remained in the levee zone of the park would gradually be idled or converted to pasture over the next several decades. A 1918 soil survey of Richland County observed that there was evidence of "more extensive cultivation [in the lower Congaree floodplain] in times past, certain old fields now being grown up in small trees and underbrush."[58]

The abandonment of formerly productive fields suggests that the interests of white landowners and black laborers converged when it came to floodplain agriculture on the lower Congaree: both sought to concentrate their efforts on the uplands and cotton, leaving much of the floodplain to their cattle and hogs. The soil survey of 1918 noted that the lower Congaree floodplain was one of the least important areas of Richland County in terms of agriculture, there being "no present demand for land of this type for farming." Only a few scattered areas were then in cultivation, mostly narrow fields near the river. In the Beidler Tract the last riverside fields remained open until around the 1930s, when they began to be invaded by trees.[59]

Although floodplain cultivation in the postwar period was mostly limited to the river margin, tree-ring data suggest that some cleared areas in the northern half of the park were not abandoned until around the turn of the twentieth century. It is possible that some of these areas were cowpens rather than cultivated fields. Alternatively, the presence of older pines immediately adjacent to some younger pine stands may be evidence of farmers reentering fields abandoned in the early to mid–nineteenth century, possibly with the intent of practicing "girdle farming"—that is, farming around deadened trees. Such a scenario would be consistent with the state of the farming economy at the end of the nineteenth century. Throughout South Carolina, farming had been depressed since the Civil War, with corn production not reaching its prewar levels until 1900. As plantations were broken up and sharecropping became prevalent, many smaller holdings were created, resulting in even less crop diversification than before the war. Cotton cultivation spread rapidly into increasingly marginal agricultural lands as tenants and sharecroppers engaged in a "frantic effort to make the land yield ever more cotton in a vain attempt to pay off liens." At the same time, the proliferation of railroad lines made provisions so cheap that many farmers neglected to grow food crops in favor of the bigger financial returns that a large cotton crop would bring. By 1900 the amount of improved farmland in the state had increased from 28 percent in 1860 to more than 40 percent. The result was land butchery on a massive scale. These pressures may have forced some farmers down into the floodplain to risk a cotton crop or to grow corn for food.[60]

For those determined to try their hand at floodplain agriculture, one additional obstacle remained: transportation. Even in years when crops could be successfully grown and harvested in the bottomlands, getting them to market at a profit was a major hurdle. This point was made forcefully in 1893 by the president of the Columbia Board of Trade:

[The Congaree River] flows through one of the most fertile portions of this or any State, not surpassed by the Mississippi bottom lands, capable of producing thousands of bushels of corn annually, acres of which have been known to produce with ordinary culture 80 bushels of corn per acre. The greater part of these lands are now neglected for the want of river naviga-tion, being too far to haul in wagons and then pay high freights to reach the markets. Steamers coming to Columbia would give them relief, thus causing thousands of acres to be cultivated that now are entirely neglected; there is now on the Congaree five or six hay meadows producing about 1,800 tons annually and need a market, which would give the relief they ask if the steamers could come up to Columbia.

Limited steamboat traffic resumed on the Congaree in the 1890s and roads be-gan to be upgraded in the early 1900s to accommodate automobile traffic. This helped the situation somewhat. The *State* reported in 1907 that a rehabilitated road leading to the abandoned Bates (formerly McCord's) Ferry "has already served a good purpose, so far as Columbia is concerned, for it has enabled the farmers to market in Columbia their hay and produce which had been shipped down the river rather than haul it through swamps. Heretofore it required four mules to pull a ton of hay, now two mules can pull 1 1–2 tons on this road." But even after rehabilitation, visitors to this area "were struck with the fact that though this soil is rich and alluvial, like that of the Mississippi delta, yet there are hundreds and hundreds of acres not under cultivation."[61]

The reason for this relative neglect was not just flooding, or labor shortages, or reliance on imported foodstuffs. Changes in the nation at large meant that the Beidler Tract and adjacent lands were now valued far more for their old-growth timber than for their agricultural potential.

The first sale of land in the Beidler Tract to a northern lumberman occurred in 1890, and more sales soon followed. Northern investors were drawn to the tract primarily because of its extensive stands of old-growth bald cypress, but other species were of interest too, when it was cost-effective to log them. These species included such traditionally sought-after species as pine, oak, and ash, but also the formerly "worthless" sweet gum. In fact, when the U.S. Bureau of Forestry undertook a study of the harvesting, milling, and sale of "red gum" (that is, sweet gum) in the winter of 1903–04, it chose the Congaree holdings of the Santee River Cypress Lumber Company as one of its two principal study sites (the other site was in Missouri).[62] These lands, which one day would form the heart of the park, were chosen in part because they represented a good ex-ample of a "virgin" bottomland hardwood forest in the Atlantic Coastal Plain. Alfred K. Chittenden, the author of the study, provides a rare description of the Santee lands as they existed over a century ago:

Figure 10. "A Large [Sweet Gum], Richland County, S.C." From Chittenden, *The Red Gum* (1906).

The forest on the hardwood bottoms of the Congaree River, in South Carolina, consists chiefly of red gum, cottonwood, white ash, elm, sycamore, hackberry, some few oaks, and red and silver maples. In the sloughs and perpetual swamps are large quantities of cypress and tupelo gum, and there is some black gum on the ridges. The forest is, for the most part, dense and fairly even-aged. There is little young growth beneath the older trees. Canebrakes are common and are very dense, the cane often reaching a height of 20 feet. This cane, with the briars and rattans, makes a very heavy undergrowth, so that where it occurs no tree reproduction can take place. The result is that the forest gradually becomes rather open in character.[63]

For present purposes, the Bureau of Forestry study is most useful for what it suggests about the extent of human disturbance to the Congaree Swamp in the eighteenth and nineteenth centuries. Chittenden's description of the forest as "dense and fairly even-aged," plus his references elsewhere in the text to cane and vines in the understory, suggests that much of the forest had been disturbed by storms or fires in the relatively recent past. Interestingly, stand data generated by the study (said to be collected on "acres . . . all carefully selected, so as to obtain average conditions in respect to both the size and the number of the trees") indicate a basal area similar to that found in the aftermath of Hurricane

Figure 11. "Dense Cane-brake, in Which No Tree Reproduction Can Take Place, South Carolina." From Chittenden, *The Red Gum* (1906).

Figure 12. "Tupelo Gum Slough, Congaree River, South Carolina." From Chittenden, *The Red Gum* (1906).

Figure 13. "A Cypress Slough in the Dry Season, South Carolina." From Chittenden, *The Red Gum* (1906).

Figure 14. "A Large Cottonwood—One of the Associates of [Sweet Gum] on the Hardwood Bottoms—Richland County, S.C." From Chittenden, *The Red Gum* (1906).

Hugo.[64] Nevertheless, the working assumption of the foresters who studied it was that the Congaree Swamp was essentially an old-growth forest. These men knew what second-growth forest looked like, and they acknowledged that second-growth forest existed along the Congaree (figure 15). They even reported data on a second-growth stand in the park dating back around to the 1820s.[65] However, the bulk of their work in South Carolina was devoted to the "virgin" Congaree holdings of the Santee River Cypress Lumber Company. This point bears emphasizing, because whatever amount of human disturbance the Santee lands may have experienced in the past, it was not enough for observers in the early 1900s to consider them mostly "cut over" or regenerating.

Ultimately, it is simply not possible to determine the precise extent of clearing in the park before 1900. One can point to physical factors limiting the extent of floodplain cultivation, or describe historic circumstances that reduced the amount of clearing that might otherwise have occurred, but doing so only reveals so much. What can be said for sure is that the places most likely to have been cleared were those that were easiest for people to get to—and that justified the time and expense of clearing. This translates to the levee zone along the river, as well as the more elevated floodplain ridges below the northern bluff line. Perhaps the best indicator of the state of the floodplain at century's end is

Figure 15. "Second-Growth [Sweet Gum], Ash, Cottonwood, and Sycamore, on Hardwood Bottomland, South Carolina." From Chittenden, *The Red Gum* (1906).

the advent of northern lumbermen in search of cheap timber and a big payoff. The arrival of investors from Syracuse, Chicago, and Philadelphia is mute testimony to the amount of timber still available for exploitation in the floodplain. It may even be a sign that clearing in large parts of the floodplain had been quite limited, notwithstanding the preference of settlers and planters for fertile floodplain tracts. Be that as it may, the arrival of the northern lumbermen would soon give rise to a level of human disturbance never before seen in the postsettlement era.

Industrial Logging FIRST INROADS, 1870–1918

My father's principal recreation consisted of trips from Chicago to the South to view his superb trees. . . . One suspects he had more enjoyment in strolling through the woods than in cutting them down.

Francis Beidler II to Christopher Reed, 1981

THOSE FAMILIAR WITH THE CAMPAIGN to protect the Beidler Tract have long acknowledged the pioneering efforts of conservationist Harry Hampton, whose advocacy in the 1950s and 1960s helped pave the way for the eventual establishment of Congaree National Park. Less well known is that Hampton was not the first to call for preserving the old-growth forests at Congaree. That distinction belongs to an early-twentieth-century firm of landscape architects from Boston. In a 1905 report to the Civic League of Columbia, the firm of Kelsey and Guild presented a number of recommendations for improving the city, among which was one for establishing a "reservation" in the swamps below Columbia:

> If Columbia realizes its hopes of having the Congaree River made navigable from the southern limits of the city to the sea, an avenue will be opened by which it will be possible to operate pleasure craft for excursions down the river. Fringing the banks of the river, at least as far as where its waters join the Wateree below Kingsville, is a magnificent growth of heavily timbered swamp forest almost tropical in luxuriance, and covering many thousands of acres. Undoubtedly, in time, this will disappear before the axe unless steps are taken for its protection, thus saving one of the finest natural features of the state from ruin and the wonderful beauty of the river's banks for the perpetual enjoyment of the people of Columbia and the state.

It may be said that these swamp jungles are inaccessible and, therefore, in no danger of destruction,—and this was said of the Adirondacks and the White mountains at one time,—but if so, no harm can come if the state should make a permanent reservation of a tract along the river banks wide enough to forever keep the wild beauty of the river inviolate.

From the vantage point of history it is easy to appreciate the visionary reach of this proposal, while acknowledging how utterly contrary it was to the commercial tenor of the times. By the time the Kelsey and Guild report landed on people's doorsteps, dutifully excerpted in the *State,* large-scale industrial logging had already been underway along the Congaree for more than a decade. Indeed, exploitation of the Congaree bottomland was only accelerating.[1]

The Timber Barons Look South

For much of the last half of the nineteenth century, the Great Lakes states were the major source of commercial timber in the United States, supplying tremendous quantities of white pine *(Pinus strobus)* and other woods for a growing nation. By the end of the century, however, the timber in the lake states had begun to play out and timber companies and northern investors turned their attention to the relatively untapped forests of the Southeast. Scouts sent south by major timber concerns reported back that the region contained a seemingly inexhaustible supply of old-growth timber that could be had for next to nothing. At first longleaf pine was the principal attraction for northern investors, but soon bald cypress drew their attention as well. Land that would have been highly productive if reclaimed was now valued primarily in terms of the quality of its standing timber and the ease with which it could be logged. It was not long before large tracts of South Carolina bottomland began to change hands.[2]

As had been the case in the lake states, hardwoods were of relatively little interest to the new arrivals. The principal demand at century's end was for white pine and similar conifers—wood that was strong, durable, and easily worked. While local southern producers continued to cut hardwoods for tool handles, barrel staves, railroad ties, and furniture, northern investors were drawn primarily by longleaf pine and bald cypress, woods ideal for use in the building trades. With their access to capital and the latest technological advances, these large operators were able to generate lumber in volumes sufficient to meet demand from both domestic homebuilders and the export market. Almost immediately, longleaf pine was viewed by the major producers as a logical substitute for white pine. Not only was it very strong and durable, longleaf had the further advantage of growing across vast stretches of the Atlantic and Gulf coastal plains. Bald cypress, in contrast, was more restricted in range and harder to get to, being limited primarily to swamps and floodplains below the fall line. But bald cypress had one great advantage that most other woods did not: it was highly resistant to decay. The heartwood of bald cypress was ideal for shingles, siding, gutters, cisterns, fencing, and any other structures exposed to the elements. Thus, when northern investors started buying up large swaths of southern bottomland, it was primarily bald cypress they were after, not oak, ash, or sweet gum.[3]

The special qualities of bald cypress were well known in lower Richland, and it can be assumed that cypress had been cut in the park on a small scale for decades, mostly for local use. However, so far as can be determined from surviving records, the first large-scale effort to log cypress in the park did not occur until the 1870s. On December 1, 1871, Joseph Bates conveyed a timber lease on his large Fork Swamp tract to Walter S. Monteith, a Columbia businessman and lawyer. The lease granted Monteith "the privilege of cutting Cypress timber in my Swamp Tract of land bounded by Wateree & Congaree Rivers for such length of time as he shall keep up his Mill in Richland Fork." This lease was subsequently assigned to the firm of McMaster, Monteith and Roath, the entity actually logging the area. Soon Monteith and his partners were making additional acquisitions of land and timber. In February 1872 Monteith acquired a 400-acre parcel on the north bank of Bates Old River, a short distance west of present-day U.S. Highway 601. Here the firm built its sawmill, probably on uplands north of the swamp (see entry 29 in appendix A). A little more than a year later, McMaster, Monteith and Roath obtained a separate timber lease (cypress only) on the adjacent tract to the west. This lease covered 579 acres about halfway between the railroad track and the future Highway 601 right-of-way.[4]

On the surface, this acquisition and the ones before it appear to bespeak a growing enterprise. McMaster, Monteith and Roath placed an advertisement on March 16, 1873, informing the public that they were "prepared to furnish our first class CYPRESS SAWED SHINGLES, in any desired quantity and upon the shortest notice." However, in June 1873, when Monteith moved to acquire a 620-acre tract west of the railroad (today's Beidler Tract Parcel 19), trouble loomed on the horizon. Monteith never made any payments on the mortgage for this tract, probably because the timber operation that would have justified its acquisition was already in serious trouble. The firm's fortunes apparently continued to deteriorate, and by early 1874 it was bankrupt.[5]

Just why McMaster, Monteith and Roath failed is not known. Low prices in the lumber market likely played a role, as did high production costs. A major contributor to the latter was the high cost of transportation. When real estate agents Gibbes and Thomas published an advertisement in 1869 offering "600 acres of Cypress Land, near Gadsden," a key selling point was that the acreage was "convenient to [the] North-Eastern Railroad" between Charleston and New

York. Even when "convenient," however, transportation by rail was not cheap. The impact of high shipping costs on the local timber industry is evident from an 1884 letter from S. A. Pearce, president of the Columbia Board of Trade, to the U.S. Army Corps of Engineers:

> There are immense growths of the most valuable timber in the upper part of the State which could be rafted down Broad River and find its way to a profitable market, if it can have a water transportation from Columbia. . . . The great cypress swamp below Columbia, which has an almost inexhaustible supply of this valuable timber growing upon it, would turn out from its stagnant pools that which makes to the wealth of the country. All efforts to utilize this wood in the manufacture of shingles and wooden ware have failed for want of cheap transportation and a convenient outlet. To the cypress must be added a great growth of hard pine timber, which will be made profitable to cut and saw for the markets of the world [if navigation is improved on the Congaree].

Naturally, not all riverside landowners in South Carolina faced identical transportation problems; access to markets varied from place to place. The U.S. Department of Agriculture had noted in 1876 that the heavy growth of oak along streams in Barnwell County was "being hewed into square logs and rafted to sea-ports," while in Clarendon County, which "has 60,000 acres in Santee Swamp . . . all heavily timbered with cypress, oaks, sweet-gum, with some pine, etc.[,] [the] timber as now situated is of little market value." The difference, apparently, was that the Savannah River fed directly into the port of Savannah, whereas the Santee emptied into the Atlantic at some distance from the ports of Charleston and Georgetown, neither of which could be reached by water except by passing over a dangerous bar at the river's mouth.[6]

To address this problem, Congress passed legislation in the 1880s directing the Corps of Engineers to remove snags and overhanging branches from the Congaree, Wateree, and Santee Rivers, and to improve access to Georgetown by digging a canal from the Santee River to Winyah Bay. These efforts apparently produced the desired result. On May 26, 1891, L. S. Ehrich, president of the Georgetown, South Carolina, Board of Trade, advised the Corps that shipments of farm products had increased considerably on the Santee due to the recent clearing work, as had timber receipts. He also noted, "This section of country has been visited and inspected during the past 12 months by many Western lumber dealers and land speculators, resulting in sales of over 65,000 acres of swamp land along the [Santee] river at steadily increasing prices."[7]

The clearing of the Congaree River meant that suddenly large portions of the Congaree Swamp—including thousands of acres thought worthless after the war and abandoned to avoid payment of taxes—now had significant economic value. William H. Gallup of Syracuse, New York, was among the first northern investors to focus serious attention on the Congaree. Gallup acquired a 3,368-acre tract in 1890 (today's Beidler Tract Parcel 15), and by the late summer of 1892 his firm, the Palmetto Lumber Company, had acquired the Fork Swamp tract (2,665 acres) at the confluence of the Congaree and Wateree Rivers. With these two acquisitions, the push to amass timber holdings in the future Congaree National Park was underway in earnest. In the mid-1890s local investors such as William L. Buyck, Mrs. David D. Buyck, and William W. Weston also acquired property in the Congaree Swamp, including tracts that would eventually form part of the Beidler Tract. Many of these tracts had, until recently, been considered virtually worthless. One such tract, Beidler Tract Parcel 13, had been held by the South Carolina Sinking Fund Commission for almost twenty-six years without a successful buyer (see entry 18 in appendix A).[8]

Judging from contemporary news accounts, the first major logging effort to take place in the lower Congaree bottomlands during this period was spearheaded by James A. Peterkin, an innovating agriculturalist well known for having developed the Peterkin variety of upland cotton. Formerly of Marlboro County, Peterkin had taken up residence in present-day Calhoun County after the Civil War and acquired Lang Syne Plantation in 1883. In 1884 he and his son John began acquiring swampland on either side of the railroad track below Kingville, assembling a tract that, Peterkin claimed, stretched roughly from the Beidler Tract to Bates Old River.[9] With a veneer mill south of the river near Fort Motte ("about a thousand yards above the Congaree [rail] bridge") and easy access to the rail line, Peterkin was in a position to start logging these new lands in the mid-1880s. However, in 1888 he decided to convey his recently acquired swampland and most of his mill equipment to a group of investors operating as the Congaree Lumber and Veneer Company.[10]

Not much is known about Congaree Lumber and Veneer, other than that it appears to have been the continuation of a veneer operation Peterkin had begun not long before. Less than two months prior to the sale, Peterkin had traveled to a cotton press in Columbia to test the feasibility of substituting "poplar" veneer for jute bagging as a covering for cotton bales.[11] (This was probably eastern cottonwood [Populus deltoides] or swamp cottonwood [P. heterophylla], both of which traded under the name poplar at the time.) Congaree Lumber and Veneer appears to have had a similar focus, producing low-grade packaging rather than furniture-grade material.[12] Based on trends in the state as a whole, the veneer part of Congaree's operation likely relied on yellow pine, sweet gum, and riverside hardwoods, but the "lumber" side of the operation may have cut other species too, including cypress from the swamp below Kingville.[13]

Congaree Lumber and Veneer was not as large as some of the companies that would come after it, but it was still a substantial concern—in ambition, at least, if not accomplishment. An idea of the scope and nature of Congaree's operation can be gleaned from a list of its assets, compiled in July 1890:

Table 5 Assets of Congaree Lumber and Veneer Company, July 1890

ASSET	VALUE
5,000 acres of land @ $5.00	25,000.00
Veneer mill buildings, dry sheds, dry kiln building, and steam tanks	3,000.00
Steam pipes and steam fittings	1,000.00
Drag saw machine with 5 h.p. engine	300.00
Dake engine, 3 h.p.	125.00
1 Skinner engine, 25 h.p.	400.00
2 table saws ($75.00 ea.)	150.00
3 yard cars	100.00
Log carts	400.00
Sawmill with 40 h.p. engine and batting of 2 boilers 60 h.p.	3,000.00
Manufactured stock on hand	150.00
22 ½ acres of land (mill site) @ $5.00	500.00 [sic]
Grading and yard implements	1,000.00
Batting of boilers 150 h.p. and setting same	2,000.00
Log track to river with hoisting rig and 12 h.p. engine	1,000.00
Shafting pulleys, belts & erecting same	1,000.00
1 automatic knife grinder	400.00
1 automatic gang saw	350.00
Extra saws and other small tools	200.00
Office sofa	75.00
Freight paid to bring machinery to place	700.00
Am't paid for erecting machinery	1,000.00

Source: Richland County Deed Book U, p. 313.

Of these assets, the "log track to river with hoisting rig and 12 h.p. engine" is of particular interest. The existence of this equipment suggests that Congaree could have, and probably did, float timber to the Orangeburg side of the river from the swamps in Richland County. Moreover, it is possible that this equipment was among the original physical assets acquired from Peterkin in late 1888, since a landing serving Peterkin's mill was already in existence by January of that year.[14] If so, then it is all the more likely that Peterkin had begun cutting his land north of the river in the mid-1880s.

Like many timber startups of the period, Congaree Lumber and Veneer was not a success. By July 1890, less than two years after beginning operations, the company was underwater financially and at the mercy of its creditors. In the meantime, James A. Peterkin had begun buying up swampland in the Santee watershed on behalf of the Santee River Cypress Lumber Company of Chicago. Seizing an opportunity, Peterkin bought back his old swampland at auction with the intent of flipping it to Santee.[15] When that sale fell through, Peterkin made other arrangements. The *State* trumpeted the results in April 1892:

CONGAREE SWAMP'S CYPRESS.

AT LAST IT IS TO BE UTILIZED BY CAPITALISTS.

Big Company With a Northern Manager Formed—A Charter to be Applied For Tomorrow—Rich Virgin Forests.

For many years the rich and heavy virgin forests of cypress trees lying in Congaree swamp, on both sides of the Congaree river lying partly in this and partly in Orangeburg counties has been the envy of investors from all over the country who have seen the territory and realized the untold and undeveloped resources that lay slumbering there.

Steadily for many years Capt. J. A. Peterkin, knowing the value of this great cypress property, lying so near Columbia, has been buying up all the lands as he could. Now when he has succeeded in getting all the property lying between Kingville and the Congaree and on the other side of the river, he has organized a big company of capitalists, and they propose to enter at once upon the manufacturing of lumber and shingles of cypress wood. . . .

. . . Northern capitalists are deeply concerned in the enterprise. Mr. Peterkin himself will be the president of the company; Mr. James Watkins of Philadelphia is to be the manager, and Mr. Charles Fraser, also of Philadelphia, is to be the secretary and treasurer.[16]

The new entity, known as the Fort Motte Lumber and Shingle Company, began operations in Richland County using sawmill equipment previously owned by Congaree Lumber and Veneer. It was not long before the new company had taken Congaree's boilers, machinery, and sheds and moved them from south of the river to a new site "on or near the South Carolina Railway in Congaree Swamp." The new mill, which appears to have operated as Fort Motte's main plant, was located in the floodplain below Kingville at a spot almost immediately adjacent to the railroad trestle. Fort Motte also erected new equipment for a shingle mill at this location. To deal with flooding, the boilers and other parts of the plant were built on top of "pens" on the swamp floor. Fort Motte may also have operated sawmills outside of the swamp, including one located at Kingville near the railroad track.[17]

Fort Motte differed from Congaree Lumber and Veneer in that its principal focus was sawing and milling bald cypress. However, like Congaree, Fort Motte was unable to turn a consistent profit. In December 1892, a mere seven months after its formation had been announced in the *State*, Fort Motte was forced to surrender the new equipment in its shingle mill to its primary lender. Eight months later, a fire at the shingle mill caused an estimated $10,000 in damage and destroyed about 80 percent of the 1 million shingles stored at the site. These losses were not insured, and it is possible that the mill was not rebuilt. With or without the shingle mill, Fort Motte's finances continued to deteriorate. In 1896 Fort Motte's primary lender brought a foreclosure action against Peterkin and his associates for default. Four years later, on July 17, 1900, the swampland that had once supported Fort Motte passed to the bank.[18]

Ironically, the demise of Peterkin's logging venture coincided with a general upsurge for the timber industry along the Congaree. Courthouse records from the mid- to late 1890s show landowners in the future Beidler Tract beginning to grant timber deeds and leases on their bottomland timber. Between 1896 and 1899, at least five landowners in or immediately adjacent to the Beidler Tract granted timber leases on their property (see table 8 below). The increased logging activity in the Beidler Tract and elsewhere is reflected by the growing volume of timber shipped down the Congaree River during the 1890s. The jump in production from 1896 to 1897 is particularly dramatic:

Table 6 Timber Shipments on the Congaree River, 1894–97

TIMBER OUTWARD FREIGHT	1894	1895	1896	1897
No. of Stems	3,000	4,000	7,000	20,000
Tons	6,000	8,000	14,000	40,000
Value	$18,000	$20,000	$28,000	$80,000

Source: U.S. Army, *Annual Reports of the War Department for the Fiscal Year Ended June 30, 1897.*

Timber shipments would increase still more after 1899, when the Santee River Cypress Lumber Company began to cut timber in the swamp.

Francis Beidler and the Santee River Cypress Lumber Company

Over the course of the 1890s and on through the turn of the century, a number of northern investors acquired either the timber rights or the fee to several large tracts along the Congaree River. By early 1906 the lion's share of this acreage had

Figure 16. Francis Beidler, about 1906. Courtesy of the Forest History Society, Durham, North Carolina.

been consolidated in the hands of just one of these investors—the Santee River Cypress Lumber Company. In time, Santee would come to own or hold the timber rights to over nineteen thousand acres on the north bank of the Congaree River. Preeminent among these holdings was the collection of parcels known as the Beidler Tract.

The guiding light of the Santee River Cypress Lumber Company was Francis Beidler (1854–1924) of Chicago. Beidler was the son of Jacob Beidler, a Pennsylvania Mennonite farmer, who as a young man had moved to Illinois to become a Springfield grocer and carpenter, and then, in 1847, the proprietor of a Chicago lumber yard. Francis entered the family business in 1870 at the age of fifteen, working in the office and yard of J. Beidler and Brother, a lumber wholesaler run by his father and uncle. A young man of obvious ability, Francis was tapped by his father in 1873 to serve as secretary of the newly formed South Branch Lumber Company. South Branch rose to become one of the most successful wholesale lumber distributors in the Midwest, and it continued to thrive until being absorbed by Francis Beidler and Company in 1893.[19]

In some ways Francis Beidler's business life was defined by an experience he had as a young man traveling in the American West. While on a business trip to

Colorado in 1875, the twenty-year-old Beidler took a month off to go exploring. Setting off from Denver with a guide and pack horses, he traveled four hundred miles northwest to Yellowstone National Park, arriving at Old Faithful just as it was about to erupt. According to Francis Beidler II, his father's experience of Yellowstone inspired in him a lifelong commitment to conservation. Beidler does not appear to have left behind any writings describing his conservation philosophy, but it seems clear that he saw his timber holdings in South Carolina as a long-term investment rather than an asset to be liquidated as quickly as possible. Unlike many lumbermen of the "cut and get out" era, Beidler strove to develop a sustained-yield system of forestry. He consulted with the U.S. Bureau of Forestry (soon to become the U.S. Forest Service) regarding sustainable practices and in 1907 traveled to Europe to learn European conservation methods so that he could apply them to his lands in South Carolina.[20]

Relatively early in his career, Beidler developed a consuming interest in the commercial possibilities of bald cypress. In 1888 he left Chicago's LaSalle Street Station for South Carolina, intent on exploring the great river swamps of the Santee, Wateree, and Congaree Rivers. He was so impressed with the trees of these great river-bottom forests that he returned home, borrowed $1 million from the University of Chicago, and set about acquiring South Carolina swampland.[21]

Beidler did not go it alone in South Carolina. Other investors included B. F. Ferguson and Joseph Rathborne of Chicago, Robert B. Dolsen of Bay City, Michigan, and others. Ferguson was a long-time business associate of the Beidler family, having served as vice president of both the South Branch Lumber Company and the Eastern Lumber Company of Tonawanda, New York, a South Branch offshoot. Rathborne was a fellow Chicago lumber wholesaler who did business as J. H. Rathborne and Company.[22]

In the summer of 1889, Beidler and Rathborne traveled to South Carolina to acquire land in the swamps along the Santee River. On that trip alone they acquired around seventeen thousand acres. By February 1890 Beidler and his colleagues had formed the Santee River Cypress Lumber Company to do business in the state.[23] B. F. Ferguson was appointed president of the new company, and Beidler the vice president and treasurer.[24] Santee set up operations in present-day Orangeburg County, South Carolina, where it soon built a sawmill and related facilities using a crew from Michigan directed on the ground by Robert B. Dolsen. The town that grew up around the mill was known as Ferguson, reportedly in honor of the company president.[25]

About fifty workers began to cut timber in early 1890 in anticipation that a mill would be completed later that year. The facility that ultimately emerged was a "monster mill" located on 132 acres at Pond Bluff, near Eutaw Springs.[26] The

Pond Bluff site had been chosen because of a large natural pond that lay within one mile of the Santee River. Santee cut a canal between the pond and river, which allowed it to raft forty thousand logs downstream for storage in the pond. According to some, the pond was the best site for storing logs along the entire river. The new mill had a projected daily capacity of one hundred thousand board feet of lumber and sixty thousand cypress shingles.[27]

At the same time he was contributing capital to Santee, Rathborne was also investing heavily in Louisiana cypress. Rathborne made a major acquisition of Louisiana timberland in 1889 and in 1890 constructed a double band sawmill in Harvey, Louisiana, opposite New Orleans. By 1894 he was reportedly manufacturing 15 million board feet annually at Ferguson (in the form of output from Santee), and 30 million board feet at Harvey. But by that point he had been living in Louisiana for several years and may not have been actively involved in the management of Santee.[28]

Beidler entered the Santee venture with ambitious goals, intending to build not just one of the largest and most complete mills in the South but also one that used the latest machinery for sawing and seasoning lumber. For a time the Ferguson facility was the largest lumber mill in the entire state. When it finally ceased operations in 1914, the facility was still among the largest in South Carolina, being surpassed only by the Atlantic Coast Lumber Company mill in Georgetown. At one time or another, the Ferguson complex featured a double-band sawmill, planing and lath mills, machinery for the manufacture of moldings and fine house finish, a ten-block shingle mill, a box factory, and extensive storage areas for curing cut boards.[29]

The town of Ferguson would grow to become bigger than many other towns in the state, eventually employing as many as one thousand people. To help accommodate its workers, the company built fifty-three cottages with indoor plumbing to house "the better class of employees," as well as ninety-seven houses "of a sufficiently high grade to make them attractive for good [common] labor." By 1912 the town of Ferguson had electric lights powered by current from a steam turbine at the sawmill. It also had a water supply system powered by a four-hundred-horsepower engine formerly used by the City of Columbia waterworks. Unlike many South Carolina communities, Ferguson even had a hospital, supported financially by employees of the company. The hospital was needed primarily because of the constant threat of malaria and hemorrhagic fever.[30]

Little is known about the men who did the actual logging on Santee's timberlands. According to Fred Seeley, who served as general manager at Ferguson around 1896–1904 and 1909–11,[31] the company worked "200 to 250 negroes and 100 to 150 whites. . . . The owners came only three or four times per year and all the balance of us lived together. Some got more pay and some less but the mills [cut (?)] steadily. The pay was more than the other mills paid. Advancement was possible. . . . We were a great big happy family. Never during [twenty-four] years of operations was there any feeling between the owners and the employees." This rather idyllic picture of company life does not tell the full story, however. Workers at the Santee mill may have been paid more than workers at other mills, but for the men out logging the swamps life was harsh. The company recruited experienced white loggers from other parts of the country, including Michiganders from the North Woods and mountaineer lumbermen from western North Carolina, but because malaria was endemic to the area and the pay low, white loggers generally avoided the swamp. Logging was mostly done by African American laborers.[32]

From roughly 1889 to 1918, Santee acquired extensive holdings of bottomland hardwood forest in South Carolina, with most of its holdings concentrated along the Santee River and its tributaries. According to some accounts, the locals thought Beidler and Ferguson were crazy for believing they could remove virgin cypress from the muddy swamps of the Santee. Undeterred, the company eventually acquired over 140,000 acres in fee along the Congaree, Wateree, and Santee rivers, much of it for as little as one to two dollars an acre, or less. At the time, the Santee River and its tributaries held some of the largest remaining stands of old-growth bald cypress in the nation outside the lower Mississippi valley and Florida.[33]

Santee began acquiring land in what is now the park in the summer of 1899.[34] Between July and September it acquired a total of five parcels in the Beidler Tract, ranging in size from 493 to 1,186 acres. Over the next several years Santee continued to acquire property along the Congaree and Wateree Rivers, including land within the park. A major acquisition in September 1903 covered over 9,000 acres in Richland and Sumter counties, together with "rights of way to the river for floating purposes." The 1903 acquisition included two large tracts in the park, namely, Parcel 15 of the Beidler Tract and the Fork Swamp tract, a 2,665-acre tract bounded by the Congaree and Wateree Rivers. By March 1906 Santee had assembled most of the Beidler Tract, with deeded acreage totaling approximately 13,433 acres.[35] (See map 2 for the location of the various Beidler Tract parcels.) Table 7 lists acquisition data for the Beidler Tract.[36]

As indicated in the table, some of the parcels acquired by Santee (Parcels 10, 11, 12, 13, 14, and 18) were encumbered by timber deeds at the time of purchase. In the case of Parcels 10, 11, and 12, Santee obtained an assignment of the timber deed at the time it acquired the fee. No such assignment was necessary in the case of Parcels 13, 14, and 18 because Santee was the holder of the outstanding timber rights at the time of acquisition. Table 8 below provides additional information on all known timber sales that predated Santee's acquisition of the fee.

Table 7 Acquisition Data, Beidler Tract Parcels

PARCEL NUMBER	ACQUISITION DATE	ACREAGE	ACQUIRED FROM	PRIOR TIMBER DEED/LEASE ON THE PARCEL?
Parcel 1	Apr. 23, 1903	3,948	Benjamin Graham (Deed Book AG, p. 243)	No
Parcel 2	Sept. 28, 1899	493	W. B. and Frank R. Frost (Deed Book AC, p. 297)	No
Parcel 3	Jan. 14, 1972	101.27	F. B. Creech [Creech Lumber Co.] (Deed Book D231, p. 70)	N/A
Parcel 4	Aug. 12, 1902	188	Tucker H. Fisher (Deed Book AF, p. 544)	No
Parcel 5	Aug. 12, 1899	595	William W. Weston (Deed Book AC, p. 271)	No
Parcel 6	July 11, 1899, Aug. 2, 1899	1,111	Harry W. Adams et al. (Deed Book AC, pp. 266, 268)	No
Parcel 7	May 18, 1970	2.32	Marion T. Burnside Jr. (Deed Book D176, p. 558)	N/A
Parcel 8	Feb. 17, 1903	965	William L. Buyck (Deed Book AG, p. 226)	No[37]
Parcel 9	Apr. 19, 1904	119	J. S. Hildebrand and Frank W. Wise (Deed Book AG, p. 496)	No
Parcel 10	Aug. 12, 1899	1,186	William W. Weston (Deed Book AC, p. 271)	Yes. Timber rights previously acquired by James E. Faulkner. Rights assigned to Santee.
Parcels 11 and 12	July 31, 1899	715	W. J. and W. K. Duffie (Deed Book AD, p. 172)	Yes. Timber rights previously acquired by James E. Faulkner. Rights assigned to Santee.

Table 7 (continued)

PARCEL NUMBER	ACQUISITION DATE	ACREAGE	ACQUIRED FROM	PRIOR TIMBER DEED/LEASE ON THE PARCEL?
Parcel 13	March 14, 1918	998	David D. Buyck (Deed Book BU, p. 101)	Yes. Timber rights previously acquired by Santee.
Parcel 14	Aug. 1, 1928	474	James B. Williams et al. (Deed Book DC, p. 586)	Yes. Timber rights previously acquired by Santee.
Parcel 15	Aug. 1, 1903	3,368	Francis M. Perkins and Edward B. Taylor (Deed Book AG, p. 291)	Yes. Limited timber rights had been acquired previously by John M. Bates; these may have expired by the time of the sale to Santee. There is no recorded assignment of rights to Santee.
Parcel 16	Jan. 25, 1961	49	U. S. Plywood (Deed Book 295, p. 71)	N/A
Parcel 17	Jan. 25, 1961	80	U. S. Plywood (Deed Book 295, p. 71)	N/A
Parcel 18	Feb. 16, 1906	164	Vassar H. Taylor (wife of Edward B. Taylor) (Deed Book AM, p. 429)	Yes. Timber rights previously acquired by Santee.
Parcel 19	Oct. 29, 1904	581	Sultan W. McKenzie Jr. (Deed Book AK, p. 48)	Yes. Santee had previously paid "R[oss] S McKenzie and Bro" $2.00 per log for "2730 Logs from Congaree." However, no timber deed or assignment of rights to Santee was ever recorded.

In some instances Santee acquired the timber rights, but not the fee, to a particular tract. In all, Santee acquired timber deeds or timber leases on at least fifteen hundred acres of land immediately adjacent to the Beidler Tract. The terms of these agreements are of particular interest because they provide information about Santee's day-to-day logging operations, something its fee-simple deeds do not. Among other things, these agreements specify the type(s) of timber acquired by Santee, how the company was to obtain access to the timber, and how the timber was to be transported off-site. None of this had to be spelled out when Santee bought property outright.

Table 8 lists all recorded timber deeds/timber leases on swampland bordering the Beidler Tract (whether or not the timber rights were ever conveyed or assigned to Santee). Salient details about logging methods are included in the "Interest Conveyed" column. See map 2 for location of parcels/tracts.

An important point to note is that Santee did not restrict itself to bald cypress when acquiring timber rights on the Congaree. Many of the timber deeds acquired by Santee granted it the right to cut species such as pine, oak, ash, and cottonwood—or even all timber "both standing and fallen." The cutting of species other than cypress likely carried over to Santee's fee lands as well, since by this time the company was milling a variety of species at Ferguson. In 1903, the superintendent of Santee's logging department told the *State* that the company had on hand at the mill "15,000,000 feet of cypress, 4,000,000 feet of pine, 1,000,000 feet of ash, 1,000 feet of cottonwood and a lot of oak, gum and sycamore." These figures tell two stories, however. While confirming that Santee harvested a variety of species on its lands, they also suggest that cypress likely made up most of the timber cut on the Beidler Tract.[39]

Santee began logging timber in the Beidler Tract sometime around 1899 and by 1910 had completed the bulk of its cutting in the tract. A 1906 study by the U.S. Bureau of Forestry found that cypress on the company's Congaree lands was already "being rapidly thinned out" at that time. A published summary of the report noted that the demand for cypress was so great that "there are few trees left in this section of the country."[40] Yet despite reduced timber volumes, activity apparently continued on the tract for almost another decade. The company mapped its Congaree holdings in 1909 and conducted a timber cruise of the Beidler Tract in 1911. A fact sheet prepared by the Beidler family in 1975 stated that "most of the large cypress trees on this tract were harvested between 1900 and 1914."[41]

Santee's standard practice on its large tracts was to establish logging camps in multiple locations, from which workers would travel to perform their daily task of girdling and felling trees. An advertisement from the *Muskegon (Mich.) Chronicle* describes the company's logging methods in the early 1890s:

Table 8 Beidler Tract and Vicinity: Timber Deeds/Timber Leases, 1896–1907

DATE OF TIMBER DEED/LEASE	PARCEL/TRACT NO.	SELLER & BUYER OF TIMBER RIGHTS	INTEREST CONVEYED	TIMBER DEED/LEASE ASSIGNED TO SANTEE ?
Dec. 21, 1896	Parcel 10	Seller: William W. Weston Buyer: James E. Faulkner (Deed Book Z, p. 453)	Cypress and ash only (1,125 acres). Five-year term. Faulkner allowed to cut other timber, but only so much as may be necessary to create rights-of-way and roads for utilizing cypress and ash timber.	Yes. J. E. Faulkner assigns timber deed to Santee on June 14, 1899. [38] Santee acquires fee on Aug. 12, 1899.
Mar. 16, 1897	Parcel 13 (portion of)	Seller: Mrs. Elizabeth B. Wise Buyck (wife of David D Buyck) and Mrs. H. A. D. Herlong Buyer: James E. Faulkner (Deed Book Z, p. 508)	Cypress only, on lands north of "Cypress creek or gut" (500 acres out of 774-acre tract). Five-year term. Faulkner allowed to cut other types of timber, but only so much as may be necessary to create rights-of-way and roads for utilizing cypress timber. Rights of way granted on the entire 774-acre tract so Faulkner may have full use of his right to cut cypress timber.	Yes. J. E. Faulkner assigns timber deed to Santee on June 14, 1899. Santee acquires fee on Mar. 14, 1918.
Mar. 31, 1897	Parcels 11 & 12	Seller: W. J. and W. K. Duffie Buyer: James E. Faulkner (Deed Book Z, p. 521)	Cypress only (600 acres). Five-year term. Faulkner allowed to cut other timber, but only so much as may be necessary to create rights-of-way and roads for utilizing cypress timber. (Note: Faulkner was prohibited from logging until purchase money had been paid in full. He had two years to complete payment.)	Yes. J. E. Faulkner assigns timber deed to Santee on June 14, 1899. Santee acquires fee on July 31, 1899.
Dec. 19, 1899	Parcel 14	Seller: James B. Williams et al. Buyer: Santee (Deed Book AC, p. 425)	All timber on parcel (474 acres). Twenty-year term, with right of access to open cart ways, roadways, or such other ways as buyer needs to ring, cut, float, or haul timber from this tract, or to float and haul timber from any other tract controlled by Santee.	N/A: Santee is original grantee of timber. Elizabeth Beidler (widow of Francis Beidler I) acquires fee on Aug. 1, 1928.

Date	Tract	Seller/Buyer	Description	Santee Acquisition
Dec. 27, 1899	Tracts 101-24 and 101-25, and adjacent lands north of park boundary	Seller: John M. Bates Buyer: Santee (Deed Book AC, p. 423)	All cypress timber and all other timber standing and growing on tract (182 acres). Twenty-year term, with right of access to ring, cut, float, and haul timber from this tract, or to float and haul timber from any other tract controlled by Santee.	N/A: Santee is original grantee of timber. Santee never acquires fee.
Aug. 7, 1900	Tract 101-32 (western portion of)	Seller: Arthur J. Garick and James P. Garick Jr. Buyer: John M. Bates (Deed Book AC, p. 539; Deed Book AG, pp. 100, 101)	All merchantable timber 10 in. or more in diameter (158 acres). Ten-year term for timber, with right of access to open cart ways, roadways, or such other ways as buyer needs to ring, cut, haul, and float timber from this tract, or to float and haul timber from any other tract controlled by Bates. Also granted is a 20-year right-of-way through Cedar Creek and "Cypress gut" to move trees.	Yes. John M. Bates assigns timber lease to Santee on April 17, 1902. Santee never acquires fee.
Sept. 13, 1900	Parcel 15	Seller: Palmetto Lumber Company Buyer: John M. Bates (Deed Book AC, p. 613)	1,000 cypress trees. Note: total sale is for not less than 1 million board feet. Bates must make additional payment to the extent the 1,000 cypress trees exceed 1 million board feet. If necessary, Bates can cut additional trees to reach minimum board footage. Bates may cut a 75-foot float road leading from Cedar Creek in the direction of the trestle of the South Carolina & Georgia Railroad, plus any side float roads necessary to reach the 1,000 trees. Can cut trees from float roads without paying, except for cypress and ash. Bates may use the main float road to float out any timber located above the lands of Palmetto now owned or later acquired by himself or the Santee River Cypress Lumber Company.	Possibly. On November 7, 1901, John M. Bates and Santee enter into an unrecorded contract covering the removal of "logs" from Palmetto Lumber Company lands and the use of specified creeks and sluice ways. The precise terms of this agreement are not known, but it may constitute an assignment of the "1,000 cypress trees" sale from Bates to Santee (see Deed Book AG, p. 81). Santee acquires fee to Parcel 15 on Sept. 4, 1903.

Table 8. (continued)

DATE OF TIMBER DEED/LEASE	PARCEL/TRACT NO.	SELLER & BUYER OF TIMBER RIGHTS	INTEREST CONVEYED	TIMBER DEED/LEASE ASSIGNED TO SANTEE ?
May 28, 1901	Parcel 18	Sellers: Edward B. Taylor, Vassar H. Taylor, and Charles D. Stanley Buyer: Santee (Deed Book AC, pp. 621, 623)	All cypress timber (150 acres). Fifteen-year term, with right of access to open creeks or make cart ways, roadways, or such other ways as buyer needs to cut, haul, float or otherwise transport timber from this tract, or to float and haul timber from any other tract controlled by Santee.	N/A: Santee is original grantee of timber. Santee acquires fee on Feb. 16, 1906.
Mar. 22, 1902	Parcel 19	Sellers: Ross S. McKenzie and Sultan W. McKenzie Jr. Buyer: Santee (No timber deed recorded. Receipt of sale exists in private McKenzie family collection)	2,730 "Logs from Congaree."	N/A: Santee is original buyer of timber. Santee acquires fee on Oct. 29, 1904.
Mar. 26, 1902	Parcel 15	Seller: Palmetto Lumber Company Buyer: Santee (per memorandum of agreement) (Deed Book AG, p. 81)	300 cypress trees, to be cleared in the construction of float roads. These trees are to be cut at the same rate and in the same manner as set forth in the existing contract for 1,000 cypress trees between John M. Bates and Palmetto Lumber Company (see entry above for Sept. 13, 1900). Note: this timber sale is contained in a memorandum of agreement among Palmetto Lumber Company, Santee, and E. B. and V. H. Taylor. The agreement allows Santee to select and use permanent (main) float roads over the lands of Palmetto known as the Weston tract, including one specifically to Cedar Creek, as well as "the necessary subways from various directions and localities,	N/A: Santee is original grantee of timber. Santee acquires fee on Aug. 1, 1903.

			said subways not to exceed three in number, to the said main or permanent float roads." The purpose of these float roads is to allow Santee to remove present or future timber from its lands or the lands of other parties. The agreement also grants Santee and John M. Bates the right to extend indefinitely a separate agreement (unrecorded), dated Nov. 7, 1901, "with regard to removing logs from Palmetto Lumber Company's land and of using certain creeks and sluice ways referred to and provided for in [that] agreement."	
Feb. 17, 1903	Tract 101-41	Seller: William L. Buyck Buyer: Santee (Deed Book AG, p. 226)	All timber both standing and fallen (139 acres). Twenty-year term, with authority to construct ditches, canals, dykes, railroads, tramways, roadways, cart and wagon ways, or any other ways for the purpose of hauling and removing timber.	N/A: Santee is original grantee of timber. Santee never acquires fee.
Oct. 23, 1903	Tract 101-32 (central portion of)	Seller: John J. Kaminer Buyer: Santee (Deed Book AG, p. 319)	All timber of any and all description, including pine, cypress, ash, oak, etc., on 150 acres of swampland. Ten-year term, with the right to lay such tracks, tramways, roads, or other ways as may be necessary for removing timber.	N/A: Santee is original grantee of timber. Santee never acquires fee.
April 19, 1904	Tract 101-37	Seller: J. S. Hildebrand and Frank W. Wise Buyer: Santee (Deed Book AG, p. 496)	All timber both standing and fallen (80 acres). No term specified. Authority granted to construct ditches, canals, dykes, railroads, tramways, roadways, cart and wagon ways, or any other ways for the purpose of hauling and removing timber.	N/A: Santee is original grantee of timber. Santee never acquires fee.

Table 8. (continued)

DATE OF TIMBER DEED/LEASE	PARCEL/TRACT NO.	SELLER & BUYER OF TIMBER RIGHTS	INTEREST CONVEYED	TIMBER DEED/LEASE ASSIGNED TO SANTEE ?
Feb. 7, 1905	Tract 101-36	Seller: Moses Felder Wise Buyer: Santee (Deed Book AG, p. 582)	All cottonwood, ash, and cypress trees 12 in. diameter and over (692 acres). Fifteen-year term, with authority to construct ditches, canals, dykes, railroads, tramways, roadways, cart and wagon ways, or any other ways for the purpose of hauling and removing timber. Deed states that lands shall be cut over in regular course and complete, and no second series of cutting after an interval of years shall be made.	N/A: Santee is original grantee of timber. Santee never acquires fee.
Sept. 16, 1905	Tract 101-34	Seller: Mrs. M. E. Antley (Executrix of Estate of A. P. Bruner) Buyer: Santee (Deed Book AL, p. 37)	Cottonwood, ash, cypress, and pine on tract known as "Glover Field." Acreage not specified in deed; probably about 70 acres of timber sold. Ten-year term, with authority to construct ditches, canals, dykes, railroads, tramways, roadways, cart and wagon ways, or any other ways for the purpose of hauling and removing timber.	N/A: Santee is original grantee of timber. Santee never acquires fee.
Oct. 12, 1905	Parcel 13	Seller: David D. Buyck Buyer: Santee (Deed Book AG, p. 613)	All timber both standing and fallen (944 acres) [sic]. Three-year term, with authority to construct ditches, canals, dykes, railroads, tramways, roadways, cart and wagon ways, or any other ways for the purpose of hauling and removing timber.	N/A: Santee is original grantee of timber. Santee acquires fee on Mar. 14, 1918.
July 16, 1907	Tract 101-44 (northwest portion of)	Seller: Mary D. Rawls Buyer: John M. Bates (Deed Book AL, pp. 55, 56; Deed Book AN, p. 177)	An estimated 156,630 board feet of cypress timber, being all of the cypress timber standing on Mary D. Rawls's portion of the "Silver Lake Stock Farm" in Congaree Swamp. No acreage specified in deed.	Yes. John M. Bates assigns timber lease to Santee on July 17, 1907. Santee never acquires fee.

		(Mary D. Rawls's portion of Silver Lake Stock Farm contained 232 acres, but only a portion of that was cypress swamp.) Trees in sale already girdled by Bates. Three-year term (all timber to be cut in first two years), with right of access to open cart ways, roadways, float ways, and such other ways as are needed to cut and remove timber from this tract, or to float and haul timber from any other tract controlled by John M. Bates.	
Feb. 29, 1924	Tract 101-32 (eastern portion of)	Seller: Laura J. McKenzie Buyer: Hoffman Lumber Company (Deed Book CN, p. 106)	All timber of every character now standing or lying in the swamp portion of the tract (184 acres). Five-year term, with right to use any machinery or build any railroad to remove timber.	No.

WANTED—100 GOOD MEN

accustomed to working in woods and driving logs, to work in swamp on
Santee River, getting out cypress logs. Driving is mainly poling logs out of
flats when water is up. Chopping and sawing is done from boats, and land
when water is low. Good camps and good grub. Can work the year round.
Wages from $24 to $30 per month and board. . . . Santee River Cypress
Lumber Co., Ferguson, Berkeley Co., S.C.[42]

Santee may have made less use of boats in the Congaree Swamp than in
the substantially wetter Santee, but otherwise its logging methods in the park
appear to have been as described in the advertisement. No logging camps are
known from within the Beidler Tract itself, but a 1909 plat prepared for Santee
shows a logging camp on the edge of the river near Starling's Mound (see entry
14 in appendix A). The 1909 plat also shows five camps scattered on the edge of
the bluff east of the Cedar Creek landing at South Cedar Creek Road. One of
these, identified as "Bates Camp," was probably named after local businessman
and logging contractor John M. Bates. Bates acquired the underlying property
in 1899 and immediately sold the timber to Santee. Bates is also known to have
been a Santee manager from 1905 to at least 1908. The other bluff camps may
have been rather transient affairs, as each is denoted with a tent symbol rather
than the squares used to identify the riverside and Bates camps. See entries 12
and 13 in appendix A.[43]

Most of the timber cut by Santee was floated down the Congaree and Santee
Rivers to be processed at Ferguson. But getting logs to the river was no easy
task. The main difficulty was the need to move huge logs, some of them six to
seven feet in diameter above the buttress, over long distances through difficult,
swampy terrain. The cheapest method of getting logs out of the swamp was to
construct "float roads" leading to the principal creeks and guts or directly to
the river itself. To make a float road, loggers waited for low water and then cut
trees along a main route through the swamp. At high water, logs could be floated
down the route to Cedar Creek or some other waterway, and from there to the
river.

The practice is illustrated by a 1902 Memorandum of Agreement between
Santee and the Palmetto Lumber Company. Under the terms of the agreement,
Palmetto granted Santee the right to select and use rights of way over Beidler
Tract Parcel 15 (then owned by Palmetto) to remove timber from adjacent lands.
These rights of way were to "include not only the main or permanent float roads,
including especially one to Cedar Creek, but also the necessary subways from
various directions and localities, said subways not to exceed three in number,
to the said main or permanent float roads." Similarly, a previous agreement involving the same tract had granted John M. Bates the right to clear "a 75 foot

float road to be made and located by Mr. Bates, leading from Cedar Creek over the lands of the Palmetto Lumber Company in the direction of the trestle of the South Carolina & Georgia Railroad."[44]

Until the autumn of 1905, Santee allowed many logs to float loose down the river to Ferguson because this was the cheapest way to get logs to the mill. The cost savings were such that Santee adhered to this practice even though many of its logs sank or were otherwise lost along the way. Not even the hazard posed to snag boats and other vessels was enough to discourage the practice. However, with the launching of the steamboat *City of Columbia* in 1905, Santee agreed to end the floating of loose logs. Thereafter, logs from the park were assembled into rafts and floated to the mill by raftsmen. At other times, especially during periods of slack water, rafts were towed to the mill by tug or other vessel.[45]

To make it more likely that the huge cypress logs would float, workers girdled each tree with an ax so that the sap would run out and allow the tree to "cure." Faster drying was achieved by cutting through the sapwood all the way to the heartwood. After six months to a year, the tree would be ready for cutting, and two men would fell it with a crosscut saw, standing on "springboards" inserted in the buttress. When the tree was down, the bole would be cut into sixteen-foot sections, and the logs left to be floated out during next spring's floods. All too often this was wasted effort, as trees had not been given enough time to dry out. Today, sunken cypress logs can still be seen in streams and guts in the park.[46]

Although the preferred method for cutting Congaree cypress was to "ring, cut, and float" logs, conditions in the floodplain were generally dry for much of the year, and floods often came with short notice and receded quickly. As a result, the time available for floating logs to the river was limited. Making a virtue of necessity, Santee used draft animals to skid logs to clearings in the forest or to staging areas along the principal streams and float roads.[47] Logs skidded to clearings could be hauled to the river during dry periods, while logs staged along waterways could be floated out during high water. The company asked a lot of its draft animals. In one instance, logs hauled from the Congaree were so large that they broke down a steel wagon having wheels twelve feet in diameter.[48] The use of draft animals may have been especially prevalent in stands within a mile or so of the river. Here it would have been feasible to skid or haul logs to the riverbank rather than wait for high water. Logging with animals may actually have been a necessity in stands along the natural levee, as these were among the last areas to flood.[49]

"Log fords" consistent with animal-powered logging have been found in the eastern half of the Beidler Tract, including three near the northern bluff. These fords, which tend to be visible only during periods of low water, consist of timbers laid down at the bottom of guts to enable wheeled vehicles to cross. The fords are about eight feet wide and may date to the time of Santee's logging operations, although this has not been confirmed. In some cases, the fords may have been used to haul logs to the railroad near Kingville, from where they could be shipped to points beyond. Alternatively, the fords may have afforded access to a local sawmill north of the floodplain. No evidence of such a mill has yet been discovered, but it is worth noting that by 1909 Santee was "operating a number of saw mills in different sections of the State," including one in the lower part of Lexington County. A sawmill is known to have existed at Kingville in the mid-1890s, and it is possible that a mill was still operating there after the turn of the century.[50]

One question that remains to be considered is whether Santee used steam logging equipment on its Congaree holdings. The question arises not only because of the difficulty of using animals to log wet areas but also because skidding and hauling were two of the largest expenses associated with logging wet terrain. In 1914, the year Santee ceased its logging operations in South Carolina, the average cost of logging southern bottomlands broke down more or less as follows:

Table 9 Average Cost to Log Bottomland Sites in 1914

TASK	COST (PER THOUSAND BOARD FT.)
Deadening	$0.15
Felling and logmaking	0.60
Skidding	3.25
Hauling or driving to mill	1.00
Milling and kiln drying	4.00
Total	9.00

Source: Woodward, *The Valuation of American Timberlands*, 68, citing figures from U.S. Forest Service.

Faced with this cost structure, companies were always looking for faster, less labor-intensive ways of getting felled logs to the mill. In certain circumstances the initial expense of steam skidders and logging trams more than paid for itself by reducing the time between stump and mill, and by ensuring a steady supply of timber when the float roads were dry. More fundamentally, railroads and steam skidders allowed loggers to cut in areas where large log sizes and soft ground combined to make animal logging impractical.[51]

Santee is known to have made extensive use of logging trams and steam skidders on its wetter properties near Ferguson. But even upstream from the mill, Santee made frequent use of steam logging equipment, as this advertisement from 1909 makes clear:

> Wanted—Men who are familiar with logging work to work in swamp logging on the Santee river. The work is located near Elloree and may be reached from that station. Logging is being done by pull boat and other steam logging machinery, but laborers who are familiar with cutting timber or any other logging work can find work by going to Elloree and going into the camp from there. Santee River Cypress Lumber Company, Ferguson, S.C.

The reason steam-powered equipment was so desirable was spelled out in a 1915 bulletin by Wilbur Mattoon of the U.S. Forest Service:

> The present logging of cypress is attended by difficulties of a kind unknown in handling any other commercial timber. The bulk of all cypress timber is now logged by massive steam machinery moved from place to place on railroads built into the deepest parts of swamps over soft and treacherous ground. Periods of high water interfere with both the cutting and the moving of logs. For many years only the timber accessible to streams subject to flooding was taken. The soft nature of the soil and the great weight of the logs made it impossible to move the timber by the usual method—with oxen or mules. . . . The decline of the eastern white-pine industry sent into the South lumbermen who solved the difficult problem of logging cypress. Logging progressed from the float method in the eighties to the pull boat in the nineties, and from that to overhead-cableway skidding, the method now in use. . . . The advent of railroad swamp logging with the overhead cableway skidder was the principal factor in opening up vast regions of cypress previously considered inaccessible because not sufficiently inundated.

Thus, railroad logging was useful both in wet areas that were hard to reach by conventional means and in relatively dry areas where floating opportunities were more limited and of short duration. The latter would have been the case in the Congaree Swamp, which was generally higher and drier than many areas downstream.[52]

The suggestion that Santee used a mixture of float roads and tram roads to log the Congaree receives some limited support in the historic record. In 1953 former general manager Fred Seeley recalled that "in the woods, animals hauling to portable saw mills, moving about to be near the logs or to dinky little railroads with dinky little locomotives, fired with wood, was the rule. . . . Logwoods machinery came in at the turn of the century. It was with much experimenting and discarding. It was costly from first cost and upkeep. Often resulted in higher costs than the older, primitive method." While this observation does not necessarily apply to Santee's Congaree lands, other evidence suggests that

Santee could have used rail trams and steam skidders to log parts of the park. In 1903, after interviewing the superintendent of Santee's logging department, the *State* reported that the "company is building tramroads through the swamps in order to get the logs to the Congaree river." From here they would be "rafted to the big mills at Ferguson." Three years later a representative of the U.S. Weather Bureau suggested that an enhanced flood signal service would be of great bene-fit to lumbermen in the Santee basin because it would make them less depen-dent on rail trams than they currently were. According to the representative, "the advance notices of the coming of high water [would enable lumbermen] to make preparations for getting lumber out of the woods and floating it down to the mills. During the low water season the logs are brought to the river banks largely by steam power, a somewhat expensive process." The latter statement appears to have been based in part on information obtained from Santee repre-sentative John M. Bates, as well as observations made on tours of the Congaree and Santee Rivers on Santee's launch.[53]

Taken at face value, these sources seem to confirm that railroad logging took place in the Beidler Tract and adjacent lands. It may also be relevant that after February 1903 almost all of Santee's timber deeds in the Congaree Swamp con-tained an express grant of authority to construct "ditches, canals, dykes, *rail-roads, tramways,* roadways, cart and wagon ways, or any other ways" for the purpose of hauling and removing timber (see table 8 above). (Such an express grant of authority was usually required before the courts would recognize a right to construct logging railroads on a servient estate.)[54] The feasibility of rail-road construction in the tract is pointed up by the fact that logging railroads are known to have been constructed in upstream portions of the Congaree Swamp. In 1915, less than a year after Santee ceased operations at Ferguson, a large hard-wood stave mill near Columbia began constructing a logging railway through the swamps below the city. The mill eventually completed at least eighteen miles of track on ten thousand acres of swampland.[55]

However, all this having been said, it is still a mystery how much use Santee actually made of tram roads or steam skidders in the park. No remnant rail beds or trestles appear to have survived in the Beidler Tract, and local tradition, such as it is, comes down rather emphatically on the side of "ringing, cutting, and floating."[56] On the other hand, logging trams were often rudimentary, ephem-eral affairs, built quickly and with a minimum of expense (see chapter 8).[57] It is possible, therefore, that Santee used logging trams in the park even though no physical evidence of their use has ever been found. But granting this possibility, there is reason to believe that any mechanized logging by Santee was relatively limited in scope.

In July 1904, more than a year after Santee was reported to be building tram roads to the Congaree River, its St. Matthews office advertised for "8 or 10 head of heavy horses for logging. Must weigh not less than 1,200 or 1,250 [pounds]."[58] This and other evidence suggests that Santee logged the Beidler Tract with a relatively light hand and may have made only limited use of steam equipment in the park. The NPS team sent to study the Beidler Tract in 1961 observed that "some baldcypress has been cut in the area, but there appeared to be considerable uncut cypress, and the lumbering occurred so long ago (circa 1900 . . .) that objectionable scars have largely disappeared." [59] Coming only fifty or so years after logging ceased, when the impacts of widespread, heavy cutting would still have been clearly evident, this statement provides strong evidence that Santee focused principally on the largest trees when logging cypress in the tract. One has to assume that Santee would have logged the tract much more heavily had it constructed extensive tram roads through the swamp, not only because of the improved access to timber afforded by rail but also to maximize return on investment.

Furthermore, when Santee moved to expand its mechanized logging operations, as it did between 1908 and 1910, its focus was the Santee Swamp, not the Congaree. In retrospect, the years 1908–10 constituted something of a watershed moment for the company. Prior to that time Santee appears to have cut most of its timber from lands upstream from Ferguson, as doing so allowed it to keep equipment costs relatively low. Logs could be floated to the mill cheaply and then be held for processing in the company's large holding pond. In time, though, timber on the more accessible of the company's upstream lands began to dwindle. Moreover, the company's reliance on the river for moving logs meant that it was forced to shut the mill down for weeks at a time during periods of low water. With Santee needing a steady and reliable source of logs to feed its mill, the time had come by 1908 for the company to ramp up its railroad logging operations. The decision was therefore made to invest in the lines and equipment necessary to exploit the company's extensive holdings across the river from Ferguson.[60] Congress authorized a steel drawbridge over the Santee in early 1909, and soon the company was constructing rail lines through the Santee Swamp.[61]

No records documenting the amount of cypress logged from the Beidler Tract appear to have survived. According to William Milliken, the Beidler family's consulting forester, Santee cut only large cypress trees from the tract, leaving behind many small- to medium-sized trees, as well as a number of large trees that were hollow or crooked.[62] Many of these old-growth cull trees are still standing today, as are most of the smaller trees, which have since grown to large size. Additional details can be found in the recollections of Fred Seeley. Seeley reported that the average age of Congaree cypress was between five hundred and seven hundred years, although some trees were considerably older. Seeley once counted a stump in the Santee drainage with sixteen hundred rings (making it around one thousand years old or older), and there were other large stumps he had not bothered to count.[63] It was common for cypress trees to be four to five feet in diameter above the butt swell and to be remarkably tall as well. As a rule, the company cut nothing below sixteen inches on the stump. Cut trees typically yielded four sixteen-foot logs between the stump and the limbs, although the top log was sometimes only ten or twelve feet long. Some of Santee's recorded timber contracts provided that the small end of the top log in a tree could be no less than eight (or ten) inches across inside the bark, and this requirement may have reflected general practice.[64]

Improved manufacturing methods and dwindling hardwood supplies in other parts of the country meant that Santee also logged hardwoods on its Congaree holdings when it was profitable to do so (figure 17).[65] A description of Santee's plant from early 1905 noted, "The leading specialties in [Santee's] lumber line are cypress and ash, which they have in all thicknesses and sizes up to 40 inches wide .... In addition . . . they make cottonwood and gum lumber, the two southern woods that are now so prominent in the box trade, and claim to have a very superior class of cottonwood, something that is nearer poplar than the general run, and also a fair amount of South Carolina pine."[66] Santee and its competitors increasingly supplied the needs of businesses making interior finishing, boxes, and other wood products, including furniture. When asked by the *State*

Figure 17. "Hardwood Bottomland Recently Logged, Richland County, S.C."
From Chittenden, *The Red Gum* (1906).

in 1903 whether there was enough hardwood timber in the swamps to justify the construction of a furniture factory in Columbia, John M. Bates replied that "the supply is practically inexhaustible." It does not appear that a furniture factory of any size was built in Columbia during this period, but it seems clear that the Congaree's vast supply of sweet gum was now an asset rather than a liability.[67]

By the end of the decade, sweet gum was the third most utilized species at South Carolina sawmills, falling just behind bald cypress in amount sawed. South Carolina mills sawed 15.1 million board feet of sweet gum in 1911, compared to 18.4 million board feet of cypress. Much of the sweet gum cut in South Carolina was shipped as logs or rough lumber to northern manufacturers for further processing. A large market for sweet gum also existed overseas, where it was used for furniture, interior finishing, newel posts, stair railings, and the like.[68]

In 1903, responding to the growing commercial importance of sweet gum, the U.S. Bureau of Forestry undertook an early study of ways to improve logging and handling methods for the species. As discussed in chapter 6, the bureau chose the Congaree holdings of the Santee River Cypress Lumber Company as one of the two principal research sites for this study. The result was *The Red Gum*, a bulletin prepared by assistant forest inspector and recent Yale Forest School graduate Alfred K. Chittenden.

Chittenden describes at some length the customary methods for logging sweet gum, which he appears to have observed on Santee's Congaree lands. He notes that in the bottomlands of South Carolina, "the trees are frequently cut in the fall and early winter, the bark is peeled off, and the logs left for about three months in the woods to dry out before they are floated to the mills" (figure 18). This practice rendered the logs floatable but often resulted in decay of valuable sapwood. To deal with this problem, a modified procedure was soon developed that dispensed with leaving logs to dry on the ground. As before, trees were felled in the fall and early winter months to take advantage of low sap levels, but now they were immediately cut into standard lengths, skidded to the river bank, and tied into rafts with more buoyant species. The logs could then be floated to the mill when high water came.[69]

Given the Chittenden study, it is somewhat surprising to find the *State* reporting in 1908 that sweet gum and cottonwood "have been despised by the lumber concerns which have been cutting timber in the swamps" near Columbia.[70] Chittenden, however, provides a more nuanced view of the situation, allowing this statement to be put in perspective. Though a valuable hardwood, sweet gum was not as valuable as cypress, and difficult to reach stands were not worth cutting. As Chittenden noted, the "[sweet gum] which is now being cut is comparatively easy to remove from the woods. It is usually located within 1 or 2 miles of the river or railroad to which it must be hauled. Otherwise it could not be handled profitably at present prices. Beyond this there lies a supply, the

Figure 18. "Peeled [Sweet Gum] Logs Seasoning in the Woods, South Carolina."
From Chittenden, *The Red Gum* (1906).

amount of which is only vaguely known, which is unprofitable to cut."[71] The
same went for other hardwoods. According to Chittenden, "With the exception
of ash it hardly pays to take out logs less than 10 inches in diameter at the small
end, or 13 inches in diameter breasthigh. Trees under 12 inches breasthigh are
seldom taken."[72] Yet in the right circumstances, the sweet gum, cottonwood,
and other hardwoods on the Beidler Tract had definite economic value. Some,
such as green ash and oak, were potentially more profitable than bald cypress,
as the following figures from the U.S. Forest Service make clear:

Table 10 Profitability of Various Bottomland Species in 1914

SPECIES	PRODUCTION COSTS (PER THOUSAND BOARD FEET)	AVERAGE SALE VALUE	MARGIN FOR PROFIT AND STUMPAGE
Ash	$9.00	$35.00	$24.00
Cottonwood	9.00	15.00	6.00
Cypress	9.00	24.50	15.50
Sweet gum	9.00	20.00	11.00
Water tupelo	9.00	18.00	9.00
Oak	9.00	25.00	16.00

Source: Woodward, *The Valuation of American Timberlands* (1921), 69.

In the end, neither cypress nor hardwood made much difference to Santee's fortunes: the company struggled for profitability from the outset. Santee had initially been considered something of an experiment by its owners, whose main business, after all, was lumber wholesaling.[73] In the early years, local management expended a great deal of effort to maintain a steady supply of logs for the mill, but with only mixed success. Any interruption in felling and floating timber would shut down the mill, and the mill reportedly sat idle two-thirds of the time. To deal with this situation, Francis Beidler brought in Fred Seeley as general manager in the mid-1890s, telling him to either meet the company's desired production quota or else junk the mill. Seeley immediately went to work "logging the mill" and within two and a half years had produced more lumber than his predecessors had generated in seven and a half. This, together with effective cost cutting and the higher timber prices of the McKinley boom years (1897–1901), allowed the company to pay off debt incurred in earlier years and still turn a profit. To help ensure the company's long-term self-sufficiency, many of the profits from this period were used to acquire additional timberlands in the Santee drainage. Among these were a number of Santee's properties on the Congaree River.[74]

Santee produced a variety of products for the market but was particularly well known for its cypress shingles and the quality of its ornamental wood moldings. In 1900 the Ferguson mill was sawing up to eighty thousand board feet per day (approximately 25 million feet per year), mostly cypress, from the company's various land holdings. By 1903 production had increased to approximately 35 million board feet, with twenty carloads of lumber leaving the mill per day. But despite this large output, Santee had a hard time maintaining profitability as the new century progressed.[75]

By its very nature cypress was more costly to produce than most other types of lumber. The practice of girdling trees in advance of cutting meant that labor costs were relatively high, and workers were at constant risk of contracting malaria, with attendant costs in down time and healthcare. More significantly, producing cypress lumber required expensive equipment for logging wet terrain, plus extended holding times in the yard so that the green lumber could season properly.[76] All of this cost money. Francis Beidler was certainly not averse to spending money to make money, as his decision to bridge the Santee and construct rail lines through the swamp near Ferguson shows. In the words of the *Hardwood Record,* "Everybody knows Francis Beidler . . . as a man that is always 'from Missouri' and is always wide awake to new and improved machinery for logging or milling." Yet Beidler's desire to run a modern, high-production operation eventually collided head-on with a nationwide glut in the cypress market. As a result, when it was not operating at a loss, Santee was only marginally profitable. Santee was hardly alone in this, however. Throughout the industry, "chronic overproduction of timber products guaranteed a 'profitless prosperity' at best and bankruptcy sooner or later."[77]

When Santee president B. F. Ferguson died in 1905, Beidler bought out his interest and assumed full control of the company. Soon he was upgrading Santee's operations and investing large sums of money in new facilities and equipment. Beidler held fast to this course despite a series of major setbacks, which followed in rapid succession. The first was a devastating fire in early May 1906 that destroyed the sawmill and possibly other buildings as well. Determined to bounce back, Beidler traveled to Ferguson in June to oversee preparations for rebuilding. Construction got underway by the end of the year, with workers housed in a new eighty-room hotel, complete with electric lights. But the more Beidler invested, the more unlucky he became. In early August 1910 fire destroyed the mill's main warehouse and machine shops. In September 1912 the planing mill and box factory burned. Hard work by several hundred employees prevented the 1912 fire from consuming the sawmill and stored lumber in the kilns and lumber yards, but the combined loss from this and the 1910 fire was estimated to be more than $130,000.[78]

Once more Beidler resolved to rebuild, this time using structural steel, concrete flooring, and the most modern, fireproof designs. By the fall of 1913, grading had been completed on about seven acres of land for a large new planing mill, a box factory, and sheds for dressed and rough lumber. Construction followed soon thereafter.[79]

For all this activity, however, Santee continued to struggle. Not the least of its problems was the fact that the period from 1908 to 1914 was "one of distinct stagnation if not depression" for the American lumber industry. This was precisely the time that Santee was making huge new capital investments both at its Ferguson plant and in the swamps across the river. Another, more critical problem lay closer to home: Beidler was gradually losing his eyesight. In an attempt to improve Santee's situation, Beidler eventually turned all operations over to his general manager, M. B. Cross, and extended the company a loan of almost $557,000 from his personal account. But it was all for naught. At last, with his vision gone and lacking the ability to personally oversee the financial affairs of the company, Beidler sent word to Cross to shutter the Ferguson plant. Santee terminated its "woods operations" in the summer of 1914 and closed the mill complex indefinitely by the end of November. The mill never reopened. Final closure took place in the fall of 1916, and within a short time Beidler had sold the mill buildings—"mostly for scrap prices"—and suspended most operations of the company.[80]

For the next fifty years, the forests of the Beidler Tract remained largely untouched. While other lumbermen furiously liquidated their timber in an effort to generate profits, Beidler held on to his trees in the belief that they would one day have significant value. This decision paid off relatively quickly in the case of his Santee Swamp timber. Not long before his death in 1924, "timber went up in price to what was then fantastic prices," allowing Beidler to sell $5 million worth of stumpage in the swamp to the Brooklyn Cooperage Company, a subsidiary of the American Sugar Refining Company. In the years that followed, Beidler's descendants continued to make sales of the family's remaining timber, but on a limited, sustained-yield basis. Little logging of any consequence took place in the Beidler Tract during this period.[81]

Many of the scars from Santee's operation in the park are now largely obscured, but the remnants of some very impressive cypress stumps still dot the swamp, giving an idea of the massive trees that once grew here. The cutting and hauling of such trees over hundreds, even thousands, of acres must have had a number of adverse environmental impacts, including compacted and eroded soils, diminished water quality, shredded vegetation, and lost wildlife habitat—to name only the most obvious. To the extent that Santee used steam-powered skidders in the tract, these impacts would have been even more pronounced. As forester Wilbur Mattoon observed in 1915, the efficiencies of logging cypress with mechanized equipment came at a heavy price: "The early float method of logging destroyed very little growing stock, the pull-boat method considerable, and under present methods of clean cutting the overhead-cableway skidder effects almost complete destruction of any part of the forest which happens not to be taken."[82]

On the whole, though, it would seem that the immediate impacts of logging on the Beidler Tract were relatively transitory. As noted previously, cutting levels across much of the tract do not appear to have been particularly intense, at least as compared to the company's heavily mechanized operations downstream. Viewing the forest today, it is evident that Santee left behind a considerable number of intermediate-size trees during its time on the tract, especially in those areas where only float logging took place—which, despite published indications to the contrary, may have been most or all of the tract.[83]

Nevertheless, there are parts of the tract where the impacts of Santee's tenure may persist long into the future. This is especially so in places where significant concentrations of large cypress trees triggered heavy logging activity. Here Santee may have effected a long-term reduction of bald cypress in favor of water tupelo (Nyssa aquatica). On other river systems in the South, intensive logging of bald cypress has allowed water tupelo to assume a more dominant position in the canopy than it otherwise would have had, and such a shift has also been documented in parts of the Beidler Tract. Regeneration of cypress depends in large part on the availability of adequate light, but in heavily cut areas, the crowns of remnant tupelo trees spread quickly to fill canopy gaps, shading out cypress seedlings. Moreover, cypress seedlings are often out-competed by young water tupelo stems, especially in cutover areas. Water tupelo sprouts prolifically, produces seed more regularly and in larger quantities than cypress, and grows faster. One does not have to look far in the Beidler Tract today to find sloughs dominated by water tupelo. Some of these sloughs once supported giant cypress trees, as the still-moldering stumps attest.[84]

If Santee's operations triggered a shift to water tupelo in parts of the tract, it may take a very long time for bald cypress to reassert its former dominance in these areas, if it ever does. The combined effects of increased sedimentation, altered hydrology (from upstream dams), and climate change may precipitate a successional shift to less wetland-obligate species on some sites. This shift is most likely to occur in areas closer to the river where sediment accumulation is most pronounced. However, even on sites that are more hydrologically intact, cypress recovery may be slow to nonexistent in areas that were heavily cut over. Water tupelo is a long-lived species, and young tupelo stands that established in the wake of Santee's logging operations could conceivably persist for hundreds of years. In contrast, where logging was only moderately intense, the death of senescent tupelo stems could allow new cohorts of cypress and tupelo to establish comparatively quickly in canopy gaps. Much therefore depends on how intensively Santee logged particular sites.[85]

How widespread the shift to tupelo might be on the tract is impossible to say in the absence of detailed descriptions of the forest before it was cut. Not every stand of water tupelo on the tract necessarily originated from intense timber harvest; some may have resulted from factors completely unrelated to past logging. On this question and others, historic stand-composition data would be particularly illuminating, if only it existed. The lack of such data is felt all the more acutely because Santee's long-term impacts were by no means limited to the logging of cypress sloughs, or even to actual logging. In some ways it was Santee's post-logging management practices that produced the most pervasive impacts on the tract.

Following closure of the mill at Ferguson, Santee continued to treat its timber base as a long-term economic investment. The company actively sought to protect its trees from loss or damage during this period, hiring caretakers to mark boundaries, prevent timber theft and destruction, and control forest fires. In some cases the company allowed local farmers to graze cattle on company land for free in exchange for protecting the timber from trespass and fire. Even low-intensity surface fires were felt by foresters to have a deleterious impact on floodplain forests, and their suppression was encouraged to minimize butt-rot and decay.[86]

Assuming that Santee adopted a policy of full fire suppression on the Beidler Tract, any stockmen igniting canebrakes at the turn of the century would have been rapidly brought to heel. This approach to management may have produced a marked reduction in disturbance on the tract. Meanwhile, a lull in major hurricane activity characterized the inner coastal plain for much of the twentieth century, continuing more or less uninterrupted until Hurricane Hugo in September 1989.[87] With fewer floods and wind events setting back the successional clock, trees in the tract matured rapidly and shade cover increased. In time, the ever-deepening shade, spreading over larger and larger areas, spelled the final demise of the tract's giant cane. The brakes that had once been a defining feature of the landscape were soon gone, apparently for good.

By the mid-1970s parts of the Beidler Tract had assumed a grove-like aspect, a quality not lost on those seeking protection of the tract as a national park. From the forester's standpoint, Santee's efforts to safeguard its investment had worked all too well, for in some respects the Beidler Tract was now too valuable to cut. As Francis Beidler III would later observe, "My father was right that those trees would become uniquely valuable. We did not foresee that they would become uniquely valuable to the nation." The heirs of Francis Beidler would still see an economic return from the tract. Now, however, that return would come from sale to the National Park Service, not from periodic logging.[88]

After Santee

The closure of Santee's mill complex at Ferguson brought to an end the most extensive commercial logging operation ever to operate in the lower Congaree floodplain. While it is possible that Santee sold timber to third parties over the course of the following decade, there is no indication in the Richland County Register of Deeds that it ever did so. But this does not necessarily mean that logging in the future national park came to a complete halt. By June 1913 the Sumter Stave Company had purchased a seven-year supply of "hard wood from the Wateree, Congaree and Santee swamps" to run in its new mill in Sumter. It is possible that this entity cut parts of the park during these years to produce barrel staves. Another company that may have logged the park at this time was a new firm in Columbia called the Carolina Veneer Company. Carolina Veneer began logging somewhere on the lower Congaree in 1916 and continued to do so until late 1917 or early 1918.[89]

The chartering of Carolina Veneer is significant because it marks the beginning of a decisive shift away from old-growth cypress, which by now was mostly logged out, to bottomland hardwoods. Carolina Veneer completed construction of a new veneer plant in Columbia in May 1916 and about this time began to cut and process logs from the Congaree Swamp. Three times a week logs from the swamp were loaded on the company's one-hundred-ton stern wheeler, the *Kochaline*, and its barge, *Elliott*, and towed to Columbia. The logs were cut from lands where Carolina Veneer had purchased timber rights some time before.[90]

Carolina Veneer was reputed to be the largest veneer plant between Louisville and the Atlantic. Its chief products were veneer and glued panels for use in furniture and interior housework. In late 1916 the company was shipping 800,000 feet of product per week, with plans to increase output to 1.2 million feet. To meet its production goals, the plant used a number of different woods, including poplar, oak, pine, and gum, about half of which came from the Congaree Swamp. The *State* reported in December 1916 that "twenty men are stationed about 50 miles down the Congaree river and they cut every day to supply the 50 per cent of the plant's raw material." Just where Carolina Veneer was cutting is not known because it did not record its timber deeds. However, if the *State* report is accurate, much of the company's raw material probably came from the Bates Old River area, as well as from the lands southeast of Kingville formerly owned by James A. Peterkin.[91]

Despite its initial success, Carolina Veneer's business fell off dramatically in 1917, and it soon began to face lawsuits from creditors. Disaster struck in the early morning hours of January 11, 1918, when its entire plant burned. Not long thereafter, the company was forced into receivership.[92]

Carolina Veneer's time on the scene may have been brief, but its operation pointed the way to the future. Hardwood logging would continue in the floodplain for years to come and would affect many parts of the future national park. Only the Beidler Tract would be spared and then only for a time.

Logging after 1920

The [Beidlers] certainly [have] not exploited the area. The vast number of old growth trees testifies to that. On the contrary, [they have] erred on the side of timidity in harvesting the forest, both hardwood and pine.

J. Sid McKnight, consulting forester, statement to South Carolina House
of Representatives, October 23, 1975

WITH THE CESSATION OF SANTEE'S WOODS OPERATIONS in 1914, any logging still taking place in the Beidler Tract came to an immediate halt. Apart from a limited amount of timber that may (or may not) have been sold to third parties during the next few years, the tract remained free from intensive logging for the next fifty years and more. Only in 1969 did the Beidler family reinitiate systematic cutting on the tract.

On adjacent properties the situation was different. Here, intermittent logging took place over the course of the entire twentieth century. Most of the adjoining tracts were logged more than once, leaving behind few extensive stands of old trees. In time, efforts to regularize the park boundary and protect additional bottomland habitat would bring many of these cut-over tracts into NPS ownership. The second-growth forest on these lands now augments and buffers the remaining old-growth forest of the Beidler Tract.

Logging the Beidler Tract, 1969–1976

The Beidler Tract comprises 15,138.25 acres in nineteen contiguous parcels. No major commercial logging appears to have occurred on any of these parcels during the period 1914–69. The only known cutting during this period is some salvage logging that took place in the wake of Hurricane Gracie, a category 3 storm that struck South Carolina on September 29, 1959.[1]

The National Park Service acknowledged this salvage operation briefly in its 1963 study evaluating the Beidler Tract for possible inclusion in the National Park System. According to the study, "The most notable inroad to area preservation has been the recent cutting and subsequent removal of several dying trees and a small number felled by a severe hurricane. Fortunately these forestry activities have been limited in scope, confined to a relatively restricted area, and have not penetrated the heart of the study area. Thus, the prime qualities of the forest remain virtually intact." Additional confirmation of this logging activity comes from Julian T. Buxton, former president of the Williams Furniture Corporation of Sumter, South Carolina. Testifying before Congress in 1976, Buxton noted that "our plywood plant found signs of incipient decay in some fine sweet gum logs salvaged from trees" taken from the Beidler Tract after Hurricane Gracie. These trees had been "damaged when Hurricane Gracie passed through the tract in 1959."[2]

To understand how the Beidler Tract remained largely untouched from 1914 to 1969, one need only look at the size of the Beidler family's land base and the philosophy of the man who managed it. At one time the Beidler family owned or controlled the rights to more than 176,000 acres of South Carolina timberland. Despite losing approximately 60,000 acres of these lands in the 1930s to the Santee Cooper hydroelectric project, the family's land base still contained tremendous quantities of bottomland timber after World War II—more than enough, as it turned out, to keep the family occupied in succeeding decades. Overseeing management of these lands was Francis Beidler II (1897–1984), who took over at Santee in 1924 and resolved to follow in his father's footsteps: "I assumed an uneasy control of our South Carolina forests at the age of 26. My father's friends and associates viewed these as 'Beidler's Folly,' and vehemently urged me to sell out or to cut and run like everyone else. However, I shared my father's conservational views and decided to dig in my heels and hold on. I sold some Chicago real estate to pay the . . . taxes [on my father's estate]. Then came the Depression, during which I grudgingly sold logging rights for enough cash to insure our survival."[3] As time went on, Francis Beidler II attempted to perpetuate his father's conservation ethic by harvesting timber on a relatively slow, sustained-yield basis. His objective was to log at such a rate that once the old-growth timber had been cut, the family could turn its attention to cutting the regrowth on lands logged sixty or more years earlier.[4] Consequently, the family did not reach the Beidler Tract—its last old-growth holding—until the late 1960s. It then began what was intended to be a thirty-year program of timber sales.

By that point the Santee River Cypress Lumber Company was no more. Santee's shareholders had voted to liquidate and dissolve the company in 1934, ten years after the death of Francis Beidler. It was not until many years later, however, that the company was finally dissolved.[5] In 1967 the company's trustees in dissolution and liquidation began conveying the parcels in the Beidler Tract to Francis Beidler II individually and to Francis Beidler II and J. Beidler Camp as trustees of various family trusts.[6] Beidler and Camp then began to log the Beidler Tract in order to meet their fiduciary obligations to generate income for trust beneficiaries. Between 1969 and 1976 the family sold approximately thirty-six hundred acres of timber in the tract to be selectively logged or clear-cut.[7] This figure represents almost 24 percent of the entire tract. About this same time the owners of a number of properties bordering the tract logged their timber as well.

The Beidlers limited the sale of timber to approximately five hundred acres per year, with each sale consisting mostly of miscellaneous bottomland hardwoods other than cypress. As these sales went forward, the public began to voice increasing concern that logging would destroy the tract's tremendous ecological and scenic value. But to the Beidler trustees the tract was first and foremost commercial forestland—land that would allow them to meet their obligations to beneficiaries of the family trusts. On a more philosophical level, the sales also reflected the view of Francis Beidler II that the tract's exceptional potential for timber growth should not be lost to future generations. Thus, the family's legal obligations and strong business orientation spurred the commercial utilization of all its lands, including the Beidler Tract.[8] Even so, the impact of the family's timber sales was relatively light compared to the effect logging was having on most other bottomland forests of the period. This was due in no small part to Francis Beidler II. As his son noted in 1981, "My father realized that timber was going to become an increasingly scarce and valuable resource, that it was worth more standing than cut. He was reluctant to make a great many sales. As a result of his unusually foresighted forbearance from timber harvesting, the untouched forests we owned on the Congaree River and in Four Holes Swamp became the last of their kind. Everything around them had been logged. They became unique."[9]

To an extent that has perhaps not been fully appreciated, Francis Beidler II made possible the creation of Congaree National Park. In the face of strong social and economic pressures to liquidate the family's timber, he insisted on pursuing sustained-yield forestry. His resolve left the Beidler Tract largely intact and, notwithstanding the limited logging of the 1970s, worthy of inclusion in the National Park System.

After Congress declared the Beidler Tract a national monument in October 1976, the National Park Service and the Beidler family entered into negotiations for sale of the tract to the government. These efforts were prolonged but not successful. The NPS initially filed a declaration of taking[10] on three small subtracts (the "timber sale tracts") to prevent them from being cut under outstanding timber contracts. Eventually, and at the urging of the Beidler family, the Park Service decided to file a declaration of taking on the remainder of the tract as well. Title to the main tract passed to the government on February 22, 1980.[11]

Not much information has survived regarding the Beidler family's timber management practices in the early to mid-1970s. What little information there is suggests that logging activities on the Beidler Tract were conducted in accordance with standard industry practice of the time. The typical objective of forest management in the early 1970s was high-quality sawtimber rather than pulpwood, since few pulpwood markets then existed across the South. To obtain high-quality trees of at least forty inches dbh (diameter at breast height), foresters typically recommended uneven-aged management, using both single-tree and group selection. In addition, foresters recommended relatively light partial harvests on a ten-year cutting cycle to maintain well-stocked stands. Harvests were based on tree-marking rules designed to evaluate critical characteristics of individual trees in the stand.[12]

Based on correspondence submitted in evidence during the condemnation case, the Beidlers' consulting forester appears to have recommended a ten-year cutting cycle for the selectively logged portions of the Beidler Tract. The amounts cut in these areas may have been somewhat greater than was customary elsewhere in the region because many of the trees on the tract were considered "overmature" and thus ripe for removal in an "improvement cut." For example, a letter describing a sale in Parcel 1 of the tract states that sale trees were "selectively marked, taking out the over-mature, many of the mature trees and all trees showing excessive defect and those trees considered poor risks to hold for another decade." No cypress was sold from the Beidler Tract during this period because cypress had been extensively logged at the turn of the century and hence was not perceived to have an "overmaturity problem." Researchers in the 1980s reported that selective cuts on the Beidler Tract removed as much as 50 percent of the overstory canopy.[13]

By the early 1970s clear-cutting was becoming an increasingly favored method for managing bottomland hardwood timber throughout the South. The first clear-cut on the Beidler Tract occurred between late 1973 and early 1974, around four years after the Beidlers resumed logging operations. The following year, the Beidlers retained prominent forester Sid McKnight to advise them and their consulting forester, R. F. Knoth, regarding the best harvesting methods to use on the tract. McKnight had spent the majority of his career as a researcher with the U.S. Forest Service, specializing in bottomland and swamp hardwood forests of the Southeast. After touring the Beidler Tract, McKnight recommended that the property be managed for commercial shade-intolerant species "by removing old growth timber that now stands. Small areas at a time should be clearcut of all stems and allowed to regenerate naturally." By following this approach, the entire tract could be cut in about thirty to forty years, after which a variety of age classes would be present in the forest.[14]

In keeping with this recommendation, much of the timber sold off the tract in 1975 and 1976 was clear-cut. The clear-cuts ranged in size from 85 to 240 acres in size and generally removed the entire overstory canopy except cypress. Other species were occasionally retained as well, depending on the terms of individual sales.[15]

Companies bidding for cutting rights on the Beidler Tract were required to submit lump-sum bids for all species included in a sale, even if they only had use for a portion of those species. As a result, successful bidders often subcontracted with other firms to cut species of trees that did not meet their needs. For instance, sawmills and producers of hardwood squares were primarily interested in green ash, sugarberry, and various oaks. These mills had little use for sweet gum and sycamore and would typically resell all or a large part of these species to a hardwood veneer mill. Conversely, veneer mills were primarily in the market for sweet gum and sycamore and usually sought to resell other hardwood species to a sawmill or square mill.

The mechanics of lump-sum bidding are illustrated by the experience of Council Brothers, Inc., which entered successful bids on nine of the twenty-five Beidler Tract sales. Council Brothers was a manufacturer of furniture squares and as such sought to acquire quantities of high-quality green ash, sugarberry, and "black gum" trees. It resold remaining species to other timber users in the area, including veneer mills. One of its known subcontractors was the Swansea Lumber Company, which also operated as a prime contractor elsewhere in the park.[16]

A number of veneer mills vied for the high-grade logs on the Beidler Tract, either as a subcontractor or as principal bidder. Among them were the Kearse Manufacturing Company of Olar, South Carolina, and the Williams Furniture Division of Georgia-Pacific Corporation, located in Sumter. The Williams plant was dependent on high-grade veneer logs to make hardwood plywood for its furniture. In 1975 close to one-third of all the veneer logs sawed in the Williams plant came from the Beidler Tract.[17]

Despite its value to the furniture industry, the Beidler Tract timber presented significant logistical challenges, both in the field and at the mill. Naturalist L. L. Gaddy has written that the tract routinely yielded hardwoods over five feet in diameter, although many proved to be hollow and commercially worthless. Even when sound, old-growth logs could be difficult to get out of the swamp over wet, slippery logging roads. A more fundamental problem lay in the fact that many of the tract's old-growth trees were too big for regional mills to handle. Gaddy observed that oftentimes trees had to be cut six to ten feet above the buttress to produce logs that could be sawed at the mill. When Gaddy took Lieutenant

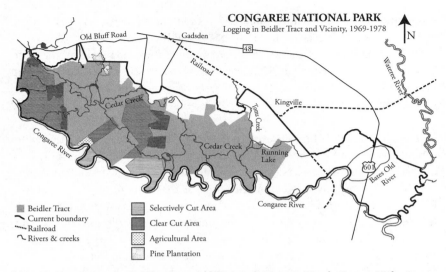

CONGAREE NATIONAL PARK
Logging in Beidler Tract and Vicinity, 1969-1978

N

Old Bluff Road   Gadsden   48   Wateree River

Railroad

Cedar Creek   Kingville

Congaree River   Toms Creek   Cedar Creek   Running Lake   601   Bates Old River

Congaree River

- ▦ Beidler Tract
- ∿ Current boundary
- ‑‑‑‑ Railroad
- ∿ Rivers & creeks
- ▦ Selectively Cut Area
- ▦ Clear Cut Area
- ▦ Agricultural Area
- ▦ Pine Plantation

Map 10. Logging in the Beidler Tract and Vicinity, 1969–78. Map by Lynne Parker.

Governor Brantley Harvey on a tour of the swamp in 1975, what struck Harvey most was the great waste of wood he saw.[18]

Some confusion has existed about the precise extent of logging on the tract before it was acquired by the Park Service. The single best source of information on this subject is the series of documents filed with the court in the condemnation case. In one of these documents, the Beidlers informed the court that "over the period 1969–1976, approximately 800 acres have been clearcut and 2,800 acres have been selectively cut over," for a total of 3,600 acres, or about 24 percent of the tract. These same figures are found in an appraisal of the tract prepared for the Beidler family. Map 10 shows the parts of the tract where logging took place during the 1970s.[19]

Logging Outside the Beidler Tract, 1918–2004

At the time it established Congaree Swamp National Monument, Congress directed the secretary of the interior to identify any additional "lands adjacent or related to the monument which are deemed necessary or desirable for the purposes of resource protection, scenic integrity, or management and administration of the area." Over the next twelve years, the NPS considered a range of possible boundary configurations without settling on a preferred option. Finally, Congress adopted a "Citizens' Proposal" in 1988 that expanded the monument by almost 7,000 acres. The 1988 expansion added several important tracts between the Beidler Tract and the Congaree River, as well as significant areas to the east and north. In 2003 Congress expanded the park yet again, adding over 4,500 acres between the Norfolk Southern rail line on the west and the Wateree River on the east. The 2003 expansion linked the park to the Upper Santee Swamp Natural Area, a 16,700-acre area on the headwaters of Lake Marion managed by the South Carolina Public Service Authority (also known as Santee Cooper).[20]

Each of the tracts added to the park in 1988 and 2003 had a long history of logging. Many experienced additional cutting just prior to their acquisition by the National Park Service.

Logging North of the Beidler Tract

HOLLY HILL TRACT (TRACT 101-32)

The 661-acre Holly Hill tract is located due east of South Cedar Creek Road (map 2). The parcels originally making up this tract were owned at the turn of the twentieth century by various private individuals, two of whom made sales of bottomland timber totaling 308 acres between 1900 and 1903.[21] In 1924 a third landowner sold bottomland timber in the far eastern part of the tract to the Hoffman Lumber Company. The latter sale covered "all timber of every character now standing or lying" on approximately 184 acres.[22]

The original parcels of this tract were consolidated into the timber base of the Holly Hill Lumber Company beginning in the 1940s.[23] At that time the floodplain portion of the tract still held extensive stands of mature timber, while most of the adjoining bluff was farmland, pasture, and brush.[24] Holly Hill began cutting the floodplain portion of the tract in the early to mid-1950s and by 1959 had selectively cut most of the tract's forested wetlands. In the mid-1970s, it converted over 150 acres on the northern bluff to pine plantations.[25]

Holly Hill sold this and other nearby tracts to Georgia-Pacific Corporation on June 28, 1978. Georgia-Pacific (G-P) was one of the period's major producers of wood and paper products, both regionally and nationally. Between 1984 and 1990 Georgia-Pacific clear-cut approximately 20 percent of the tract's 661 acres, with the cutting about evenly split between the floodplain and uplands. No significant cutting appears to have occurred during this time in any of the tract's cypress-tupelo sloughs.[26]

This tract is crossed by a particularly scenic stretch of Cedar Creek. In 1986, with park expansion on the horizon, Senator Strom Thurmond asked G-P to refrain from cutting that part of the tract between Cedar Creek on the north and the Beidler Tract on the south, an area of approximately 160 acres (map 1). Georgia-Pacific not only honored this request, it held off logging much of the rest of the tract as well. When the NPS acquired the tract in 1990, it contained about 400 acres of merchantable hardwoods.[27]

ELLIOTT TRACT (TRACT 101-33)

This 238-acre tract lies just to the east of the Holly Hill tract. Formerly owned by the Elliott family, the tract consists of approximately 203 acres of floodplain and 35 acres of upland. Aerial photos from the late 1930s show a logging road traversing the tract from its northwestern corner to its southeastern edge, together with signs of logging in the southeastern portion of the tract.[28] However, extensive logging had clearly taken place quite a bit earlier than this because the outline of the tract's southern boundary is faintly evident even in places where no obvious logging was taking place in the 1930s.

In April 1980 John E. Elliott Jr. provided park superintendent Robert McDaniel with some limited information on the logging history of the tract. According to Elliott, the last time this tract had been cut prior to the 1980s was around 1950. McDaniel did not record which species had been cut or how much of the tract had been logged. Aerial photographs from 1955 suggest that the cutting was selective and took place in the southwestern part of the tract.[29]

Some of the higher parts of the tract were clear-cut in 1982. Much of the western portion of the tract appears to have been cut around this time, except for stands of cypress-tupelo.[30] The last logging to take place on the tract occurred around 1989 in the central and northeastern sections of the property.

By the time the NPS acquired this tract in 1994, the only merchantable timber still standing was about one hundred acres of mature cypress-tupelo.[31]

Logging East of the Beidler Tract

Over 7,400 acres of the floodplain east of the Beidler Tract is in federal ownership. Before acquisition by the NPS, the tracts in this area sorted into three principal compartments: Kingville West (2,940 acres, between the Beidler Tract and the Norfolk Southern rail line), Kingville East (1,840 acres, between the rail line and the far arm of Bates Old River), and Fork Swamp (2,665 acres, in the fork of the Congaree and Wateree Rivers). Each of these areas has a separate history of commercial logging.

KINGVILLE WEST (TRACTS 101-44, 45, AND 46)

Parts of Kingville West were logged at least as far back as the late nineteenth century. As discussed in chapter 7, a succession of owners (specifically James A. Peterkin, the Congaree Lumber and Veneer Company, and the Fort Motte Lumber and Shingle Company) logged timber in the vicinity of the railroad line in the late 1880s and 1890s. In the early twentieth century, the Carolina Veneer Company cut hardwoods on the lower Congaree from mid-1916 until late 1917. Whether Carolina Veneer cut timber in Kingville West is not known.

No records exist to suggest that the Santee River Cypress Lumber Company ever held an interest in Kingville West or Kingville East. While it is possible that some of the timber cut from the Kingville tracts was sent to the mill at Ferguson, no evidence of any timber sales to Santee has survived.

The first modern logging in Kingville West began in the mid- to late 1930s on lands of the Holly Hill Lumber Company. Holly Hill began buying up land in Kingville West around 1935 and continued to make purchases of land and timber rights into the 1940s. By 1950 it had acquired most of the interests that came to constitute Kingville West.[32]

The full extent of Holly Hill's logging in Kingville West is not known. The relatively small size of the cypress and tupelo still standing on the tract suggests that Holly Hill cut most of the sloughs and depressions on the tract during its ownership.[33] This conclusion is borne out by the recollections of Belton Harmon, who visited Kingville during the early 1940s when he was fourteen years old. Harmon recorded his memories of the Holly Hill logging operation in an e-mail message to his cousin Sam Watson in 2009:

> I first visited the Utseys [at Kingville] around 1941. [Marion] Utsey had taken a job with the Holly Hill Lumber Co. to manage their commissary for their large sawmill at Kingville. The mill was the only employer in that remote area. The only residents were the black sawmill hands that lived in shacks forming a small community. I believe the Utseys were the only whites within several miles. . . .
>
> . . . the sawmill was Kingville's reason for being. Its log supply came mostly from the river bottoms which had very large hardwoods and cypress. It had its own logging railroad which ran from the sawmill down into the swamps at the river. It was three to five miles long. The rails were laid on ties cut from trees as it advanced into the forest. Much of the track crossed water and the rails were spiked right on top of stumps that had been cut at water level. Needless to say, this was a crooked and rough track not suitable for passenger travel. The engine was a wood burning steam engine. Each log car carried three tremendous logs. Arrangements were made for three of us to make a turn with the train one day.
>
> We met at the sawmill early in the AM. The engine was already fired up ready to go. We were perched right in the cab where we could see everything going on. The whistle sounded and off we went with smoke billowing out the stack as it picked up speed. Soon we were crossing water on those stumps. The engine seemed to literally jump from stump to stump and swing from side to side as we rumbled through the woods as the fireman threw more slabs in the fire box and sparks flew out of the stack. You can imagine the excitement of this experience for three young boys.

When we got to the logging site, the cars were positioned for loading. A steam cable skidder was used to drag the logs from where they were cut to the train for loading. We spent most of the day watching this operation and then it was back to the sawmill with a train load of logs. This was one of the few remaining railroad logging operations in the US. I think the mill and the logging operation ended before 1955. I visited one other logging railroad operated by the Savannah River Lumber Co. at Savannah, GA. This was around 1952. I think Kingville died along with the sawmill. I never heard when the sawmill started, but I do know it was an old one. I heard a story that during World War [II] cypress was logged in the swamp and some of the logs were left for some reason. They sank into the water after a few years and were recovered many years later in perfect condition.[34]

Aerial photographs give some idea of the extent of logging by Holly Hill. By 1939 fairly widespread selective logging had occurred in the central and south-central parts of the tract. Logging had progressed considerably to the southeast by 1943, as well as westward into Running Lake Slough. By the mid- to late 1950s, Holly Hill had completed additional selective logging over much of the northern part of the tract. The area immediately north and east of Beidler Tract Parcel 18 was known as a "big tree" area in the 1970s, so in this area at least, the logging of the 1950s apparently left many mature trees untouched.[35]

The 1950s also saw additional cutting in the southern part of Kingville West. One aerial photograph from 1951 shows a logging road extending north from the river into the southwestern part of the tract.[36] Secondary logging tracks are visible branching away from the main road, with cutting occurring in places up to the boundary of the Beidler Tract. Logs from this area were transported south to the riverbank and from there to the opposite shore. Once across, the logs were pulled up the steep southern bluff to a log deck overlooking the river.

Holly Hill sold its fee lands in Kingville West to Georgia-Pacific in 1978. The following year, Georgia-Pacific acquired the remainder of the area (specifically, NPS Tract 101-45) from the Lorick family.[37] Georgia-Pacific began logging Kingville West in 1980 and continued logging through 1988.

When word leaked out in May 1980 that Georgia-Pacific intended to log Kingville West, alarm bells went off among conservationists and the Department of the Interior. Only six years earlier the department had included Kingville West in the newly designated Congaree River Swamp National Natural Landmark, an area consisting of the Beidler Tract and various adjacent parcels.[38] Department officials feared that the proposed logging in Kingville West threatened the loss of nationally significant resources in the new landmark. Furthermore, by March 1980 the Park Service had made the preliminary decision to recommend expansion of the monument to take in the entire national natural landmark, including Kingville West. The prospect of cutting by Georgia-Pacific made this proposed boundary harder to justify.[39]

Faced with the possibility of major losses in the landmark and hoping that Georgia-Pacific lands could be considered for eventual acquisition by the Park Service, Superintendent Robert McDaniel attempted to convince Georgia-Pacific to observe a logging moratorium on lands adjacent to the Beidler Tract. In May 1980, McDaniel asked the National Audubon Society and the South Carolina Wildlife Federation to write letters to Georgia-Pacific in support of such a moratorium. The Audubon Society duly weighed in on behalf of the Park Service, but the executive committee of the South Carolina Wildlife Federation declined to do so. At the time most members of the committee opposed the federal government's acquiring any more land in South Carolina.[40]

Efforts to protect the Georgia-Pacific lands accelerated in early summer. On June 16, 1980, Secretary of the Interior Cecil Andrus wrote to G-P, asking that it suspend planned logging operations pending a decision by Congress on a revised boundary. Company president T. Marshall Hahn responded that it would be very difficult to accede to this request, noting that G-P had acquired Kingville West at a bargain price in 1978 to supply timber to its Williams Furniture Division in Sumter and its hardwood sawmill in Alcolu. Nevertheless, Hahn expressed a willingness to discuss selling G-P property to the government so long as the company was fully compensated for its losses.[41]

In July, signaling a serious intent to expand the monument, members of the U.S. House of Representatives introduced legislation to protect the entire national natural landmark, including about 3,860 acres owned by Georgia-Pacific. At that point the Park Service abruptly changed course. Concerned about the projected costs of land acquisition, the NPS expressed opposition to the new bill and scrapped the internal-expansion proposal underlying it. By late August 1980, additional internal deliberations and a reconnaissance survey with G-P personnel yielded a much-reduced expansion proposal. The Park Service now recommended acquiring only 1,396 acres from G-P, including just 700 acres in Kingville West. The House bill was soon amended to reflect this proposal, but the legislation failed to move.[42]

All along, Georgia-Pacific maintained that Kingville West was "commercial, second-growth forest, that [had] long been managed for timber production."[43] While essentially true, this contention elided the fact that the higher areas of Kingville West still contained substantial areas of mature timber at the time G-P began cutting. John Cely pressed this point to the Park Service in 1986, observing that "there are still significant patches of mature bottomland hardwood, some with near record-size trees, that have been uncut."[44] Ultimately, Georgia-Pacific was just not willing to spare Kingville West. Given the increasing scarcity of furniture-grade logs in the vicinity of its South Carolina plants, G-P's reluctance to forego logging the area is readily explained.[45]

Georgia-Pacific began logging Kingville West during the summer of 1980 and by late 1988 had clear-cut almost two-thirds of the tract. G-P's standard practice was to log in ten- and twenty-acre-patch clear-cuts, although some places were logged in larger blocks. The first cuts occurred in the northeastern portion of Kingville West. By September 1980 a clear-cut in the central part of the tract extended to the park boundary, touching the park at the northwestern corner of Beidler Tract Parcel 19. By late 1988, when the park boundary was expanded to take in the entire national natural landmark, only around 1,000 acres of the 2,940 acres in Kingville West remained uncut.[46]

For the most part, Georgia-Pacific restricted cutting to the more elevated parts of the tract. Sloughs containing cypress and tupelo generally were not cut. In part this was because much of the cypress and tupelo left by Holly Hill was too small to be commercially desirable. A more important factor, however, was market demand. Georgia-Pacific relied on Kingville West (and other nearby lands) to supply oak and other furniture-grade hardwoods to its local mills.

In May 1988, as logging in Kingville West was drawing to a close, G-P laid off about a third of its employees at the Alcolu mill because of a shortage of oak trees. G-P informed the *Sumter Item* that furniture makers served by the Alcolu mill preferred oak to other, more readily available species. Experiments sawing sweet gum, cypress, and pine to meet the needs of furniture makers had not been successful.[47]

KINGVILLE EAST (TRACT 101-73)

The middle portion of Kingville East was originally logged in the early 1870s by McMaster, Monteith and Roath (see chapter 7). The scale of logging expanded significantly in the late 1880s and 1890s, when James A. Peterkin, the Congaree Lumber and Veneer Company, and the Fort Motte Lumber and Shingle Company cut timber in the area north and west of Bates Old River.[48]

In the early years of the twentieth century, timber in the Buckhead Island part of the tract may have been cut by John M. Bates. A 1909 plat of the lower Congaree shows a mill on the northeastern side of Bates Old River that it identifies as the "Bates sawmill." Still more cutting in Kingville East may have been conducted from mid-1916 until late 1917 by the Carolina Veneer Company.[49]

Kingville East was assembled as a single tract between the mid-1930s and the mid-1950s by the Holly Hill Lumber Company. Holly Hill seems to have cut its lands in Kingville East somewhat later and more intensively than its Kingville West lands. When the South Carolina Department of Natural Resources Heritage Trust Program assessed the Kingville bottomlands in the mid-1980s, it concluded that the river swamp east of the railroad was considerably less mature and more disturbed than the land west of the line.[50]

Aerial photos indicate that Holly Hill logged much of Kingville East between the early 1940s and mid-1960s.[51] Information on Holly Hill's logging practices in this area is generally lacking, but the one recorded timber deed for the area, given in 1943, granted Holly Hill cutting rights on all hardwood timber twelve inches in diameter and above at the stump, together with all pine timber ten inches in diameter and above. (Such "diameter-limit" logging, also known as high-grading, "cuts the best, and leaves the rest." If repeated over time, high-grading can seriously degrade the quality of a forest by removing disproportionate amounts of certain high-value species [for example, oaks] and allowing less commercially valuable species to proliferate.) The grant to Holly Hill applied to a 950-acre tract bounded on the south by Bates Old River, on the north by the Camden branch of the Southern Railway line, and on all other sides by the Holly Hill Lumber Company.[52] Within the present park boundary, the deed apparently authorized cutting in the area south of Little Lake and Big Lake on Running Lake Slough.

Holly Hill probably finished its most intensive logging in the tract by the mid-1950s, but additional logging took place in the 1960s and 1970s.[53] Logging along Running Lake Slough in the mid-1960s was followed in the early to mid-1970s by selective cutting of the part of the tract lying west of U.S. Highway 601 and north of Bates Old River. Additional cutting took place in the ear-shaped area east of the highway.[54] During this same period, the company clear-cut a number of areas on the south side of the historic road linking U.S. Highway 601 and the river (sometimes referred to as the Bates Old River causeway; see entry 30 in appendix A). Holly Hill subsequently established loblolly pine plantations in these clear-cuts. Between 1970 and 1973, Holly Hill planted approximately 150 acres of loblolly pine in this location.[55]

Holly Hill sold Kingville East to Georgia-Pacific Corporation in 1978. Georgia-Pacific then clear-cut and selectively cut the more elevated, western part of the tract beginning in the mid- to late 1980s. Of the approximately 471 acres cut at this time, about 346 acres were clear-cut between 1984 and 1988, and 125 acres were selectively cut in 1988. The 1988 cut was reportedly a "minimal" selective cut owing to water levels at the time of harvest. Georgia-Pacific's local forester reported that some parts of the selectively cut area were "close to being clearcut," while a few spots were not cut at all. This observation is consistent with aerial photos taken in 1989, which show a substantial amount of standing timber in the selectively cut area.[56]

After a pause of about six years, G-P reinitiated logging in parts of Kingville East in 1994.[57] Most of the cutting during this period took place on the 150 acres of planted pine south of the Bates Old River causeway. These areas were then allowed to regenerate naturally in pine. North of the causeway, the company selectively cut mature stands of sweet gum–mixed bottomland hardwoods and laurel oak–mixed bottomland hardwoods.[58] Cutting principally took place along a new logging road running north from the causeway. This road and the tracks branching off from it were built to reach hardwoods lying below the northern arc of Running Lake Slough.

Cutting was much less extensive east of Highway 601. Here Georgia-Pacific clear-cut a small area south of Bates Old River but otherwise seems to have left the area intact.

In 1995 and 1996, Georgia-Pacific logged the area west of Highway 601 a final time by helicopter. (Indications are that G-P did not use helicopters to log any of the stands east of the highway.) The helicopter logging was not designed to do an extensive harvest of the tract but only to remove the highest quality stems of cypress, ash, maple, and oak. Most of the logs from the helicopter logging operation were sent to Georgia-Pacific's sawmill in Alcolu.[59]

FORK SWAMP (TRACTS 101-74 AND 75)

The Fork Swamp area is the site of the oldest documented postwar timber sale in Congaree National Park. On December 1, 1871, Joseph Bates granted a timber lease on his "fork" tract to Walter S. Monteith. The lease granted Monteith the right to cut cypress timber for as long as he maintained his sawmill in the area.[60] The lease was subsequently assigned to McMaster, Monteith and Roath and recorded on November 15, 1872.

In the following decades, the Fork Swamp tract passed through a succession of owners. Among them were the Columbia Furniture and Manufacturing Company and the Palmetto Lumber Company. The amount of logging undertaken by the latter concerns, if any, is unknown. In 1903 control of the tract passed to Francis Beidler, acting through the Santee River Cypress Lumber Company. The Beidler family maintained a legal interest in the Fork Swamp tract for the next 102 years, longer than for any of its other Congaree properties.[61]

Although specific information is limited, it is evident that the Beidlers authorized logging on the Fork Swamp tract during the first half of the twentieth century, beginning, presumably, with the cutting of old-growth cypress in the early 1900s. Aerial photos taken in 1943 show clear evidence of past cutting.[62] After World War II, the area east of Highway 601 (2,395 acres, now often referred to as the "Bates Fork tract") was logged under a long-term cutting agreement with U.S. Plywood Corporation. Cutting likely commenced soon after December 14, 1944, the date on which the Beidlers temporarily conveyed the tract to U.S. Plywood. The conveyance was made subject to an agreement that the family would reacquire the property at one of two times, whichever came earlier: (a) after twenty years, or (b) the date on which U.S. Plywood completed cutting all the timber it was authorized to cut under a purchase-money mortgage held by the Beidlers. The sale was thus akin to a timber lease but with the added benefit that it relieved the Beidlers of property taxes and other expenses during the time the property was owned by U.S. Plywood.

Under the terms of the purchase agreement, U.S. Plywood was authorized to cut timber on a diameter-limit basis. Specifically, it was allowed to cut trees not less than twelve inches in diameter, as measured at the ground or above the swell. Among the more noteworthy provisions of the contract was one prohibiting U.S. Plywood from returning to any area of the tract once it had "cut over" that area the first time. In addition, U.S. Plywood was authorized to "make selective cuttings of over-matured timber wherever located, excluding areas which the Grantee [had] previously cut over," or had selectively logged. Cutting of "over-matured timber" was initially capped at 3.55 million board feet but was increased in 1950 to 6 million board feet.[63]

U.S. Plywood and its successors in interest cut the Bates Fork tract more or less continually for a period of nineteen years. Aerial photos from 1951 show one logging road entering the tract from U.S. Highway 601 and another from the agricultural lands north of Bates Old River. The photos show a number of secondary logging roads in different parts of the tract, but large areas still remained without roads at that time. The rate of cutting appears to have picked up considerably after 1959, when U.S. Plywood conveyed the tract to Vestal Lumber and Manufacturing Company.[64] By the fall of 1961 evidence of intensive logging is clearly evident across the central part of the tract and in places along the Congaree and Wateree Rivers. Aerial photos from April 1964 show an extensive network of logging roads throughout the entire tract, and by this point the tract appears to be largely cut over. It was during this period that cutting took place in much of the cypress-tupelo community that dominates large parts of the tract.[65]

The Beidlers reacquired the Bates Fork tract on December 19, 1963. Timber harvesting continued thereafter, and by the mid-1970s most of the tract had been thoroughly logged.

Around 1998, after a break of twenty-plus years, cutting once more commenced on the Bates Fork tract. This time logging activities were focused on the green ash–mixed bottomland hardwood community that characterizes much of the more elevated parts of the tract. By September 2002, approximately 150 acres of the tract had been cut, including 50 or so acres converted to "openings" to provide improved waterfowl habitat.[66] In August 2003 the Beidlers sold timber on an additional 133 acres to the Rebel Lumber Company. Yet another timber sale was initiated in late 2003, covering up to 300 acres. The latter sale was suspended, however, after the Trust for Public Land optioned the Bates Fork tract for eventual conveyance to the National Park Service.[67] In all, approximately 285 acres were cut on the tract between 1998 and 2003. As of July 2004, the forested portions of this tract consisted of approximately 1,658 acres of low flat and ridge hardwood timber and 414 acres of cypress-tupelo flats.[68]

The many years of logging on this tract left it with a predominately young stand of timber. When the NPS acquired the tract in November 2005, "many acres" of the tract were said to be covered in trees ranging in age from thirty to fifty years old.[69]

Much less is known about the logging history of the Beidlers' other Fork Swamp property, the 265-acre, triangular-shaped tract located west of U.S. Highway 601. It is possible that McMaster, Monteith and Roath cut old-growth cypress in this area during the early 1870s. Such cutting would have taken place pursuant to the timber lease with Joseph Bates discussed above. It is also possible that the Santee River Cypress Lumber Company logged this area at the turn of the twentieth century.

This property may also have been cut in the 1940s, when it was owned by L. Russell Smith and Nellie G. Smith. The Smiths acquired the tract from the Beidler family in 1943.[70] The Beidlers conveyed the tract subject to a reversion clause that allowed them to buy back the property, which they did in 1951.

Over one hundred acres of this tract were clear-cut around 1990 in the wake of Hurricane Hugo. The southern part of the tract, fronting on the Congaree River, was not cut.

Logging South of the Beidler Tract

Six principal tracts lie directly south of the Beidler Tract. These tracts range in size from 110 to 699 acres; all include land on the natural levee of the Congaree River. At least four of the tracts contained cleared fields at the turn of the twentieth century.

The Santee River Cypress Lumber Company bought timber rights to four of the six tracts between 1903 and 1905. Santee typically sought to acquire floodplain tracts in fee simple, so the fact that it never acquired the fee to these tracts may indicate that parts were still being actively used to graze cattle, or to grow corn, hay, or cotton.

All six of the tracts were cut more than once between 1914 and 1990.

BRADY TRACT (TRACT 101-42)

The Brady tract (390.60 acres) is the western-most (and second-largest) of the six tracts lying south of the Beidler Tract (see map 2 and entry 8 in appendix A). Recorded timber deeds and other documentation indicate that logging took place on this tract during the periods 1916–19, 1928–43, 1967–70, and 1977–78.[71] Logging may have taken place during earlier periods as well. There is no record that the Santee River Cypress Lumber Company ever acquired a timber deed to this tract.

Of the cuts for which records are available, all but the last were done on a diameter-limit basis. In the 1967 sale, for example, Council Brothers, Inc., was authorized to cut all timber on the tract sixteen inches and over except mulberry and persimmon. Also excepted were not more than sixty oak trees to be selected and paid for by Leo Brady.

Aerial photographs taken in 1970 and 1971 make clear the extent of logging on the tract during the late 1960s. In these photographs the outlines of the Brady tract are distinctly visible against the old-growth Beidler Tract, indicating that most of the larger trees on the tract had been cut by 1971. The tract is similarly, though less sharply, outlined in aerial photographs from 1939.[72] These photographs and the relatively mature timber now found on portions of the tract confirm that logging operations took place on the entire tract over the course of many years. A somewhat idealized description of these operations (that is, it conflicts with aerial photographs and the express terms of recorded timber deeds) was provided by Jack Brady in a 1975 magazine piece:

> "Some of the trees they want to save [for the proposed national park unit] are on land my grandfather used to farm. My family has been protecting the really big trees for as long as they've owned the land." For Jack Brady that means more than 100 years. He and his father own about 1,000 acres of the river bottoms, half of it in soybeans and corn or rough pasture for their cattle and hogs. . . . Jack says the family has cut some trees every 20 years or so for generations. That it's more than 100 years before the same piece of land is likely to be cut a second time. "And the trees are selected for harvest by experts, rather than taking out all the trees on an acre at the same time. That means a lot of trees will be more than 150 years old before they're harvested. By that time a lot of older trees will have died of storm or insect damage or just from old age anyway."

Brady reiterated this description of the family's logging philosophy in October 1975, when he appeared before the Agriculture and Natural Resources Committee of the South Carolina House of Representatives to discuss the proposed park. He testified that "my father, Leo Brady, my brother Larry Brady and I own about 1000 acres located on the Congaree River. . . . This property has been in our family for about 200 years. . . . Some champion size hardwood are on our property. They are there because we have select cut our timber when we have cut, usually about every 10 or 15 years in various places. We have never cut our entire acreage at one time. The income from the trees have helped us to put two children through college and also to build dikes on the river side to help control flooding in our area."[73]

The last timber harvest on this tract took place in 1977–78, about a year after an unsuccessful attempt by Leo Brady to sell the tract to the National Park

Service.[74] Brady had approached the NPS with an offer to sell in October 1976, just days after Congress passed the legislation establishing Congaree Swamp National Monument. The NPS immediately declined the offer, notifying Brady that it had no legislative authority to acquire the tract. However, in an attempt to be encouraging, the Park Service informed Brady that the government would be studying a revised boundary in due course as required by the legislation and thus might be authorized to acquire the property at some point in the future. With his offer rejected and needing money, Leo Brady and his son Jack initiated a timber sale to the Swansea Lumber Company. Swansea soon clear-cut portions of the property.[75]

According to the Park Service's *Assessment of [Management] Alternatives* for the then-new national monument, approximately two hundred acres of the Brady tract were clear-cut between the late summer of 1977 and the end of 1978. These clear-cuts were concentrated in the middle and eastern portions of the tract.[76]

KATIE WISE TRACT (TRACT 101-41)

The Santee River Cypress Lumber Company acquired a timber deed to this tract in 1903. The deed granted Santee the right to cut all timber on the tract, standing and fallen.[77]

On January 15, 1951, members of the Wise family of Calhoun County conveyed a timber deed on the tract to Holly Hill Lumber Company. The deed conveyed "all trees and timber, except oak trees and persimmon, measuring twelve inches and upward in diameter" at the time of cutting. Trees were to be measured at twelve inches from the ground.[78]

The NPS *Assessment of Alternatives* indicates that the Wise tract was selectively cut in 1978. It appears likely that loggers on this tract made use of the road system opened up on the Brady tract the previous year (see discussion of Brady tract logging above).[79] According to the NPS *Assessment of Alternatives,* the 1978 selective cut covered approximately 100 acres of this (then) 139-acre tract. In places this "selective" cut was fairly extensive.[80]

FRANK W. WISE TRACT (TRACT 101-37)

The Santee River Cypress Lumber Company acquired timber rights to the northern 80 acres of this 110-acre tract in 1904. The deed granted Santee the right to cut all timber on the tract, standing and fallen.[81]

Between 1916 and 1975 the tract was owned by members of the Wise family. There is little doubt that additional cutting took place during these years. When the tract passed to the National Park Service in 1993, the volume of timber on the tract was comparable to that on the W. Peter Buyck Sr. and A.P. Bruner tracts (see below), both of which appear to have been selectively logged in the 1950s and 1960s.

On August 29, 1975, Frank W. Wise Jr. and others sold the tract to Council Lumber Company, Inc. Council, in turn, sold the tract to the Beidler family in 1977. It is possible that the tract was logged again after one or both of these sales, but aerial photos taken in 1981 show no obvious signs of the tract having been logged in the recent past.[82]

Regardless of when, or if, cutting took place after 1975, the tract was observed in the mid-1990s to contain a number of "medium-sized trees" that had the potential to reach champion size "in one or two decades."[83] Thus, any logging that may have taken place during the 1970s and 1980s was probably relatively light.

RUSSELL L. BUYCK TRACT (TRACT 101-36)

The Santee River Cypress Lumber Company acquired a timber deed to this tract (699 acres) in 1905. The deed granted Santee the right to cut all cottonwood, ash, and cypress trees twelve inches in diameter and above.[84]

Sometime in the late 1920s or early 1930s, the Wise family granted a timber deed on the tract to Marion McKenzie.[85] This deed expired in August 1936. (By that time the property had passed from the Wise family to Russell L. Buyck and W. Peter Buyck Sr.)[86] Aerial photos taken in 1939 appear to show evidence of recent logging in the middle and eastern portions of the tract, but the extent of logging is difficult to make out. Subsequent photos from May 1943 show no obvious evidence of logging at all. Given the number of champion-size trees still present on the tract later in the century, the amount of cutting done at this time may have been relatively limited. In contrast, the logging that occurred a few years later on the tract's southern peninsula was intense. Aerial photos clearly show that logging occurred on much of this area sometime between 1939 and 1943.[87]

In the late 1960s and possibly into the early to mid-1970s, the concentration of champion trees standing on the Russell Buyck tract was second only to that on the Beidler Tract. Two national champions—a sweet gum and a bitternut hickory—were measured in May 1970, and ten state champions were identified around this same time. It is not known how long these trees survived into the 1970s and 1980s; the landowner denied access to the tract soon after local citizens proposed it for acquisition by the federal government.[88]

The entire tract was selectively logged beginning around the summer of 1970. Loggers entered the tract via the river on the south and the "New Road" on the north, the latter having been constructed in 1970 to facilitate logging in the central portion of the Beidler Tract.[89] It is also possible that logging took place on the tract in the late 1970s. The Park Service did not acquire title to the Beidler Tract until February 1980, and it was not until then that the New Road could be closed to vehicle traffic. However, aerial photos taken in 1978 and 1981 do not show any major new cutting in the Buyck tract during that time.[90]

Congress included the Russell Buyck tract in the park boundary in 1988. Shortly thereafter the landowner made a sale of selected persimmon trees on the tract for use in the manufacture of golf clubs.[91] The sale consisted of marked trees on approximately two hundred acres. Cutting began in late August 1989, and substantial cutting had occurred by the time Hurricane Hugo struck in the early morning hours of September 22, 1989.[92]

The last logging to occur on the tract was a salvage operation undertaken in 1990 after the hurricane. A November 4, 1989, public notice issued by the South Carolina Department of Natural Resources names "Milliken Forestry Company, Inc. . . . . Attn: Chester M. Kearse Jr." as the applicant for a permit to install a temporary double-overhead-cable rehaul system to remove timber from the tract and transport it to the south side of the river.[93]

The 1990 salvage operation involved both the removal of downed timber and the harvest of a portion of the still-standing timber on the tract.[94] Aerial photographs indicate that approximately two hundred acres of the western half of the property were virtually clear-cut by the logger, with only scattered merchantable trees left behind. In other areas only damaged trees and some high-value undamaged trees were removed. At least a third of the tract was not logged at all. The combined effects of wind damage and logging resulted in the loss of around half the timber on the tract by the fall of 1990. No champion trees remained on the tract after the hurricane and subsequent salvage logging.[95]

W. PETER BUYCK SR. TRACT (TRACT 101-35)

There is no record that the Santee River Cypress Lumber Company ever acquired a timber deed to this 111-acre tract.

Aerial photos from 1939 show what looks to be a network of logging roads in the northern part of the tract, suggesting that this area had been logged some years before. Subsequent photos suggest that the tract was next selectively logged in the 1950s, with cutting being concentrated in the southern half of the tract.[96] Prior to Hurricane Hugo, the last time the tract was logged was in the mid-1960s. An internal document prepared by the NPS Planning Division in 1986 noted that this tract was "cut but regenerating."[97]

W. Peter Buyck Jr. offered to sell this tract to NPS in 1988. In his offer letter Buyck described his forestry practices as follows: "I do not cut timber for the sake of cutting timber, only when the trees are mature or are falling down do I cut them. My trees are managed as well as possible. The trees were last cut approximately 20–25 years ago. If [my forester] sees any extremely large trees he does not mark them to be cut. He leaves a buffer zone around them and measures them to see if they are record trees. For this reason, the world's record Cottonwood tree, plus several state record trees, and other large trees were located on my property."[98] Years before, Buyck's father, W. Peter Buyck Sr., had likewise stated that "every time our forester finds a tree that should be saved for posterity he leaves it. It is marked and its position is denoted on an aerial map." As a result, he said, "on my land stands the largest cottonwood tree in the United States." Correspondence in NPS files indicates that the tree in question was a swamp cottonwood *(Populus heterophylla)*.[99]

Any champion trees still present on the tract at the time of acquisition by NPS would have had to survive not only the selective logging in the first half of the century and the cutting from the 1960s but also salvage logging after Hurricane Hugo. The northern half of the tract was subject to post-hurricane salvage logging around 1989–90. Approximately twenty acres of the tract were cut at that time.[100]

A. P. BRUNER TRACT (TRACT 101-34)

The Santee River Cypress Lumber Company acquired a timber deed to this tract in 1905. The deed granted Santee the right to cut cottonwood, ash, cypress, and pine on about seventy of the tract's one hundred acres.[101] Aerial photos taken in 1943 show the trees on the southern quarter of the tract to be noticeably shorter than those to the north, suggesting that the southern quarter of this tract had been open land in the early 1900s.[102]

The Bruner tract reportedly was last logged about 1965. (No post-hurricane salvage logging took place on this tract.) The logging in the 1960s does not appear to have been extensive, since a low-altitude aerial photo published in 1974 does not show evidence of recent cutting.[103] Aerial photos from 1939, 1943, and 1951 also show no obvious evidence of recent cutting.[104] However, tree-crown size in a 1959 aerial photo appears to be smaller than that on the Beidler Tract to the north, suggesting that the tract may have been selectively logged in the 1950s or earlier.[105]

All told, about 57 percent of the park (floodplain and bluff) was logged between 1914 and 2003. The last cutting to occur in most parts of the park took place between 1969 and 1990, but additional cutting occurred in the Bates Fork tract as late as 2003. Since that time logged areas have continued to recover year by year—so much so that virtually all the floodplain west of the railroad has been designated wilderness under the Wilderness Act of 1964. But while logged portions of the park may be recovering, some areas are regenerating more quickly than others. For clear-cut areas in particular, it will be many years before the forest exhibits the age diversity and structural complexity characteristic of old-growth bottomland hardwoods.

Conclusion THE IMPACT OF HUMAN DISTURBANCE

*It's not a primeval forest—these trees were intensively managed. Probably less than
10 percent—at most 20 percent—existed prior to the 1860's.*

Robert Knoth, Beidler family consulting forester, to Luke Popovich, 1975

FORMING A CLEAR PICTURE of the impact of human disturbance on Congaree
National Park is made difficult by a lack of direct, concrete evidence about what
activities took place in the floodplain, and where. Very little archaeological data
has been unearthed from the lower Congaree valley, and few written accounts
survive of past land-disturbing activities in the immediate vicinity of the park.
The task is made all the more difficult by the fact that the floodplain is subject
to frequent windstorms and flooding, such that distinguishing "natural" from
human disturbance is not always easy to do. For now, any assessment of the
impacts of human disturbance on the park must be based in large part on infer-
ence and informed speculation. Uncertainty abounds, and yet enough evidence
is available to permit some initial conclusions regarding the impact of human
disturbance on the park's vegetative cover. Before doing so, however, it is important to consider the setting in which this disturbance occurs.[1]

The southern bottomland hardwood forest is a disturbance-mediated ecosystem, and all human disturbance that occurs here does so within a context of
ongoing biotic and abiotic disturbance. In this forest abiotic disturbance primarily takes the form of windfall gaps and periodic flooding. Storms ranging in
intensity from afternoon thunderstorms to tropical hurricanes blow down trees
in the forest, creating light gaps in the canopy. Whether the size of an individual
mature tree or considerably larger, these gaps allow direct sunlight to reach the
forest floor, releasing seedlings and filling the gaps with a dense layer of woody
and herbaceous vegetation. As the forest regenerates, intense competition ensues

for a place in the canopy. Catastrophic flooding can also produce light gaps in the canopy, but flooding more typically affects regeneration by suppressing species not adapted to extended hydroperiods. Flooding is more frequent and lasts longer on lower flats and depressions than on higher bottomland ridges, suppressing all but the most flood-tolerant species. Flooding also disturbs the landscape itself by depositing alluvium or scouring the ground surface. Impacts vary by position in the landscape and the severity of the flood.

Historically, wind and flooding disturbance were accompanied by disturbance from fire. In the days before habitat fragmentation and modern fire-suppression measures, fires burned frequently on vast upland terraces, edging into floodplains in those places where fuel was available. Most surface fires in floodplains tended to be mild and did not substantially alter species composition or forest structure. Canebrake fires, on the other hand, whether ignited by lightning or set by Indians, could be quite intense and cover large areas. Today, stand-replacing fires in southern bottomlands are rare.

Complementing these types of abiotic disturbance is disturbance from biotic forces, principally insect outbreaks and beaver activity. Insect outbreaks are uncommon in closed canopy forests, but impacts from beaver activity are increasingly noticeable as the numbers of this once nearly extirpated species continue to grow. Beavers kill trees for food and building materials, and their impoundments alter hydrology. Not infrequently, beaver impoundments convert hardwood stands to cypress-tupelo wetlands, or even open water.[2]

It is against this backdrop of natural disturbance that human disturbance has operated at Congaree for hundreds, indeed thousands, of years. Most types of natural disturbance are still at work in the park today, although the impacts of some, such as fire and flooding, have changed to a greater or lesser extent because of human modification of the landscape. As a result, the absence of large numbers of old trees in a particular area is not necessarily a sign that it has been "intensively managed," to use the words of the Beidlers' consulting forester. Natural disturbance alone is enough to ensure that old-growth parts of the floodplain consist mostly of small to medium-sized trees. As James Tanner noted of the Singer Tract in Louisiana, old-growth bottomland forests possess "a wide range of size classes . . . and many young trees as well as a number of large, old ones."[3]

Distinguishing Human from Non-Human Disturbance

Archaeological evidence and historic testimony make clear that both Indians and settlers of European and African descent worked the land of the lower Congaree Swamp. Each cleared land for crops, cut trees for fuel and building materials, and established dwelling sites in less flood-prone areas. Of course, the nature and intensity of human disturbance changed dramatically over time, especially in the years after settlement. Unlike the Indians, Europeans and their slaves cleared land for pastures, introduced large numbers of free-ranging cows and pigs, and in time engaged in extensive logging operations.

By the early twentieth century, the combined effects of farming, hunting, burning, grazing, and logging were evident over much of the floodplain, affecting the regeneration of vegetative cover in potentially significant ways. For example, as discussed in chapter 7, it is likely that the clearing and burning of floodplain fields caused some parts of the park to be dominated by stands of even-age sweet gum and others to have more pine than was typical prior to European settlement. Likewise, intensive logging of sloughs and guts may have favored the regeneration of water tupelo over bald cypress in some areas. But it is possible that human disturbance has produced other, more subtle changes to the park's vegetation, changes that have been obscured by the floodplain's natural-disturbance regime. A closer look at successional pathways in the park allows a better appreciation of how and to what extent human disturbance has affected the park's vegetative associations over time.

Old plats indicate that the dominant tree species in the park today are the same as those that were present at the time of first settlement. Then as now, the forest canopy appears to have been dominated by sweet gum and various species of shade-intolerant and intermediately intolerant oak.[4] But the means by which these species have maintained or even increased their numbers over the past two centuries remains somewhat uncertain.

In the years just after Hurricane Hugo, Robert Jones collected data in the park indicating that many large individuals of loblolly pine, sweet gum, cherrybark oak, and persimmon "had no conspecific saplings beneath their crowns, and thus, had no evidence of potential self-replacement." The large number of shade-intolerants in the overstory may therefore be the result of major, widespread disturbance of a type that has not been repeated in decades. Jones also suggested that "disturbances other than hurricanes (or more destructive than Hugo) may be needed to maintain large populations of some shade intolerant species."[5] Drawing on the latter idea, one might speculate that the prevalence of shade-intolerants in today's forest stems in significant part from the agricultural and logging activities of the eighteenth through early twentieth centuries—that is, from the activities discussed at length in this book. Indeed, as noted previously, John Cely's map of the park shows fairly extensive areas of loblolly pine and even-age sweet gum, telltale signs of past cultivation, historic logging, or both. A close look at Cely's map reveals that most of the identified stands of even-age sweet gum are concentrated in the western third of the Beidler Tract, which is higher and drier than the rest of the tract. This is precisely what one would expect if human disturbance were responsible for the widespread regeneration of early successional, shade-intolerant species. Not only is this area the best part of the park for cultivating crops, but it also tends to grow the largest specimens of the most commercially valuable hardwoods.

Nevertheless, there are certain rather obvious problems with attributing the present concentration of shade-intolerants in the park to human disturbance. Above all, sweet gum and other shade-intolerants are not restricted to young or even-age stands in the park, but also dominate in areas that bear no obvious imprint of human disturbance. Throughout the Beidler Tract, mature sweet gum and shade-intolerant oaks populate the canopy of species-rich, uneven-age stands. In addition, the impacts from past logging and clearing, although locally severe, are not uniform across the floodplain. Most logging appears to have taken place mostly near waterways, and most agricultural disturbance was concentrated in and near the levee zone and along floodplain ridges, especially in the western part of the park. Thus, except for areas dominated by loblolly pine, human disturbance is not sufficient in and of itself to account for the current concentration of shade-intolerants in the park.

An alternate possibility, following the suggestion of Jones, is that a hurricane more powerful than Hugo is responsible for the composition of today's forest. Research conducted in the park after Hurricane Hugo suggests that intense wind events are critical for maintaining the dominance of shade-intolerants in the canopy because it is these events that produce the level of disturbance necessary for such species to regenerate in large numbers. Yet the idea that the composition of today's forest is the result of a storm more powerful than Hugo has its own set of problems. Climate researcher Cary Mock believes that Hurricane Hugo was an unusual event, likely exhibiting the highest sustained wind speeds to have hit lower Richland in centuries. Moreover, a model developed by Tom Doyle and others suggests that Hugo was the strongest storm to have hit the park since at least the mid-1880s, the starting point of the model. Evidence is therefore lacking that a storm more powerful than Hugo has occurred during the lifetime of most of the trees in today's forest.[6]

A more likely scenario is that storms less powerful but more destructive than Hugo have struck the park over time. Both the hurricane of 1822 and the great Sea Islands Hurricane of 1893 were probably almost as strong as Hugo, and the latter was particularly destructive. The 1893 hurricane appears to have crossed the midlands quite slowly, uprooting hundreds of shade trees in Columbia over the course of eight to ten hours and bringing with it almost four and a half inches of rain. It is possible that the slow progress of this hurricane, combined with floods below the city reportedly ten feet deep, generated even more vegetative disturbance along the lower Congaree than did Hugo's higher wind speeds.[7]

Still, this one storm or ones earlier in the century can hardly be responsible for the composition of the bulk of today's forest. When Tom Doyle sampled tree rings in the floodplain just after the year 2000, he found that most of the hardwoods in his samples were less than one hundred years old, an indicator of "past logging activity and disturbance history." This finding is consistent with research conducted by Paul Harcombe and colleagues in a mature bottomland forest in the Neches Bottom Unit of Big Thicket National Preserve in southeast Texas. Harcombe's team found a turnover rate for local bottomland hardwoods on the order of seventy-seven-plus years. This rapid rate of turnover is due primarily to the perturbing effects of flooding in combination with the relatively short life spans of bottomland species, their high growth rates, and favorable conditions for rapid recruitment. Since these same factors obtain at Congaree, a similar turnover rate may apply. In any case, the rapid turnover implicit in Doyle's findings suggests that little, if any, of the hardwood tree cover at Congaree can be attributed to a storm more destructive than Hugo. In the long run, perpetuation of shade-intolerants in the forest canopy appears to depend less on isolated, catastrophic events than on repeated disturbances of moderate to major intensity. Even Hugo, strong as it was, had highly variable impacts across the floodplain. The most severe damage (for instance, snapped or uprooted trees) was usually rather localized, while minor to moderate damage (branch loss) was more widespread.[8]

Ultimately, then, it would appear that the concentration of shade-intolerants in the Beidler tract derives not from human disturbance or a single catastrophic disturbance event but from repeated disturbance on a scale less intense than Hurricane Hugo. The importance of frequent disturbance at Congaree is manifested by the large number of intermediately shade-tolerant trees in the floodplain, such as green ash and bottomland oaks. These species often need to be released from overstory competition multiple times before they can reach the canopy. In fact, without frequent disturbance much of the sweet gum–red oak forest at Congaree would succeed to elm-ash-sugarberry forest. The latter is a community of shade-tolerant to intermediately intolerant species capable of perpetuating itself for long periods if site conditions remain relatively stable.[9] It seems probable, therefore, that the park's present canopy stems in large part from a combination of frequent, small-scale wind disturbance and the occasional major event, such as a hurricane moving inland from the coast. Storms as powerful as Hugo may be rare, but hurricane force winds may strike the park every fifty to sixty years, augmenting the effects of high winds from more common but weaker storms.[10]

As for the lack of advance regeneration noted by Jones, this phenomenon does not necessarily signal a shift from shade-intolerant to shade-tolerant species. The absence of shade-intolerants in the seedling and sapling layers has been noted in a number of other southern floodplain forests. More to the point, it is not a recent development.[11] The U.S. Forest Service observed as long ago as 1906 that sweet gum reproduction was "extremely scanty" over the greater part of the southern bottomland hardwood forest. (This finding is particularly significant because it was based, in part, on a study of the Richland County holdings of the Santee River Cypress Lumber Company—holding that are now protected within Congaree National Park.) Yet despite this lack of historic advance regeneration, young shade-intolerants, especially sweet gum, are prevalent throughout the park today, even in its old-growth core. The apparent explanation for this is that shade-intolerants regenerate in pulses—pulses brought about by periodic but irregular abiotic disturbance. Considering that such pulses have clearly occurred at Congaree, the prevalence of shade-intolerants in the park appears attributable in large part to recurrent disturbance and, in particular, intense wind events.[12]

Another factor facilitating the persistence of shade-intolerants is floodplain hydrology. Flooding has long been thought to favor shade-intolerants because of a presumed tradeoff between flood tolerance and shade tolerance. Few species can withstand the double stresses of flooding and low light, so most shade-tolerant species are intolerant of flooding, generating instead on drier, less flood-prone sites. In contrast, many of the more shade-intolerant species, such as green ash and various species of oak, are able to survive wetter environments by growing quickly under an open canopy. In the field these relationships are not always so straightforward; some shade-tolerants, for example, are more tolerant of flooding when released from shade in canopy gaps.[13] Moreover, most floodplain species respond to flooding in complex, species-specific ways, allowing them to establish over a range of flooding conditions, up to some threshold beyond which they cannot survive.[14] On average, however, shade-tolerant species tend to establish on sites that are shaded and drier, whereas less shade-tolerant species establish on sites that are wetter and more open. Because wet conditions predominate in floodplain environments, most floodplain species have evolved to exhibit some combination of flood tolerance and shade intolerance, with individual species sorting themselves along a flooding and light gradient. Flooding therefore ranks in importance with wind disturbance as a driver of community dynamics in southern bottomland forests. At Congaree the two types of disturbance appear to work in concert to inhibit shade tolerant species from succeeding shade intolerant species in the canopy.[15]

Before leaving this discussion, it is important to highlight one of its principal underlying assumptions—the idea that repeated wind disturbance, interacting with floodplain geomorphic processes, hydrologic conditions, and the life-history characteristics of individual species, will set back the successional clock rather than move it forward. Judging from the early to mid-successional species that dominate the canopy at Congaree, this assumption would appear to be reasonably well founded. However, research conducted on post-Hugo vegetation plots in the park does not entirely bear it out. One study, noting an increase in the importance values of several shade-tolerant species, suggests that Hurricane Hugo may actually have served to accelerate succession by releasing shade-tolerant species in the understory. But the shift identified in the study was small, was concentrated in subcanopy species, and was masked by a large number of shade-intolerant and intermediately intolerant recruits that will grow to dominate the canopy in future years.[16] Furthermore, no significant shift to shade-tolerants was identified by Rebecca Sharitz and Bruce Allen in a subsequent, comprehensive analysis of data collected across vegetation plots in the park. They concluded that any shift to shade-tolerants that may be occurring is only happening in a very limited way and is not widespread. Taking the long view, it seems evident that intolerant and intermediately intolerant species have dominated the canopy at Congaree since before the time of first settlement and continue to do so today, even in areas of low human disturbance. No clear shift to shade-tolerant species appears to be occurring at the present time.[17]

Human Disturbance and Ecological Change

So where does this leave us? Has human disturbance had any lasting impact on the vegetative associations of the Beidler Tract, apart from the presence of even-age sweet gum, increased numbers of loblolly pine and, possibly, greater concentrations of water tupelo? Given that the overall species composition of the Congaree forest has remained more or less unchanged for the past three hundred years and more, the initial answer to this question might be a more or less confident "no." To date, scientific studies have failed to identify any significant shift in species composition in the floodplain due to human disturbance. As part of his doctoral research at Congaree, Bruce Allen compared the impacts of Hurricane Hugo on the Beidler Tract with those resulting from the selective logging and clear-cuts of the 1970s. His findings are striking. Apart from the existence of greater structural complexity in areas hit by Hugo, each of Allen's study sites displayed a basic similarity, regardless of type of disturbance. More specifically, species composition did not differ significantly among the sites that were logged and those that suffered hurricane damage. This is not to say that no differences existed. Rather, such differences as there were appeared to be small and not easily discerned. According to Allen, the species richness of the Congaree forest may mask any relationship between disturbance type and species composition at the community level.[18]

In a similar vein, Harcombe and colleagues failed to observe a strong correlation between disturbance and species composition in the mature forest of the Neches Bottom Unit of Big Thicket National Preserve. The team reported that "species composition and forest structure over large areas do not appear greatly different than in remnant old-growth forests from other parts of the Coastal Plain (e.g., Congaree Swamp National Monument, South Carolina)."

Any logging in this forest had not significantly affected species composition, and extensive natural disturbance had likewise resulted in only a low shift in species composition, with most recruits being of the dominant, shade-intolerant species. The team suggested that the compositional stability of this forest may stem not only from frequent disturbance, but also from the long dispersal distances between large, homogeneous river bottomlands and adjacent uplands, which are characterized by other, more mesic species. They concluded that the Big Thicket site, despite possibly having been logged at some point in the past, "probably [does] not differ greatly from old-growth forest in most ecologically meaningful parameters."[19]

Accordingly, even if it is assumed that logging was pervasive across the Beidler Tract at the turn of the twentieth century—an assumption that does not appear warranted given the clear weight of evidence—the actual changes wrought by such disturbance may be relatively limited, especially as compared to climatic factors or outright clearing. The latter inhibits the generation of heavy-seeded species such as oaks and favors light-seeded shade intolerants like sweet gum. As noted at various points throughout this book, the signs of such clearing are still evident in the Beidler Tract today. But even these impacts may dissipate over time.[20]

There is at least one respect, however, in which human disturbance appears to have brought about changes much different and more enduring than what natural disturbance alone would have produced. These changes stem not from clearing and logging but from sustained, long-term manipulation of the floodplain's fire regime. This manipulation has produced a fundamental alteration to the bottomland ecosystem as it existed in presettlement times.

Long before contact, lightning fires and fires set by Indians burned with some regularity through parts of the lower Congaree floodplain. Igniting in highly flammable brakes of giant cane, the fires burned with great intensity and spread quickly, generating enough heat to reach into adjacent forest dry enough to sustain fire. Cane fires served as both a disturbance element for the forest as a whole and a regenerative agent for the canebrakes themselves, allowing the cycle to continue. Anthropogenic fires continued after the arrival of Europeans but at much shorter intervals, primarily to improve forage for free-ranging livestock. Over the course of decades, a combination of intensive cattle grazing, land clearing, and frequent burning radically diminished the cane savannahs and pure brakes of giant cane that once figured so prominently in the landscape.

The final and critical blow came in the form of a *decrease* in disturbance. Although the customary practice of "setting the woods on fire" may have persisted in the floodplain through the early to mid–nineteenth century—and in places into the first part of the twentieth—it gradually began to die out over time. As it did, the moderate disturbance needed to maintain canebrakes occurred less and less often. Full shade gradually increased in the levee zone and along ridges, suppressing the growth of giant cane and leading to the more or less permanent replacement of canebrakes by forest.[21]

With its principal ignition source gone, fire has now been almost completely eliminated from the Congaree floodplain. Like other bottomland hardwood forests throughout the South, Congaree is now virtually fireproof.[22] The failure of loblolly pine to reproduce in large numbers at Congaree, even after a storm as strong as Hugo, provides strong circumstantial evidence that fire once played an important role in creating the conditions necessary for pine to perpetuate itself (that is, mineral soil substrate and reduced competition from hardwoods). With fire no longer playing its historic role and with clearing and logging prohibited in the park, the population of loblolly pine in the floodplain seems destined to decline significantly in the coming decades.

A more subtle factor than the absence of fire and one that only recently has begun to receive detailed study, is the impact of altered hydrology on vegetation patterns and successional pathways. With hydrology playing such an important role in floodplain succession, the integrity of the hydrologic regime is important for the perpetuation of early to mid-successional forests. Today, few rivers in the Southeast retain an intact hydrological regime; most have seen their hydrology disrupted by the proliferation of dams built for hydropower or flood control. On some rivers, dams have disrupted flooding patterns to such an extent that parts of the floodplain have effectively been rendered uplands, allowing flood-intolerant/shade-tolerant species to gain a foothold where they formerly could not compete. Examples of this shift can be found along the lower Roanoke River in eastern North Carolina, where dams have so altered natural hydrologic conditions that the shade-tolerant American beech (*Fagus grandifolia*) is starting to invade parts of the floodplain that once flooded on a regular basis but now rarely do.[23]

A reduction in peak flows has also been observed in the Congaree floodplain. At one time it was thought that dams on the Saluda and Broad Rivers might be responsible for this reduction, especially since reduced peaks became particularly noticeable after completion of the Saluda Dam in 1930. Now, however, it appears that lower flows have more to do with climate variability and an absence of large floods than with the operation of the Saluda and other dams. Recent studies indicate that dams have affected peak flows on the Congaree River far less than has been the case on many other major southern rivers, in large part because the Broad River, which supplies roughly two-thirds of the flow of the Congaree, is a relatively free-flowing stream. But even if the Saluda Dam has not had a major impact on the frequency and magnitude of peak flows, it appears to be having a potentially significant impact on the subsurface water levels of the surficial floodplain aquifer. Operation of the dam has lowered seasonal surficial groundwater levels in the first half of the year, when conditions should be wetter, and raised them in the second half of the year, when conditions normally are drier. These shifts may be having an effect on the root zone of the swamp and a corresponding impact on vegetative community structure.[24] The latter effects have yet to be studied in detail, but preliminary field evidence suggests that artificially high flows during the growing season are inhibiting the successful recruitment of bald cypress, a species that cannot survive prolonged inundation during the seedling stage of its life cycle.[25] On higher ground, the observed shift in seasonal surficial groundwater levels is likely having much greater impacts on mature, established trees than it is on seedlings and saplings.[26] The nature and extent of these impacts and their implications for long-term successional pathways will need to be the subject of future study.

A related concern is the possibility that vegetation communities and successional pathways in the park are being affected by elevated rates of sedimentation, a phenomenon that dates back to the mass wasting of Piedmont soils in the nineteenth and early twentieth centuries. Even though mass wasting was largely over by the late 1930s, elevated sediment loads continue to enter the park today as Piedmont streams cut their way down through sediments that accumulated decades ago. Elevated sediment loads can influence rates of floodplain accretion, affect floodplain morphology, and alter water levels and flow patterns through the floodplain. Rates of sedimentation can also affect the development of floodplain soils, with corresponding impacts on soil chemistry and structure. Preliminary studies have begun to explore the ways in which physical and chemical soil properties interact with water levels and light availability to influence early successional pathways in the park. These studies highlight the potential significance of historic and current sedimentation rates, and point up the need for more in-depth studies in this area.[27]

Finally, it is possible that the elimination of large predators and fluctuations in the local deer population have wrought material changes to the park's vegetation communities. Over thousands of years, herbivory from locally dense numbers of white-tailed deer probably affected to some extent the development of vegetation associations in the Congaree floodplain. Given that Indians actively managed the landscape to increase the deer population, it is likely that deer numbers became sufficiently high in the floodplain to limit the growth and distribution of certain preferred plant species. At the same time, impacts from herbivory may have been mitigated by periodic flooding, which would have forced deer up out of the floodplain and onto the low bluff, where they would have faced increased competition for food and greater exposure to predation by large carnivores and human hunters.[28] Whatever the precise effects of presettlement herbivory may have been, conditions changed dramatically with the arrival of European traders and settlers. Beginning with the colonial hide trade, Europeans engaged in the wholesale slaughter of deer throughout the state and in so doing may have released the park's vegetation associations from some of the impacts of deer herbivory. In the nineteenth and early twentieth centuries, deer herbivory decreased still further as subsistence and market hunting caused populations to plummet, especially in the straitened decades between the Civil War and the end of the Great Depression.[29] At the same time, grazing by semiferal cattle and rooting by nonnative hogs affected the regeneration of vegetation in ways never before seen in the floodplain. The long-term impact of these changes on local plant communities is not known but may have been substantial.

Today, cattle have not grazed the Beidler Tract in decades, but a prohibition on hunting in the tract since the early 1980s has caused the deer population to rebound. It is even possible that for a time deer numbers reached levels comparable to those of the presettlement era.[30] (The recent spread of coyotes into the park has likely driven deer numbers back down to an extent.) More ominously, the absence of hunting pressure and the availability of optimal habitat have caused the wild hog population, already present in comparatively small numbers in the early 1970s, to increase dramatically. Many of the wild hogs present in the park today are descendants of pigs introduced by hunters on adjacent lands. Others are descended from a hybrid strain of wild boar (Sus scrofa) and feral pig that the Cedar Creek Hunt Club introduced sometime in the early to mid-1960s. The interplay of deer browsing and wild hog rooting continues to this day, as does the spread of invasive exotic plants such as privet (Ligustrum spp.) and Japanese stilt grass (Microstegium vimineum). Propagules of exotics float into and through the park during flood events, finding ready substrates for germination in the soils disturbed by wild hogs. Taken together, these forces may be inducing long-term changes in the park's vegetative communities, the full extent of which may not be evident for many years to come.[31]

As noted at the outset of this book, Congaree National Park is often thought of as a window onto the distant past, where visitors can still experience one of the great American landscapes more or less as it existed before the arrival of Europeans. Years of study by teams of researchers have shown that this notion, while not entirely accurate, is closer to the truth than anyone today might reasonably have expected. Given the extent to which humans have altered bottomland forests throughout the Southeast, the fact that the park's hydrology is still comparatively intact and that so much of the Beidler Tract managed to escaped the ax is little short of miraculous.

But if Congaree is a window onto the past, it is one with a number of wavy and clouded panes. Today's forest may still contain the "the vast burden of mighty trees" observed by Mark Catesby in the bottomlands of the early 1700s, but in other important respects it surely differs from the forest known to the

Indians and first settlers. And these differences are not limited simply to those brought on by fire exclusion, altered hydrology, and disrupted predator-prey relationships. Like all natural systems, the Congaree forest has been constantly changing through time. Such change will continue and even accelerate in the future, due in large part to expanding upstream development, the spread of invasive nonnative species, and global climate change.[32]

For the National Park Service, change on this scale will present a difficult management challenge. Charged with preserving the park's resources unimpaired for future generations, the Park Service will have to determine what "unimpaired" means in the face of forces it cannot control and then strive to prevent impairment from occurring. Continued scientific research and a commitment to long-term monitoring will be essential if these efforts are to have any chance of success.

Appendix A SELECTED FLOODPLAIN CULTURAL FEATURES

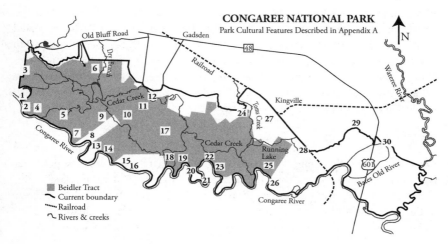

Map 11. Park Cultural Features Described in Appendix A.

1. Barber's Cutoff
2. Shad fishery
3. Northwest Boundary Dike
4. Adams Pond Dike and two smaller, nearby dikes
5. Old road, with bridge over Boggy Gut
6. Open area in floodplain
7. Adams' Quarter/Starling's Upper Stock Farm
8. Gillon's Retreat/Wm. Scott's Quarter/Braddy's Cattle Mound/Braddy's fields
9. Dwelling, road, and possible site of old cowpen
10. Cooner's Mound
11. Old field north of Cowpen Gut
12. Bates camp
13. Logging camp
14. Zeigler's Ferry/ Starling's Mound/Starling's Quarter/riverside fields
15. Round dike (Buyck's Ring)
16. Field on bank of old river channel
17. Road from northern bluff to Congaree River
18. Old Dead River Dike and cattle mound
19. "Negro cabin"
20. Spigener's fields
21. Cooner's Cut
22. Mazyck's Cut
23. Dr. Weston's Quarter
24. Antebellum dike
25. Huger's Ferry and approach road
26. Site of William R. Thomson's indigo vats/ John A. Mitchell's Quarter, with cattle mound
27. Silver Lake Stock Farm
28. Railroad line and causeway/sawmill
29. Sawmill
30. Joyner's Ferry/McCord's Ferry/Bates' Ferry

Map by Lynne Parker

The following entries describe selected areas within the park boundary (proceeding west to east) that were occupied or otherwise modified by human disturbance between the onset of settlement and the early twentieth century. Locations are shown by number in map 11. Except where noted, wills, plats, and maps referred to in the text below are on file at the South Carolina Department of Archives and History. For a more complete listing of the park's cultural features, with specific citations to sources, see Kinzer, *Annotated Checklist of Floodplain Cultural Features, Congaree National Park.*

1. Barber's Cutoff

In January 1819, Mordecai Barbour was retained to clear snags, logs, and other obstructions from the Congaree and Wateree Rivers. Later that year Barbour created a cutoff across a neck of the Congaree River at the location subsequently referred to as "Barber's Cutoff" or "Barber's Cut." The resulting oxbow lake is known today as Cooks Lake. A road from the northern bluff to the Congaree River was in existence prior to the creation of the cut. The road ended at a landing on the north bank of Cooks Lake, at that time the main channel of the Congaree River.

2. Shad fishery

This fishery was reached via a large point bar that extended out into the Congaree River. Joel Adams Sr. obtained access to the fishery when he acquired the point bar and adjacent land sometime prior to the creation of Barber's Cut. Adams later maintained that Barber's Cut had destroyed the fishery. The fishery tract likely had access to the northern bluff via a road or an oxcart path. A fishery was a valuable asset for a planter because fish could be an inexpensive source of protein to feed to slaves.

3. Northwest Boundary Dike

This dike was begun sometime prior to 1840 by James Adams Sr. His will, signed on July 11, 1840, stated that if his children "become unwilling to continue embanking the swamp lands as I have commenced, then, they may sell their interest in the same, giving to my brothers Joel [Jr.] and Robert Adams, the refusal thereof." It appears that the children chose not to complete the dike system. A 1909 map by R. C. Cantwell entitled *Plat of the Swamp Lands and Timber Holdings of the Santee River Cypress Lumber Company Lying on the Northern Side of the Congaree River* (see bibliography) shows the dike as extending approximately 3,350 feet along the northwest boundary of the Beidler Tract, without any indications of washouts or gaps. The plat also depicts an "old ditch" bounding the lower portion of the dike on the west. The dike's upper portion is depicted as extending north of the Beidler Tract for an additional 1,750 feet, making the entire dike approximately fifty-one hundred feet long.

4. Adams Pond Dike (also known as Southwest Boundary Dike)
and two smaller, nearby dikes

The Adams Pond Dike is often referred to as the Southwest Boundary Dike. It is a linear, double-ridged feature constructed on the north bank of Adams Pond. Its double-ridge construction is unique in the park. NPS ranger Guy Taylor suggested that this dike closely resembles rice canals seen near Charleston. He speculated that it may have been built as a canal to irrigate rice. Two nearby dikes are located on the banks of guts within the former Adams swamp plantation. Both are strictly linear in configuration and may be unfinished.

5. Old road, with bridge over Boggy Gut
This road and bridge appear on a plat of a thirty-five-acre tract prepared in 1790 for Joel Adams Sr. The plat shows the road bordering the tract on the south side. The road deviates slightly from an "old path" at the point where it crosses Boggy Gut. The road may therefore have followed the track of an older route through the swamp for part of its length. The precise location of the road is not known, but it was somewhere on the Joel Adams Sr. land shown in map 6.

6. Open area in floodplain
Aerial photos from 1939 show a large open area (or early successional forest) in the floodplain just below the northern bluff, a short distance east of where the elevated boardwalk now runs. Charcoal in the soil indicates that this area was kept open, at least in part, by fire. The area also shows clear evidence of historic cultivation and logging, including fence-row pines, a drainage ditch, and scattered stumps. Most of the pines in this area seeded in during the 1930s.

7. Adams' Quarter/Starling's Upper Stock Farm
In Marmaduke Coate's *Survey of Richland District* (1820), Adams' Quarter is shown on the north bank of the Congaree River, just upstream from the mouth of Big Beaver Creek (figure 7). It consists of two parallel rows of dots along the river, denoting slave houses. Adams' Quarter was owned by Joel Adams Sr.

In later years the site of Adams' Quarter was known as Starling's Upper Stock Farm. Captain Wesley D. Starling owned this cattle operation between 1885 and 1889. The designation "upper stock farm" was presumably intended to distinguish this property from Starling's other property a short distance downstream, known as "Starling's Quarter" (see entry 14 below).

8. Gillon's Retreat/ Wm. Scott's Quarter /Braddy's
   Cattle Mound/Braddy's fields
Commodore Alexander Gillon acquired his plantation "Gillon's Retreat" before the Revolutionary War. The bulk of this large plantation lay south of the river across from the park, but Gillon also owned approximately 586 acres on the north bank. The northern tracts consisted of the modern-day Brady tract (Tract 101-42, 400 acres) as well as two smaller tracts to the west. Gillon sold the northern tracts to Francis Goodwyn in 1777.

By 1806, ownership of Tract 101-42 was split between William Scott Jr. (see appendix B) and his brother Samuel. William survived Samuel and appears to have owned the entire tract by the time of his death around 1822. Marmaduke Coate's *Survey of Richland District* (1820) shows "Wm. Scott's Quarter" lying in Tract 101-42, a short distance downstream from "Adams' Quarter" (figure 7). As with Adams'

Quarter, Coate shows "Wm. Scott's Quarter" as comprising two parallel rows of small structures along the river.

In the twentieth century Tract 101-42 was owned by various members of the Brady (formerly Braddy) family. Braddy's Cattle Mound is located near the river and is generally assumed to have been constructed in the early 1900s. Braddy's fields are clearly visible in an aerial photo from 1939 and date, in one form or another, to at least 1884. They may be much older. An 1884 map of the Congaree River by the U.S. Army Corps of Engineers (see bibliography) shows the fields being served by a cluster of structures on the river's north bank. When acquired by NPS in 2001, the fields covered about sixty-five acres along the riverbank. The fields were cultivated as late as 1999 but are now reverting to tree cover.

9. Dwelling, road, and possible site of old cowpen
A plat of a hundred-acre tract certified in 1799 for Isaac Tucker shows a house and a road—more likely a path—in the floodplain near Frenchman's Gut. The house was probably a slave dwelling, built to serve an agricultural field or cowpen. Today this area is an even-aged stand of old-growth sweet gum. A number of old-growth pine trees grew in this area until blown down by a wind storm in 2000. (Regarding Frenchman's Gut, see "John Frentz" in appendix B.)

10. Cooner's Mound
Local tradition holds that this mound was built around 1840. However, the rectangular shape of the mound may indicate that it is actually an old Indian mound that was adapted and enlarged for use as a cattle mound. The name probably derives from Frederick Cooner, who owned the site of the mound in 1851. Cooner also owned land across the river from the park in present-day Calhoun County (see entry 21 below).

11. Old field north of Cowpen Gut
This large field may have been in existence by 1789. A plat of the Joseph Martin tract prepared between 1789 and 1802 (see map 6 and chapter 2, note 60) shows the field just to the north of a waterway called "Cowpen Gut," indicating that the field was likely a cowpen. The field was probably located east of the Kingsnake Trail and north of Big Snake Slough (see map 3 for location of trail and slough).

12. Bates camp
The Bates camp was presumably a logging camp run by John M. Bates, a logging contractor and eventual employee of the Santee River Cypress Lumber Company. According to Francis Dawson, who sold the underlying property to the NPS, Santee once had a logging camp on the tract.

13. Logging camp
This camp was operated by the Santee River Cypress Lumber Company in the early 1900s. It is the only logging camp specifically identified as such in Cantwell's 1909 plat of Santee's holdings in lower Richland. Cantwell depicts the camp using a total

of seven small squares clustered near the river. Five of these squares are the same size and may be intended to indicate living quarters.

14. Zeigler's Ferry/Starling's Mound/Starling's Quarter/riverside fields

Daniel Zeigler operated a private ferry connecting his land south of the river to his extensive holdings on the north bank (map 7). The ferry was in operation by 1850. In the mid-1870s, the Court of Common Pleas of Orangeburg County marshaled the assets of the estate of Daniel Zeigler and set aside deeds whereby Zeigler had attempted to convey equal portions of his remaining land north of the river to members of his family. In 1879 the State of South Carolina sold six hundred acres of this same area to W. D. Starling. Known as "Starling's Quarter," this area formed the bulk of what would later become Parcel 8 of the Beidler Tract.

Starling was seriously affected by the flood of May 1886, with losses in stock and grain crops estimated at $3,000. Some of these losses were sustained at Starling's Quarter, including the area around Starling's Mound. The latter was an old Indian mound that later saw use as a cattle mound. (Almost all of the mound has now eroded into the river.) Other losses may have been incurred at Starling's Upper Stock Farm (see entry 7 above).

Beidler Tract Parcel 8 included agricultural fields along the river well into the twentieth century. It is possible, but not established, that these fields date back to the time of Starlings' Quarter or before. One big field in this area was substantial, on the order of seventy-five acres. Aerial photos from the early 1940s show a series of four fields along the riverbank, one of which may be a remnant of the big field.

15. Round dike (Buyck's Ring)

This circular levee-like structure measures approximately 440 feet in circumference, with an interior diameter of 110 feet. The structure is approximately 4 to 5 feet high and 6 to 8 feet wide at the top. Its age is not known. Buyck family tradition holds that the ring was built at the direction of Augustine Buyck (see appendix B) to protect his cattle from floods. It is possible that Buyck leased the ring property from its long-time owner, Charles Cotesworth Pinckney. Buyck's home plantation (the former "Gillon's Retreat") was located south of the river and upstream from Pinckney's plantation.

16. Field on bank of old river channel

At some point in the nineteenth century, Pinckney's Creek (figure 7) became the main channel of the Congaree River. By late in the century, if not before, a large field snaked along the east bank of the old river channel. The field appears to have expanded considerably between the 1880s and the early 1900s. By 1903 a series of six small structures were present near the old river channel.

17. Road from northern bluff to Congaree River

This road dates to the late 1780s or earlier. The road entered the Joseph Martin tract (map 6) from the west along the northern bluff line. It continued some distance east along the bluff to "Martin's Old House," at which point it descended into the floodplain and immediately crossed a bridge over Cedar Creek. Proceeding in a southerly direction, the road traveled a little over half a mile before entering a large old field north of Cowpen Gut (see entry 11 above). Traversing the field, the road turned to the southeast, crossed a bridge over Cowpen Gut and eventually entered the property of an adjoining landowner.

The plat of the Joseph Martin tract does not show the route of the road after it leaves the Martin tract but merely refers to it as the "Road to Mouth of Running Gut." In the late eighteenth century, the mouth of Running Gut emptied into the Congaree River at what is today Old Dead River (maps 1, 6). The road thus appears to have linked the northern bluff and a landing on the river.

18. Old Dead River Dike and cattle mound

This old dike is a three-sided structure that extends approximately seventy-five hundred feet along and near the banks of Horsepen Gut, Old Dead River, and the main channel of the Congaree River (map 6). Inside the dike is the Old Dead River Cattle Mound.

The dike probably dates from the antebellum period, even though it does not appear on an 1861 plat prepared for Alfred M. Hunt, or on a subsequent plat completed around 1870 for the South Carolina Land Commission.[1] The Land Commission plat shows what appears to be about one hundred acres of cleared land along the river, so it is possible that the dike system already existed at that time but was simply omitted by the surveyor. It seems doubtful that such a large and costly project would have been initiated after the war.

The commission divided the tract into twenty-one lots, three of which were purchased by African American buyers. Lot 15 was sold to Jerry Williams in November 1870. That same month, the commission sold lots 16 and 17 to Aesop Goodson (1826–ca. 1914), an African American state legislator from Gadsden. (Neither individual completed payment.) These three lots, which together included the cleared land depicted in the Land Commission plat, totaled approximately 123 acres. It is not known whether Williams or Goodson ever occupied and farmed their lots in the Hunt tract. There is no record in the Richland County Register of Deeds that either man ever acquired title to property in the park.

Harry Hampton contended in his book *Woods and Waters and Some Asides* that the dike later enclosed the "Jim Williams Old Field." If Hampton is correct, then at least part of the area within the Old Dead River Dike may have been farmed by James B. Williams, a local landowner who resided in Gadsden in the late nineteenth and early twentieth centuries. Williams may have leased this land, as there is no record of him ever having owned it. However, he did own the adjacent tract to the east—that is, Beidler Tract Parcel 14—which he acquired with John G. Williams in 1882.

19. "Negro cabin"

The 1861 plat prepared for Alfred M. Hunt (see entry 18 above) shows a "Negro Cabin" on the eastern edge of Beidler Tract Parcel 13, near the confluence of a gut and the Congaree River. This cabin would appear to have been well situated for tending fields within the Old Dead River Dike.

20. Spigener's fields

Two fields are shown on a plat of land regranted to Paul Spigener in 1839 (see figure 8). The smaller of the two fields fronted on the river at the tract's south end. Spigener sold this area (NPS Tract 101-35) around 1860 (?), keeping the remainder of the regrant (Beidler Tract Parcel 14) for himself.

21. Cooner's Cut

This cutoff, the subject of a court case heard by the South Carolina Court of Appeals in Law, was built by Frederick Cooner on land owned by Paul Spigener. (See *Spigener v. Cooner*, 42 S.C.L. [8 Rich.] 301 [1855].) The cutoff appears to have been located at the southern end of Beidler Tract Parcel 14 or somewhere on Tract 101-35, but this cannot be confirmed.

During the middle of the nineteenth century, the Congaree River flowed in two channels on Spigener's property. According to the court case, at some point prior to 1855 Cooner paid Paul Spigener for the privilege of opening "a ditch from the old to the new river through a point of [Spigener's] land." When Cooner opened the ditch, the "new river running through [Spigener's] land forced its way through the cut, and left the old bed generally dry." The purpose of constructing the cutoff was to "preserve [Cooner's] dam" on the Orangeburgh side of the river.

22. Mazyck's Cut

Mazyck's Cut has also been called Mazyck's Break or Mazyck's Breakover. The "cut" is an outfall from Cedar Creek to the Congaree River at the point where the creek makes its closest southerly approach to the river's north bank (before emptying into the river farther downstream). The cut does not have a constructed appearance but winds and twists like a natural stream, which may testify to its age. The cut may have been made by Peter Mazyck or another member of the Mazyck family in the 1770s or 1780s.

The cut does not appear in surviving nineteenth-century maps of the swamp. If the latter maps are accurate, Mazyck's Cut may actually be a twentieth-century feature. One possibility is that the cut was created by the Santee River Cypress Lumber Company to shorten the distance for floating logs to the river. Another possibility is that Santee (or someone else) reopened a cut originally made many years before. Locals reportedly used generous supplies of dynamite to open (or at least maintain) the cut as late as the 1950s.

23. Dr. Weston's Quarter

An 1884 map of the Congaree River by the U.S. Army Corps of Engineers (see bibliography) shows "Dr. Weston's Quarter" as including four small structures on the north bank of the river a short distance downstream from Mazyck's Cut. The structures stand next to a field that may have been of fairly substantial size. While the boundaries of the field are not shown, the manner in which the field is indicated in the survey suggests that it may have extended some distance back from the river. The occupied portion of "Dr. Weston's Quarter" was part of a much larger tract (over thirty-three hundred acres) owned by Dr. William Weston IV and his wife after 1862.

24. Antebellum dike

The eastern edge of this "old dam" is in the Beidler Tract; the rest is on land once part of Stoney Hill Plantation. Stoney Hill was owned by Governor James Hopkins Adams before the Civil War. It is not known who built the dike or when. Possible builders include David Myers, who owned the underlying property in the 1820s, and Governor Adams, who acquired the property in the early 1830s. The dike originally tied into the northern bluff on either end and enclosed about twenty-five acres.

25. Huger's Ferry and approach road

Isaac Huger's ferry was located approximately six river miles upstream from the site of McCord's Ferry, where a ferry had operated since the 1750s (see entry 30 below). After the charter to McCord's Ferry lapsed during the Revolution, citizens petitioned the legislature to establish a public ferry upriver at Huger's plantation. The General Assembly authorized Huger's Ferry on March 22, 1786. The ferry and much of the northern approach road were located on what later became Beidler Tract Parcel 19. A major purpose of the ferry was to facilitate the transportation of produce and livestock to the coast, as well as to places such as Charlotte and Camden.

The act authorizing the ferry charged three commissioners with constructing a public road to Huger's Ferry along a route that passed, "through part of Edward Lightwood's land, to the said ferry . . . at Isaac Huger's plantation" (map 6). (The property of Edward Lightwood referred to in the statute is separate from and to the east of the Lightwood's Old Field tract on Cedar Creek.) In 1788 the General Assembly enacted legislation prohibiting the keeping of any private ferry within seven miles of Huger's Ferry. The stated purpose of this law was to protect General Huger, who had "with great labour and expence erected a causeway and sundry bridges over the swamp, and opened all the roads leading to the . . . ferry, without any assistance." Three pair of earthen bridge abutments survive in the swamp along the northern approach road. The abutments vary in size from five to ten feet high and ten to fifteen feet wide. One set of ramps is for a bridge over Running Lake.

Notwithstanding the new public ferry at Huger's plantation, citizens petitioned the legislature in 1787, 1789, and 1791 to reestablish a public ferry at the old McCord's Ferry site. The General Assembly rechartered McCord's Ferry in December 1792. Huger's Ferry still appears to have been in operation in 1797, but it probably ceased to operate soon thereafter. The charter for the ferry expired in 1800.

26. Site of William R. Thomson's indigo vats/John A. Mitchell's Quarter, with cattle mound

A set of "William R. Thomson's Indigo Vattes" is noted on a map of Huger's Landing and vicinity prepared for the General Assembly around 1791. The vats are shown on the north bank of the Congaree River just downstream from Beidler Tract Parcel 19. Thomson was the son of Colonel William Thomson.

In the late nineteenth century, John A. Mitchell owned about seven hundred acres in this same location. The 1884 Corps of Engineers' map (see entry 23 above) identifies "J. A. Mitchell's Quarter" as being on the riverbank, a half mile downstream from the Beidler Tract. The quarter is depicted with four small squares along the river, denoting multiple structures. A field of unknown size is indicated northeast of the structures. The quarter also included a cattle mound.

John A. Mitchell and his mother, Eliza, conveyed this property to John A. Peterkin on April 7, 1884. As part of the conveyance, Mitchell reserved for life the right to pasture cattle and stock in the swamp and to cultivate as much of the tract as he wished, so long as he kept the cultivated areas under a durable fence.

27. Silver Lake Stock Farm
The Silver Lake Stock Farm was the name given to an eleven-hundred-acre tract assembled by Benjamin A. Rawls in the 1880s. The stock farm included NPS Tract 101-45, part of Tract 101-44, and other land to the north and east.

28. Railroad line and causeway/sawmill
Completed in 1842, the rail line between Branchville and Columbia is the second oldest rail line in South Carolina and one of the oldest in the country. The earthen embankment north of the Congaree River trestle dates to 1840–41. When first built, the embankment was lower than it is today. The bridge over the river was rebuilt at least three times before the Civil War.

Troops of Major General William T. Sherman burned the bridge in February 1865, and it was not until 1867 that a permanent replacement was finally constructed. At some point, probably because of a shift in the low-water channel of the river, the draw of this bridge appears to have become unusable, rendering the bridge an impediment to navigation for a number of years. Between 1889 and 1891, the railroad raised the embankment two to three feet and rebuilt the trestle. Pressure by the state and shipping interests prompted the railroad to install a new draw at this same time.

In the 1890s the Fort Motte Lumber and Shingle Company operated a saw and shingle mill in the floodplain, on or near the rail line.

29. Sawmill
The firm of McMaster, Monteith and Roath logged bald cypress in the eastern end of Congaree Swamp in 1872 and 1873. The firm built its sawmill on a four-hundred-acre tract located a short distance west of present-day U.S. Highway 601. The mill was probably located on the uplands above Singleton Creek, outside the park boundary.

30. Joyner's Ferry/McCord's Ferry/Bates' Ferry
Joyner's Ferry, which dates from the late 1740s, was a private ferry located on the Congaree River at the northern end of Buckhead Neck. It apparently succeeded a private ferry operated earlier in the decade by Miles Jackson. The precise location of Joyner's Ferry is not known, but it appears to have been located near where U.S.

Highway 601 crosses the northern arm of Bates Old River. The ferry was located along an ancient Indian travel route. In the sixteenth century, Spanish explorer Juan Pardo used this route twice on expeditions north from the coast.

Joyner's Ferry was discontinued in the 1750s. By late 1756 John McCord was operating a private ferry on the adjacent tract to the east. In 1766 the provincial government authorized McCord to operate a public ferry from the north side of the river to Buckhead Neck.

Accounts of the Revolution describe combatants on both sides using McCord's Ferry to cross the Congaree River. It is reported that on one of these crossings the British lieutenant colonel Banastre Tarleton burned the house of John McCord's widow, Sophianisba, in retaliation for her assistance to the patriot cause. During the siege of Fort Motte, American soldiers camped near the landing at McCord's Ferry. Some were stationed at the landing itself to protect the troops laying siege to the fort. After the capture of the fort in May 1781, Major General Nathanael Greene crossed south over the river at McCord's Ferry to confer with Francis Marion and Henry "Light-Horse Harry" Lee and issue orders.

The charter to McCord's Ferry lapsed during the course of the war. The charter was not reissued until 1792, when it was vested in David McCord. McCord was required to maintain a bridge over a big "lake" that had formed at the southern end of Buckhead Neck, in the area that would eventually become the river's new main channel. Thereafter, two ferries operated at McCord's Ferry, one over the lake to the south and the other over the river to the north. The great flood of August 1852 cut off Buckhead Neck once and for all, creating a new main channel on the south and leaving behind a large oxbow lake. It is not known how the flood affected ferry operations in succeeding years.

By early 1865 a ferry over the new main channel of the Congaree River was known as "Bates' Ferry." On February 15, 1865, Union troops marching north from Orangeburg skirmished with Confederate troops at Bates' Ferry as part of an effort to create a diversion from Sherman's main attack on Columbia.

By 1907 service at Bates' Ferry had long since been discontinued. Ferry service was finally reinstituted on the main river channel in 1910, owing largely to the efforts of John M. Bates. To facilitate the reopening of the ferry, Bates constructed a wood bridge over Bates Old River at his own expense. He also donated a right of way on Buckhead Island to be used for the approach road to the ferry. The ferry operated until 1923, when a toll bridge finally opened to the public. In 1949 the bridge was replaced by a new structure, two miles downstream, on the realigned highway to St. Matthews (U.S. Highway 601).

Appendix B BIOGRAPHICAL SKETCHES

Individuals in bold below have separate entries in this appendix.

Joel Adams Sr. (1750–1830) moved to lower Richland County from Virginia about 1768, at around the age of eighteen. He soon courted and married Grace Weston, daughter of **William Weston I**. Ambitious and hardworking, Adams began his life in lower Richland managing the lands of others, while also planting his own lands and slowly building up a huge estate. During the course of his life, he reportedly acquired some twenty-five thousand acres north of the Congaree River, including a substantial part of the future Congaree National Park. His first known acquisition in the park, completed by September 1790, consisted of over four hundred acres on Boggy Gut formerly owned by **Wade Hampton I**. By 1799 he also owned land on the river west of Tract 101-42, identified in subsequent maps as "Adams' Quarter." At his death in 1830 Adams still owned over four thousand acres in the park.

James Adams Sr. (1776–ca. 1840), Joel Adams Jr. (1784–1859), and Robert Adams (1793–1850) were sons of **Joel Adams Sr**. They each owned substantial plantations north of the park. In 1839 the state formally conveyed 5,188 acres of Congaree bottomland and adjacent uplands to the three brothers, all or most of which had been previously acquired by their father. The floodplain part of this regrant, known as the "swamp plantation," was located in the western end of the park and included the area along the river known as "Adams' Quarter" (figure 7). The upland portion of the regrant was referred to as the "bluff plantation." Although each brother held an undivided one-third interest in the regranted tract, James managed the swamp plantation, while Robert worked the bluff. James's home place was Pea Ridge Plantation, which consisted of 1,111 acres of swampland near the middle of the Beidler Tract plus adjacent uplands to the north. The upland portion of Pea Ridge bordered the Weston family's Gum Tree Plantation on the east. James probably obtained the initial acreage at Pea Ridge from his father in the first part of the nineteenth century. He appears to have conveyed the bulk of Pea Ridge to his son **James U. Adams** sometime prior to 1840.

James U. Adams (1812–1871), was a son of **James Adams Sr**. He owned 309 slaves in 1860, making him the second largest slaveholder (out of around 600) in Richland District. At the outbreak of the war he either owned or had an undivided interest in over five thousand acres in the Beidler Tract. Of these lands, he owned Pea Ridge Plantation outright and held an undivided one-sixth interest in the Adams swamp and bluff plantations, which had been regranted to his father and uncles in 1839. Responsibility for managing the swamp plantation apparently fell to him after his father's death around 1840. Adams was an ardent secessionist before the war. Active in politics, he was an intimate and advisor to his cousin James Hopkins Adams (governor of South Carolina, 1854–1856). He himself served in the South Carolina House of Representatives in 1864. Besides a large house in Columbia, he maintained a home in Gadsden at the former Stage-coach Inn, which he enlarged and remodeled with his wife, Sarah "Sallie" H. Adams.

James Hopkins Adams (1812–1861) served as governor of South Carolina from December 1854 to December 1856. While governor, he ignited controversy by endorsing resumption of the transatlantic slave trade. In 1857 his name was put forward by friends as a candidate for the U.S. Senate, but he lost decisively to James Henry Hammond, who went on to deliver the famous "Cotton is King" speech on the Senate floor. In 1858 he lost another senate run, this time to James Chesnut Jr., who was considered a more moderate figure. Adams was a signatory to the South Carolina Ordinance of Secession in December 1860 and one of three commissioners sent to Washington to negotiate the transfer of federal property to the state. At the time of his death in 1861 he owned a large amount of improved and unimproved land in lower Richland District, including almost 240 acres within the present park boundary. This tract (Tract 101-33) was part of the much larger Stoney Hill Plantation. His main plantation and residence was Live Oak Plantation, located where the McEntire Joint National Guard Base now stands.

John Bates (1787–1866) owned fifty-eight slaves in 1850 and approximately twenty-three hundred acres of land, nine hundred of which were improved. A significant portion of Bates's land was located east of the railroad and north of the park boundary. Within the park, Bates appears to have owned two tracts fronting on the north arm of Bates Old River. Bates may have acquired the easternmost of these two tracts from Thomas Seay in the 1830s or 1840s. The two Bates tracts were separated by a large tract owned by the Adams family. By the end of the Civil War, if not considerably earlier, Bates also appears to have owned some part of Buckhead Island.

John M. Bates (1871–1924), the son of Joseph Bates and grandson of John Bates, was intimately involved in all aspects of commercial life in lower Richland. For much of his life he lived in Gadsden but later moved to his late father's plantation near the now defunct settlement of Wateree. In the 1890s he was a logging contractor in the Congaree Swamp. The following decade he was employed directly by the Santee River Cypress Lumber Company. Later he was involved in the sale of automobiles. Public spirited, Bates played a major role in reestablishing a ferry and later a toll-bridge over the southern reach of the Congaree River. The bridge, located about two miles upstream from the current U.S. 601 bridge, opened in 1923.

Francis Beidler I (1854–1924), a Chicago lumber wholesaler, served as vice president and treasurer and later president of the Santee River Cypress Lumber Company. In addition to managing Santee, Beidler participated in various other business ventures. In 1893 he established and served as president of the lumber firm of Francis Beidler and Company of Chicago, successor to the South Branch Lumber Company. He also served as president of Beidler and Robinson Lumber Company (operator of lumber yards in North Dakota); vice-president of the Eastern Lumber Company of Tonawanda, New York; president of the Lumbermen's Mutual Insurance Company of Chicago; and president of the Junction Mining Company of Springfield, Illinois.

William Bull Jr. (1710–1791) served as lieutenant governor of the colony of South Carolina from 1759 until 1775. During this time he was appointed acting royal governor five times, serving a total of eight years. A major planter and landowner, Bull advocated expansion of the colony into the backcountry. He lived at Ashley Hall plantation on the Ashley River but had major plantations on St. Helena Island and the Congaree River. He also owned a number of other properties, including a large tract on the Satilla River in Georgia. Loyal to the Crown, Bull was forced out of politics and eventually into exile. He died in London, unsuccessful in his efforts to return to South Carolina, where he had been born.

Bull began acquiring the land for his Congaree plantation in the early 1770s or perhaps earlier. The plantation consisted of about 1,750 acres of upland and swamp that spanned the river just below the plantation of **Isaac Huger**. It was managed by Bull's neighbor, **William Thomson**, who oversaw the cultivation of indigo and corn on the property. More than 400 acres were in cultivation in 1780. One hundred years later the high southern bluff overlooking the river was still known as "Bulls Hill." Today Bulls Hill is part of the Congaree Bluffs Heritage Preserve owned by the South Carolina Department of Natural Resources.

Augustine Buyck (1761–1824) was the son of Pieter Buyck of Ghent (1712–1803). The elder Buyck loaned money to Commodore **Alexander Gillon** during the Revolutionary War in connection with the lease of the frigate *South Carolina*. When Gillon failed to repay the loan, Pieter sent Augustine to South Carolina to obtain payment. Pieter followed himself a year later when Augustine failed to collect. It was only after Gillon's death in 1794 that Augustine Buyck finally received compensation in the form of "Gillon's Retreat," Gillon's plantation on the south bank of the Congaree River.

David D. Buyck (1861–1920), grandson of **Augustine Buyck**, lived for much of his life as a prominent citizen of St. Matthews, South Carolina. As a young man he operated a mercantile store in Fort Motte. In 1895 his wife Elizabeth B. Wise Buyck acquired a 998-acre tract that would become Beidler Tract Parcel 13. For a number of years Mr. Buyck operated a farm south of the Congaree River and grazed cattle on the swamp tract to the north. In 1918 he sold the swamp tract to the Santee River

Cypress Lumber Company but reserved the exclusive right to graze stock on the conveyed lands during his life and the life of his children.

Russell Buyck (1897–1974) and W. Peter Buyck Sr. (1905–1984), sons of **David D. Buyck** and Elizabeth B. Wise Buyck, jointly operated the Buyck Cotton Company for a time. In addition to being a cotton broker, Peter Buyck Sr. was also a member of the South Carolina Bar and raised polo ponies. Russell Buyck and W. Peter Buyck Sr. together acquired Tract 101-36 in 1936 and Tract 101-35 in 1942. In 1960 they split the two tracts between them, with Russell Buyck getting Tract 101-36.

William L. Buyck (1854–1930) was an older brother of **David D. Buyck**. He acquired Parcels 8 and 9 of the Beidler Tract in 1893, together with Tract 101-41 and the northern part of Tract 101-37. He grew swamp hay on part of his land and ran cattle on both sides of the river.

Joy Buyck Carpenter (1932–2015), daughter of **Russell Buyck** and Celia Kennerly Buyck, sold her interest in Tract 101-36 to the National Park Service in 1996.

Frederick Cooner (b. ca. 1804) owned the site of Cooner's Mound inside the park. A resident of Orangeburg District, he also owned a 3,135-acre tract on the south side of the Congaree River lying on both sides of High Hill Creek (now known as Bates Mill Creek). This tract lay opposite a tract on the north side of the river acquired by **Paul Spigener** in 1839. The census of 1850 lists twelve hundred of Cooner's thirty-two hundred acres as improved. Cooner owned 103 slaves in 1850, the fourth largest number of slaves in the area north of the Belleville Road.

Barnard Elliott (1740–1778), a lowcountry rice planter, served on the Royal Council prior to the Revolution. He married his second wife, Susannah Smith Elliott, in 1775. Susannah Smith had been orphaned at an early age and was raised by her aunt, **Rebecca Brewton Motte**. Elliott acquired a large tract in the park adjacent to land owned by Miles Brewton and not far from other lands owned by Jacob Motte Jr. (Miles Brewton and Jacob Motte Jr. were Rebecca Motte's brother and husband, respectively). The Elliott tract was said to contain between nine hundred and one thousand acres and to be located on the Congaree River about three miles from Colonel **William Thomson**.

Elliott resigned from the Royal Council on May 10, 1775. In June he was elected captain in Colonel William Moultrie's 2nd South Carolina Regiment (Infantry). He was promoted to lieutenant colonel of the 4th South Carolina Regiment (Artillery) in 1776 and given command of Fort Johnson in Charleston Harbor in 1777.

Benjamin Farrar (1740–1790), doctor, planter (?), and real estate speculator, originally settled in South Carolina in 1755. In August 1764 he was said to be living in St. Johns Parish, Berkeley County. Later he lived in Saxe-Gotha Township. He married a widow of property and accumulated estates on the Congaree River. His second marriage, in 1771, was to Elizabeth Gaillard, daughter of Tacitus Gaillard. In 1779 he settled in Point Coupee, Louisiana. He died in Philadelphia.

B. F. Ferguson (1839–1905) grew up in Columbia, Pennsylvania, working at his father's lumber yard. Mustered out of the Union army in 1865, he later set up a planing mill on Chicago's south side, working with partner Philip L. Auten until the facility was destroyed by the Great Chicago Fire of 1871. He then joined forces with Jacob Beidler, who named him vice president and treasurer of the newly organized South Branch Lumber Company in 1873. Ferguson became vice president of the Eastern Lumber Company of Tonawanda, New York, in 1886, and by February 1890 he had been named president of the newly formed Santee River Cypress Lumber Company. He partly disengaged from his business responsibilities beginning around 1893–95 and spent a large portion of his time traveling at home and abroad. A childless widower, he left almost all of his estate in trust to the Art Institute of Chicago. His will directed that the income from a $1 million corpus be used to fund statuary and monuments for public spaces in Chicago.

William H. Fishburne Jr. (1760–1819) was the son of William and Ann Fishburne. Fishburne served under Francis Marion and Charles Cotesworth Pinckney during the Revolutionary War. In later years he and Pinckney were friends. On January 29, 1778, he became the stepson of Major **Samuel Wise**, his mother's third husband. Fishburne had charge of the South Carolina coast as a major general in the War of 1812. He was also a wealthy lowcountry planter. Fishburne owned two hundred slaves in Colleton District in 1810 and by 1815 owned around twenty-five thousand acres of land. Beginning in the mid- to late 1780s, Fishburne acquired six hundred acres near the middle of the Beidler Tract, as well as land on the uplands to the north.

John Frentz (d. ca. 1768?) was a barber and peruke maker (that is, a maker of men's powdered wigs). In 1761 he obtained a grant to a two-hundred-acre tract bordered on the northwest by today's Oak Ridge Trail. The tract included the waterways later known as Frenchmans Pond and Frenchmans Gut. Frentz sold the tract to Michael Muckenfuss in April 1768. At the time of the sale, Frentz and his wife, Margaret, were living in Savannah, Georgia. The Frentz marriage was not a happy one. In July 1768 John shot and killed Margaret when she refused to be reconciled with him and return home.

Alexander Gillon (1741–1794) was born in Rotterdam of a Scottish father and Anglophone mother. He settled in South Carolina in 1766, where he became one of the colony's wealthier merchants. Among his landholdings was a five-thousand-acre plantation on the Congaree River known as Gillon's Retreat. Most of Gillon's Retreat lay south of the river across from the park, but at one time it also included 586 acres in the park itself. The latter acreage consisted of the modern-day Brady tract (Tract 101-42), as well two tracts to the west totaling 186 acres. Gillon sold the land north of the river to **Francis Goodwyn** in 1777.

Proficient in several languages, Gillon approached contacts on the continent during the Revolution for loans in support of the South Carolina war effort. These loans, which he personally secured, were used to lease the frigate *L'Indien* on behalf of the State of South Carolina and the South Carolina Navy. Rechristened the *South Carolina*, this ship was the largest man-of-war under American command during the Revolution. Gillon achieved some limited military success while at the helm of the *South Carolina*, including, most notably, assisting the Spanish in capturing the Bahamas in May 1782. In 1788 he served as a delegate to the state convention that ratified the federal constitution. In 1793 financial difficulties forced him to sell his lowcountry seat and make "Gillon's Retreat" his sole residence.

Francis Goodwyn (1749–1785) moved to lower Richland from Virginia in 1760 with other members of his family. Among those making the move were his older brothers Jesse, Boswell, and Robert, each of whom would obtain land in park. Francis was a lieutenant colonel of militia in the Revolution and provided supplies to Continental forces. Among his land holdings in lower Richland were four contiguous tracts in the park totaling 1,036 acres. Three of these tracts, including NPS Tract 101-42, he acquired from **Alexander Gillon** in 1777. Tract 101-42 would later be owned by **William Scott Jr.** and would include the site of "Wm. Scott's Quarter." Much of the fourth tract, bordering Tract 101-42 on the north, would be acquired by **William H. Fishburne Jr.** not long after Goodwyn's death in 1785.

Wade Hampton I (1754–1835) immigrated to the upcountry of South Carolina in 1774 from Virginia by way of North Carolina. He had moved to the Congarees by late 1780 and was a commander of state troops during the last part of the Revolutionary War. Beginning in 1779, Hampton served multiple terms in the General Assembly and was twice elected to the U.S. House of Representatives. He was an important figure in the War of 1812, rising to the level of major general. Hampton became hugely wealthy from his extensive land holdings on the Congaree River just below Columbia. For a time Hampton owned over four hundred acres inside what is now Congaree National Park. He obtained this property in 1783 via marriage to Martha Epps Goodwyn, his first wife. By 1790 he (or an intervening owner) had sold these lands to **Joel Adams Sr.**

Harry R. E. Hampton (1897–1980) was one of the foremost South Carolina conservationists of the twentieth century. A writer for the *State* newspaper, he penned the popular "Woods and Waters" column, which he used to advocate for protection of the state's natural resources. Hampton was instrumental in the formation of the South Carolina Wildlife and Marine Resources Department, forerunner of the South Carolina Department of Natural Resources. A member of the hunt club that held the lease on the Beidler Tract, Hampton began campaigning for its preservation in the 1950s. His efforts inspired the citizen campaign that eventually resulted in the establishment of Congaree Swamp National Monument in 1976.

Isaac Huger (1743–1797) was born at Limerick Plantation on the Cooper River, the son of prominent Huguenot merchant and planter Daniel Huger. His status as a landowner in St. Matthews Parish allowed him to represent the parish in the

Commons House of Assembly in 1772. In 1775 he was commissioned a lieutenant colonel in the First South Carolina Regiment (Infantry), rising to the rank of colonel the following year. On January 9, 1779, he was promoted to brigadier general in the Continental Army. Huger was wounded at the Battle of Stono Ferry in June 1779. He also saw action at the unsuccessful patriot siege of Savannah later that year and at the British siege of Charleston in the spring of 1780. On March 15, 1781, Huger commanded a brigade of Virginia continental regiments at the Battle of Guilford Courthouse and was slightly wounded in action. After the war, Huger served in the General Assembly for six years before resigning in 1785 to serve as sheriff of Charleston District. He was appointed the first federal marshal of South Carolina in 1789, a position he held for five years.

Huger was a major landowner in South Carolina, with holdings in various parts of the state. His Congaree plantation contained around 1,750 acres, split between the high bluffs south of the river and the bottomlands to the north. Almost 900 acres of the plantation lay north of the river inside the park. In 1786 the General Assembly authorized a public road and ferry on Huger's plantation.

Alfred M. Hunt (b. ca. 1800) owned the United States Hotel in Columbia. He acquired Beidler Tract Parcel 13 in the 1850s, as well as a large contiguous tract to the north. In November 1860 a large crowd gathered in front of Hunt's hotel to hear a series of speakers agitate in favor of secession. Hunt was forced into bankruptcy after the war and lost all his land in what is now the park.

Edward Lightwood (ca. 1740–1797) was a Charleston ship owner, merchant, and insurer. He operated the slave-trading firm of Lightwood and Everleigh with his partner, Thomas Everleigh. He also owned and lived part-time on a 250-acre plantation on James Island. This plantation, much expanded by subsequent owners, is today the McLeod Plantation Historic Site (Charleston County Parks). Lightwood owned a Congaree plantation that consisted of six tracts totaling 1,164 acres. The largest tract (500 acres), known as Lightwood's Old Field, appears to have been partly cleared and planted by the early 1780s.

John McCord (d. 1768) immigrated to South Carolina from Ireland some time before the middle of the eighteenth century. In 1748 he appears to have been a trader with the Catawba Indians. McCord married Sophianisba Russell of Amelia Township in 1751. (Sophianisba's sister Eugenia married William Thomson four years later.) In 1766 the General Assembly designated McCord's ferry over the Congaree River a public ferry. McCord, Sophianisba, and Thomson each owned property at the confluence of the Congaree and Wateree Rivers. Control of McCord's land passed to Sophianisba after his death in 1768.

Daniel McKenzie (ca. 1810–1881) lived in the former Amelia Township, Orangeburgh District. Sometime before 1862 he assembled what is today Beidler Tract Parcel 19 out of land once owned by Isaac Huger in the eighteenth century. The parcel consisted of two tracts, one of which McKenzie acquired from his brother-in-law,

Lieuellan Woodward. A part or parts of Parcel 19 may have been kept open through the last half of nineteenth century. In his will, dated April 2, 1880 (Orangeburg County), Daniel McKenzie devised his "'Swamp Tract' of about seven hundred acres in Congaree Swamp, to be equally used and enjoyed by all my children . . . for planting or pasture purposes."

Peter Mazyck (1738–1772) was trained as a merchant. After traveling extensively in Europe, he made a fortune in trade and then retired to live the life of a private gentleman in Charleston. He died of consumption, aged thirty-four, in 1772. Between around 1769 and the year of his death, Mazyck assembled a tract of 3,150 contiguous acres in the heart of the park. This tract included land on either side of the feature known today as Mazyck's Cut. At his death, the tract passed into the control of his brother William, who died three years later. All or some part of the tract (including land close to the cut) remained in the estate of **William Mazyck** as late as 1786.

William Mazyck (1740–1775) trained as a lawyer under Charles Pinckney, Esq. He practiced law for a brief period before retiring to private life in Charleston, where he enjoyed a considerable estate. He died of consumption at the age of thirty-five.

John Mitchell (d. 1771) was a colonial deputy surveyor working out of St. Matthews Parish. His eldest brother was Ephraim Mitchell, who did survey work for the Mouzon map of the Carolinas (1775) and subsequently served as surveyor general of South Carolina.

Washington Mitchell (ca. 1799–1850s) lived in St Matthews Parish, Orangeburgh District. He owned an approximately seven-hundred-acre tract on the north bank of the Congaree River, which extended a short distance northeast of the rail line. All or most of this acreage appears to have been part of the former **William Bull Jr.** plantation. Mitchell was a small farmer rather than a planter, owning just eight slaves in 1830 and seven in 1840. His Congaree tract later passed to his wife Eliza Mitchell (b. ca. 1810) and sons William A. Mitchell (b. ca. 1831) and John A. Mitchell (b. ca. 1843).

Mary Brewton Motte (1769–1838) was the youngest daughter of Jacob Motte Jr. and **Rebecca Brewton Motte.** She received Buckhead Plantation (500-plus acres) in 1784 as part of a judicial partition of her deceased father's property.

Rebecca Brewton Motte (1737–1815) owned Mount Joseph Plantation, which spanned the Congaree River west of Buckhead Neck. Her brother Miles Brewton, a wealthy Charleston merchant, slave trader, and planter, had purchased the principal tracts making up the plantation between 1771 and 1774. The bulk of the seventeen-hundred-acre plantation was located on the uplands south of the river, but the plantation also contained six hundred acres of swampland on the opposite bank. Brewton and his entire immediate family died at sea in 1775, after which the Congaree plantation and much other valuable property passed to Rebecca. Among the various bequests in his will (filed in the South Carolina state archives), Brewton specifically listed "all my stock of Cattle, horses & other stock and plantation Tools and utensils at my mount Joseph plantation on the Congaree river."

Rebecca Motte was living at her deceased brother's house in Charleston when the British occupied the city in May 1780. Recently widowed and heir to the fortunes of both her brother and her husband, Jacob Motte Jr., Mrs. Motte was one of the wealthiest individuals in South Carolina and a fervent supporter of the patriot cause. When her house was chosen as the headquarters of British commander Sir Henry Clinton, she sought and received permission to remove to Mount Joseph with her three daughters, Frances, Elizabeth, and Mary. Elizabeth Motte was the wife of Thomas Pinckney, younger brother of **Charles Cotesworth Pinckney**.

Around January 1781 the British seized and fortified the Motte home at Mount Joseph. Four months later, Brigadier General Francis Marion and Lieutenant Colonel Henry "Light-Horse Harry" Lee mounted a siege of the fortified house. On May 12, with enemy reinforcements believed to be on the way, Lee informed Mrs. Motte that patriot forces needed to oust the British troops from her house. Mrs. Motte not only voiced no objection, she reportedly provided combustible arrows to assist with the task. (Another account states that a patriot soldier slung burning rosin onto the roof.) The British surrendered when the roof caught fire, and troops from both sides then put out the fire to save the structure.

Charles Neuffer (ca. 1805–1862) immigrated to Richland District from Germany. He lived in Columbia and served as sheriff of the district from 1851 to 1854. At some point he acquired 330 acres on the Congaree River inside the park. This Charles Neuffer is quite likely the "Carles Neufer" listed in the 1850 census as owning fifty-nine slaves in Orangeburgh District north of the Belleville Road, on or near Lang Syne Plantation. Neuffer sold the Congaree tract in 1859 to James Trumble and Joseph Bates. The tract was the site of the "Bates Big Field" in the 1880s.

James A. Peterkin (1834–1909) moved to Orangeburg County from Marlboro County in 1880. In 1883 he purchased Lang Syne plantation on the Congaree River, formerly the seat of David and Louisa Cheves McCord. Peterkin was widely known for having developed the Peterkin variety of cottonseed beginning about 1870. By the time of his death, he was said to have the most extensive farming operation in Calhoun County. With his son John A. Peterkin, he purchased large tracts of timberland on the north side of the river across from Lang Syne. For a time he operated a sawmill and veneer mill on the south side of the river.

Charles Cotesworth Pinckney (1746–1825), second cousin of Governor Charles Pinckney, was an influential soldier, diplomat, and legislator. He served on George Washington's general staff during the Revolution, where he made contacts with key officers that would later propel him to a place on the national and international stage. Pinckney represented South Carolina at the Constitutional Convention of 1787, arguing against abolition of the slave trade and advocating the counting of slaves as a basis for representation. Pinckney's arguments were influential in the drafting of the Constitution, and he subsequently helped secure South Carolina's ratification of the document. Pinckney was twice a candidate for president of the United States on the Federalist ticket. He ran against Thomas Jefferson in 1804 and James Madison in 1808.

In 1783 Pinckney and his business partner **Edward Rutledge** acquired a 2,910-acre plantation on the Congaree River known then or later as "the Precipice." Pinckney and Rutledge acquired the plantation from Henry Middleton, who was the father-in-law of both men. Pinckney and Rutledge subsequently acquired a 693-acre tract north of the Precipice known as the Joseph Martin tract. In all, the Precipice comprised approximately 3,600 acres on both sides of the river, including almost 1,950 acres of river swamp. The Martin tract alone contained about 550 acres of swampland.

Edward Rutledge (1749–1800) represented South Carolina in both the First and Second Continental Congresses, together with his older brother John. He signed the Declaration of Independence at age twenty-six, the youngest person to do so. From 1782 to 1798 he served in the South Carolina legislature. He was elected governor in 1798 but suffered a stroke and died a little over a year into his term.

William Scott Jr. (d. ca. 1822) owned a plantation on the river corresponding to today's Tract 101-42 (four hundred acres). The part of the tract nearest the river is referred to as "Wm. Scott's Quarter" in Marmaduke Coate's *Survey of Richland District* (1820; see figure 7). The plantation was at one time the property of **Francis Goodwyn**, who had acquired it from **Alexander Gillon**. Scott first obtained an interest in the plantation from his father sometime before 1806. The will of William Scott Sr., dated April 20, 1806 (South Carolina state archives), states that "I have already given the Riverswamp tract of Land unto my Sons William Scott and Samuel Scott to be Equell [sic] devided [sic] between them." The inventory of William Jr.'s estate appears to indicate that he owned the entire swamp tract (and other nearby property) at the time of his death around 1822. William Scott Jr. owned multiple plantations in lower Richland, which he worked in 1820 with 129 slaves. The Scott family's home plantation, known as Whitehall, was located between the villages of Congaree and Gadsden.

James H. Seay (ca. 1798–1866) and his younger brother **Thomas Seay** (b. ca. 1801) planted land in the Kingville area. Thomas Seay owned land east of the railroad, including two tracts partly within the park boundary. Thomas completed the sale of his lands in the mid- to late 1840s and was living in Murray County, Georgia, by 1850. James H. Seay remained in lower Richland, where he owned sixty-two slaves in 1850 and approximately 2,500 acres of land, 600 of which were improved. Among his various properties in the vicinity of Kingville were three tracts, mostly in the park, totaling 966 acres. Almost all of this land was located in the floodplain southwest of Kingville station. James Seay lived the latter part of his life in the mansion now known as Laurelwood, north of Eastover.

Paul Spigener (1789–1867) lived in Orangeburgh District near **Frederick Cooner**. According to the census of 1850, Paul "Speigner" owned 2,700 acres (300 of them improved) and thirty-six slaves. His holdings included a 370-acre tract in the park granted to him by the state in 1839. Spigener sold the southern portion of his park tract (NPS Tract 101-35) around 1860 (?). In 1869 the amount of cleared land on the remaining 300 acres was said to be about 60 acres, with the rest being well timbered.

Wesley D. Starling (1843–1922) was trained as a butcher. He rose to the level of sergeant during the Civil War, dividing his time between the front lines and selecting cattle to be foraged by General Joseph B. Kershaw's Confederate troops. He ran a livery stable in Columbia after the war. Starling earned the honorific "captain" during Reconstruction, when he commanded the company of Red Shirts that reportedly broke up Republican control of Richland County. In the 1880s he owned land on either side of the lower Congaree River, which he used for stock farming. He served as Richland County supervisor between 1905 and 1908, where he worked to improve the county road system, including Old Bluff Road and the route to the Bates Ferry area.

Thomas Taylor (1743–1833) served under Brigadier General Thomas Sumter in the Revolution and went on to become a principal founder of the city of Columbia and Richland County. During his lifetime, he and **Wade Hampton I** were perhaps the two most influential men in Columbia and the surrounding area.

William Thomson (1727–1796) was raised on the frontier in Amelia Township. By the 1750s he was an occasional trader with the Cherokees. After serving as major commandant of Rangers during the Anglo-Cherokee War, he received grants of at least 1,921 acres in Amelia and Orangeburgh townships and St. Matthews Parish. He administered these and other lands from his home at Belleville Plantation, located just south of the Congaree River and to the west of present-day U.S. Highway 601. In 1775 he was commissioned a lieutenant colonel of the South Carolina Third Regiment (Rangers) and campaigned against loyalists at Ninety Six and Great Cane Brake. In June 1776 he and his Rangers played a pivotal role in the Battle of Sullivan's Island, successfully preventing the British from attacking Fort Sullivan (later known as Fort Moultrie) from the rear. On November 23, 1776, Thomson was promoted to colonel in the Continental Army. He was captured in the fall of Charleston in May 1780, after which the British commandeered Belleville and established a garrison there until the spring of 1781. (By April 7, 1781, the British had abandoned Belleville and were occupying the fortified plantation house of **Rebecca Brewton Motte**.) Thomson was exchanged in June 1781 and served as an advisor to General Nathanael Greene for the remainder of the war. In later years Thomson held a variety of elective offices, including delegate to the state convention to ratify the U.S. Constitution.

Thomson eventually came to own well over four thousand acres in Orangeburgh District and more land elsewhere. His lands included various tracts in the far eastern part of the park. He was reputedly a major producer of indigo before shifting to cotton in the mid-1790s.

William Russell Thomson (1761–1807), son of **William Thomson,** served as a lieutenant in the 3rd South Carolina Regiment (Rangers) but resigned in 1778 to serve in the militia, where he eventually attained the rank of lieutenant colonel. He was appointed a justice of the peace for Orangeburgh District in 1785 and was elected to the South Carolina House of Representatives from St. Matthews Parish in 1790. Thomson owned at least two plantations with home sites in present-day Calhoun County. One, known as Midway, was located about five miles south of Fort Motte.

Reverend Isaac Raiford Tucker (1772–1811) was the son of Dr. William Tucker (d. 1779), who moved to lower Richland from Virginia in 1760. The Tuckers were closely associated with the Goodwyn family. Reverend Tucker married Sarah Adams, daughter of **Joel Adams Sr.,** in 1796. His daughter Christian Grace Tucker married Dr. **William Weston III** in 1818. Reverend Tucker reportedly preached and conducted religious services in a grove of trees near the site where his grandson, Dr. **William Weston IV,** would one day help found the Episcopal Church of St. John's, Congaree.

William Weston I (ca. 1716–ca. 1771) moved to lower Richland from Edenton, North Carolina, around 1769. He may have followed his brothers Thomas and Malachi to the area, as a Thomas Weston was present in the area by 1762, and a Malachi "Western" obtained a plat for land on the west bank of the Wateree in 1765. William himself may have made previous trips to the area to scout for land. He disposed of his property in North Carolina in 1769 and settled permanently in lower Richland soon thereafter. He established Brite Savannah Plantation about three miles northeast of the park.

William Weston II (ca. 1750–1821), son of **William Weston I,** established Gum Tree Plantation on land located below Old Bluff Road, a short distance south of his father's Brite Savannah Plantation. William II may have begun assembling Gum Tree around the time of his marriage in the early 1770s. At his death the plantation appears to have extended south past Weston Lake, which probably takes its name from him. The plantation covered about 1,896 acres in 1873, of which 1,634 acres are now in the park. William II fought on the American side in the Revolutionary War and saw action in the siege of Charleston in 1780. He lived at Brite Savannah from the early 1790s until his death in 1821.

Dr. William Weston III (1795–1848) was the grandson of **William Weston I** and a major planter in lower Richland during the 1830s and 1840s. Weston was said to be a sober, retiring man who shunned politics and public life despite his wealth. He owned at least two properties within what became the Beidler Tract. The first derived from Gum Tree Plantation, which he had inherited from his father, **William Weston II.** The other was a 774-acre tract on the east side of Old Dead River.

Isaac Tucker Weston (1827–1885) was the second surviving son of Dr. **William Weston III**. In 1857 he sold his interest in Grovewood Plantation to his younger brother Dr. **William Weston IV** and took possession of Gum Tree Plantation. He served as a private in the 6th Regiment South Carolina Infantry during the Civil War. In 1862 he was seriously wounded at Frazier's Farm (the fifth of the Seven Days' Battles outside Richmond). He experienced serious financial difficulties after the war and contemplated moving to Florida, where his wife Elizabeth had grown up. He lived for a time at Pine Bluff Plantation (formerly Gum Tree Plantation) but moved around 1872 to the future site of Melrose, Florida, which he helped found. He died there in 1885.

Dr. William Weston IV (1829–1896) was the third surviving son of Dr. **William Weston III** and younger brother of **Isaac Tucker Weston**. In 1861 he left Grovewood to join the Confederate forces as a surgeon. From 1862 until 1890 he held an ownership interest in a 3,368- acre tract in the middle part of the park that would come to form Beidler Tract Parcel 15. This tract included an area on the river known as "Dr. Weston's Quarter" (see entry 23 in Appendix A). Many, if not all, of the constituent tracts of Parcel 15 had once been owned by **Isom Woodward** and **Lieuellan Woodward**, the grandfather and father, respectively, of Weston's wife Caroline. For much of his adult life Weston lived at the Woodward family home plantation near Eastover, known as the Oaks.

William W. Weston (1853–1931), son of **Isaac Tucker Weston**, moved to Florida with his family around 1872 but returned to lower Richland after a year to manage his father's lands and collect rents. For a number of years he lived at Grovewood, which he rented from his uncle Dr. **William Weston IV**. During this time Pine Bluff Plantation was being actively marketed to help resolve his father's debts. In 1881 he acquired the remaining 1,554 acres of Pine Bluff out of foreclosure and moved there with his family around 1884. Between 1889 and 1899 he oversaw the sale of the Weston family's Congaree Swamp lands (three tracts totaling 5,743 acres) to outside buyers, including the Santee River Cypress Lumber Company.

Samuel Wise (d. 1779) immigrated to South Carolina from England, becoming a merchant in Charleston by 1766. Within a few years he had settled on the east side of the Pee Dee River just below the North Carolina line. Wise actively acquired property in the Congaree region and eventually relocated to the Midlands sometime during the mid-1770s. Promoted to major of the South Carolina 3rd Regiment (Rangers) in the spring of 1776, Wise served under **William Thomson** at the Battle of Sullivan's Island in June of that year. On December 29, 1778, Wise took part in the failed defense of Savannah, Georgia. His detachment of the 3rd Regiment was part of the right wing of Major General Robert Howe's army, under the command of Brigadier General **Isaac Huger**. In the autumn of 1779, Wise participated in the patriot siege of Savannah (Second Battle of Savannah). He was killed on October 9, 1779, in the Franco-American attempt to retake the city.

Major Wise owned 1,250 acres in the vicinity of Cedar Creek and Wise Lake. This plantation remained in his estate for many years after his death. While part of the estate, it appears to have been worked to help pay off debts. The plantation was advertised for judicial sale in 1806 and was probably acquired by **Joel Adams Sr.**

Major Wise was not related to the Wise family of Calhoun County. His only heir was a daughter, Jane Ann Wise.

Isom Woodward (d. 1847) and his son **Lieuellan Woodward** (ca. 1796–1862) were major landowners in lower Richland and together owned substantial acreage in the eastern half of the Beidler Tract. They had acquired at least some part of their Beidler Tract plantation by the early 1820s. To reach the plantation, the Woodwards used a road over property to the north owned by David Myers and later **James H. Adams.** The road led to a bridge over a large "gum pond," providing the Woodwards and others in the neighborhood with access to the swamp and river beyond. (See figure 12 for the type of terrain crossed by the bridge. The bridge appears to have been located in or near the far southeastern part of Tract 101-32 [Map 2].). In later years the Woodward swamp plantation consisted of about 3,368 acres (Beidler Tract Parcel 15), which Lieuellan Woodward managed from his home at the Oaks Plantation near Eastover. Much of this land appears to have been devised or otherwise conveyed to Lieuellan by his father, although Lieuellan acquired other property in Parcel 15 independently. Lieuellan, in turn, devised ownership interests in Parcel 15 to his daughter Caroline E. Woodward (1840–1899) and her husband, Dr. **William Weston IV.**

Daniel Zeigler (ca. 1785–1872) was a significant planter living in Orangeburgh District. The census of 1850 shows him owning twenty-seven hundred acres, of which three hundred were improved. He owned more than twenty-five hundred acres in the park, including a large tract that extended west from Old Dead River to the eastern boundary of the Adams swamp plantation. He operated a private ferry at his landing on the south side of the Congaree River.

Notes

Abbreviations

ASCS   Agricultural Stabilization and Conservation Service
AO   Audit Office Records, London
CNP   Congaree National Park
CSNM   Congaree Swamp National Monument
NAPP   National Aerial Photography Program
NPS   National Park Service
PD   Planning Division, Southeast Region, National Park Service
RG   Record Group
SCDAH   South Carolina Department of Archives and History
SCDACI   South Carolina Department of Agriculture, Commerce, and Immigration
SER   Southeast Region, National Park Service
USGS   United States Geological Survey

Introduction

1. James T. Tanner, quoted in Soucie, "Congaree," 78 ("virgin stand"); Tanner, *Ivory-Billed Woodpecker*, 37, 87–89; Jackson, *In Search of the Ivory-Billed Woodpecker*, 140–43; Cokinos, *Hope Is the Thing with Feathers*, 102.

2. Jackson, *In Search of the Ivory-Billed Woodpecker*, 142; Cokinos, *Hope Is the Thing with Feathers*, 104–5.

3. NPS, *Specific Area Report*, 2.

4. Act of October 18, 1976, Public Law 94–545, 90 Stat. 2517 (1976).

5. Gaddy et al., *Vegetation Analysis of Preserve Alternatives*, 35, 38 (table 5). See also Pederson, Jones, and Sharitz, "Origins of Old *Pinus taeda* Stands," 114, 116. Researcher Bruce P. Allen has found that the growth rate of oaks at Congaree can be quite high: "When you think about the giant Cherrybark oaks in the Congaree, growth rates have likely been 2–3 cm dbh/year for the fastest growing individuals (even for young trees after a disturbance) so ages may be as low as 100 years for some of those monsters. Most of the oak species in the Congaree grow almost as fast. When [you] grow that fast you don't have to survive that many storms [to] reach the canopy but your life expectancy is short" (quoted from discussion thread on website of Native Tree Society, January 30, 2005, http://www .nativetreesociety.org/). Allen has also suggested that the Congaree's nutrient-rich flood-waters dramatically affect tree growth: "I have had the opportunity to look at tree growth in the Savannah and Congaree floodplain[s]. The results are startling—fewer than 10 trees have grown 1 cm/yr in the Savannah while several species of oaks in the Congaree average

better [than] a cm/yr over a similar time period. The difference, I believe, is the flood regime. The Savannah River floodplain below Augusta almost never floods since the last dam was built" (quoted from note posted on website of Native Tree Society, June 13, 2003).

6. Lyell, *Second Visit to the United States*, 344–45; Trimble, *Man-Induced Soil Erosion*, 9–10; Patterson, Speiran, and Whetstone, *Hydrology and Its Effects on Distribution of Vegetation*, 6; Knowles et al., *Water Resources Management Plan*, 7, 37. Erosion rates postsettlement were dramatically higher than those in the centuries before European contact, when limited sediment deposition took place in many southern floodplains. A site in the upper Congaree valley investigated by James Michie showed only eighteen inches of soil deposition between the years 10 B.C.E. and 1590 C.E. Prehistoric sedimentation rates may have been higher in the park than they were in the upper valley, but even if they were, the park saw a substantial increase in vertical accumulation rates after contact. Point bars and levees along the modern river channel contain numerous fresh litter horizons to a depth of almost twelve feet (three and a half meters), suggesting recent and rapid sedimentation in the park. Stumps of cypress trees that generated before 1660 C.E. have been found in some cutbanks, buried by more than seven to ten feet (two to three meters) of laminated mud deposits. See Williams and Evans, *Archaeological Excavations at the Bullard Landing Site*, 1, 11, 15; Michie, *Discovery of Old Fort Congaree*, 38–40; Shelley et al., "Radiocarbon Controls on Late Quaternary Development"; Shelley, "Geology, Geomorphology, and Tectonics," 48.

7. Barnes et al., *Forest Ecology*, 462–64; Sharitz and Mitsch, "Southern Floodplain Forests," 328; Battaglia and Sharitz, "Effects of Natural Disturbance," 131; Thompson, "Ecological Inventory and Classification," 30–32.

8. Sharitz and Mitch, "Southern Floodplain Forests," 316, 326; Carroll et al., "Historical Overview of the Southern Forest Landscape," 597–98; Delcourt et al., "History, Evolution, and Organization," 62–63; Cohen et al., "Palynology and Paleoecology"; Anderson, "Initial Human Occupation"; Goodyear, "Evidence for Pre-Clovis Sites," 107–11.

9. Cely, "Tree Species . . . Used as Boundary Markers"; Rangel, "Account of the Northern Conquest," 280; Carroll et al., "Historical Overview of the Southern Forest Landscape," 593, 600.

Chapter 1: Managing the Presettlement Landscape

1. Rangel, "Account of the Northern Conquest," 275 ("Governor arrived"); South Carolina State Historic Preservation Office, "Native American Time Periods," n.p. The periods assigned to the time before European settlement identify basic shifts in culture, social organization, and subsistence methods in American Indian life. The date ranges are approximate and are based on ranges proposed by the South Carolina State Historic Preservation Office (SHPO), as modified by the findings of Gail E. Wagner at the Wateree archeological complex. See Wagner, "National Register of Historic Places Registration Form"; and Wagner, "Mississippian Landscape Managers." The South Carolina SHPO differs from other authorities in defining the Woodland period as extending until 1670 C.E. This difference is meant to emphasize that in South Carolina the Woodland period overlaps both the Mississippian period and the period of European exploration (1520–1670 C.E.).

2. Delcourt and Delcourt, "Pre-Columbian Native American Use of Fire"; Delcourt et al., "History, Evolution, and Organization," 69–71.

3. Hardy, "Brief Introduction to the Prehistoric Communities," 7; Michie, *Archeological Survey of Congaree Swamp*, 53–59. See also Howe, "Essay on the Antiquities"; and Steen and Taylor, *Archeological Survey of the Congaree Bluffs*.

4. Hardy and Prentice, "Cultural Overview," 41–42; Carruth and Joy, *Archaeological and Architectural Survey Report;* Banschbach et al., "Long-Term Changes."

5. Hardy and Prentice, "Cultural Overview," 42–43. At Congaree a substantial Middle Woodland occupation has been discovered in the floodplain on a bench adjacent to Toms Creek. This site was occupied intermittently for some three thousand years but was used most intensively during the Middle Woodland period. See King, *Environmental and Cultural History.*

6. Keel, Cornelison, and Brewer, *Regionwide Archeological Survey Plan,* 26; Hardy, *Archeological Survey of Sampson Island,* 60, 61. The use of sand ridges as burial sites has been documented elsewhere in the Congaree floodplain, most notably at Green Hill Mound, about seven miles west of the park. Within the park itself, ranger Guy Taylor discovered five sherds from a suspected burial urn in 1981, buried under about ten feet of alluvium. The sherds were eroding into the Congaree River from the remnants of a suspected Indian mound known as Starling's Mound (38RD1237). Most of the mound eroded away before it could be investigated further, but in 2012 archaeologists from the NPS Southeast Archeological Center unearthed ceramics at the site suggesting a Middle to Late Woodland (100–800 C.E.) timeframe for the mound. See Guy Taylor, "Archeology," memorandum to superintendent CSNM, August 3, 1981, CNP files; and Seibert, Hardy, and Fry, *Archeological Investigations of Starling's Mound,* 18, 21–28.

7. Keel, Cornelison, and Brewer, *Regionwide Archeological Survey Plan,* 24; Seibert, Hardy, and Fry, *Archeological Investigations of Starling's Mound,* 19, 29–40, 52; Dennis, *Preliminary Report on the Woody Plants,* 2; Hardy, *Congaree National Park,* 95–97.

8. Cobb and Nassaney, "Domesticating Self and Society," 538; Steen and Taylor, *Archeological Survey of the Congaree Bluffs,* 62.

9. NPS, "Southeastern Prehistory"; Gremillion, "Development and Dispersal," 483, 490.

10. Hardy and Prentice, "Cultural Overview," 43; Gremillion, "Development and Dispersal," 490, 498.

11. Wagner, "Mississippian Landscape Managers"; Carruth and Joy, *Archaeological and Architectural Survey Report,* 9; Vanier, "Ceramic Vessel Function Analysis," 12, 20–21, 118–19.

12. Wagner, "National Register of Historic Places Registration Form," 12; Wagner, "Mississippian Landscape Managers."

13. Anderson, "Mississippian in South Carolina," 113–15; Hudson, *Juan Pardo Expeditions,* 53; Vanier, "Ceramic Vessel Function Analysis," 16–18.

14. Prentice, "Ninety Six National Historic Site"; Hudson, *Juan Pardo Expeditions,* 53–58, 73.

15. See generally Wharton et al., *Ecology of Bottomland Hardwood Swamps,* 9–10, 23–27, 37–38.

16. Hudson, *Southeastern Indians,* 295; Doolittle, "Permanent vs. Shifting Cultivation," 184–86; Doolittle, "Agriculture in North America," 393; Hilton, *Relation of a Discovery,* 13; Hudson, *Knights of Spain,* 153–54.

17. Anderson, *Savannah River Chiefdoms,* 260–61, 270–71, 273.

18. Wagner, "National Register of Historic Places Registration Form," 5, 14; Hudson et al., "On Interpreting Cofitachequi," 469, 475; Hudson, *Juan Pardo Expeditions,* 71–72.

19. Prentice, "Ninety Six National Historic Site"; Wagner, "National Register of Historic Places Registration Form," 12; Wagner, "Mississippian Landscape Managers"; Gagnon, Passmore, and Platt, "Multi-Year Salutary Effects," 63–64; United States Forest Service, United

States Department of the Interior, and the Nature Conservancy, "LANDFIRE National Bio-physical Setting Model," 78–80; Croy and Frost, "Reference Conditions, Potential Natural Vegetation Group."

20. Hudson, *Juan Pardo Expeditions*, 59; Delcourt et al., "History, Evolution, and Organization," 71.

21. Hudson et al., "On Interpreting Cofitachequi," 468–70, 481; Bandera, ["Long" Juan de la Bandera relation], 260; Hudson, *Knights of Spain*, 172, 178.

22. Hudson et al., "On Interpreting Cofitachequi," 475; Hudson, "Social Context of the Chiefdom of Ichisi," 177; DePratter, "Chiefdom of Cofitachequi," 220–21; Hudson, *Knights of Spain*, 183–84.

23. Steen and Taylor, *Archeological Survey of the Congaree Bluffs*, 10; Hardy and Prentice, "Cultural Overview," 48–49; Michie, *Archeological Survey of Congaree Swamp*, 59.

24. Michie, *Archeological Survey of Congaree Swamp*, 6–7, 72–74, 102; Hudson, *Southeastern Indians*, 291–92, 297; Goodyear and Wilkinson, "Prehistory at High Creek Plantation," 37, 42; Steen and Taylor, *Archeological Survey of the Congaree Bluffs*, 2; Seibert, Hardy, and Fry, *Archeological Investigations of Starling's Mound*, 52.

25. Christopher Judge in discussion with the author, December 2002; Hudson, *Juan Pardo Expeditions*, 72–73; DePratter and Judge, "Wateree River [Chronology and Phase Characteristics]," 34, 59.

26. Grego, "Pottery Shard Early Mississippian"; Hudson, *Juan Pardo Expeditions*, 72; Steen and Judge, *Archaeology at the Great Pee Dee*.

27. Hudson, *Knights of Spain*, 150–165, 171; Bandera, ["Long" Juan de la Bandera relation], 288; Gentleman from Elvas, "Account by a Gentleman from Elvas," 78 ("a lean land"; "a rich land"), 83 ("very pleasing and fertile"); Delcourt and Delcourt, *Prehistoric Native Americans*, 70.

28. Carruth and Joy, *Archaeological and Architectural Survey Report*; Hardy, *Archeological Survey of Sampson Island*, 50, 59–60; Steen and Taylor, *Archeological Survey of the Congaree Bluffs*, 62, 93, 113.

29. Ferguson, "South Appalachian Mississippian," 246; Larson, *Aboriginal Subsistence Technology*, 36, 49, 65.

30. Wagner, "Mississippian Landscape Managers."

31. Ibid. At the Bullard Landing site in Georgia, residents lived on what may have been an island in the Ocmulgee River. Their houses were built on low mounds. The relatively small size of the site (ca. 2.5 hectares) has prompted speculation that the Bullard Landing site was a chiefly compound with unrelated common people living on farms for miles around. The first town on the Ocmulgee to be visited by De Soto in 1540 was a site very much like the Bullard Landing site. De Soto subsequently visited the Lamar Mounds and Village site, a fortified Late Mississippian town in the Ocmulgee floodplain about one mile below the fall line. This site has also yielded evidence of residential structures built on low mounds. Today the Lamar Mounds and Village site is part of Ocmulgee National Monument. See Williams and Evans, *Archaeological Excavations at the Bullard Landing Site*, 1, 11–14, 66; and Hudson, *Knights of Spain*, 160.

32. Anderson, *Savannah River Chiefdoms*, 260, 283, 288–89; Hudson, *Knights of Spain*, 182–83; Hudson, *Juan Pardo Expeditions*, 73.

33. Hudson, *Knights of Spain*, 163–64, 168–69. See also Hudson, *Juan Pardo Expeditions*, 61, 68, 79.

34. Hudson, *Knights of Spain*, 171.

35. Biedma, "Relation of the Island of Florida," 230; Garcilaso, "La Florida," 280.

36. Rangel, "Account of the Northern Conquest," 275; Garcilaso, "La Florida," 280. Garcilaso actually said the Spaniards traveled upstream along the river, but this contradicts the accounts of the other three chroniclers, each of whom stated that the soldiers traveled downriver to the southeast. Garcilaso was not an eyewitness to the events he describes, and he composed his narrative years after the fact. This may account for many of the discrepancies between his version of events and those of the other chroniclers.

37. Rangel, "Account of the Northern Conquest," 275; Biedma, "Relation of the Island of Florida," 230; Garcilaso, "La Florida," 280.

38. DePratter, "The Chiefdom of Cofitachequi," 201; Hudson, *Juan Pardo Expeditions,* 79, 134; Delcourt et al., "History, Evolution, and Organization," 69; Williams, *Americans and Their Forests,* 39.

39. Hudson, *Juan Pardo Expeditions,* 134. See also McLendon, "Soil Survey of Clarendon County," 448–49; Van Duyne, McLendon, and Rice, *Soil Survey of Richland County,* 64, 66; and Platt and Brantley, "Canebrakes," 12–13.

40. Bandera, ["Long" Juan de la Bandera relation"], 259.

41. Ibid., 288, 293 ("sow a large quantity"); Barnes, "National Historic Landmark Nomination Form," 24.

42. Meitzen, "Lateral Channel Migration Effects," 472.

43. Wagner, "Mississippian Landscape Managers"; Foster, Black, and Abrams, "Witness Tree Analysis," 44–45.

44. DePratter, "Chiefdom of Cofitachequi," 215–19; Hudson et al., "On Interpreting Cofitachequi," 469–70; Hudson, *Juan Pardo Expeditions,* 64, 67.

45. Steckel and Rose, *Backbone of History;* Hudson, *Knights of Spain,* 422–25; Green, *History of Richland County,* 12–13; Moore, *Columbia and Richland County,* 5, 8; Moore, *World of Toil and Strife,* 15–17.

46. Lawson, *New Voyage to Carolina,* 29–38; DePratter and Green, "John Lawson and the Great Catawba Trading Path," 17, 19; Michie, *Archeological Survey of Congaree Swamp,* 64; Waddell, "Cofitachequi," 360n10; Green, *History of Richland County,* 13. The Congarees appear to have moved to the Columbia area sometime after their encounter with John Lawson. By 1715 conflicts with European settlers had prompted the Congarees to join various other tribes in fighting the Yamassee War (1715–18). The settlers won this conflict decisively with disastrous consequences for the tribe. Half were sold into slavery and sent to the West Indies, while the remainder were apparently absorbed into the Catawba. Steen and Taylor, *Archeological Survey of the Congaree Bluffs,* 12.

47. Green, *History of Richland County,* 8; Meriwether, *Expansion of South Carolina,* 61; Moore, *World of Toil and Strife,* 11, 16.

48. Platt and Brantley, "Canebrakes," 12–13; Catesby, "Account of Carolina," 142.

49. Gagnon, "Fire in Floodplain Forests," 522; Steinberg, "Importance of Cultural Ecological Landscapes."

50. Gagnon, Platt, and Moser, "Response of a Native Bamboo," 289, 292–93; Delcourt et al., "History, Evolution, and Organization," 61; Gagnon, "Fire in Floodplain Forests," 522.

51. This discussion of the disturbance regime underlying the formation and spread of canebrakes is largely drawn from a series of studies by Paul Gagnon and colleagues. See Gagnon, Passmore, and Platt, "Multi-Year Salutary Effects"; Gagnon, "Population Biology and Disturbance Ecology," 61–63; Gagnon, "Fire in Floodplain Forests," 524.

52. Gagnon, Platt, and Moser, "Response of a Native Bamboo," 292–93; see also Lossing, *Pictoral Field-Book of the Revolution*, 682–83.

53. Platt and Brantley, "Canebrakes," 13; Lawson, *New Voyage to Carolina*, 17 (emphasis in original); Foster and Cohen, "Palynological Evidence of the Effects of the Deerskin Trade," 37, 45.

54. Gagnon, Platt, and Moser, "Response of a Native Bamboo," 289; Roosevelt, "In the Louisiana Canebrakes," 47.

55. Noss, LaRoe, and Scott, *Endangered Ecosystems of the United States*; Chittenden, *Red Gum*, 11 ("common"); Calkins, *History of the One Hundred and Fourth Regiment*, 529–30, 531 (quotation).

56. See plat, 440-acre tract, certified November 8, 1757 for Elizabeth Mercier, Colonial Plats, SCDAH. See also plat, 400-acre tract, certified September 10, 1759, for Willis Monk, Colonial Plats, SCDAH ("cane swamp"); and plat, 300-acre tract, certified September 11, 1759 for Joseph Jackson, Colonial Plats, SCDAH ("impassable cane swamp"). For references to "cane swamp" near what are today park trails, see plat, 450-acre tract, certified August 16, 1756, for Walter McDaniel, Colonial Plats, SCDAH (Weston Lake Loop Trail); and plat, 300-acre tract, certified July 9, 1765, for Robert Goodwyn, Colonial Plats, SCDAH (Kingsnake Trail).

57. In the early 2000s researchers extracted a core from the muck rimswamp southwest of the visitor's center that yielded a single corn (*Zea mays*) pollen grain. Although analysis of the core lacked tight age control, this grain was found at a depth consistent with pre-European settlement. *Zea mays* is a large, relatively heavy pollen that does not disperse well over long distances. Its presence in the core suggests prehistoric corn cultivation nearby, though more pollen samples and dates are needed for confirmation. David Shelley in discussion with the author, September 2006. See also Cohen, Shelley, and Bartley, "Pollen and Palynofacies," 111.

58. Gagnon, "Fire in Floodplain Forests," 522–23, 524; Brantley and Platt, "Canebrake Conservation in the Southeastern United States," 1175–77, 1179.

59. Medlin, *Richland County Landmarks*, 93; Glen, "Description of South Carolina," 14; Land grant, 100-acre tract to John Cole, March 4, 1760, Colonial Land Grants, SCDAH; Kovacik and Winberry, *South Carolina*, 69; Meriwether, *Expansion of South Carolina*, 102.

60. Pederson, Jones, and Sharitz, "Age Structure and Possible Origins," 111, 118–19; Wagner, "Mississippian Landscape Managers"; Sharitz and Allen, *Quantify Change in the Old-Growth Forests*, 37, citing data compiled by John E. Cely; John E. Cely in discussion with the author, January 2012.

61. Ramsay, *History of South Carolina*, 594–95.

62. Scharf, "Archeology, Land Use, Pollen"; Ouchley et al., "Historic and Present-Day Forest Conditions."

Chapter 2: First Settlement, Land Clearing, and the Open Range

1. Catesby, "Account of Carolina," 142; Moore, *Columbia and Richland County*, 9, 60; Mills, *Statistics of South Carolina*, 692; Groover and Brooks, "Catherine Brown Cowpen," 96–97; Platt and Brantley, "Canebrakes," 14.

2. Drayton, *View of South Carolina*, 62; Platt and Brantley, "Canebrakes," 14–15.

3. Meriwether, *Expansion of South Carolina*, 59–60; Green, *History of Richland County*, 23, 30.

4. Meriwether, *Expansion of South Carolina*, 33, 53, 61, 99; Green, *History of Richland County*, 8, 26; Medlin, *Richland County Landmarks*, 94.

5. Meriwether, *Expansion of South Carolina*, 59–60; Medlin, *Richland County Landmarks*, 95; Moore, *Columbia and Richland County*, 64.

6. Ackerman, *South Carolina Colonial Land Policies*, 95, 106, 109; Kovacik and Winberry, *South Carolina*, 68, 69; Meriwether, *Expansion of South Carolina*, 19–20, 20n9.

7. Meriwether, *Expansion of South Carolina*, 59–61.

8. Ibid., 61; Frost and Wilds, *Presettlement Vegetation and Natural Fire Regimes*, 11.

9. See, for example, advertisements in *Columbian Herald* (Charleston), April 24, 1786, 3; *Charleston City Gazette*, December 31, 1800, 4; and *Charleston Courier*, December 12, 1810, 4.

10. Green, *History of Richland County*, 138. See also Sitton, *Backwoodsmen*, 6; Williams, *Americans and Their Forests*, 67–68. Within a few decades of settlement, the forests of the Southeast were overrun with feral cattle, horses, and swine. Feral stock was especially abundant in wild and difficult terrain such as river swamps. Feral hogs reached saturation density throughout the range of longleaf pine by 1860. Frost and Wilds, *Presettlement Vegetation and Natural Fire Regimes*, 21.

11. Groover and Brooks, "The Catherine Brown Cowpen," 94, 97; Klein, *Unification of a Slave State*, 28–30, 34–35; United States Department of Commerce and Labor, *Heads of Families*. The term "planter" is often defined as a person owning twenty or more slaves. However, in the eighteenth-century backcountry, a planter arguably was any slaveholder wealthy enough to engage in activities other than farm labor. See Klein, *Unification of a Slave State*, 7.

12. De Brahm, "Philosophico-Historico-Hydrogeography," 198–99.

13. Hammond, *South Carolina*, 9, 612; Edelson, "Clearing Swamps, Harvesting Forests," 390–91, 393–95; *South-Carolina and American General Gazette* (Charleston), December 9, 1774, 4; Edelson, *Plantation Enterprise in Colonial South Carolina*, 123–24, 212.

14. This information comes from the diary of James Henry Hammond (Harry's father), whose Silver Bluff Plantation was located on the Savannah River just below the fall line. In his diary, Hammond recounts a conversation with a slave named Jacob about a millpond on the plantation. Jacob tells Hammond that "his old master . . . ran 8 saws and 2 sets of stones on this stream before the Revolution and sold his lumber in Savannah at $8 pr. M." Bleser, *Secret and Sacred*, 51.

15. *South Carolina Gazette and Country Journal* (Charleston), September 27, 1774, 2. See also *Gazette of the State of South Carolina* (Charleston), June 24, 1778, 4.

16. Holcomb, *South Carolina Deed Abstracts 1783–1788*, 257–58 (conveyance from Wade Hampton and Martha Epps Hampton to John Hall); Green, *History of Richland County*, 33; Coate, *Survey of Richland District*.

17. Mills, *Statistics of South Carolina*, 211–12; Downey, *Planting a Capitalist South*, 56–58.

18. Citizens of Lexington District, Petition asking that Congaree Creek be made navigable to provide for the rafting of timber to market, ca. 1835, SCDAH Series S165015, Item 3006. Between 1800 and the mid-1850s, it was possible to ship rafts of lumber directly to Charleston via the Santee Canal, which linked the Santee and Cooper rivers over a distance of twenty-two miles. However, serious design flaws plagued the canal from the start. During droughts, low water at the canal's northern end forced it to close for extended periods. Further limiting traffic was the completion of rail lines to Columbia and Camden

in the 1840s. By the late 1840s, trade on the canal was largely reduced to the local neighborhood. Faced with this fall-off in traffic, the Santee Canal Company sought revocation of its
charter, and the General Assembly obliged in 1853. See Bennett, "Santee Canal, 1785–1939";
Phillips, *History of Transportation,* 36–44.

19. Joel Adams Sr., Petition and supporting papers asking remuneration for injuries
resulting from a change in course made in the Congaree River, ca. 1828, SCDAH Series
S165015, Item 1618; *South Carolina State Gazette* (Columbia), December 3, 1828, 1; see also
entry 1 in appendix A.

Marmaduke Coate's 1820 *Survey of Richland District* contains the legend "Joel Adams
Mills" near the north end of the dam at Duffies Pond (figure 7). An 1839 plat of the Adams "bluff" and "swamp" plantations shows a "Saw Mill" and "Grist Mill" in this same
location. Taken together, these plats indicate that Joel Adams Sr. had operated water-
powered saw and grist mills at the pond since sometime before 1820. In 1850 Joel's grandson James U. Adams was running two water-powered "grist & saw" mills in Richland District, quite possibly in the same location. However, at the time he was surveyed for the
census, James U. Adams was only producing ground corn. By 1867 the younger Adams
was operating two steam-powered sawmills on a three-thousand-acre tract north of where
the park's visitor center would one day stand. These mills were probably cutting longleaf
pine. See Coate, *Survey of Richland District;* Tomlinson Engineering Co., *Plan of Five Thousand One Hundred and Eighty Eight Acres;* United States Census Office, Manuscript Census Returns, 1850 (Industry), Richland District, SCDAH; Richland County Deed Book D,
p. 583.

20. The *James Adams* was successor to a pole boat of the same name. Both vessels were
named after Joel Adams Sr.'s oldest son, James. The steamboat was sold to the U.S. government around 1818 to transport troops to Florida for the First Seminole War. Green, *History
of Richland County,* 144; James P. Adams, letter to the editor, *State* (Columbia), March 4,
1904, 6.

21. *South-Carolina Gazette and Public Advertiser,* February 5–9, 1785, 4. James Henry
Hammond estimated that his ten-thousand-plus acres of swamp and pineland at Silver
Bluff could produce between 800,000 and 1,000,000 board feet of lumber per year. In
1832 Hammond produced 670,000 board feet of lumber for shipment to Savannah. Scurry,
Joseph, and Hamer, *Initial Archeological Investigations,* 27.

22. South Carolina House of Representatives, *Hearing on H 3097* (statement of Joy
Buyck Carpenter).

23. SCDACI, *Handbook of South Carolina,* 542, 544, 546, 549; Walker, *Southern Forest,*
88–101, 125; Southerlin et al., *Occupation of Socastee Bluff,* 98–101.

24. Sitton, *Backwoodsmen,* 109–10; Edelson, "Clearing Swamps, Harvesting Forests,"
391, 393–95; Ball, *Slavery in the United States,* 210–11; *South Carolina State Gazette* (Charleston), April 13, 1802, 1 ("largest cypress trees").

25. Along the Edisto and elsewhere, some people cut trees directly into the river, floating the best parts of the tree to market and leaving the rest in the channel. The tops and
limbs left behind obstructed the river and caught driftwood, creating a hazard to navigation. The legislature eventually made it a misdemeanor to cut "any trees or tree tops, brush
or logs, or [throw] any refuse material whatever into any navigable river." S.C. Code § 49-1-
20. This practice probably occurred along the Congaree, too, but how prevalent it may have
been is not known.

26. Raoul, John Louis, of St. Mathews [*sic*] Parish, Petition to alter the route of the road

to McCords Ferry on the Congaree River, n.d. [ca. 1820], SCDAH Series S165015, Item 3586. Buckhead Neck became Buckhead Island after the great flood of August 1852. See "Buckhead Island" on map 1.

27. Bryant, *Logging*, 19, 373–74; SCDACI, *Handbook of South Carolina*, 546; Chittenden, *Red Gum*, 7 (quotation), 18; Walker, *Southern Forest*, 115; Woodward, *Valuation of American Timberlands*, 67; Smith, *Gone to the Swamp*, 50; Ayers, *Promise of the New South*, 123; United States Senate, *Making Appropriations for . . . Rivers and Harbors*, 212 (notes on Altamaha River, Ga.).

28. Kohn and Glenn, *Internal Improvement in South Carolina*, 10–11, 280; United States Army, "Annual Report of the Chief of Engineers . . . 1887," 1093–97; United States Department of Agriculture, *Report of the Commissioner of Agriculture*, 271.

29. Early, *Looking for Longleaf*, 124, 156–57; Williams, *Americans and Their Forests*, 245–46. In 1978 ranger Guy Taylor found a log raft buried in the sand and silt of Dead River Gut (a remnant of Old Dead River) about half a mile north of the Congaree River. The raft consisted of twenty squared-off pine logs, each approximately twelve to fourteen inches square, held in place by a perpendicular log (six by eight inches by twenty-two feet) at each (?) edge of the raft. (Only one of these perpendicular logs was visible above the sand.) The perpendicular log was lashed to the raft in two places by lengths of chain, with each chain held in place by wedge-shaped spikes driven into the underlying logs. A second raft was later found under the first. Guy Taylor, "Report of the Discovery of Intact Timber Raft in Horsepen Creek," memorandum to archaeological resources file, CSNM, 1980, CNP files; Cely, *Map of Congaree National Park*.

30. United States Census Office, Manuscript Census Returns, 1850 (Industry), Richland District, SCDAH; United States Department of Agriculture, *Report of the Commissioner of Agriculture*, 271; Sargent, *Report on the Forests of North America*, 518 ("vast quantities still remain"); Wolfe, *Wood-Using Industries of South Carolina*, 7; SCDACI, *Handbook of South Carolina*, 542, 546.

31. W. J. Murray to Reid Whitford, June 1, 1893, in United States Army, "Annual Report of the Chief of Engineers . . . 1893," 1494. See also Edelson, "Clearing Swamps, Harvesting Forests," 393–94; and Stroyer, *My Life in the South*, 18–19.

32. *State*, November 5, 1917, 2; Williams, *Americans and Their Forests*, 77, 156; SCDACI, *Handbook of South Carolina*, 547.

33. Williams, *Americans and their Forests*, 156–57, 332–35; *Charleston City Gazette*, May 11, 1797, 3. The name "Congaree boat" referred to vessels built for carrying on commerce between Charleston and Columbia. Besides cordwood, these boats moved cotton and other products. Many advertisements for Congaree boats and "Camden boats" were published over the years.

34. *Charleston City Gazette*, March 31, 1821, 1; Woodward, *Valuation of American Timberlands*, 67.

35. *State*, November 5, 1917, 2; Williams, *Americans and Their Forests*, 153, 154, 156; Hunter, *Steamboats on the Western Rivers*, 264–67; Derrick, *Centennial History of South Carolina Railroad*, 42, 49; Bleser, *Secret and Sacred*, 44, 66–7; *Charleston City Gazette*, February 16, 1820, 2.

36. *Charleston Southern Patriot*, October 16, 1837, 2; *State*, April 1, 1909, 10; Moore, *Columbia and Richland County*, 92.

37. *Charleston City Gazette*, September 28, 1818, 2; Kohn and Glenn, *Internal Improvement in South Carolina*, 10–11, 280; Moore, *Columbia and Richland County*, 91–92; Mills,

Statistics of South Carolina, 708; Committee on Columbia Trade, "South Carolina—Trade and Manufactures," 206.

38. The Louisville, Cincinnati, and Charleston Railroad (LC&CRR) reached lower Richland from Branchville in 1841. (The LC&CRR was consolidated into the South Carolina Rail Road Company in 1844.) After the completion of a branch line to Camden in 1848, the junction of the two lines—originally known as "Junction" but later called "Kingsville" and then "Kingville"—grew in importance as a transportation hub. A station building was completed at Kingsville in the mid-1850s, and a hotel, maintenance sheds, and houses followed soon thereafter. See Derrick, *South Carolina Railroad,* 187, 228; Fetters, *Charleston & Hamburg,* 93–94; *South Carolina Railroad Co. v. Wilmington, Columbia and Augusta Railroad Co.,* 7 S.C. 410, 413 (1875).

39. In his diary James Henry Hammond complained that completion of the rail line to Augusta had cost him about $2,500 per year of the amount that he formerly earned supplying wood for steamboats on the Savannah River. Bleser, *Secret and Sacred,* 66–67.

40. Moore, *Columbia and Richland County,* 92; United States Army, "Annual Report of the Chief of Engineers . . . 1885," 1140–41; *Charleston Mercury,* October 25, 1856, 2; Resolutions to provide for the examination of the Congaree and Santee Rivers and aid the Columbia Steamboat Company in clearing obstructions, 1856, SCDAH Series S165018, Item 24.

41. Derrick, *South Carolina Railroad,* 216, 224; Jones, *South Carolina, a Synoptic History,* 150; Cecilia, "Memories of Home Travels," 142.

42. *Charleston Daily News,* September 20, 1869, 3.

43. United States Army, "Annual Report of the Chief of Engineers . . 1885," 1140–41; *State v. South Carolina Railroad Company,* 4 S.E. 796, 799 (S.C. 1888); United States Army, "Annual Report of the Chief of Engineers . . . 1889," 1194; SCDACI, *Handbook of South Carolina,* 497.

44. United States Army, "Annual Reports of the War Department . . . June 30, 1897," 1470–71; *Charleston Evening Post,* December 10, 1912, 4; *State,* May 24, 1914, pt. 1, 12, January 24, 1917, 10, January 27, 1907, 5, July 13, 1913, sec. 1, 5, March 21, 1904, 8.

45. *State,* May 9, 1896, 8.

46. See Michie, *Archeological Survey of Congaree Swamp,* 132–33; Ball, *Slavery in the United States,* 198, 329–30; Klein, *Unification of a Slave State,* 17–18; Winberry, "Indigo in South Carolina."

47. Sitton, *Backwoodsmen,* 6–7.

48. See Gray, *History of Agriculture,* 1:138–39; McWhiney, *Cracker Culture,* 52–53.

49. Stroyer, *My Life in the South,* 6; Groover and Brooks, "Catherine Brown Cowpen," 99; Morgan, *Slave Counterpoint,* 5, 52–53; Edgar, *South Carolina,* 133–34; Meynard, *History of Lower Richland,* 218.

50. *State,* May 31, 1906, 2; *Charleston Mercury,* January 5, 1856, 2; *Orangeburg (S.C.) Times and Democrat,* June 3, 1886, 8.

51. Michie, *Archeological Survey of Congaree Swamp,* 104–11; Hardy, *Congaree National Park,* 95–97.

52. *Columbia Register,* May 26, 1886, 2.

53. See Richland County Deed Book AR, p. 185. A photo by Dr. J. Heyward Gibbes, published in Harry Hampton's *Woods and Waters and Some Asides* (p. 268), shows livestock using the Beckham Meadow Mound during the flood of August 1928. This mound

was located well upstream of the park near the end of Beckham Swamp Road. Gibbes also took film footage of this same event (see Heyward Gibbes home movie collection at the University of South Carolina film library).

54. Hardy, *Congaree National Park*, 85, 95–97.

55. NPS, "Multiple Property Documentation Form."

56. Williams, *Americans and Their Forests*, 68; Ball, *Slavery in the United States*, 196.

57. Groover and Brooks, "Catherine Brown Cowpen," 100, 107; Groover, "Archaeology of Cattle Raisers," n.p.; Thomas Howell, Inventories of Estates, 1760, Charleston County, vol. T, 394–95, SCDAH.

58. William Howell, Inventories of Estates, 1757, Charleston County, vol. S, 178–79, SCDAH; Chappell, "Names Old, New, and Forgotten," 17; Green, *History of Richland County*, 140; Medlin, *Richland County Landmarks*, 44.

59. Land grants to Martha Howell: 100-acre tract, granted August 1, 1758, and 247-acre tract, granted September 19, 1758, Colonial Land Grants, SCDAH; Cely, *Map of Original Land Grants*; Groover and Brooks, "Catherine Brown Cowpen," 93.

60. Plat of Joseph Martin tract, n.d. [1789 or after], in Charles Cotesworth Pinckney Family Papers, Box OV3, Manuscript Division, Library of Congress. The Martin tract included the 600-acre tract originally laid out to David Peeples [*sic*] in 1764. See plat, 600-acre tract, certified March 12, 1764 for David Peeples, Colonial Plats, SCDAH; and Cely, *Map of Original Land Grants*.

61. Kinzer, *Partial Chain of Title*; John E. Cely in discussion with the author, November 2011; Cely, *Map of Congaree National Park*.

62. Joseph Martin Sr., will date October 22, 1804, proved February 6, 1805, Will Transcripts, Book D, 198, SCDAH; estate records for Joseph Martin Sr., Richland County Estate Papers, Box 19, Package 470, SCDAH.

63. Dunbar, "Colonial Carolina Cowpens," 126.

64. Hammond, *South Carolina*, 80, 100–101; Moore, *Columbia and Richland County*, 210–11; United States Census Office, Manuscript Census Returns, 1860 (Agriculture), Richland District, SCDAH.

65. Ayers, *Promise of the New South*, 188–90.

66. "An Act . . . [Authorizing Alteration] of the Fence Laws," 306; Moore, *Columbia and Richland County*, 230; Dennis, "Big Trees of the Congaree Swamp," 18–22; Adams, *Tales of the Congaree*, 9, 32; SCDACI, *Handbook of South Carolina*, 548–49.

67. Richland County Deed Book Q, p. 125 ("lawful fence"); Richland County Deed Book BU, p. 101. See also "Daniel McKenzie" in appendix B.

68. Cely, *Map of Congaree National Park*. See entries 8 and 14 in appendix A.

69. *State*, October 8, 1891, 2, May 31, 1906, 2, January 11, 1956, 6-B; ASCS, aerial photo no. 45079–11c-051, May 22, 1943; *Orangeburg Times and Democrat*, August 20, 1910, 1; Dr. Robert Taylor in discussion with the author, January 2010. All ASCS photos cited in this chapter were downloaded from the University of South Carolina, University Libraries Digital Collections, Aerial Photographs of Richland County, S.C., http://library.sc.edu/digital/collections/aerials/sccola.html

70. ASCS, aerial photo no. 45079–3h-091, May 13, 1951; NPS, *Specific Area Report*, 15.

71. Chittenden, *Red Gum*, 39; SCDACI, *Handbook of South Carolina*, 548–49.

72. Gallagher, *Grail Bird*, 93–94; Watson, *Reflections on the Neches*, 39–40, 321; cf. Stroyer, *My Life in the South*, 38.

73. Hopkins, *Lower Richland Planters,* 393, quoting written recollections (July 1932) of Thomas Philip Weston, grandson of Dr. William Weston III; Cely, "Is the Beidler Tract in Congaree Swamp Virgin? An Update."

74. Chittenden, *Red Gum,* 15; Hammond, *South Carolina,* 79; Watson, *Reflections on the Neches,* 39; Platt and Brantley, "Canebrakes," 12–15.

75. Pederson, Jones, and Sharitz, "Age Structure and Possible Origins," 112, 114, 118.

Chapter 3: The Rise of Plantation Agriculture

1. Diary entry, February 10, 1797, Joshua Evans Diary and Autobiography, no. 249-z, Southern Historical Collection, Wilson Library, University of North Carolina at Chapel Hill ("Me glad it rain"); Moore, *World of Toil and Strife,* 23; Meriwether, *Expansion of South Carolina,* 165.

2. Moore, *Columbia and Richland County,* 60–61; Williams, *Americans and Their Forests,* 62–63; De Brahm, "Philosophico-Historico-Hydrogeography," 198–99.

3. Green, *History of Richland County,* 26–27, 32, 63, 141; Medlin, *Richland County Landmarks,* 95–97; Edelson, *Plantation Enterprise in Colonial South Carolina,* 11.

4. Klein, *Unification of a Slave State,* 19–23; Medlin, *Richland County Landmarks,* 95–97; Meriwether, *Expansion of South Carolina,* 56, 59, 61; *Charleston Courier,* September 29, 1824, 5; *Charleston City Gazette,* May 26, 1810, 4; Caughman, "Agricultural Resources of Lexington District," 134; *State,* May 23, 1909, pt. 1, 9; *News and Courier* (Charleston), September 13, 1888, 1.

5. *State,* May 23, 1909, pt. 1, 9; Van Duyne, McLendon, and Rice, *Soil Survey of Richland County,* 64, 66; Mills, *Statistics of South Carolina,* 712.

6. "An Act for Raising and Paying," 627–28. During the antebellum period, oak and hickory highlands were rated at only $3.00 per acre, while "all high river swamp, and low grounds, cultivated and uncultivated, including such as are commonly called second low grounds" were rated as follows: first quality, $13.00, second quality, $8.50, and third quality, $4.00, excepting in each case "such as may be clearly proven to the Collectors to be incapable of immediate cultivation, which shall be rated at one dollar per acre." Pickens, "Report of the Comptroller General . . . 1861," 97. See also Drayton, *View of South Carolina,* 110–11; Mills, *Statistics of South Carolina,* 697.

7. This system of valuing land only persisted as long as it did because the state drew the bulk of its revenue from taxes on slaves. See Pickens, "Report of the Comptroller-General . . . 1859," 4; Ford, *Origins of Southern Radicalism,* 309–12.

8. Blanding, "Address...on the Subject of Internal Improvement," 135.

9. *Charleston City Gazette,* November 23, 1821, 4 ("first quality Swamp Land"); Richard H. Fishburne to Mary C. Fishburne, ca. December 1821, in Fishburne Papers ("too insignificant"); tax return of William H. Fishburne Jr. for tax year 1799, in Fishburne Papers ("3d quality second low grounds"); H. A. De Saussure to Mary C. Fishburne, June 7, 1832, quoting letter from W. F. De Saussure to H. A. De Saussure, in Fishburne Papers; plat, 375 acre-tract on Running Gut, resurveyed for Robert Fishburn [*sic*], certified December 10, 1850, State Plats, SCDAH.

10. Cely, *Map of Original Land Grants;* Cely, *Map of Early Land Grants.*

11. Cely, "Is the Beidler Tract in Congaree Swamp Virgin?" 92–93; Green, *History of Richland County,* 63; Meriwether, *Expansion of South Carolina,* 104, 106; Jones, *South Carolina, a Synoptic History,* 55.

12. Green, *History of Richland County,* 23, 26; Langley, *South Carolina Deed Abstracts,*

3:374; Cely, *Map of Original Land Grants*; Brown, *South Carolina Regulators*, 145; Meriwether, *Expansion of South Carolina*, 64, 64n37; Holcomb, *South Carolina Deed Abstracts 1783–1788*, 183; Langley, *South Carolina Deed Abstracts*, 4:8. Creighton and Sullivan obtained their land in the park via grants, but Muckenfuss purchased his land. Muckenfuss acquired at least two tracts within the present park boundary. One of these he acquired in 1768 from John Frentz, another lowcountry (?) speculator (see Holcomb, *South Carolina Deed Abstracts 1773–1778*, 98; and "John Frentz" in appendix B). The Frentz tract bordered today's Oak Ridge Trail on the southeast. By 1784 a slough on the tract was known as "Frenchmans Pond." See plat, sixty-acre tract on Running Gut, certified July 30, 1784, for John Cook, state plats, SCDAH.

13. Langley, *South Carolina Deed Abstracts*, 4:183, 279; *South Carolina Gazette and Country Journal*, September 27, 1774, 2, January 10, 1775, supplement, 1.

14. Peter Moore argues that most grants held for five years or less were never intended for use by the original grantee. See Moore, *World of Toil and Strife*, 131n29.

15. Beginning in the late seventeenth century, a number of French Huguenot families fled religious persecution in France and settled in the South Carolina lowcountry. The descendants of the first Isaac Mazyck (William's grandfather) rose to prominence in the ensuing decades. See Ruymbeke, "Huguenots of Proprietary South Carolina"; Hirsch, *Huguenots of Colonial South Carolina*, 232–34.

16. Cely, *Map of Original Land Grants*; Holcomb, *South Carolina Deed Abstracts 1773–1778*, 182, 232; Langley, *South Carolina Deed Abstracts*, 4:183. Dr. Farrar was a leader in the Regulator movement of the late 1760s. The Regulators sought to end the banditry, lawlessness, and chaos that plagued the South Carolina backcountry in the wake of the Anglo-Cherokee War (1759–1761). They were led by a coalition of around 120 small planters and leading men. One of the Regulators' principal aims was to establish a system of courts, jails, and garrisons for the protection of property and commerce. However, some Regulators resorted to extreme violence to punish persons they considered idle and immoral. These tactics soon triggered a reaction by the so-called Moderators, prosperous backcountry settlers who approved of the Regulators' efforts to establish order but not the use of violence to check immorality. Other Regulators who owned land in the park included John Cook and possibly Moses Kirkland. For information on the activities of the Regulators at the Congarees, see Moore, *Columbia and Richland County*, 24–27; and Brown, *South Carolina Regulators*.

17. Cely, *Map of Congaree National Park*.

18. Mills, *Statistics of South Carolina*, 695; *Carolina Gazette* (Charleston), October 2, 1824, 2 ("hazard of freshets"); *Charleston City Gazette*, May 26, 1810, 4 ("increasingly so"). Flooding on the Congaree was nothing new. Flooding had induced some settlers along the upper Congaree to abandon or sell their lands as early as the 1750s, and this pattern may have been even more prevalent farther downriver. See Meriwether, *Expansion of South Carolina*, 62.

19. Mathew, *Agriculture, Geology, and Society*, 157–59. See also Edelson, "Clearing Swamps, Harvesting Forests," 391.

20. Stroyer, *My Life in the South*, 18–19; Mills, *Statistics of South Carolina*, 712.

21. Thomas B. Clarkson to Matthew Singleton, August 3, 1852, Singleton Family Papers, SCDAH.

22. Winberry, "Indigo in South Carolina," 91, 92–95, 100n13; Ramsay, *History of South Carolina*, 284; Worcester, *Geographical Dictionary*, 337; Edelson, *Plantation Enterprise in*

Colonial South Carolina, 123; Klein, *Unification of a Slave State,* 16, 20–21; Morgan, *Slave Counterpoint,* 37, 162.

23. Morgan, *Slave Counterpoint,* 160; Huneycutt, "The Economics of the Indigo Industry," 13.

24. Glen, "Description of South Carolina," 17–18; Moore, *Columbia and Richland County,* 64; Winberry, "Indigo in South Carolina," 96.

25. Winberry, "Indigo in South Carolina," 91–92; Edgar, *South Carolina,* 146.

26. Winberry, "Indigo in South Carolina," 92; Meriwether, *Expansion of South Carolina,* 62; Moore, *Columbia and Richland County,* 64; South Carolina House of Representatives, *Hearing on H 3097* (statement of W. Peter Buyck Sr.).

27. Klein, *Unification of a Slave State,* 20–23; Morgan, *Slave Counterpoint,* 62.

28. Ackerman, *South Carolina Colonial Land Policies,* 106; Klein, *Unification of a Slave State,* 36; William Howell, will date February 2, 1757, proved May 6, 1757, Will Transcripts, Charleston County, vol. 8, 74, SCDAH; William Howell, 1757, Inventories of Estates, Charleston County, vol. S, 178–79, SCDAH.

29. Winberry, "Indigo in South Carolina," 96–97; United States Department of Commerce and Labor, *Heads of Families . . . 1790,* 26–27, 95, 97; Klein, *Unification of a Slave State,* 22–23.

30. Gray, *History of Agriculture,* 1:294; Winberry, "Indigo in South Carolina," 98; Dubose, "Reminiscences of St. Stephen's Parish," 75 ("well cleared, drained"); Woodmason, "Different Species of the Indigo Plant," 202 ("at the hoe").

31. Schoepf, *Travels in the Confederation,* 157; Dubose, "Reminiscences of St. Stephen's Parish," 76–77; Woodmason, "Different Species of the Indigo Plant," 202 ("very able ones").

32. Edgar, *South Carolina,* 146, 266; Green, *History of Richland County,* 139 ("old indigo fields").

33. Shelley et al., "Bluff to Bluff," 87–88; Tomlinson Engineering Co., *Plan of Five Thousand One Hundred and Eighty Eight Acres.*

34. South Carolina General Assembly, Committee Report and supporting papers (including map of Huger's Landing and related features [n.d.]) on the petition of the inhabitants of Camden District, asking for a ferry over Congaree River at General Huger's Landing, 1786, SCDAH Series S165005, Item 172; United States Department of Commerce and Labor, *Heads of Families,* 95.

35. Schafer, *Governor James Grant's Villa;* Wagner, "National Register of Historic Places Registration Form"; Woodmason, "Different Species of the Indigo Plant," 203, 256 (quotation); Floyd, "On the Cultivation and Preparation of Indigo," 154; Edelson, *Plantation Enterprise in Colonial South Carolina,* 111, 160; plat, 60-acre tract on Cedar Creek, certified October 7, 1803, for John Hamelton, State Plats, SCDAH; Cely, *Map of Early Land Grants.* The age of the dam across Running Lake Slough is not known.

36. Floyd, "On the Cultivation and Preparation of Indigo," 157.

37. Woodmason, "Different Species of the Indigo Plant," 256–58; Dubose, "Reminiscences of St. Stephen's Parish," 74–77; Beeson, "Indigo Production in the Eighteenth Century."

38. Huneycutt, "Economics of the Indigo Industry," 16; Beeson, "Indigo Production in the Eighteenth Century," 215; Schafer, *Governor James Grant's Villa;* Walsh, "Work and the Slave Economy," 108–9; Morgan, *Slave Counterpoint,* 163–64.

39. Winberry, "Indigo in South Carolina," 98–99; Mendenhall, "History of Agriculture," 49–51, 52; Elliott, "Reflections on the State of Our Agriculture," 64–65.

40. Meriwether, *Expansion of South Carolina*, 4, 59, 109; Moore, *Columbia and Richland County*, 10, 172; Klein, *Unification of a Slave State*, 16.

41. Simms, *Geography of South Carolina*, appendix, 154; Wicks, "Culture of Upland Rice"; Richardson, *Cultural Resource Survey*, 48, 55; Jaeger Company, *Survey Report*, 25.

42. Dubose, "Address [to] the Black Oak Agricultural Society," 6; Edgar, *South Carolina*, 266–67; Drayton, *View of South Carolina*, 116; Moore, *Columbia and Richland County*, 172, 174.

43. Meriwether, *Expansion of South Carolina*, 59, 61; Guy Taylor, "Old Dead River Dike II, Historic Rice Plantation Remnants," site inventory record, n.d., CNP files; Guy Taylor, "Location of Levee," memorandum to superintendent, CSNM, September 28, 1979, CNP files.

44. United States Census Office, Manuscript Census Returns, 1850 (Agriculture), Richland District, SCDAH; Trinkley and Fick, *Rice Cultivation, Processing, and Marketing*, 5, 14, 22; Gibbes, "Agricultural Survey of the Parish of St. Mathews [*sic*]," 149 ("somewhat like corn"); *Columbia (S.C.) Daily Phoenix*, April 15, 1869, 3.

45. Kinzer, "Partial Chain of Title"; Michie, *Archeological Survey of Congaree Swamp*, 68; Carney, "Landscapes of Technology Transfer," 86; Trinkley and Fick, *Rice Cultivation, Processing, and Marketing*, 3, 7–8.

46. Romans, *Concise Natural History*, 126. See also Bennett and Griffen, "Soil Survey of the Orangeburg Area," 200.

47. Ball, *Slavery in the United States*. Ball's narrative was written by a "Mr. Fisher," based on Ball's personal recollections. Ball provides the best available account of life along the upper Congaree during the early national period.

48. Ibid., 137 (quotation), 193, 316; Blassingame, introduction, *Slave Testimony*, xxv; Meynard, *Venturers*, 106–8. Wade Hampton I had acquired various tracts in and near the park via his marriage to Martha Epps Goodwyn in 1783. These included the "Mill Place" (that is, the Duffies Pond area on Cedar Creek) and three parcels in the western end of the Beidler Tract totaling over four hundred acres. It is not known when Hampton sold the Beidler Tract acreage or to whom. However, Joel Adams Sr. had acquired this land by September 1790. See Holcomb, *South Carolina Deed Abstracts 1783–1788*, 257–58; plat, 35-acre tract on Boggy Gut, certified September 6, 1790, for Joel Adams Sr., State Plats, SCDAH. The latter document identifies Adams as the adjoining landowner on three sides.

49. Ball, *Slavery in the United States*, 293 ("made his rice fields"), 203–4 ("clearing and ditching").

50. Meriwether, *Expansion of South Carolina*, 56, 58, 106, 165–66, 170; *Charleston Southern Patriot*, October 17, 1845, 2; Mills, *Statistics of South Carolina*, 696–97.

51. South Carolina Department of Agriculture, Commerce and Industries and Clemson College, *South Carolina: A Handbook*, 135; Phillips, *History of Transportation*, 42; Smith, *Economic Readjustment of an Old Cotton State*, 52, 74–75; Hilliard, *Hog Meat and Hoecake*, 154–55, 200–201, 210–11, 224; Mendenhall, "History of Agriculture," 326–27.

52. Drayton, *View of South Carolina*, 10 ("fifty to seventy bushels"), 113 ("brought down the rivers"), 138 ("only spoken of").

53. Mills, *Statistics of South Carolina*, 694. See also Allen, "Letters from the South," 21; Robinson, "Statistics of Cotton Growing," 339, 340.

54. Ford, "Self-Sufficiency, Cotton, and Economic Development"; Gallman, "Self-Sufficiency in the Cotton Economy of the Antebellum South"; Battalio and Kagel, "Structure of Antebellum Southern Agriculture," 33–34; Mendenhall, "History of Agriculture," 119.

55. Hilliard, *Hog Meat and Hoecake*, 22–25, 151–52, 198, 211, 234–35; Ford, *Origins of Southern Radicalism*, 254–55; Lieber, "Stray Notes on the Agricultural Capacities," 265.

56. Mendenhall, "History of Agriculture," 62, 103–4, 112–13, 166; Edgar, *South Carolina*, 273–74; Ford, *Origins of Southern Radicalism*, 14, 249–55; Moore, *Columbia and Richland County*, 174. The district's cotton-to-corn ratio, calculated by dividing pounds of cotton by bushels of corn, went from 10.47 in 1850 to 19.18 in 1860.

57. United States Census Office, Manuscript Census Returns, 1850 and 1860 (Agriculture), Richland District, SCDAH.

58. See Miller and Smith, *Dictionary of Afro-American Slavery*, 145–48.

59. Most of the individuals who owned land in the Beidler Tract in 1860 resided in Richland District. Zeigler, Spigener, and McKenzie lived across the river in Orangeburgh District.

60. Michie, *Archeological Survey of Congaree Swamp*, 133, 135; Charles Cotesworth Pinckney to Thomas Pinckney, May 25, 1792, Pinckney Family Papers, Box 1 ; Charles Cotesworth Pinckney to Thomas Pinckney, July 17, 1793, Pinckney Family Papers, Box 9; Estate records for Joel Adams Sr., Richland County Estate Papers, Box 1, Package 5, SCDAH.

61. Guy Taylor, "Mound and Structural Remains," memorandum to archaeological resources file, CSNM, February 2, 1983, CNP files; Drayton, *View of South Carolina*, 130, 137 (quotation); Ball, *Slavery in the United States*, 211; Hammond, *South Carolina*, 89.

62. Mendenhall, "History of Agriculture," 54; Edgar, *South Carolina*, 270–71; Gray, *History of Agriculture*, 1:294; Drayton, *View of South Carolina*, 127; Floyd, "On the Cultivation and Preparation of Indigo," 106; Klein, *Unification of a Slave State*, 151, 251–52.

63. Drayton, *View of South Carolina*, 129 (emphasis in original); Mills, *Statistics of South Carolina*, 694; Allen, "Letters from the South," 21 (cf. Robinson, "Statistics of Cotton Growing," 339, 340); Webster, *Private Correspondence of Daniel Webster*, 252; Rosengarten, *Tombee*, 75–76.

64. On cotton cultivation in the floodplain below Columbia, see *Carolina Gazette*, October 2, 1824, 2; *South Carolina State Gazette* (Columbia), June 2, 1827, 3; and *Charleston Courier*, August 30, 1831, 2.

65. Van Duyne, McLendon, and Rice, *Soil Survey of Richland County*, 66; Wicks, "Culture of Upland Rice"; North Carolina Agricultural Experiment Station, "On the Temperature of the Soil," 181; Mathew, *Agriculture, Geology, and Society*, 160; Hammond, *South Carolina*, 78; Sitton, *Backwoodsmen*, 68–69.

66. Lossing, *Pictorial Field-Book of the Revolution*, 683n1; Coate, *Survey of Richland District; Columbia Daily Phoenix*, November 3, 1869, 2 ("productive lands"); United States Fish and Wildlife Service, National Wetlands Inventory Mapper, accessed August 1, 2015, http://www.fws.gov/wetlands/data/mapper.HTML; Natural Resources Conservation Service, *Assessment of the Congaree Subbasin*, 9.

The O'Hanlon plantation consisted of two tracts, mostly floodplain, totaling 5,164 acres. The two tracts were known as the Singleton tract and the Log Castle tract. In 1865 these "superior cotton and grain lands" were advertised for rent with the suggestion that sixty or seventy hands could be "advantageously employed" on the Singleton tract, and twenty-five or thirty on the Log Castle tract. The 1860 census shows that of the "6,000" total acres of O'Hanlon land, 2,000 were improved. See *Columbia Daily Phoenix*, December 24, 1865, 2, November 4, 1869, 3; United States Census Office, Manuscript Census Returns 1860 (Agriculture), Richland District, SCDAH.

67. Mathew, *Agriculture, Geology, and Society*, 160. Major Porcher's embankment was situated on the south bank of the Santee River in Berkeley County, just below where the Lake Marion Dam stands today. When he visited Mexico Plantation in March 1843, Edmund Ruffin observed that Major Porcher

> has by many years of labor executed a work of which he has a right to be proud . . . his embankment of swamp lands on the Santee. . . . This embankment extends from the northern outlet of the [Santee] canal, 4¼ miles, on the swamp land of Major P. & 300 yards farther through his next neighbor's land, for the greater safety of his own. Its height varies from 8 to 14 feet of perpendicular height, & averages 10. The base varies from 35 to 60 feet, & most of it is over 50 feet. It protects fully, for dry culture 800 acres, & embraces about 1400. This great work was begun in 1817, & was not deemed complete until 1841; & even now, it is designed to add to its height considerably through its entire length. Besides the first construction, there have been at different times breaches made, & parts swept away, so as to cause about a mile of bank to be re-constructed. This is one of the greatest private works known; & is the more remarkable as being the work of one individual, & who was sustained by no encouragement of concurrent opinion or hope of other persons. (Mathew, *Agriculture, Geology, and Society*, 156–57.)

68. Seabrook, "Reclamation of the Swamps"; Natural Resources Conservation Service, *Assessment of the Congaree Subbasin*, 9; Richland County, S.C., *Prime Agricultural Soils*; Webster, *Correspondence of Daniel Webster*, 253.

69. Quoted in Jones, *South Carolina, a Synoptic History*, 148.

Chapter 4: Early Park Plantations

1. Statement of C. C. Pinckney in Elliot, *Debates in the Several State Conventions*, 285 ("raise my voice"); United States Department of Commerce and Labor, *Heads of Families . . . 1790*, 26–27, 94–98. On the loss of slaves in the Revolutionary War, see Klein, *Unification of a Slave State*, 105–7, 114.

2. Meriwether, *Expansion of South Carolina*, 105–6; Klein, *Unification of a Slave State*, 20; Mendenhall, "History of Agriculture," 218–19; Richardson, *Cultural Resource Survey*, 24.

3. Meriwether, *Expansion of South Carolina*, 106; Edelson, *Plantation Enterprise in Colonial South Carolina*, 7.

4. Edelson, *Plantation Enterprise in Colonial South Carolina*, 257, 258–59; Cely, *Cowasee Basin*, 40–41; Blanding, "Address . . . on the Subject of Internal Improvement," 135; Trenholm, "History and Present Condition," 638, citing statistics compiled by Robert Mills.

5. Kinzer, *Partial Chain of Title*; Salley, "Col. Miles Brewton and Some of his Descendants," 148. For a discussion of slaves supervised by local overseers, see Edelson, *Plantation Enterprise*, 153–54. See also Wagner, "National Register of Historic Places Registration Form."

6. Winberry, "Indigo in South Carolina," 92–93; plat, 35-acre tract on Boggy Gut, certified September 6, 1790, for Joel Adams Sr., State Plats, SCDAH (identifying Major Wise as adjoining landowner); *South-Carolina Gazette and General Advertiser*, December 16, 1783, 1 ("To Be SOLD"); *Clifton, Administrator of [Jane Ann Wise] Campbell v. Executors of Haig, et al.*, 3 S.C. Eq. (3 Des Eq.) 330 (1812); *South Carolina State Gazette* (Columbia), July 12, 1806, 3.

7. One of the tracts in the plantation was laid out to Middleton in the fall of 1772. See plat, 206-acre tract, certified November 25, 1772, for Henry Middleton, Colonial Plats, SCDAH. By then the tract was surrounded on three sides by other Middleton land, suggesting that Middleton had already acquired a large part of his Congaree plantation by late 1772. The approximate boundary of the plantation as it existed in the early to mid-1770s (?) is shown in an undated, unlabeled plat located in the South Carolina state archives. See plat, 2,546-acre tract, divided among 14 individuals [including James McKelvey [sic]] , n.d., McCrady plats, SCDAH.

8. *South-Carolina Gazette and General Advertiser*, May 10, 1783, 2 ("those valuable Indigo lands"); plat, 2,546-acre tract, divided among 14 individuals [including James McKelvey [sic]], n.d., McCrady plats, SCDAH; *Carolina Gazette*, January 14, 1802, 3.

9. Charles Drayton to Edward Rutledge, ca. 1797, Charles Cotesworth Pinckney Family Papers, Box 15, Manuscript Division, Library of Congress; *South Carolina Gazette*, January 25, 1772, 1; Neuffer, "Calhoun County Plantations," 46; Cely, *Cowasee Basin*, 38–39.

10. This undated map is filed in the state archives together with an apparently unrelated legislative committee report on Huger's Ferry dated February 10, 1786. The inclusion of distance information in the map suggests that it was actually prepared in or about 1791, the year the General Assembly appointed commissioners to investigate the feasibility of rechartering a public ferry at McCord's Landing. The commissioners in that matter were expressly directed to ascertain the distance between Huger's Ferry and the former site of McCord's Ferry. See Committee Report and supporting papers on the Petition of the inhabitants of Camden District, asking for a ferry over Congaree River at General Huger's Landing, 1786, SCDAH Series S165005, Item 172; Resolution directing the appointment of commissioners to ascertain the distance between Huger's Ferry and McCord's Ferry, 1791, SCDAH Series S165018, Item 18.

11. See map of Huger's Landing and related features (n.d.), filed with Committee Report on the Petition of the inhabitants of Camden District, asking for a ferry over Congaree River at Gen. Huger's Landing, 1786, SCDAH Ser. S165005, Item 172.

12. Charles Drayton to Edward Rutledge, ca. 1797, Pinckney Family Papers, Box 15 ("family consideration"); Haw, *John and Edward Rutledge*, 180, 225, 262; Williams, *Founding Family*, 206, 295, 421n54.

13. Charles Drayton to Edward Rutledge, ca. 1797, Pinckney Family Papers, Box 15; Thomas Middleton to Charles Cotesworth Pinckney, November 9, 1795, Pinckney Family Papers, Box 14 ("'prime' swampland"); Kinzer, *Partial Chain of Title;* George Butler, will date November 21, 1840, proved October 8, 1841, CNP files; *Carolina Gazette*, January 14, 1802, 3; plat of Joseph Martin tract, n.d. [1789 or after], in Pinckney Family Papers, Box OV3. The Pinckney/Rutledge plantation may have played a small role in the debate over relocating the state capital away from Charleston to a spot closer to the center of the state. Rutledge argued that if the capital was not to remain in Charleston, which he and C. C. Pinckney strongly preferred, then it should be located near the confluence of the Congaree and Wateree Rivers. Rutledge adduced various reasons in support of this location, but the fact that he and Pinckney owned a large plantation nearby was perhaps more than coincidental. Certainly other prominent landowners such as Wade Hampton I and Thomas Sumter sought to influence selection of the new site to increase the value of their local holdings. The legislature ultimately chose to locate the capital at Columbia, due in no small part to the maneuverings of Hampton. *Charleston Morning Post,* March 21, 1786, 2; Haw, *John and Edward Rutledge,* 190; Moore, *Columbia and Richland County,* 43–44.

14. Charles Drayton to Edward Rutledge, ca. 1797, Pinckney Family Papers, Box 15; Adams, *History and Sketches*; Meynard, *History of Lower Richland*, 8, 215–17; Isaac Rivers, will date April 26, 1777, proved n.d., Will Transcripts, Charleston County, vol. 17, 697–98, SCDAH.

15. Green, *History of Richland County*, 33; Morse, "South Carolina"; United States Census Office, Manuscript Census Returns, 1820 (Population), Richland District, SCDAH; Congaree Land Trust, "Adams Conserves Wavering Place"; [Charles Cotesworth Pinckney and ?], Gen. Charles Cotesworth Pinckney account book, 1784–1791, in Pinckney Family Papers, Box 5.

16. Thomas Taylor (see appendix B).

17. William Weston II (see appendix B).

18. Zahniser, *Charles Cotesworth Pinckney*, 76–78; Williams, *Founding Family*, 206; Charles Drayton to Edward Rutledge, ca. 1797, Pinckney Family Papers, Box 15; Thomas Middleton to Charles Cotesworth Pinckney, with certification, November 9, 1795, Pinckney Family Papers, Box 14 ("indigo or corn"); Charles Cotesworth Pinckney to Thomas Pinckney, July 17, 1793, Pinckney Family Papers, Box 9 ("a fourth time"). See also Charles Cotesworth Pinckney to Thomas Pinckney, May 25, 1792, Pinckney Family Papers, Box 1.

19. *Carolina Gazette*, January 14, 1802, 3 ("Public Auction"); Dubose, "Address [to] the Black Oak Agricultural Society," 22; Matthews, *Forgotten Founder*, 70–71; Edgar, *South Carolina*, 271; Haw, *John and Edward Rutledge*, 262.

20. See deed of conveyance to William Rouse, February 16, 1802, in Pinckney Family Papers, Box OV3. For mention of Pinckney tracts north of the river after 1802, see, for example, plat, eighty-eight-acre tract, certified December 30, 1828, for Moses Braddy, State Plats, SCDAH. On Joel Adams Sr.'s role as agent and the possibility that Pinckney leased out his Congaree plantation, see Charles Cotesworth Pinckney to the Reverend Mr. De la Vaux, Rector of St. Matthews, January 29, 1821, in Ann Heatly Reid Lovell Papers, 1786–1854, 1103.03.01, South Carolina Historical Society, Charleston.

After Pinckney's death, the Congaree plantation passed to his daughters Maria Henrietta and Harriott. They in turn sold a fourteen-hundred- to fifteen-hundred-acre portion of the plantation, mostly south of the river, to George Butler of Orangeburgh District. The only area north of the river sold to Butler appears to have been Pinckney's Neck—that is, the area surrounded today by the remnants of Old Dead River. George Butler later devised this land, including Pinckney's Neck, to his son Joel in 1840 (the neck was eventually known as "Butler's Island"). See Charles Cotesworth Pinckney, will date April 7, 1824, proved September 23, 1825, Will Transcripts, Charleston County, vol. 36, 1168–71, SCDAH; George Butler, will date November 21, 1840, CNP files.

21. Information about Gillon's Retreat can be found in Bailey and Cooper, *Biographical Directory of the South Carolina House of Representatives*, 268. See also *South Carolina Gazette and General Advertiser*, May 10, 1783, 2; and map of Orangeburgh District, with notation for "A. Buyck's" land, in Mills, *Atlas of State of South Carolina* (Augustine Buyck was the subsequent owner of Gillon's Retreat). The part of the plantation north of the river consisted of the modern-day Brady tract (Tract 101-42) as well as 186 acres to the west originally granted to Elizabeth Ricker (100 acres) and Bartholomew Vawser (86 acres). Gillon conveyed this acreage to Francis Goodwyn in 1777. See plat, 86-acre tract, certified February 12, 1770, for Bartholomew Vanser [*sic*], Colonial Plats, SCDAH; Memorial, 86-acre tract granted to Bartholomew Vawser, July 14, 1770, Memorial Books, SCDAH; Holcomb, *South Carolina Deed Abstracts 1773–1778*, 136 (conveyance to Goodwyn). For information

about the later history of Gillon's Retreat, see "Alexander Gillon" and "Augustine Buyck" in appendix B.

22. *Charleston City Gazette*, September 23, 1793, 4. This description appears to indicate that the plantation was located on the south side of the Congaree River. Its owner may have been the Estate of Andrew Lord. See *South Carolina Gazette and General Advertiser*, May 10, 1783, 2; and *Columbian Herald*, November 9, 1793, 3. Andrew Lord, a Charleston merchant, should not be confused with John Lord (d. 1795), who resided downriver from Gillon on a tract overlooking the park. John Lord's plantation bounded the Pinckney-Rutledge plantation on the east and included Lord Lake.

23. *South Carolina Gazette*, December 21, 1769, 1 ("Indico Plantation"), October 18, 1770, 5 ("For Sale").

24. Cely, *Map of Original Land Grants*; Kinzer, *Partial Chain of Title*; Langley, *South Carolina Deed Abstracts*, 3:374 and 4:8; Peter Mazyck, will date June 24, 1772, proved July 23, 1772, Will Transcripts, Charleston County, vol. 14, 285–90, SCDAH; William Mazyck, will date June 13, 1775, proved n.d., Will Transcripts, Charleston County, vol. 16A, 376–79, SCDAH. The Mazycks were one of the wealthiest merchant and trading families in eighteenth century South Carolina. Philip Porcher, husband of Mary Mazyck (and brother in law of Peter and William), owned a four-hundred-acre tract inside the present park boundary. Porcher sold this tract to Peter Mazyck sometime in or before 1772. See will of Peter Mazyck.

Mazyck's Cut is a short artificial outlet from Cedar Creek to the Congaree. Although the name would appear to indicate that the cut dates to the eighteenth century, other evidence suggests that it was dug (or perhaps merely reopened) sometime in the twentieth. See entry 22 in appendix A.

25. Mortgage (with plat), Gershom Kelly to Commissioners of the Loan Office, May 6, 1786, mortgages, SCDAH; Peter Mazyck, will date June 24, 1772, SCDAH.

26. United States Department of Commerce and Labor, *Heads of Families . . . 1790*, 97; *Charleston City Gazette*, September 24, 1791, 1; United States Census Office, Manuscript Census Returns 1800 (Population), Orangeburgh District, SCDAH. The 1790 population schedule for Orangeburgh District includes an entry for thirty-four slaves, "the property of William and Isaac Mazyck." No white person is identified as part of the household.

27. Holcomb, *South Carolina Deed Abstracts 1783–1788*, 182–83 (three deeds conveying five tracts to Edward Lightwood); plan representing a tract of land situated near Huger's Ferry, containing 500 acres [granted to Elias Jordan (*sic*)], [post-1786], McCrady plats (showing tracts owned by Edward Lightwood), SCDAH; *South-Carolina Weekly Gazette*, July 12, 1783, 2 ("Will be SOLD"). For information on "the proposed seat of government," see note 13 above.

28. Gagnon, "Fire in Floodplain Forests," 521, 523; Cely, *Map of Congaree National Park*; plat, 300-acre tract, certified September 11, 1759, for Joseph Jackson, Colonial Plats, SCDAH.

29. Plan representing a tract of land situated near Huger's Ferry, containing 500 acres [granted to Elias Jordan (*sic*)], SCDAH; Conrad, Parks, and King, *Papers of Nathanael Greene*, 118, 124.

30. Lightwood mortgaged most of his Congaree tracts to the state in 1786 but had not repaid the loan by the time of his death. See mortgages (with plats), Edward Lightwood to Commissioners of the Loan Office, March 28, 1786, and May 6, 1786, mortgages, SCDAH; *Charleston City Gazette*, May 25, 1801, 2. Three of the mortgaged tracts were later sold to John Bostick in 1801. See note 37 below.

31. United States Department of Commerce and Labor, *Heads of Families . . . 1790*, 34, 39.

32. *Charleston City Gazette*, February 2, 1793, supplement, 2; mortgages (with plats), Isaac Huger to Commissioners of the Loan Office, April 25, 1786, and May 10, 1786, mortgages, SCDAH.

33. Inhabitants of Camden District, Petition asking that a new ferry and road be laid out to shorten the travel time to Charleston, 1786, SCDAH Series S165015, Item 69; Green, *History of Richland County*, 113, 117; Klein, *Unification of a Slave State*, 244–46.

34. Huger, Isaac, Petition asking that his ferry be the only point for crossing the Congaree for seven miles, 1788, SCDAH Series S165015, Item 33; Cely, *Map of Congaree National Park*. See also Phillips, *History of Transportation*, 29.

35. *Columbian Herald*, November 14, 1794, 3 ("resided for some years"). The new property was probably Huger's 2,470-acre plantation on Cat Island in Prince Georges Parish. Huger paid 2,500 pounds sterling for this plantation (and other smaller tracts) in March 1787. Holcomb, *South Carolina Deed Abstracts 1783–1788*, 424–25.

36. *Columbian Herald*, September 20, 1787, 1 ("Plantation, for Sale"); Holcomb, *South Carolina Deed Abstracts 1783–1788*, 183 (1771 conveyance to Huger); *Charleston City Gazette*, August 4, 1788, 4.

37. *Charleston City Gazette*, March 11, 1797, supplement, 1; *Brailsford v. House*, 10 S.C.L. (1 Nott & McC.) 31 (1817); Draine and Skinner, *Richland District . . . Land Records*, 8; Thomas, *Slave Trade*, 268, 297; Bell, *Major Butler's Legacy*, 10, 510. John Bostick acquired the contiguous tract to the west in 1801. He acquired four other tracts in the park at the same time, three of them formerly owned by Edward Lightwood. *Charleston City Gazette*, May 25, 1801, 2; *Hampton v. Levy*, 6 S.C. Eq. (1 McCord Eq.) 107 (1825); Bostick, John, Petition asking to have deducted from his bond a sum of money, 1802, SCDAH Series S165015, Item 34; *Charleston City Gazette*, March 15, 1809, 4. Although it sold sooner, the ferry tract may not actually have been occupied until 1810, when it was leased to Reuben House by James Kennedy. Kennedy was a rival in title to Samuel Brailsford. *Brailsford v. House*, 10 S.C.L. (1 Nott & McC.) 31 (1817).

38. Bull, *Oligarchs in Colonial and Revolutionary Charleston*, 232; Bull, Memorial of Lt. Gov. William Bull Jr., AO 12/52: 90 ("River Swamp improved"); Steen and Taylor, *Archeological Survey of the Congaree Bluffs*, 22, 108–9; lease and release, Benjamin Farrar to Isaac Huger, November 19 and 20, 1771, Charleston County Deed Book Q-5, p. 222, SCDAH (conveying a 600-acre tract [today's Beidler Tract Parcel 19], bounded eastward by "a Part of the same Tract lately sold to the Hon. William Bull Esquire"); lease and release, William Bull Jr. to Robert Pringle, September 7 and 8, 1779, Charleston County Deed Book H-5, p. 40, SCDAH (conveying multiple properties in South Carolina and Georgia, including tracts of 1,170 and 576 acres on the Congaree River, the latter adjoining "Brigadier General Huger"); *Hannah Bull v. Stephen Bull and Nathaniel Russell*, final judgment (March 8, 1790), 2, Chancery Court Records, SCDAH (52 slaves). See also copy of plat accompanying indenture made June 26, 1779, between Colonel William Thomson and Dr. Robert Pringle, in maps/plats, South Carolina Historical Society, 33–44–08 (identifying Bull as adjoining landowner to Colonel Thomson north of river); and plat, 742-acre tract, certified September 18, 1804, for Henry Reese Hall, State Plats, SCDAH (encompassing, in whole or in part, land formerly owned by Bull). In 1779 Bull conveyed his various real estate interests to his nephew Stephen Bull (via Robert Pringle, see Charleston County Deed Book H-5, p. 40, cited above) in an attempt to avoid confiscation by state authorities. The conveyance

included both the 1,170- and 576-acre tracts. Bull listed "1095 [*sic*] Acres of Land at the Congarees" in a Loyalist claim (Memorial) submitted to the Crown in 1782 but made no mention of the 576-acre tract.

39. Charleston County Deed Book H-5, p. 40, SCDAH; Bull, *Oligarchs in Colonial and Revolutionary Charleston*, 232; Bull, Memorial of Lt. Gov. William Bull Jr., AO 12/52: 109, 116 ("above 400 Acres"); United States Department of Commerce and Labor, *Heads of Families . . . 1790*, 95, 97, 98. Bull fled to England in 1782. In 1790 a judicial ruling allowed him to recover his property from his nephew, who had wrongfully refused to restore it, but he was never able to return to South Carolina. He died in London in 1791.

40. Bull, Memorial of Lt. Gov. William Bull Jr., AO 12/52: 96; Thomson and Russell, Affidavit on behalf of William Bull Jr., AO 13/97: 45 (specifying, among other property taken from the Congaree plantation, 1,800 bushels of corn); Nathaniel Russell to William Bull Jr., January 29, 1785, AO 13/97: 55 (adding 2,500 bushels to the 1,800 specified in the Thomson-Russell affidavit). In his claim to the Crown, Bull sought compensation for a large group of slaves captured in the May 1781 raid. Bull's trustees had moved many of his slaves inland to the Congarees in 1779 to safeguard them from the fighting on the coast, but this proved to be a major miscalculation. General Sumter took 160 of the best slaves in the raid and distributed them as booty. The seizure did not go unnoticed by Bull's neighbor Brigadier General Isaac Huger, who lamented Sumter's plundering in a letter to a fellow patriot, Colonel Lewis Morris. Twenty of Bull's slaves were sent to Brigadier General Francis Marion to help destroy the ditch and palisade at Rebecca Motte's house ("Fort Motte"), which Marion and Lieutenant Colonel Harry "Light Horse" Lee had recently captured from the British. Bull, *The Oligarchs in Colonial and Revolutionary Charleston*, 272, 290; Bull, Memorial of Lt. Gov. William Bull Jr., AO 12/52: 96 and AO 13/97: 22–23; Isaac Huger to Lewis Morris, May 22, 1781, in Webber, "Revolutionary Letters," 78; Smith et al., "Obstinate and Strong," 34, 52.

41. Dubose, "Reminiscences of St. Stephen's Parish," 38 ("a second Egypt"); "Address [to] the Black Oak Agricultural Society," 6 ("no settlements"). See also Porcher, *History of the Santee Canal*, 6. For a discussion (and map) of settlement in and around the lower Santee floodplain, see Edelson, *Plantation Enterprise in Colonial South Carolina*, 132–33.

42. Dubose, "Address [to] the Black Oak Agricultural Society," 11, 19 ("the more fortunate"); *Charleston City Gazette*, November 5, 1794, 2.

43. Kirk, "Belvidere Plantation, Sinkler Family"; Ramsay, *History of South Carolina*, 571.

44. Joel Adams Sr. to William H. Fishburne Jr., September 20, 1792, in William Fishburne Papers, Manuscripts Division, South Caroliniana Library, University of South Carolina; *Charleston City Gazette*, November 23, 1821, 4. By 1790 Adams had acquired a substantial amount of land in the far western part of the park (map 6). He owned sixteen slaves of his own in 1790 and may have been able to rent others owned by the men whose lands he managed. United States Department of Commerce and Labor, *Heads of Families . . . 1790*, 27.

45. Ramsay, *History of South Carolina*, 571; Ford, *Origins of Southern Radicalism*, 7; Mendenhall, "History of Agriculture," 58, 62.

46. Regarding the restriction of cotton cultivation to the best-drained floodplain soils, see Mendenhall, "History of Agriculture," 58, 62, 103.

Chapter 5: Reclaiming the Floodplain

1. Seabrook, "Reclamation of the Swamps," 219–20 ("frequently in error"); Klein, *Unification of a Slave State*, 114; Edgar, *South Carolina*, 266; Winberry, "Indigo in South Carolina," 98; *Charleston City Gazette*, November 5, 1794, 2.

2. *Charleston City Gazette*, January 26, 1796, 3.

3. Trimble, *Man-Induced Soil Erosion*, 18–19, 21–22; *Carolina Gazette*, October 2, 1824, 2; *Charleston Courier*, August 30, 1831, 2; September 6, 1831, 2; April 30, 1833, 2; June 1, 1840, 2; October 17, 1845, 2; *Charleston Southern Patriot*, August 16, 1841, 2; Green, *History of Richland County*, 13.

4. Hammond, *South Carolina*, 77–78; plat, 370-acre tract, certified August 15, 1839, for Paul Spigner [*sic*], State Plats, SCDAH; *Columbia Daily Phoenix*, November 21, 1869, 3 ("cleared"); *Orangeburg Times and Democrat*, June 3, 1886, 8 ("stock and grain crops"). On flooding patterns in the park, see Patterson, Speiran, and Whetstone, *Hydrology and Its Effects*, 17–19. Care must be taken when extrapolating backward from modern data. It is possible that flooding pulses in the mid- to late nineteenth century were more exaggerated than those experienced today, given the amount of land-clearing and runoff occurring in the Piedmont at the time. Moreover, the elevation of the modern floodplain, particularly the levee zone, is higher now than it was before the mass wasting of piedmont soils, which peaked in the latter part of the nineteenth century. Observations of the modern meander belt in the middle part of the park indicate that the levee has aggraded up to eight feet above the adjoining backswamp. See Knowles et al., *Water Resources Management Plan*, 37, 141–42; Shelley, "Geology, Geomorphology, and Tectonics," 48; Minchin and Sharitz, *Age Structure and Potential Long-Term Dynamics*, 31.

5. Mathew, *Agriculture, Geology, and Society*, 248.

6. Hammond, *South Carolina*, 77; Edgar, *South Carolina*, 274.

7. Cook, *Life and Legacy of David Rogerson Williams*, 170–73; Edelson, *Plantation Enterprise in Colonial South Carolina*, 112.

8. *Charleston City Gazette*, November 22, 1793, 3 ("affected by the freshes"), September 19, 1796, 3 ("highest Freshes").

9. Richardson, *Cultural Resource Survey*, 19, 28–29, 33–34, 40, 49; Wallace, *South Carolina*, 362.

10. Quoted in Cook, *Life and Legacy of David Rogerson Williams*, 168–69.

11. Cook, *Life and Legacy of David Rogerson Williams*, 169–170; Mills, *Statistics of South Carolina*, 518–19; Mathew, *Agriculture, Geology, and Society*, 157, 159; Dubose, "Address [to] the Black Oak Agricultural Society," 28.

12. Mathew, *Agriculture, Geology, and Society*, 260; Gibbes, "Extraordinary Freshet."

13. Martineau, *Society in America*, 42.

14. Mathew, *Agriculture, Geology, and Society*, 260.

15. Allen, "Letters from the South," 20; cf. Robinson, "Statistics of Cotton Growing," 339.

16. South Carolina House of Representatives, *Hearing on H 3097* (statement of W. Peter Buyck Sr.). The Buycks descended from Augustine Buyck of Belgium, who immigrated to South Carolina in 1784.

17. *Charleston Mercury*, April 26, 1856, 2. According to the *Mercury*, Frederick Cooner had recently prevailed in a legal dispute with his neighbor, Paul Spigener, over injuries

allegedly caused by Cooner's Dam. Spigener argued that Cooner's Dam "obstructed the flow of the water in time of freshets and backed it up the river, thereby causing his tract to be submerged." At the time of the dispute, Cooner owned a large tract spanning "High Hill Creek," which included the future Buyck property. Spigener owned a smaller tract across the river from Cooner, making up what would later become Beidler Tract Parcel 14 and Tract 101-35. The phrase "backed it up the river" suggests that Cooner's Dam was located across the river and to the east of Parcel 14 and Tract 101-35. If so, this would place the dam on the Buyck property. See entry 21 in appendix A.

18. Adams, *History and Sketches;* United States Census Office, Manuscript Census Returns 1850 (Agriculture, Slave Schedules), Richland District, SCDAH.

19. Joel Adams Sr., will date October 30, 1829, proved July 21, 1830, Will Transcripts, Book H, 362, SCDAH. The state formally regranted the devised lands to the three brothers in 1839. See plat, 5,188-acre tract, certified August 5, 1839 for James Adams Sr., Joel Adams [Jr.], and Robert Adams, State Plats, SCDAH; and also Tomlinson Engineering Company, *Plan of Five Thousand One Hundred and Eighty Eight Acres.* The regranted land consisted of 4,175 acres of swamp (over 4,000 of which were in the Beidler Tract), plus adjoining uplands. The upland portion of the tract contained 1,013 acres in the vicinity of Duffies Pond.

20. James Adams Sr., will date July 11, 1840, proved February 10, 1841, Will Transcripts, Book L, 11, SCDAH; Joel R. Adams, Memorandum of Agreement with the South-Carolina Rail-Road Company, February 1, 1846, in Cantey Family Papers. See *North American Tourist,* 447–48, on the use of slaves to construct the Branchville-to-Columbia line. The payments from the railroad came at a critical time for a number of planters, whose finances had been undermined by a depression that started with the Panic of 1837 and lasted until 1843. Slaves were also hired out between 1845 and 1848 to construct the branch line from Kingsville (originally called "Junction") to Camden. This line included almost four miles of trestle through the Wateree Swamp. Derrick, *Centennial History of South Carolina Railroad,* 184–85; Fetters, *Charleston & Hamburg,* 93–94.

21. Cely, *Map of Congaree National Park;* Michie, *Archeological Survey of Congaree Swamp,* 135; Lawrence, *Soil Survey of Richland County,* maps 55, 63 (Toccoa loam [TO]).

22. Bleser, *Secret and Sacred,* 70.

23. Ibid., 194. Hammond stayed in South Carolina. During the 1840s he drained and cleared about six hundred acres of Carolina bays at great expense.

24. Coate, *Survey of Richland District;* Tomlinson Engineering Company, *Plan of Five Thousand One Hundred and Eighty Eight Acres* (showing the Adams swamp plantation and adjoining bluff plantation).

25. Cantwell, *Plat of the Swamplands and Timber Holdings;* Green, *History of Richland County,* 13; Gibbes, "Extraordinary Freshet" ("immense dams").

26. Cely, *Map of Congaree National Park.* In 1909 the *State* reported that dikes built perpendicular to the river, well upstream from the park, "were evidently built with the intention of breaking any considerable current, and thus preventing the resulting cutting effect of the floods, but they have not bettered conditions in so far as growing crops are concerned." *State,* May 23, 1909, pt. 1, 9.

27. James Adams Sr., will date July 11, 1840, proved February 10, 1841, Will Transcripts, Book L, 11, SCDAH. See also Cely, "Is the Beidler Tract in Congaree Swamp Virgin?" The cost of the project could have been considerable. The children of James Adams may have looked at the numbers and decided that the potential returns were not worth the present

costs and future risks. Cotton prices were particularly low in 1840 because of the bumper crop of 1839. Moreover, in 1840 the nation was still in the midst of one of the worst economic depressions in its history, brought on by the Panic of 1837. Adams's children may have decided that reworking the dam at the Adams millpond (known today as Duffies Pond) was a better investment of time and money. An 1869 deed states that the dam for this millpond was "erected" between 1840 and 1845. Since the pond is known to date back to the eighteenth century, it seems likely that what was erected in the 1840s was an expansion of the original dam. See Richland County Deed Book K, p. 150.

28. Doyle, *Modeling Flood Plain Hydrology,* 14, 28; Gaddy et al., *Vegetation Analysis of Preserve Alternatives,* 38 (table 5).

29. O'Meally, introduction to Adams, *Tales of the Congaree,* xxii, xxiii; Williams, *A Devil and a Good Woman Too,* 290n68; Adams, *Tales of the Congaree,* 109 ("slave days"), 124 ("swamp fields"), 239 ("de river"). Goose Pond and the site of the former Lykes plantation are located upstream from the park.

30. William Weston I, will date October 17, 1770, proved February 25, 1772, transcribed in Hamrick, "Some Notes on the Weston Family," 138; Meynard, *History of Lower Richland,* 8, 13, 15, 18, 159–62, 279. According to Virginia Meynard, Dr. Weston's move to Grovewood was prompted by his uncle's move to Alabama and the siting of the railroad through Brite Savannah, which resulted in major disruption to life at the family home. At the time of his move to Grovewood, Weston apparently sold the majority of Brite Savannah to Joel Adams Jr. (1784–1859). This land became part of Adams's Elm Savannah Plantation. Meynard, *History of Lower Richland,* 162–63, 244, 365.

The Adams and Weston properties reportedly escaped some of the worst destruction visited by Sherman's troops on the plantations of lower Richland. According to tradition, a Union captain who had gone to school with Dr. William Weston IV in Paris ordered his troops to spare Weston's property and that of his relatives. Houses at Grovewood, Magnolia (Wavering Place), Elm Savannah, and Live Oak were not burned. Much looting of family properties occurred, however, and the house once occupied by patriarch Joel Adams Sr. (d. 1830) was destroyed. Hopkins, *Lower Richland Planters,* 37, 259.

31. Green, *History of Richland County,* 139; Meynard, *History of Lower Richland,* 161; Lowry, *Hooper and Weston Families,* 15, 17 ("a thousand acres or more," quoting Thomas Philip Weston [?]); Hopkins, *Lower Richland Planters,* 392; Tomlinson Engineering Company, *Plan of Five Thousand One Hundred and Eighty Eight Acres;* Medlin, *Richland County Landmarks,* 39.

32. Plat, 300-acre tract, certified January 16, 1765, for Malachi Western [*sic*], Colonial Plats, SCDAH. See also Hamrick, "Some Notes on the Weston Family," 140 (describing the Malachi Weston of lower Richland as possibly being William Weston I's brother of that name).

33. Old Dead River appears to have been intentionally cut off in the 1820s. Nothing in Marmaduke Coate's 1820 *Survey of Richland District* suggests that a shift in the river's main channel was imminent at that time. However, a subsequent state plat prepared for John D. A. Murphy in 1827 shows that Old Dead River had been cut off by that date. The Murphy plat shows a 130-acre island in the Congaree River bordered on the south by a small channel labeled a "cut off." See plat, 130-acre tract , certified July 30, 1827, for John D. A. Murphey [*sic*], State Plats, SCDAH.

34. The dike was located at the southern end of what is today Beidler Tract Parcel 13. By 1839 land in the middle part of this parcel was "said to belong to Mr. Westen." See

plat, 370-acre tract, certified August 15, 1839, for Paul Spigner [*sic*], State Plats, SCDAH. This "Mr. Westen" would have been Dr. William Weston III. In fact, William Weston III had likely exercised control over much of Parcel 13 since the date of his marriage to Christian Grace Tucker in 1818. Up to that point Christian Grace Tucker's real property had probably been held in trust for her in accordance with the terms of her father's will. Language from the will states that "my executors [James Adams Sr. and Joel Adams Jr.] may commit the trust of . . . properties [held in trust for my daughters] to such persons as they deem proper and worthy" (see Isaac Tucker, will date April 25, 1811, proved June 22, 1811, Will Transcripts, Book E, 220, SCDAH). Given that the Weston, Adams, and Tucker families were all interrelated by marriage, it seems safe to assume that the Adams brothers committed Christian Grace Tucker's trust to her husband, William Weston III. Among the properties apparently held in trust for Tucker was all or some portion of Parcel 13. An 1827 plat indicates that the entire area immediately to the east of Old Dead River is "supposed to belong to the Estate of Isaac Tucker De'd" (see plat, 130-acre tract, certified July 30, 1827, for John D. A. Murphey [*sic*], State Plats, SCDAH). In 1861 this same area, including the site of the dike, was said to be known as the "Weston tract" (Richland County Deed Book F, p. 28). Likewise, an 1882 deed refers to this area as "land formerly of Wm Weston" (Richland County Deed Book O, p. 349; see also Deed Book AC, p. 425). Taken together, this evidence suggests that William Weston III controlled the dike property for some indeterminate period of time between 1818 and his death in 1848.

35. Hopkins, *Lower Richland Planters,* 392, quoting written recollections (July 1932) of Thomas Philip Weston, grandson of Dr. William Weston III.

36. Plat, 370-acre tract, certified August 15, 1839, for Paul Spigner [*sic*], State Plats, SCDAH; plat of dike property prepared for A. M. Hunt, July 26, 1861, Richland County Deed Book F, p. 29; United States Census Office, Manuscript Census Returns, 1850 and 1860 (Agriculture), Richland District, entries for Alfred M. Hunt, SCDAH.

37. *State,* May 23, 1909, pt. 1, 9; Cely, *Map of Congaree National Park;* Guy Taylor, "Levee in Congaree NM," memorandum to Paul Spangle, NPS Denver Service Center, August 15, 1978, CNP files.

38. United States Census Office, Manuscript Census Returns, 1820 and 1830 (Population), Richland District, SCDAH; Morgan, *Slave Counterpoint,* 196–97; Edelson, *Plantation Enterprise in Colonial South Carolina,* 217; Dusinberre, *Them Dark Days,* 71; *Charleston City Gazette,* August 4, 1821, 3.

39. United States Census Office, Manuscript Census Returns, 1840 (Population), Richland District, SCDAH; estate records for Dr. William Weston III, Richland County Estate Papers, Box 61, Package 1519, SCDAH; Manuscript Census Returns, 1810 (Population), Darlington District, SCDAH. Slaves are not broken out by age and gender in the 1810 census, so it is not possible to compare the number of able-bodied hands available to Williams with those available to Weston.

40. See United States Census Office, Manuscript Census Returns, 1850 (Slave Schedules), Orangeburg District (slaves of Paul "Speigner"), and Manuscript Census Returns, 1860 (Slave Schedules), Richland District (slaves of A. M. Hunt), SCDAH. Although Spigener owned thirty-six slaves in 1850, only ten were males between the ages of sixteen and fifty-two. Hiring slaves was always an option, but when cotton prices were high, as they were in the 1850s, slaves could provide a greater return for their owners working the fields than by being leased out for construction projects.

41. Kinzer, *Partial Chain of Title*; Tomlinson Engineering Company, *Plan of Five Thousand One Hundred and Eighty Eight Acres* (showing "William Weston, Esq." as the owner of swampland immediately to the east of the Adams swamp plantation).

42. Governor Adams had acquired Stoney Hill Plantation by the early 1830s. A small part of the plantation lay within what is now the park. This area is designated Tract 101-33 in the park's tract map. Whether Adams constructed the dike or ever used it is not known.

43. Lossing, *Pictorial Field-Book of the Revolution*, 683n1.

44. Mathew, *Agriculture, Geology, and Society*, 271 ("high land"), 160 ("continuance of freshes").

45. *Carolina Gazette*, October 9, 1824, 2; Mills, *Statistics of South Carolina*, 299–325; Seabrook, "Reclamation of the Swamps"; *State*, May 23, 1909, pt. 1, 9.

46. Letter to the editor from Sumter District.

47. *Charleston Mercury*, July 17, 1856, 2.

48. S.C. Statutes at Large, vol. 12, Act No. 4307 (1856); Smith, *Economic Readjustment of an Old Cotton State*, 85–86; S.C. Statutes at Large, vol. 12, Act No. 4455 (1859) (incorporating the Wateree Embankment Company).

49. *State*, March 17, 1896, 4 ("lottery"), May 23, 1909, pt. 1, 9.

Chapter 6: The Location and Extent of Historic Clearing

1. Woodward, *Mary Chesnut's Civil War*, 249 ("big fish"); Jackson, *In Search of the Ivory-Billed Woodpecker*, 136; Tanner, *Ivory-Billed Woodpecker*, 37.

2. Gallagher, *Grail Bird*, 98–99 (quoting unpublished essay by James T. Tanner).

3. Cely, "Is the Beidler Tract in Congaree Swamp Virgin? An Update"; Pederson, Jones, and Sharitz, "Age Structure and Possible Origins," 118, 121; Baker and Langdon, "*Pinus taeda* L., Loblolly Pine," 501.

4. Cely, *Map of Original Land Grants*; Pederson, Jones, and Sharitz, "Age Structure and Possible Origins," 120; Pederson, [Comments on age of Weston Lake loblolly pine]; Batson, [Eligibility of Congaree Swamp]; Stalter and Batson, "Giant Loblolly near Columbia," 438. Other old pines in the park have had their ages confirmed by ring counts. A loblolly stump found by Harry Hampton had 183 rings when cut, indicating that it generated around 1785. The location of this tree is not known. See Dennis, "Woody Plants of the Congaree Forest Swamp," 36. In 2012 the author counted rings on a fallen pine located just east of the elevated boardwalk, about sixty-five paces south of the northern bluff. The cut face exhibited approximately 185 rings ten feet above the base of the tree, indicating a generation date sometime before the 1820s.

5. Doyle, *Modeling Flood Plain Hydrology*, 28; Pederson, Jones, and Sharitz, "Age Structure and Possible Origins," 114, 119, 120, 121; Stalter, "Age of a Mature Pine *(Pinus taeda)* Stand," 532; Swails, Anderson, and Batson, "A Mature Pine Stand," 83; Cely, "Is the Beidler Tract in Congaree Swamp Virgin? An Update"; Hampton, *Woods and Waters*, 296; Culler, "Forest of Champions," 16 (photo of pre-hurricane loblolly pine stand along Sims Trail). See also *Columbia Daily Phoenix*, April 15, 1869, 3.

6. Gaddy et al., *Vegetation Analysis of Preserve Alternatives*, 33. The study also tentatively determined that the Beidler Tract contained approximately ten thousand acres of seemingly undisturbed, uneven-aged hardwoods, mostly old growth. The authors concluded that no widespread human interference had taken place in these portions of the tract since at least 1775. This conclusion was based on the distribution of areas with "relict canopies" and large trees.

As part of the study's effort to characterize the uneven-aged portions of the tract, researchers counted stump rings in three selectively logged areas. Ring counts revealed that the canopy trees of "relict canopy" areas ranged in age from 80 to 300 years. The authors noted that standing trees of some species were larger in diameter than the stumps measured in the study and thus may have been even older. The oldest individuals of each species and their locations (by parcel) were as follows: cherrybark oak—165 years (Parcel 1); swamp chestnut oak—280 years (Parcel 10); shumard oak—82 years (Parcel 1); laurel oak—115 years (Parcel 10); [green] ash—160 years (Parcel 1); sweet gum—237 years (Parcel 1); sugarberry—220 years (Parcel 1); American beech—101 years (Parcel 1); loblolly pine—143 years (Parcel 1); longleaf pine—300 years (Parcel 4). See Gaddy et al., *Vegetation Analysis of Preserve Alternatives*, 3, 33, 35, 38 (Table 5), 42; and also Doyle, *Modeling Flood Plain Hydrology*, 28.

7. Presentation by L. L. Gaddy at Congaree Swamp National Monument Symposium I, January 23, 2002.

8. Cely, "Is the Beidler Tract in Congaree Swamp Virgin? An Update."

9. Mathew, *Agriculture, Geology, and Society*, 248–49 ("very little is cleared"), 251 ("narrow strip").

10. Jones, *Location and Ecology of Champion Trees*, 12, 15, 16.

11. Ibid., 15, citing Gaddy, *Natural Resources Inventory*, map 14.

12. Researcher Kimberly Meitzen has also observed pervasive evidence of human disturbance along the river. During the course of investigating succession patterns in the levee zone, Meitzen observed mounded soil, abandoned equipment, and a number of iron posts driven in to levee soils (Meitzen in discussion with the author, February 2008). Whether this disturbance dates to the timber-harvesting era or some other time has yet to be determined. With respect to the iron posts, one possibility is that they were installed in the late nineteenth and early twentieth centuries to secure snags pulled from the river by the U.S. Army Corps of Engineers. See *State*, February 2, 1904, 8.

13. Cely, *Map of Congaree National Park*; John E. Cely, e-mail message to author, April 19, 2005; Cely, "Is the Beidler Tract in Congaree Swamp Virgin? An Update"; Culler, "Forest of Champions," 20 (showing photo of the cherrybark oak stump discussed in main text); Minchin and Sharitz, *Age Structure and Potential Long-Term Dynamics*, 18. The cherrybark oak stump was located along the western portion of the river trail.

14. Cely, *Map of Congaree National Park*; Frost and Wilds, *Presettlement Vegetation and Natural Fire Regimes*. Many of the tracts along the river were owned by families living in present-day Calhoun County—for example, the Brady, Buyck, Zeigler, Spigener, Wise, Pauling, Cooner, and Thomson families. These and other families south of the river were responsible for much of the human disturbance in the levee zone and beyond.

15. *Liquidambar styraciflua-Quercus nigra-Quercus laurifolia/Arundinaria gigantea/ Carex abscondita* forest. See Landaal, Weakley, and Drake, *Classification of the Vegetation*, 27–28; and USGS and NPS, *Vegetation Map, Congaree National Park*. An updated description of this association is found in Landaal, [Association description of the sweet gum–(laurel oak, water oak)–(loblolly pine)/giant cane/thicket sedge forest].

16. *Celtis laevigata-Liquidambar styraciflua-Quercus laurifolia/Carpinus caroliniana/ Arundinaria gigantea/Carex lupulina* forest. See Landaal, Weakley, and Drake, *Classification of the Vegetation*, 20–21; USGS and NPS, *Vegetation Map, Congaree National Park*.

17. Not long after completion of the park's vegetation map, investigators concluded that the green ash phase and the sweet gum phase are not actually two phases of a single

association but rather analogues of two separate and distinct associations. The replacement association for the green ash phase is described in Landaal, [Association description of the green ash–American elm/American hornbeam/small-spike false nettle forest]. The replacement association for the sweet gum phase is described in Weakley and Schafale, [Association description of the laurel oak–swamp chestnut oak–sweet gum/American hornbeam forest]. Because the park's final vegetation map depicts the two phases rather than the later replacement associations, the discussion herein is framed in terms of the phases for the sake of consistency.

18. It is not entirely clear why the formerly cleared areas in Mitchell's Quarter are mapped as part of the main, green ash phase of the association. Perhaps these areas were too small to be mapped as a separate association. If not, perhaps they came to exhibit the characteristics of the green ash phase after a period of natural succession. Or perhaps they shifted from the sweet gum phase to the green ash phase after they were clear-cut in the 1980s. A study of historic aerial photos might help determine whether Mitchell's Quarter and other logged areas fell within the sweet gum phase before they were clear-cut. If they did, then the case for viewing the sweet gum phase as a possible indicator of past clearing would appear to have additional support.

19. According to the researchers who developed vegetation class descriptions for the park, at least some of the study plots assigned to the sweet gum phase may actually be "hurricane-battered examples" of an entirely separate, oak-dominated association, the laurel oak–swamp chestnut oak–sweet gum/American hornbeam forest (*Quercus laurifolia–Quercus michauxii–Liquidambar styraciflua/Carpinus caroliniana* forest). See Landaal, Weakley, and Drake, *Classification of the Vegetation*, 2–3, 21. As discussed in note 17 above, further deliberation resulted in the sweet gum phase being reclassified as an analogue of this association.

20. John E. Cely, e-mail message to author, April 19, 2005.

21. Kinzer, *Annotated Checklist of Floodplain Cultural Features*.

22. See, for example Woodard, Lewellen and Isom Woodard [*sic*], Petition for a road from their dwelling to their plantation on Congaree River, 1833, SCDAH Series S165015, Item 14; and also "Isom Woodward" in appendix B.

23. United States Census Office, Manuscript Census Returns, 1860 (Slave Schedules), Richland District, SCDAH. The owners of the principal tracts east of the Beidler Tract possessed fewer slaves. Proceeding from west to east, these landowners (and the number of slaves they owned in 1860) were as follows: Eliza Mitchell and William A. Mitchell (3), James H. Seay (77), James Trumble and Joseph Bates (47, collectively), John Bates (42), James U. Adams (309), Thomas R. Brown (34), and Robert Joyner, presumed owner of the Fork Swamp tract (31).

24. Davidson, *Last Foray*, 154; Mills, *Statistics of South Carolina*, 211–12.

25. Kellar, *Solon Robinson*, 392; *Columbia Daily Phoenix*, October 5, 1867, 2; United States Census Office, *Seventh Census of the United States: 1850*, 345–46; Anderson, "Animals into the Wilderness." On the availability of potentially arable land in antebellum South Carolina, see Smith, *Economic Readjustment of an Old Cotton State*, 84–85.

According to the Natural Resources Conservation Service, the bulk of the prime farmland in Richland County is located in lower Richland on the uplands to the north of the park. See Natural Resources Conservation Service, "Assessment of the Congaree Subbasin," 9; and also Richland County, S.C., *Prime Agricultural Soils*.

In the mid–nineteenth century, total "improved" farmland—defined in the 1850 census as "only such as produces crops, or in some manner adds to the productions of the farmer"—made up only 28 percent (1850) and 29 percent (1860) of farmland in Richland District. Despite these small percentages, the acreages involved (89,426 acres in 1850; 77,118 acres in 1860) are around twice the amount of "minimally limited" soil in the county—that is, soil having minimal limitations restricting its use for agriculture. In modern times it has been estimated that only 39,885 acres in the county are minimally limited. Thus, most of the best upland soils in lower Richland were probably cultivated over the course of the antebellum period. In the postwar years, the widespread use of fertilizers would bring ever more marginal lands under the plow, resulting in the mass wasting of lands across the Piedmont. See United States Census Office, *Seventh Census of the United States: 1850*, 345–46; United States Census Office, *Agriculture of the United States in 1860*, 128–29; Lawrence, *Soil Survey of Richland County*, 31, 79; Trimble, *Man-Induced Soil Erosion*, 26–28; Edgar, *South Carolina*, 428.

26. Edgar, *South Carolina*, 273–76; Kinzer, *Partial Chain of Title*; Moore, *Columbia and Richland County*, 118–21.

27. United States Census Office, Manuscript Census Returns, 1850 and 1860 (Agriculture), Richland District, SCDAH; United States Census Office, *Seventh Census of the United States: 1850*, 345–46; United States Census Office, *Agriculture of the United States in 1860*, 128–29. Seventeen farms did not report their improved acreage in 1860.

28. United States Census Office, *Seventh Census of the United States: 1850*, 346; United States Census Office, *Agriculture of the United States in 1860*, 129.

29. It is difficult to do a comprehensive assessment of the amount of cotton produced by these families in 1860 as compared to their output in 1850. Wealthy members of the Adams and Weston families died in the intervening decade, resulting in complex inheritance issues. Nevertheless, the following figures for cotton production illustrate the overall trend: James U. Adams, 475 bales in 1850, 600 bales in 1860; Lieuellan Woodward, 140 bales in 1850, 200 bales in 1860; Weston family, 280 bales in 1850, 445 bales in 1860. (Note: each bale was about 400 pounds in 1850 and 445 pounds in 1860.) It is not known how much, if any, of this cotton was grown on the Beidler Tract. See United States Census Office, Manuscript Census Returns, 1850 and 1860 (Agriculture), Richland District, SCDAH; Ford, *Origins of Southern Radicalism*, 245n2.

30. Stuckey, "Remarks on the 1850 Mortality Schedule."

31. *Columbia Daily Phoenix*, September 27, 1870, 3, October 16, 1870, 3; Meynard, *History of Lower Richland*, 165; Medlin, *Richland County Landmarks*, 39. Dr. William Weston III died intestate on July 25, 1848. See estate records for Dr. W. Weston III, Richland County Estate Papers, Box 61, Package 1519, SCDAH; and also Christian Grace Weston, will date February 20, 1854, proved April 18, 1854, Will Transcripts, Book L, 201, SCDAH.

32. United States Census Office, Manuscript Census Returns, 1860 and 1870 (Agriculture), Richland District/County, SCDAH; Richland County Deed Book H, p. 464. According to the 1873 plat, the plantation actually comprised about 1,896 acres, of which 1,634 acres are now in the park. Weston's floodplain acreage included all of Beidler Tract Parcels 2 and 5, as well as parts of Parcel 4 and Tract 101-21. A 189-acre area along Dry Branch north of the park is labeled "I. T. Weston's Homestead" in the plat. A residence (presumably the one called "the Bluffs" by the family) is shown on the north side of Old Bluff Road, just east of Dry Branch. Isaac relocated to Florida around 1872. See Lowry, *Hooper and Weston Families*, 27, 30, 32–33, 38.

33. *Columbia Daily Phoenix*, December 18, 1866, 3. The advertisement provides details

about an unnamed 1,800-acre plantation located eighteen miles below Columbia. (The size and location of the plantation identify it as Pine Bluff.) The advertisement stated that in addition to 1,000 acres of swamp, the plantation contained 350 cleared acres "well adapted to the culture of cotton," with accommodations for twenty-five to thirty hands.

34. On January 19, 1869, real estate agents Gibbes and Thomas advertised "1,800 acres, in Richland, River Swamp Lands, with a good Mill." *Columbia Daily Phoenix,* January 19, 1869, 4. The acreage figure and reference to swampland suggest that this land was Isaac T. Weston's Pine Bluff Plantation, although it is not identified as such in the advertisement. The timing of the notice suggests Pine Bluff as well: Weston would advertise Pine Bluff himself the following year, and it seems he had been trying to sell the plantation since 1866. See *Columbia Daily Phoenix,* December 18, 1866, 3, and September 27, 1870, 3.

35. Chittenden, *Red Gum,* 7.

36. Lawrence, *Soil Survey of Richland County,* 7, 9–11, 26–27, 76–77, maps 55, 56, 59–64; Knowles et al., *Water Resources Management Plan,* 39–40; Michie, *Archeological Survey of Congaree Swamp,* 133–35; Van Duyne, McLendon, and Rice, *Soil Survey of Richland County,* 66; Wicks, "Culture of Upland Rice."

37. Schweninger, "Maroonage and Flight"; Ball, *Slavery in the United States,* 325–36; Lockley, *Maroon Communities in South Carolina,* 107–8; *Carolina Gazette,* September 13, 1823, 3 ("dense and impervious swamps").

38. *Carolina Gazette,* September 13, 1823, 3; *Camden (S.C.) Southern Chronicle,* October 8, 1823, 3 ("secreted themselves," "solemn warning"); *Charleston City Gazette,* October 8, 1823, 2.

39. Mathew, *Agriculture, Geology, and Society,* 230.

40. *Columbia Daily Phoenix,* November 30, 1870, 3.

41. Pea Ridge plantation was part of the extensive landholdings of James Adams Sr., possibly serving as the center of his planting operations. According to family historian Laura Jervey Hopkins, Adams had "a large mansion at Pea Ridge between Gadsden and Congaree." Hopkins, *History of St. John's Episcopal Church,* 29.

42. Plat of Pea Ridge Plantation dated May 13, 1886, surveyed by Samuel G. Henry, CNP files.

43. Cely, *Map of Congaree National Park;* Pederson, Jones, and Sharitz, "Age Structure and Possible Origins," 119–20; Cely, "Is the Beidler Tract in Congaree Swamp Virgin?" 92; Hardy, *Congaree National Park,* 85.

44. Mathew, *Agriculture, Geology, and Society,* 162.

45. Doyle, *Modeling Flood Plain Hydrology,* 28; Stalter, "Age of a Mature Pine *(Pinus taeda)* Stand," 532; Swails, Anderson, and Batson, "Mature Pine Stand," 83; Pederson, Jones, and Sharitz, "Age Structure and Possible Origins," 114, 118, 121; Chittenden, *Red Gum,* 32–33, 35–36; *State,* May 23, 1909, pt. 1, 9.

46. Peterken, *Natural Woodland,* 185; Chittenden, *Red Gum,* 15.

47. Hammond, *South Carolina,* 77, 78 ("entire corn crop"), 81 ("not yet entirely grown up"), 86, 107–8.

48. Foner, *Reconstruction,* 124–25, 129, 130–36, 172–73, 400–401, 404–5.

49. Some planters, such as H. L. Jeffers, were amenable to new arrangements. In 1867 Jeffers employed thirty-five to forty freedmen to work land he had leased at Stoney Hill Plantation northeast of the Beidler Tract. Jeffers hired his hands by the month for cash wages and was said to run a "model plantation" with fields that "show the result of care, and promise an abundant harvest." *Charleston Daily News,* August 30, 1867, 1.

50. Moore, *Columbia and Richland County*, 216–17; *Columbia Daily Phoenix*, April 15, 1869, 3, June 19, 1868, 1 ("Immigration Society").

51. Foner, *Reconstruction*, 173–74, 405, 536–37; Moore, *Columbia and Richland County*, 230; Van Duyne, McLendon, and Rice, *Soil Survey of Richland County*, 18, 55, 63; *State*, July 21, 1916, 10; *Charlotte Daily Observer*, August 30, 1908, 1; *Orangeburg Times and Democrat*, May 27, 1886, 1.

52. Foner, *Reconstruction*, 125, 536; Williamson, *After Slavery*, 148–55; Thomas Philip Weston to Philip Weston, April 2, 1945, transcribed in Lowry, *Hooper and Weston Families*, 29 ("destitute circumstances"); Richland County Deed Book N, pp. 218, 402 (conveyance of Isaac T. Weston land to William W. Weston [deeds understate acreage actually conveyed]), and Deed Book M, p. 188 (sale of Zeigler lands for nonpayment of taxes).

53. *Columbia Register*, May 26, 1886, 2; *Orangeburg Times and Democrat*, May 27, 1886, 1, 8, June 3, 1886, 8; Moore, *Columbia and Richland County*, 229–30; Peterkin, "Ashes," 9; *Charleston News and Courier*, September 8, 1888, 1; Florschutz, *Refuge Land Acquisition Biological Reconnaissance Report*, 6.

54. Ayers, *Promise of the New South*, 13–15; Foner, *Reconstruction*, 408, 536; Moore, *Columbia and Richland County*, 211, 227n2.

55. Conrads, Feaster, and Harrelson, *Effects of the Saluda Dam*, 20–21; United States House of Representatives, "Acquiring Land for the Protection of Watersheds," 123.

56. *State*, May 31, 1906, 2.

57. SCDACI, *Handbook of South Carolina*, 552. See also Bennett and Griffen, "Soil Survey of the Orangeburg Area," 196–97.

58. Moore, *Work of the Weather Bureau*, 24 ("heavily wooded swamp land"); Van Duyne, McLendon, and Rice, *Soil Survey of Richland County*, 66 ("trees and underbrush").

59. Van Duyne, McLendon, and Rice, *Soil Survey of Richland County*, 66 ("no present demand"); Jones, *Location and Ecology of Champion Trees*, 15; ASCS, aerial photo no. 45079–11c-051, May 22, 1943.

60. Pederson, Jones, and Sharitz, "Origins of Old *Pinus taeda* Stands," 118; Edgar, *South Carolina*, 428 ("pay off liens"); Trenholm, "History and Present Condition," 635; Wright and Kunreuther, "Cotton, Corn, and Risk."

61. Chittenden, *Red Gum*, 37; W. J. Murray to Reid Whitford, June 1, 1893, in United States Army, "Annual Report of the Chief of Engineers . . . 1893," 1494; *State*, September 28, 1907, 9.

62. "Study of the Red Gum."

63. Chittenden, *Red Gum*, 11.

64. Ibid., 14, 33 (quotation); Bruce P. Allen in discussion with the author, February 2008.

65. Chittenden, *Red Gum*, 8, 15, 33, 35–36, and plate 1–fig. 2 (reproduced herein as figure 15).

Chapter 7: Industrial Logging

1. Francis Beidler II, quoted in Reed, "You, Too, Can Visit a Swamp," 55 ("father's principal recreation"); Kelsey and Guild, *Improvement of Columbia, South Carolina*, 50–51 (quoted material reprinted in *State*, April 29, 1906, pt. 3, 22).

2. Williams, *Americans and Their Forests*, 193, 198; Goodyear and Hemingway, "Report of Lumber Operation," 3–4; Bennett et al., "Soil Survey of Sumter County," 319.

3. Williams, *Americans and Their Forests*, 198; SCDACI, *Handbook of South Carolina*, 542, 550; Wolfe, *Wood-Using Industries of South Carolina*, 7; Mattoon, *Southern Cypress*, 9–10.

4. *Columbia Daily Phoenix,* January 5, 1867, 3; Richland County Deed Book H, pp.6, 238, 339 ("Mill in Richland Fork"), 603, Book J, p. 44; Kinzer, *Partial Chain of Title.*

5. *Columbia Daily Phoenix,* March 16, 1873, 3 ("cypress sawed shingles"), December 3, 1872, 3; Kinzer, *Partial Chain of Title; Columbia Daily Phoenix,* January 10, 1874, 2, February 6, 1874, 3; *State,* February 16, 1897, 1.

6. *Columbia Daily Phoenix,* January 19, 1869, 4 ("600 acres," "convenient"); S. A. Pearce to Reid Whitford, October 20, 1884, in United States Army, "Annual Report of the Chief of Engineers . . . 1885," 1142; United States Department of Agriculture, *Report of the Commissioner of Agriculture . . . 1875,* 270; L. S. Ehrich to Reid Whitford, June 15, 1885, in United States Army, "Annual Report of the Chief of Engineers . . . 1885," 1122; *State,* February 3, 1903, 8; Phillips, *History of Transportation,* 34. See note 18 for chapter 2 above.

7. L. S. Ehrich to Reid Whitford, May 26, 1891, in United States Army, "Annual Report of the Chief of Engineers . . . 1891," 1460–61.

8. SCDACI, *Handbook of South Carolina,* 546–47; *Charleston News and Courier,* August 7, 1889, 8; *State,* August 21, 1892, 5; Kinzer, *Partial Chain of Title.*

9. Regarding Peterkin's acquisition of Lang Syne, see Orangeburg County Deed Book 20, p. 334; on his acquisitions below Kingville, see Kinzer, *Partial Chain of Title.* For reasons that are not clear, Peterkin claimed to own substantially more land in the swamp than he actually did. Ambiguous deeds from his original grantors and an absence of plats created a situation where as much as 3,400 acres of the 5,000 acres that he and John Peterkin claimed to have acquired in the 1880s actually belonged to others. The records from Richland County show the true state of affairs clearly enough, but Peterkin argued strenuously that he owned the full 5,000 acres. He even went so far as to publicly accuse James G. Gibbes, the state land agent, of selling tracts in the swamp that Peterkin had acquired years before. In rebuttal, Gibbes provided evidence that Peterkin could not possibly own the disputed tracts, accusing him of overstating his holdings to obtain a larger mortgage. *State,* February 16, 1897, 1.

10. *Charleston News and Courier,* September 2, 1890, 1 ("a thousand yards above"); Richland County Deed Book T, p. 81.

11. *Charleston News and Courier,* September 8, 1888, 1.

12. On March 15, 1889, the *New Oxford (Pa.) Item* printed a short blurb announcing that a "mill for making boxes for fruit and vegetables from shavings of sweet gum, sycamore and other unmerchantable woods has just been established on the Congaree River, near Fort Motte, South Carolina" (p. 7). The notice does not identify the mill's owner, but the location suggests Congaree Lumber and Veneer.

13. Wolfe, *Wood-Using Industries of South Carolina,* 45–46.

14. *Fairfield News and Herald,* February 1, 1888, 4.

15. Richland County Deed Book U, pp. 313, 461; *Charleston News and Courier,* September 2, 1890, 1.

16. *State,* April 24, 1892, 8.

17. Richland County Deed Book U, p. 589 ("on or near the South Carolina Railway"); *State,* August 17, 1893, 2, May 18, 1895, 8.

18. *Perkins v. Loan and Exchange Bank of South Carolina,* 20 S.E. 759 (S.C. 1895); *State,* August 16, 1893, 2, August 17, 1893, 8; Richland County Deed Book AB, p. 368.

19. Fretz, *Genealogical Record of the Descendants of Jacob Beidler,* 313–19; Andreas, *History of Chicago,* 369; *American Lumbermen,* 205–6, 207; Hotchkiss, *Industrial Chicago,* 229, 468, 505; Leonard, *Book of Chicagoans,* 53.

20. Brunswig and Winton, *Francis Beidler Forest,* 3; *Charleston News and Courier,* May 10, 1974, 1-B; *Charleston Evening Post,* August 7, 1905, 8; Fred Seeley to Henry Savage, May 4, 1953, Savage Papers; *State,* April 16, 1903, 12; Soucie, "Congaree," 67.

21. Soucie, "Congaree," 67.

22. *Sumter (S.C.) Watchman and Southron,* February 26, 1890, 4.

23. *Charleston News and Courier,* August 6, 1889, 8, January 29, 1890, 8, September 14, 1891, 8; Seeley to Savage, May 4, 1953, Savage Papers.

24. Leonard, *Book of Chicagoans,* 53. Although B. F. Ferguson remained president of the company until his death in 1905, Francis Beidler was the person actually directing operations during the period that Santee acquired and logged the Beidler Tract and adjacent lands—that is, from 1899 to around 1914. "Personal," 365; *Hornellsville (N.Y.) Evening Tribune,* April 12, 1905, 2.

25. *Sumter Watchman and Southron,* February 26, 1890, 4; *Saginaw (Mich.) Evening News,* March 8, 1890, 6, August 13, 1890, 6, August 25, 1890, 3; *American Lumbermen,* 208.

26. *Charleston News and Courier,* January 29, 1890, 8, September 2, 1890, 1 ("monster mill"); *Sumter Watchman and Southron,* April 23, 1890, 2, September 3, 1890, 2.

27. *State,* April 16, 1903, 12; *Charleston News and Courier,* January 29, 1890, 8, September 2, 1890, 1; *American Lumbermen,* 208.

28. *State,* August 1, 1894, 3; *Charleston News and Courier,* September 2, 1890, 1; Hotchkiss, *Industrial Chicago,* 580c.

29. *Charleston News and Courier,* January 29, 1890, 8; *State,* July 29, 1913, 9; *Charleston News and Courier,* September 14, 1891, 8; Hotchkiss, *Industrial Chicago,* 446, 469; "Where Tank Stock Is Made"; *American Lumbermen,* 208.

30. *State,* May 12, 1909, 3; *Charleston News and Courier,* October 4, 1970, 12-A; Santee River Cypress Lumber Co., "Engineering Features of a Large Southern Lumbering Development," 458 (quotations); "Isolated Plant Digest," 29; Rogers, "Steam Turbine in Sawmill Plant"; *State,* February 3, 1902, 6; "Prominent Cypress Industry"; Goodyear and Hemingway, "Report of Lumber Operation," 21–22.

31. Seeley resigned twice from his position at Ferguson, first in 1904 and again in late 1911. He was succeeded both times as general manager by M. B. Cross. Cross transferred to South Carolina from Chicago, where he had been in charge of the pole division of Francis Beidler and Company. When Santee reorganized in 1910, Cross was named secretary of the new entity. After Seeley's second departure, Cross managed Santee's affairs in South Carolina until his death in 1943. See Seeley to Savage, May 4, 1953, Savage Papers; "A Prominent Cypress Industry"; "Tight Stave Firm Incorporates"; "Where Tank Stock Is Made"; Richland County Deed Book BA, p. 6; "Bits of Telephone News," 281; *Beidler v. Veno,* 311 F2d. 623 (4th Cir. 1962).

32. Seeley to Savage, May 4, 1953, Savage Papers; *Sumter Watchman and Southron,* February 12, 1896, 5, January 31, 1906, 6; *Charleston News and Courier,* November 12, 1911, 12; Goodyear and Hemingway, "Report of Lumber Operation," 11–12.

33. Cely, "Congaree Swamp's Virgin Cypress Trees," 4; *State,* July 2, 1891, 5, August 18, 1892, 4; Santee River Cypress Lumber Co., "Engineering Features of a Large Southern Lumbering Development," 456; Seeley to Savage, May 4, 1953, Savage Papers; Mattoon, *Southern Cypress,* 2–4. In 1911 Santee owned an interest in more than 176,000 acres of timberland in twelve South Carolina counties. Over 141,000 of these acres were owned in fee, with timber rights making up the remainder. Most of Santee's timberland was floodplain and

swamp, but it owned tracts of upland pine as well. See Goodyear and Hemingway, "Report of Lumber Operation," 5, 22.

34. Although Santee's first fee simple acquisition in the park did not occur until 1899, hints in various recorded documents suggest that it may have acquired timber from local contractors during the mid- to late 1890s. See table 8 and note 38 below.

Santee had attempted to acquire land in the Congaree Swamp at least twice before, but did not complete either transaction. As noted above, James A. Peterkin reacquired the 5,000-acre Congaree Lumber and Veneer property in1890 with the intention of selling it to Santee. See *Charleston News and Courier,* September 2, 1890, 1. However, no record of a sale to Santee appears in the Richland County Register of Deeds, and it is possible that title problems and the ready availability of land elsewhere prompted Santee to abandon the purchase (see note 9 above). About six years later, Santee entered into an agreement with the Palmetto Lumber Company of New York to buy "10,000 acres of land in [Richland] and Sumter [Counties] . . . rich in cypress trees." *State,* October 15, 1896, 8. This transaction also failed. It was not until 1903 that Santee finally acquired the Palmetto acreage. See discussion below.

35. *State,* September 11, 1903, 4 ("floating purposes"); Kinzer, "Partial Chain of Title."

36. Acreage figures are from L. A. Emerson, *Map of Holdings of the Santee River Cypress Lumber Company, in the State of South Carolina,* 1927, scale not given (CNP files), except for Parcels 3, 16, and 17, which were acquired later. The acreage figures in Emerson differ from the earlier, deeded acreage.

37. No recorded timber deed exists for Parcel 8. However, William L. Buyck had previously sold a 190-acre portion of Parcel 8 in 1900, reserving for himself the right to cut cottonwood, gum, and ash ten inches or more in diameter. He reacquired the 190-acre tract in 1903 in order to sell Parcel 8 to Santee.

38. The *State* reported in June 1899 that "Mr. J. E. Faulkner, a contractor of the Santee Cypress Lumber company, has sold out his effect to the company and will leave in a few days for the Pacific coast." *State,* June 16, 1899, 3. For details of Faulkner's work for the company in the Santee Swamp, see agreement dated February 3, 1897, recorded in Richland County Deed Book AC, p. 179. The agreement obligated Faulkner to cut timber owned by Santee and deliver it to Santee's "canal leading to [the] Mill Pond of their Mill Plant at Ferguson, S.C."

39. Seeley to Savage, May 4, 1953, Savage Papers; *State,* April 16, 1903, 12. See also "Where Tank Stock Is Made"; and "Prominent Cypress Industry."

40. Goodyear and Hemingway, "Report of Lumber Operation," 22; Soucie, "Congaree," 67; *Charleston Evening Post,* August 7, 1905, 8 (reprinted from *Florence [S.C.] Times,* summarizing lost U.S. Bureau of Forestry report). Corps of Engineers figures indicate that timber shipments down the Congaree dropped off considerably after 1907. High points in terms of tonnage shipped include the years 1900 (121,333 tons), 1903 (114,000 tons), and 1907 (67,200 tons). See annual reports of the Chief of Engineers, United States Army, http://catalog.hathitrust.org/Record/010304360 (accessed August 1, 2015). After 1910 Santee's principal focus was the immense swamp across the river from the mill at Ferguson. The company continued to cut timber higher up the Santee drainage, but the investment entailed in logging the Santee Swamp was such that most of the company's energies were focused there. See *Charleston News and Courier,* November 12, 1911, 12, and discussion below.

41. Cantwell, *Plat of Swamp Lands and Timber Holdings;* United States Senate, *Hearing on S.3497, S.3498, and S.J. Res. 181,* 46 (statement of Francis Beidler III); "Fact Sheet: Beidler

Family Congaree Swamp Timberland Holdings, June 23, 1975," in Records of the NPS Planning Division, Southeast Region, RG 79, CSNM and CNP records for the period 1963–2005 (cited hereafter as SER PD records). At the time of publication, these documents were housed at the NPS Southeast Regional Office in Atlanta, Georgia; they will eventually be archived at CNP.

42. *Muskegon (Mich.) Chronicle*, May 12, 1891, 3. See also *Santee River Cypress Lumber Company v. James*, 50 F. 360 (C.C.D.S.C. 1892).

43. Cantwell, *Plat of Swamp Lands and Timber Holdings;* Kinzer, *Partial Chain of Title; Charleston Evening Post*, August 7, 1905, 8; *State*, August 25, 1905, 8; *Charleston News and Courier*, July 30, 1908, 2. The individual who sold the Bates Camp tract to the NPS maintained that the tract had once been the site of a Santee logging camp. NPS, *Environmental Assessment: Installation of . . . Weather Station Tower*, 12. John M. Bates bought and sold timber near the Beidler Tract as late as 1907. See table 8 above.

44. Goodyear and Hemingway, "Report of Lumber Operation," 2–3; United States House of Representatives, *Hearing on H.R. 11891 and H.R. 12111*, 30 (statement of Francis Beidler III); Mattoon, *Southern Cypress*, 11; Richland County Deed Book AG, p. 81 ("float roads"); Richland County Deed Book AC, p. 613.

45. *State*, November 2, 1904, 8, February 2, 1904, 8, July 12, 1905, 4, August 25, 1905, 8; Hampton, *Woods and Waters*, 297; *Charleston News and Courier*, July 17, 1905, 3, October 4, 1970, 12-A.

46. Goodyear and Hemingway, "Report of Lumber Operation," 3; Mattoon, *Southern Cypress*, 11–12; Hampton, *Woods and Waters*, 297.

47. *State*, May 31, 1906, 2, July 11, 1904, 4. On the use of draft animals in logging, see Walker, *Southern Forest*, 107–10. On floating logs from staging areas during high water, see Smith, *Gone to the Swamp*, 42, 44–45.

48. *Charleston Evening Post*, August 7, 1905, 8.

49. In August 1979 ranger Guy Taylor was following up on a tip about an old boiler between Horsepen Gut and Mazyck's Cut when he stumbled upon the remains of a large wheel from a slip-tongue log skidder. The wheel was partially embedded in a tree, about fifty yards from the riverbank. Guy Taylor, "Artifact Located in Congaree," memorandum to superintendent, CSNM, August 29, 1979, CNP files.

50. *State*, July 19, 1909, 5 ("different sections of the State"), May 18, 1895, 8. The possibility that Santee moved some of its logs by commercial rail is suggested by its ownership of a 7.75-acre riverside tract adjacent to "Congaree," a turn-of-the-century stop just south of the Congaree River railroad bridge in present-day Calhoun County. Santee purchased this tract from Annie M. Darby in October 1908. See Cantwell, *Plat of the Swamplands and Timber Holdings;* Calhoun County Deed Book 3, p. 76. It is not known why Santee acquired this property. It may have been intended as a site for transferring logs from the rail line to the river so that they could be floated to Ferguson. Another possibility is that Santee operated a small satellite mill or log yard at this site. From here, wood could be transported by rail to the Port of Charleston, where it could then be loaded onto ships bound for northern destinations or points overseas. In 1884 Samuel Dibble of Orangeburg County outlined some of the reasons why men with mills along the railroad could ship lumber to Charleston by rail at a greater profit than those dependent on river transport: (a) trains were more reliable than rivers and were not as subject to unexpected delays; (b) with fewer delays, owners could charter ships in Charleston at less risk of being charged if a ship had to wait in the harbor; and (c) owners could cut lumber to order

of specified kinds and ship right away. In contrast, the river men had to guess what the market wanted and take their chances. See Samuel Dibble to Capt. Thomas N. Bailey, August 30, 1884, in United States Army, "Annual Report of the Chief of Engineers . . . 1888," 996.

51. Mattoon, *Southern Cypress,* 15; Bryant, *Logging,* 12, 430.

52. *State,* April 4, 1909, sec. 1, pt. 1, 6; Mattoon, *Southern Cypress,* 11–12 ("not sufficiently inundated"). See also Davies, "Facts of the Trade," 43.

53. Seeley to Savage, May 4, 1953, Savage Papers ("primitive method"); *State,* April 16, 1903, 12 ("tramroads"), May 10, 1903, 10 ("rafted"), May 31, 1906, 2 ("expensive process").

54. See *Williams v. Bruton,* 113 S.E. 319 (S.C. 1922).

55. *State,* February 6, 1915, 7; Harris, *Year Book and Sixteenth Annual Report,* 18.

56. See, for example, Hampton, *Woods and Waters,* 297. Of the twenty-eight Santee timber deeds reviewed for this study, only one contained anything approaching detailed provisions regarding railroad logging. This deed, dated May 2, 1906, covered land across the river from the park near Muller's Big Lake. See Lexington County Deed Book YY, p. 288. Santee acquired a total of eleven timber deeds in Lexington County between 1900 and 1908, in an area south-southwest of the park. Most of these deeds conveyed upland (pine) timber, and all authorized railroad logging. Santee had a mill in Lexington County that appears to have been supported by rail. See *State,* July 19, 1909, 5.

57. On the characteristics of logging trams, see Bryant, *Logging,* 249–50, 283–84; Walker, *Southern Forest,* 104–6; and Williams, *Americans and Their Forests,* 259–60.

58. *State,* July 11, 1904, 4.

59. NPS, *Appendix to Specific Area Report,* 4.

60. Goodyear and Hemingway, "Report of Lumber Operation," 22; *Charleston Evening Post,* August 7, 1905, 8, September 24, 1908, 7; *Sumter Watchman and Southron,* December 16, 1908, 4; "Crescent City News"; Santee River Cypress Lumber Co., "Engineering Features of a Large Southern Lumbering Development," 456–57. Around this same time, Beidler moved to reorganize and recapitalize the company. In 1910 the Santee River Cypress Lumber Company, an Illinois corporation, conveyed its assets to the Santee River Cypress Lumber Company, a South Carolina corporation. Beidler was named president of the new entity. Contributed capital was $1.5 million, most of which was supplied by Chicago capitalists. See *State,* May 15, 1910, pt. 2, 11; Richland County Deed Book AL, p. 332; "Hardwood News."

61. In 1911 steam skidders and railroad hauling were said to be "rapidly displacing" pullboats and canals in Santee's operation. However, the company continued to float timber to Ferguson, a point confirmed by Francis Beidler himself. In a 1911 letter to the *Charleston News and Courier,* Beidler reported, "The saw mill is temporarily closed for repairs, this being a propitious time on account of the great difficulty in securing colored labor to operate. Likewise the railroad logging operations are temporarily closed for the same reasons, and also because we have ample river logs in sight to start the mill and run during the winter without railroad logs." By that point river logs formed a small percentage of the total handled at Ferguson, leaving the large log pond to serve "only as an auxiliary or emergency facility." Goodyear and Hemingway, "Report of Lumber Operation," 3 ("rapidly displacing"), 22; *Charleston News and Courier,* November 12, 1911, 12; Santee River Cypress Lumber Co., "Engineering Features of a Large Southern Lumbering Development," 457 ("emergency facility").

62. Knowles et al., *Water Resources Management Plan,* 8.

63. Fred Seeley to Henry Savage, May 27, 1953, Savage Papers. Cypress trees often generate false rings, possibly in response to fluctuations in soil moisture conditions. One study found that conventional ring counts averaged about 1.6 times a tree's actual age. See Wilhite and Toliver, "*Taxodium distichum* (L.) Rich., Baldcypress," 566.

64. Seeley to Savage, May 4, 1953, and May 27, 1953, Savage Papers; Richland County Deed Book AC, p. 179, and Deed Book AL, p. 55.

65. Chittenden, *Red Gum*, 8, and plate 2–fig. 2 (reproduced herein as figure 17).

66. "Where Tank Stock Is Made." Santee was still milling both cypress and hardwoods in 1910. An advertisement from that year states: "Experienced log scaler wanted to scale on sawmill deck. Must be familiar with ash, cottonwood, gum, oak, sycamore, sugarberry, hickory, elm, persimmon and cypress. None but experienced scalers need apply. . . . Santee River Cypress Lumber Co., Ferguson, S.C." *State*, March 13, 1910, pt. 1, 6. In May 1912 the journal *Hardwood Record* reported that Santee "at present is engaged in the manufacture of cypress lumber, but within a few days will turn its big mill over to the production of red gum for some months." "Hardwood News, Notes."

67. Chittenden, *Red Gum*, 19–22; *Macon Telegraph*, January 18, 1899, 6; *State*, December 1, 1903, 5. Beginning in 1908, the huge quantities of sweet gum and other hardwoods in the swamps below Columbia prompted investors to periodically eye the city as the possible site of a veneer plant. Construction of one such plant apparently started in 1914, but there is no indication that the facility ever actually opened. The first known veneer plant to conduct business in Columbia began operations in 1916, as discussed below. See *State*, September 1, 1908, 2, April 25, 1914, 12.

68. Wolfe, *Wood-Using Industries of South Carolina*, 10, 12–13, 46; *State*, April 25, 1914, 12; Chittenden, *Red Gum*, 20.

69. Chittenden, *Red Gum*, 8, 17 ("floated to the mills"), 18, and plate 3–fig. 2 (reproduced herein as figure 18).

70. *State*, September 1, 1908, 2.

71. Chittenden, *Red Gum*, 18. See also Goodyear and Hemingway, "Report of Lumber Operation," 3; Walker, *Southern Forest*, 125.

72. Chittenden, *Red Gum*, 38. See also *Charleston Evening Post*, August 7, 1905, 8.

73. *Santee River Cypress Lumber Company v. James*, 50 F. at 360.

74. Seeley to Savage, May 4, 1953, Savage Papers. Santee commissioned a study by the U.S. Bureau of Forestry in the early 1900s to identify ways to conduct sustained-yield forestry on company lands. The resulting report, which appears to have been a companion piece to *The Red Gum*, was submitted to Fred Seeley in 1905. See "Study of the Red Gum." A published summary of the report noted that Santee had "practically an inexhaustible supply" of timber but was no longer able to cut cypress on a sustained yield basis on its Congaree lands because (a) bald cypress takes over a hundred years to mature, and (b) most of the cypress in this vicinity had already been cut. *Charleston Evening Post*, August 7, 1905, 8. However, the report also asserted that if Santee were to expand its overall land base and employ "scientific means," it would have the wherewithal to cut other species for two hundred years. Seeley responded to the report by buying more land: "I said, 'we have 70,000 acres, our mill cuts 35 million feet per year. How much more do I need to make operations continuous?' They worked on the % of each wood, growth per year, each wood time to mature, and came up: 'buy 12,000 acres!' I bought 27,000 more." In 1909 survey crews were sent out to look for more timber along the Congaree, but this time the company encountered local resistance. Some thought the timber below Columbia should be used

to encourage the development of local enterprises rather than benefit a mill on the Santee and its absentee owner in Chicago. Seeley to Savage, May 4, 1953, Savage Papers; *Charleston Evening Post,* April 16, 1909, 7.

75. Hotchkiss, *Industrial Chicago,* 446; Fetters, *Logging Railroads of South Carolina,* 127; *State,* April 15, 1900, pt. 2, 12, April 16, 1903, 12; Seeley to Savage, May 4, 1953, Savage Papers.

76. Mattoon, *Southern Cypress,* 9–10, 15, 17; Santee River Cypress Lumber Co., "Engineering Features of a Large Southern Lumbering Development," 457–58. In the early part of the twentieth century, purchasers of cypress lumber typically specified a preference for air seasoning over use of the dry kiln. The latter was generally not favored except to augment air drying. Air seasoning for doors and other high-grade products generally lasted ten to sixteen months, followed by a short period of time in the kiln. Kiln drying was especially disfavored for the best grades of cypress, since it often caused checks and raised grain to appear. The dry kiln was therefore mostly used for the "commons" grade of lumber and for shingles and lath. Kiln drying was particularly useful for reducing the weight of green cypress shingles, which tended to have a very high moisture content going into the kiln. See Mattoon, *Southern Cypress,* 10, 17.

Kiln drying was also important for other timber species, such as sweet gum and loblolly pine. In 1911 Santee had two concrete, tile-lined dry kilns, both "especially adapted for the successful drying of gum." Goodyear and Hemingway, "Report of Lumber Operation," 18–19. Pine could not be air-dried because the sap would stain so badly (a fungal condition known as "bluing") that the value of the wood would be seriously diminished.

77. "$30,000 Skidder," 41 ("new and improved machinery"); "Steam Turbine in Sawmill Plant"; Seeley to Savage, May 4, 1953, Savage Papers; United States House of Representatives, *Hearing on H.R. 11891 and H.R. 12111,* 30 (statement of Francis Beidler III); Silver, "Hardwood Producers Come of Age," 427 ("bankruptcy").

78. Seeley to Savage, May 4, 1953, Savage Papers; *American Lumbermen,* 208; *State,* May 2, 1906, 1, June 21, 1906, 9, October 29, 1906, 8, August 7, 1910, pt. 1, 1, September 26, 1912, 2; "Miscellaneous Notes."

79. [Notice of contracting opportunity at Ferguson, S.C.]; *State,* July 29, 1913, 9; *News and Courier,* July 26, 1914, pt. 2, 1; "Installed Electric Plant," 28.

80. Woodward, *Valuation of American Timberlands,* 209 ("distinct stagnation"); *Beidler et al. v. South Carolina Tax Commission,* 282 U.S. 1, 6 (1930); "Installed Electric Plant," 28; *Charleston News and Courier,* June 17, 1914, 7, July 26, 1914, pt. 2, 1 ("woods operations"), October 4, 1970, 12-A; *State,* November 5, 1914, 6, September 12, 1916, 6; Seeley to Savage, May 4, 1953, Savage Papers ("scrap prices").

81. Doyle, *Modeling Flood Plain Hydrology,* 30; Seeley to Savage, May 4, 1953, Savage Papers ("fantastic prices"); *Beidler et al. v. South Carolina Tax Commission,* 160 S.E. 264 (S.C. 1927).

82. Mattoon, *Southern Cypress,* 33.

83. See Doyle, *Modeling Flood Plain Hydrology,* 14, 34.

84. Wharton et al., *Ecology of Bottomland Hardwood Swamps,* 44, 78–79; Sharitz and Mitsch, "Southern Floodplain Forests," 336, 346; Rice and Peet, *Vegetation of the Lower Roanoke,* 112, 132; Meitzen, "Flood Processes, Forest Dynamics," 109–10, 113, 119; Johnson, "*Nyssa aquatica* L., Water Tupelo," 476–77.

85. Minchin and Sharitz, *Age Structure and Potential Long-Term Dynamics,* 31–32, 34; Meitzen, "Flood Processes, Forest Dynamics," 109–10.

86. *Beidler v. Veno*, 311 F.2d 623 (4th Cir. 1962); Goodyear and Hemingway, "Report of Lumber Operation," 7–8, 23; *Orangeburg Times and Democrat*, August 20, 1910, 1; *State*, January 11, 1956, 6–B; Chittenden, *Red Gum*, 15–16, and plate 5; Gagnon, "Fire in Floodplain Forests," 524.

87. Lennon et al., *Living with the South Carolina Coast*, 10–12.

88. Peterken, *Natural Woodland*, 185; Soucie, "Congaree," 76, 78; Francis Beidler III, quoted in Reed, "You, Too, Can Visit a Swamp," 60.

89. *Sumter Watchman and Southron*, June 21, 1913, 8 ("hard wood"); *State*, December 24, 1916, pt. 2, 9, March 31, 1919, 8.

90. *State*, May 27, 1916, 10, December 24, 1916, pt. 2, 9.

91. *State*, December 24, 1916, pt. 2, 9.

92. United States Army, "Broad and Congaree Rivers," 11–12; *Charleston Evening Post*, January 11, 1918, 11; *State*, January 12, 1918, 10, January 29, 1918, 2, December 30, 1919, 8.

Chapter 8: Logging after 1920

1. South Carolina House of Representatives, *Hearing on H 3097* (statement of J. Sid McKnight) ("erred on the side of timidity"); Eyre, *Survey of Proposed Natural Forest Areas*, 11.

2. NPS, *Specific Area Report*, 17; United States House of Representatives, *Hearing on H.R. 11891 and H.R. 12111*, 149 (statement of Julian T. Buxton).

3. Goodyear and Hemingway, "Report of Lumber Operation," 5; Soucie, "Congaree," 67–68; Reed, "You, Too, Can Visit a Swamp," 56 (quotation).

4. United States House of Representatives, *Hearing on H.R. 11891 and H.R. 12111*, 31 (statement of Francis Beidler III).

5. See Richland County Deed Book D336, p. 403.

6. It appears that J. Beidler Camp died in 1974. Francis Beidler III became cotrustee around 1975–76.

7. "Report of Commissioners," 24, filed March 10, 1982, Civil Action Nos. 77–652, 77–653, 77–654, 77–2046 (*United States v. 14,770.65 Acres of Land*), General Case Files, United States District Court for the District of South Carolina (Columbia), Records of District Courts of the United States, RG 21, National Archives and Records Administration—Southeast Region, Atlanta (archive hereafter cited as NARA SR).

8. South Carolina House of Representatives, *Hearing on H 3097* (statement of Francis Beidler III). This is not to suggest that the family was unmindful of the legitimate concerns of conservationists. In 1969 the family sold its large tract in Four Holes Swamp (Dorchester County, South Carolina) to the Nature Conservancy and the National Audubon Society for use as a nature preserve. This tract contained 1,783 acres of old-growth cypress-tupelo forest. (The preserve, since greatly expanded, is operated by the National Audubon Society as the Francis Beidler Forest.) By 1975 the family had also softened its position regarding the Beidler Tract. In that year family representatives informed Congress that the Beidlers were amenable to selling a portion of the tract to the federal government. See 122 Cong. Rec. 15,550 (1976) (statement of Senator Ernest Hollings). The Beidlers ultimately agreed to sell the entire tract, although family members expressed misgivings at the time about a park of this size. In the words of Francis Beidler III, the family "question[ed] the wisdom of using public funds to acquire a tract so much larger than anything the public is likely to use today." Since then, however, the family has facilitated park expansion on more than one occasion. In 2005, for example, it sold the NPS the 2,395-acre Bates Fork tract in the

far eastern end of the park. At the time Francis Beidler III observed, "My family is very pleased that this property will now be owned by the National Park Service." Francis Beidler III, quoted in Reed, "You, Too, Can Visit a Swamp," 60, and in Trust for Public Land, "2,395 Acres Protected."

9. Quoted in Reed, "You, Too, Can Visit a Swamp," 56.

10. A declaration of taking is a type of condemnation action in which title vests immediately in the United States upon filing of the action and payment into court of the estimated just compensation. If the deposited amount is later found to be inadequate, the government must pay the difference in value, plus interest, measured from the date of the taking. Because of the risk to the government, declarations of taking are rarely filed by the National Park Service.

11. *United States v. 14,770.65 Acres of Land,* 616 F. Supp. 1235 (D. S.C. 1985); Kinzer, *Chronology.*

12. Meadows and Hodges, "Silviculture of Southern Bottomland Hardwoods," 4.

13. Robert A. Knoth to Francis Beidler III, December 18, 1975, exhibit in Civil Action Nos. 77–652, 77–653, 77–654, 77–2046, RG 21, NARA SR ("another decade"); United States House of Representatives, *Hearing on H.R. 11891 and H.R. 12111,* 32 (statement of Francis Beidler III) ("overmaturity problem"); Nix and Barry, *Investigation of the Impacts of Clearcutting,* 16.

14. Meadows and Hodges, "Silviculture of Southern Bottomland Hardwoods," 4; South Carolina House of Representatives, *Hearing on H 3097* (statement of J. Sid McKnight).

15. Nix and Barry, *Investigation of the Impacts of Clearcutting,* 16.

16. James R. Council Jr. to Francis Beidler III, September 27, 1976, exhibit in Civil Action Nos. 77–652, 77–653, 77–654, 77–2046, RG 21, NARA SR; Chief, Land Acquisition Division, NPS Southeast Regional Office, memorandum to Deputy Regional Director, January 11, 1977, SER PD records.

17. United States House of Representatives, *Hearing on H.R. 11891 and H.R. 12111,* 159–60, 162 (statement of Philip L. Edwards).

18. Gaddy, *Natural History of Congaree Swamp,* 24.

19. "Defendant's Pretrial Statement," 24, filed August 29, 1980, Civil Action Nos. 77–652, 77–653, 77–654, 77–2046, RG 21, NARA SR (quotation); "Report of Commissioners," 24, filed March 10, 1982, Civil Action Nos. 77–652, 77–653, 77–654, 77–2046, RG 21, NARA SR.

20. Section 5(b)(1) of Public Law 94–545, 90 Stat. 2517 (1976) (quotation); Kinzer, *Chronology;* Public Law 100–524, 102 Stat. 2606 (1988); Title I, Section 148 of Public Law 108–108, 117 Stat. 1281 (2003).

21. Richland County Deed Book AG, pp. 100, 101, and Deed Book AG, p. 319.

22. Richland County Deed Book CN, p. 106.

23. Holly Hill was formed in 1927 when Lawrence E. Miller and William J. Colvin acquired the R. L. Moore Lumber Company of Bowyer, South Carolina, and renamed it the Holly Hill Cypress Company (later the Holly Hill Lumber Company). From their base at Four Holes near Holly Hill, South Carolina, the men branched out to acquire timberland and sawmills at Denmark, Bonneau, Pregnall, Walterboro, Black Branch, and Kingville, South Carolina. In later years the company was headed up by Colvin's son, Martin C. Colvin. The younger Colvin actively opposed legislation to establish Congaree Swamp National Monument. See Gregg, *Crane's Foot (or Pedigree),* 398; *State,* November 18, 1974, 8-A; United States House of Representatives, *Hearing on H.R. 11891 and H.R. 12111,* 69 (statement of Martin C. Colvin).

24. Richland County, S.C., aerial photography of lower Richland, 1939, 1959.

25. ASCS, "Aerial Photography Index, Richland County (S.C.) [1955]"; Richland County, S.C., aerial photography of lower Richland, 1959; USGS, aerial photo, Entity ID: NP0NAPP001366030, Project: NAPP 8942, Roll 1366, Frame 30, March 11, 1989. All ASCS photographs cited in this chapter were accessed August 1, 2015, from the University of South Carolina, University Libraries Digital Collections, Aerial Photographs of Richland County, S.C., http://library.sc.edu/digital/collections/aerials/sccola.html. All USGS, NPS, Air Force, and Navy photographs accessed August 1, 2015, from USGS Earth Explorer, http://earthexplorer.usgs.gov/.

26. Kinzer, *Partial Chain of Title;* NPS, "Congaree Swamp/Tract-by-Tract Analysis, 1986," SER PD records; USGS, aerial photo, Entity ID: NP0NAPP007462188, Project: NAPP 9414, Roll 7462, Frame 188, January 22, 1994.

27. NPS, [Section 8 report to Congress on threatened or damaged national natural landmarks] (1986); Robert M. Baker, regional director, SER, to W. Dale Allen, Trust for Public Land, January 22, 1990; Thomas W. Piehl, chief, Land Resources Division, NPS Southeast Regional Office, memorandum to file, March 29, 1990. All: SER PD records.

28. Richland County, S.C., aerial photography of lower Richland, 1939.

29. Superintendent, CSNM, memorandum to Regional Director, SER, May 29, 1980, SER PD records; ASCS, "Aerial Photography Index, Richland County (S.C.) [1955]."

30. Superintendent, CSNM, to Regional Director, SER, April 24, 1984; NPS, "Congaree Swamp/Tract-by-Tract Analysis, 1986." Both: SER PD records.

31. USGS, aerial photo, Entity ID: NP0NAPP001367017, Project: NAPP 8942, Roll 1367, Frame 17, March 19, 1989.

32. Kinzer, "Partial Chain of Title"; Gregg, *Crane's Foot (or Pedigree),* 398; Richland County, S.C., aerial photography of lower Richland, 1939.

33. See Acting Regional Director, SER, memorandum to Director, NPS, August 28, 1980, SER PD records.

34. John B. Harmon, "Memories of Kingville," e-mail message to Sam Watson, January 15, 2009 (in author's possession).

35. Richland County, S.C., aerial photography of lower Richland, 1939; ASCS, aerial photo no. 45079–04c-004, May 1, 1943; ASCS, aerial photo no. 45079–3h-024, May 13, 1951; Richland County, S.C., aerial photography of lower Richland, 1959; Gaddy, *Natural Resources Inventory,* 1.

36. ASCS, aerial photo no. 45079–3h-024.

37. Kinzer, *Partial Chain of Title.*

38. Designation of the Congaree River Swamp National Natural Landmark was approved by Secretary of the Interior Rogers Morton on May 19, 1974.

39. Superintendent, CSNM, memoranda to Regional Director, SER, March 24, 1980 and May 29, 1980. Both: SER PD records.

40. John E. Wishart, Georgia-Pacific Corporation, to W. Carlyle Blakeney Jr., National Audubon Society, May 23, 1980; Jacqueline E. Jacobs, executive director, South Carolina Wildlife Federation, to Robert S. McDaniel, superintendent, CSNM, June 4, 1980. Both: SER PD records.

41. T. Marshall Hahn Jr., Georgia-Pacific Corporation, to the Honorable Cecil D. Andrus, secretary of the interior, June 30, 1980, SER PD records. See also John E. Wishart to W. Carlyle Blakeney Jr., May 23, 1980, SER PD records; T. Marshall Hahn Jr., letter to the

editor, *Charleston Evening Post,* September 4, 1980; Acting Regional Director, SER, memorandum to Director, NPS, August 28, 1980, SER PD records.

42. Kinzer, *Chronology;* Acting Regional Director, SER, memorandum to Director, NPS, August 28, 1980, SER PD records.

43. T. Marshall Hahn Jr., letter to the editor, *Charleston Evening Post,* September 4, 1980.

44. John E. Cely, South Carolina Wildlife and Marine Resources Department, to John Fischer, NPS planner, October 17, 1986, SER PD records.

45. United States House of Representatives, *Hearing on H.R. 11891 and H.R. 12111,* 159–61 (statement of Philip L. Edwards). As it happened, Georgia-Pacific ended up selling the Williams Furniture Division in 1983, only a few years after starting to log Kingville West. High labor costs reportedly made the Sumter plant unprofitable. "Union Rejects Pact at Sumter Furniture Plant," *Charleston News and Courier,* November 24, 1983, 11-E.

46. Joseph Brown, regional director, SER, letter to the editor, *Charleston Evening Post,* September 4, 1980; USGS, aerial photo, Entity ID: NP0NAPP001367017, Project: NAPP 8942, Roll 1367, Frame 16, March 19, 1989.

47. "Ga-Pacific Lays Off 40 Workers," *Sumter (S.C.) Item,* May 6, 1988, 1.

48. *State,* February 16, 1897, 1; Kinzer, *Partial Chain of Title.*

49. Kinzer, *Partial Chain of Title;* Cantwell, *Plat of the Swamplands and Timber Holdings.*

50. Douglas A. Rayner, South Carolina Wildlife and Marine Resources Department, to John Fischer, NPS planner, October 2, 1986, SER PD records.

51. Richland County, S.C., aerial photography of lower Richland, 1939; ASCS, aerial photo no. 45079–04c-004; aerial photo no. 45079–1h-051, April 10, 1951; United States Air Force, aerial photo, Entity ID: ARB650108308109, Project 65010, Roll 83, Frame 8109, September 1, 1964.

52. Richland County Deed Book FR, p. 54. Holly Hill acquired the fee to this tract in 1956. See Richland County Deed Book 185, p. 204.

53. ASCS, aerial photo no. 45079–1h-051; ASCS, "Aerial Photography Index, Richland County (S.C.) [1955]"; Richland County, S.C., aerial photography of lower Richland, 1959.

54. United States Air Force, aerial photo, Project 65010, Roll 83, Frame 8109; Brian M. Fox, Georgia-Pacific, to Katherine A. Blaha, Trust for Public Land, May 20, 1992, SER PD records.

55. Georgia-Pacific, *Proposed Sale Area, Kingville Tract* [map], May 20, 1992, scale 1" = 20 chains (drawn by Brian M. Fox), SER PD records.

56. Georgia-Pacific, *Proposed Sale Area, Kingville Tract* [map]; Katherine A. Blaha, Trust for Public Land, to Robert McDaniel, superintendent, CSNM, June 1, 1992, SER PD records ("minimal" selective cut); Brian M. Fox to Katherine A. Blaha, May 20, 1992 ("close to being clearcut"); USGS, aerial photo, Entity ID: NP0NAPP001365196, Project: NAPP 8942, Roll 1365, Frame 196, March 11, 1989.

57. Gaddy, *Preliminary Biological/Hydrological Evaluation,* 13.

58. NPS, aerial photo, Entity ID: ARLCOSW00100010, Project COSW0, Roll 10, Frame 10, April 27, 1996; Richland County, S.C., aerial photography of lower Richland, 2000; Georgia-Pacific, *Proposed Sale Area, Kingville Tract* [map]; Gaddy, *Preliminary Biological/ Hydrological Evaluation,* 13.

59. Shaw, McLeod, Belser and Hurlbutt, Inc., "CCA Industries: Timber Inventory, Valuation, and Management Recommendations for the Richland Group (Kingville Tract) Richland County, S.C., 1,886 acres" (1999), 2, 4, SER PD records.

60. Richland County Deed Book H, p. 339.

61. Kinzer, *Partial Chain of Title*.

62. ASCS, aerial photo no. 45079–04c-048, May 1, 1943.

63. Richland County Deed Book GD, p. 92; Richland County Deed Book 195, pp. 575, 578, 581 (quotations).

64. ASCS, aerial photos, nos. 45079–1h-051, 45079–1h-053, April 10, 1951; USGS, aerial photo, Entity ID: AR1VOK000030515, Project: VOK00, Roll 3, Frame 515, April 7, 1957; Richland County, S.C., aerial photography of lower Richland, 1959; Richland County Deed Book 252, p. 73.

65. United States Navy, aerial photo, Entity ID: ARCVAP2A0090778, Project VAP2A, Roll 9, Frame 778, October 1, 1961; United States Air Force, aerial photos, Entity ID: ARB640120050728, –729, Project 64012, Roll 5, Frames 728, 729, April 1, 1964; aerial photos, Entity ID: ARB650108308109, –8110, Project 65010, Roll 83, Frames 8109, 8110, September 1, 1964; ASCS, aerial photos, nos. 45079–2gg-029, 45079–2gg-031, February 7, 1966; Gaddy, *Preliminary Biological/Hydrological Evaluation*, 17.

66. Kinzer, *Partial Chain of Title*; Milliken Forestry Company, Inc., "Proposed Sales Information, General Description, Lower Fork Swamp Tract, Santee River Limited Partnership, Richland County, SC, 2,420 acres +/-" (2002), 1, 2; *Timber Type Map, Bates Fork Tract, Santee River Limited Partnership, 2420.4 +/- Acres, Richland County, SC* [map], 2004, scale 1.25" = 3,000' ; Chrisanne Mitchell, Trust for Public Land, to Pat Ranels, NPS Southeast Regional Office, November 11, 2003. All: SER PD records.

67. Milliken Forestry Company, Inc., "Analysis of Comparable Land Sales, Bates Fork Tract, Richland County, SC," report to the Trust for Public Land (September 20, 2004), 13, SER PD records; Martha Bogle, superintendent CNP, in discussion with the author, 2003; Richard Watkins in discussion with the author, 2004.

68. Milliken Forestry Company, Inc., *Timber Type Map, Bates Fork Tract*, SER PD records.

69. Milliken Forestry Company, Inc., "Proposed Sales Information," 2, SER PD records.

70. Richland County Deed Book FN, p. 51, and Deed Book 85, p. 380.

71. Kinzer, *Partial Chain of Title*.

72. USGS, aerial photos, Entity ID: AR1VCPQ00020026, –55, –56, Project VCPQ0, Roll 2, Frames 26, 55, and 56, March 30, 1971; Lawrence, *Soil Survey of Richland County*, map 60; Richland County, S.C., aerial photography of lower Richland, 1939.

73. Jack Brady, quoted in Vincent, "Landowners Speak Out," 31; South Carolina House of Representatives, *Hearing on H 3097* (statement of Jack Brady).

74. Acting Regional Director, SER, memorandum to Chief, Office of Legislation, Washington Office, July 26, 1977; Acting Superintendent, Ninety-Six National Historic Site, memorandum to Associate Regional Director, Park Operations, SER, November 10, 1977. Both: SER PD records.

75. John G. Felder to Gary Everhardt, director, NPS, October 1, 1976; William J. Briggle, acting director, NPS, to John G. Felder, November 1, 1976; Richard Watkins, "Reference: Public Law 94–545," unpublished Sierra Club document, 1985. All: SER PD records.

Swansea Lumber Company had previously been active in the Congaree Swamp as a subcontractor to Council Brothers, Inc. To obtain access to the Brady sale, Swansea secured an easement over the "New Road" through the heart of the Beidler Tract. The "Existing Conditions" map in the NPS's 1979 *Assessment of Alternatives* shows a spur off of New Road entering Tract 101-42 near its northeast corner. See Chief, Land Acquisition Division,

NPS Southeast Regional Office, memorandum to Deputy Regional Director, January 11, 1977, SER PD records; NPS, *Assessment of Alternatives*, 9.

76. NPS, *Assessment of Alternatives*, 11, 20; personal observation by the author, 2001; Cely, *Map of Congaree National Park*.

77. Richland County Deed Book AG, p. 226.

78. Richland County Deed Book 67, p. 197. See ASCS, aerial photo no. 45079–11c-051, May 22, 1943; and aerial photo no. 45079–2aa-207, November 22, 1959.

79. NPS, *Assessment of Alternatives*, 11, 20.

80. Ibid., 11; Acting Regional Director, SER, memorandum to Director, NPS, August 28, 1980, 3, SER PD records; USGS, aerial photo, Entity ID: AR1VFAA00010013, Project VFAA0, Roll 1, Frame 13, January 1, 1981. This tract was assumed to contain 139 acres in 1979, based on a recorded deed. However, a more recent survey shows the actual acreage to be 193.51 acres.

81. Richland County Deed Book AG, p. 496.

82. Kinzer, *Partial Chain of Title*; ASCS, aerial photo no. 45079–278–62, January 24, 1981.

83. Jones, *Location and Ecology of Champion Trees*, 10.

84. Richland County Deed Book AG, p. 582.

85. Richland County Deed Book EB, p. 107.

86. Russell Buyck and his brother W. Peter Buyck Sr. purchased the Wise property on February 8, 1936. According to the recorded deed, sale of the property was subject to a preexisting timber contract with Marion McKenzie that expired on August, 1, 1936. See Richland County Deed Book EB, p. 107.

On January 16, 1960, Russell Buyck and W. Peter Buyck Sr. partitioned various jointly held properties in Richland and Calhoun Counties, including lands that would become Tracts 101-35 and 101-36. See Richland County Deed Book 324, pp. 524, 526. As a result of this transaction, Russell Buyck obtained Tract 101-36. W. Peter Buyck Sr. obtained Tract 101-35 (see below).

87. Richland County, S.C., aerial photography of lower Richland, 1939; ASCS, aerial photo no. 45079–04c-100, May 1, 1943.

88. South Carolina Wildlife and Marine Resources Department, "Record Trees of the Congaree Swamp," ca. 1976, SER PD records; Gaddy, *Natural Resources Inventory*, 1, 3–5, map 12.

89. Florschutz, *Refuge Land Acquisition Biological Reconnaissance Report*, appendix A, 2; USGS, aerial photo, Project VCPQ0, Roll 2, Frame 26; Gaddy, *Natural Resources Inventory*, 1; USGS, Gadsden, SC Quadrangle [topographic map], revised ed. 1972, scale 1:24,000.

90. USGS, aerial photo, Entity ID: AR1VEMO00020016, Project VEMO0, Roll 2, Frame 16, March 1, 1978; aerial photo, Project VFAA0, Roll 1, Frame 13.

91. Land Resources Division, NPS Southeast Regional Office, unsigned memorandum to record, September 5, 1989, SER PD records. Persimmon was among the most commercially valuable of all the bottomland hardwoods in the late 1980s and early 1990s.

92. Ibid.

93. South Carolina Water Resources Commission, [Public Notice re permit application to install a temporary double overhead cable rehaul system across Congaree River], 1989, SER PD records.

94. Robert M. Baker, regional director, SER, to Senator Strom Thurmond, May 9, 1995, SER PD records.

95. USGS, aerial photo, Entity ID: NP0NAPP007462187, Project: NAPP 9414, Roll 7462, Frame 187, January 22, 1994; Jones, *Location and Ecology of Champion Trees,* 3, 10.

96. Richland County, S.C., aerial photography of lower Richland, 1939; ASCS, aerial photo no. 45079–2aa-141, November 22, 1959.

97. W. Peter Buyck Jr. to Robert S. McDaniel, superintendent, CSNM, January 5, 1988; NPS, "Congaree Swamp/Tract-by-Tract Analysis, 1986." Both: SER PD records.

98. W. Peter Buyck Jr. to Robert S. McDaniel, January 5, 1988, SER PD records.

99. South Carolina House of Representatives, *Hearing on H 3097* (statement of W. Peter Buyck Sr.); Richard Watkins to Dr. Richard Curry, NPS Washington Office, June 12, 1976, SER PD records.

100. USGS, aerial photo, Entity ID: NP0NAPP007462186, Project: NAPP 9414, Roll 7462, Frame 186, January 22, 1994.

101. Richland County Deed Book AL, p. 37.

102. ASCS, aerial photo no. 45079–04c-107, May 1, 1943, aerial photo no. 45079–3h-030, May 13, 1951.

103. NPS, "Congaree Swamp/Tract-by-Tract Analysis, 1986," SER PD records; Sierra Club (Bachman Group), "Introduction to the Swamp Systems," 2.

104. Richland County, S.C., aerial photography of lower Richland, 1939; ASCS, aerial photo no. 45079–04c-107, aerial photo no. 45079–3h-030.

105. ASCS, aerial photo no. 45079–2aa-141.

Conclusion

1. Robert A. Knoth, quoted in Popovich, "National Highlights," 568.

2. This description of the disturbance regime in bottomland hardwood forests is adapted from United States Forest Service, United States Department of the Interior, and The Nature Conservancy, "LANDFIRE National Biophysical Setting Model," 77.

3. Tanner, "Distribution of Tree Species," 172.

4. Sharitz and Allen, *Quantify Change in the Old-Growth Forests,* 37, citing data compiled by John E. Cely.

5. Jones, "Status and Habitat of Big Trees," 28 (quotations); Robert H. Jones, e-mail message to author, September 15, 1997.

6. Sharitz and Allen, *Quantify Change in the Old-Growth Forests,* 7–24, 28–29, 34; Cary J. Mock, e-mail message to author, April 12, 2010; Mock et al., "Reconstructing South Carolina Tropical Cyclones"; Doyle, *Modeling Flood Plain Hydrology,* 10, 11.

7. *State,* August 29, 1893, 1, August 30, 1893, 8.

8. Doyle, *Modeling Flood Plain Hydrology,* 27, 42 (quotation); Allen, Goebel, and Sharitz, *Long-term Effects of Wind Disturbance,* 30; Harcombe et al., "Sensitivity of Gulf Coast Forests," 50–51, 54; Tanner, "Distribution of Tree Species," 174; Sharitz and Allen, *Quantify Change in the Old-Growth Forests,* 29.

9. Doyle, *Modeling Flood Plain Hydrology,* 30; Sharitz and Allen, *Quantify Change in the Old-Growth Forests,* 28–29, 35–38; Collins and Battaglia, "Oak Regeneration in Southeastern Bottomland Hardwood Forest," 3033; Hodges, "Development and Ecology of Bottomland Hardwood Sites," 122–23.

10. Purvis, Tyler, and Sidlow, *Hurricanes Affecting South Carolina;* Doyle, *Modeling Flood Plain Hydrology,* 10; Sharitz and Allen, *Quantify Change in the Old-Growth Forests,* 37–38; NPS, *Specific Area Report,* 17.

11. Sharitz and Allen, *Quantify Change in the Old-Growth Forests,* 9–10, 20, 24, 28–29, 31, 34.

12. Chittenden, *Red Gum,* 14, 33; Battaglia and Sharitz, "Effects of Natural Disturbance," 122, 127–28; Jones, "Status and Habitat of Big Trees," 28.

13. Harcombe, Leipzig, and Elsik, "Effects of Hurricane Rita," 97–98; Battaglia and Sharitz, "Responses of Floodplain Forest Species," 116–17.

14. Battaglia, Collins, and Sharitz, "Published Tolerance Ratings"; Hall and Harcombe, "Sapling Dynamics in a Southeastern Texas Floodplain Forest," 437; Townsend, "Vegetation Patterns and Hydroperiod."

15. Battaglia and Sharitz, "Responses of Floodplain Forest Species," 108; Hall and Harcombe, "Flooding Alters Apparent Position," 854; Kupfer, Meitzen, and Graf, *Forest Recovery and Hydrologic Modeling,* 43–48; Battaglia and Sharitz, "Effects of Natural Disturbance," 121–22. See also Lin et al., "Sapling Growth and Survivorship," 405–6.

16. Zhao, Allen, and Sharitz, "Twelve Year Response," 3139, 3146. See also Harcombe, Leipzig, and Elsik, "Effects of Hurricane Rita," 97–98.

17. Sharitz and Allen, *Quantify Change in the Old-Growth Forests,* 28–29, 37.

18. Allen, "Vegetation Dynamics and Response to Disturbance," 84–85, 88–89.

19. Harcombe et al., "Sensitivity of Gulf Coast Forests to Climate Change," 46 (quotations), 53, 54–55.

20. Ibid., 48–49; Battaglia, Collins, and Sharitz, "Published Tolerance Ratings"; Nix and Barry, *Investigation of the Impacts of Clearcutting,* 32–33, 46–48, 51.

21. Gagnon, Passmore, and Platt, "Multi-Year Salutary Effects," 63–64; Chittenden, *Red Gum,* 15–16; Platt and Brantley, "Canebrakes," 12–15; Pederson, Jones, and Sharitz, "Age Structure and Possible Origins," 114, 118; Gagnon, Platt, and Moser, "Response of a Native Bamboo," 292–93.

22. Gagnon, "Fire in Floodplain Forests," 524.

23. Townsend, "Relationships between Vegetation Patterns and Hydroperiod," 53; Rice and Peet, *Vegetation of the Lower Roanoke,* 60, 129–30.

24. Conrads, Feaster, and Harrelson, *Effects of the Saluda Dam,* 11–12, 24–27, 31–33, 41. See also Doyle, *Modeling Flood Plain Hydrology.*

25. Suggestion of Rebecca R. Sharitz, cited in NPS, American Rivers, and others, *Final Report and Recommendations,* 3. Cypress can only regenerate from seed if its exacting seedbed requirements are met. Germination generally takes place on moist, aerated seedbeds during periods of low water. The seedlings must then achieve sufficient height growth to escape prolonged inundation when flooded conditions return. Because the convergence of adequate seed crops and favorable water levels tends to occur infrequently, cypress reproduction from seed can be erratic. See Sharitz and Mitsch, "Southern Floodplain Forests," 346.

26. Landmeyer, "Determination of the Source(s) of Water Used by Wetland/Floodplain Plants."

27. Trimble, *Man-Induced Soil Erosion,* viii, 44–46; Kupfer, Meitzen, and Graf, *Forest Recovery and Hydrologic Modeling,* 47–48, 57; Kupfer, Meitzen, and Pipkin, "Hydrogeomorphic Controls of Early Post-logging Successional Pathways," 1887.

28. Heitmeyer et al., "Ecological Relationships of Warmblooded Vertebrates," 289.

29. Culler, "Whitetail Time"; cf. Hilliard, *Hog Meat and Hoecake,* 74–75, 77–78. Deer were already scarce by the 1840s, and their numbers continued to decline in succeeding

decades. In 1975 Calhoun County resident W. Peter Buyck Sr. recalled that deer were extremely scarce during his childhood: "I remember as a small boy of 10 or 12 [that is, in 1915 or 1917] there was not a single deer in the entire area. Today there are hundreds." See Gibbes, "Agricultural Survey of the Parish of St. Mathews [sic]," 150; South Carolina House of Representatives, Hearing on H 3097 (statement of W. Peter Buyck Sr.).

30. Heitmeyer et al., "Ecological Relationships of Warmblooded Vertebrates," 289; cf. Holladay, Kwit, and Collins, "Woody Regeneration," 223.

31. Kilgo et al., "Coyote Removal"; Florschutz, Refuge Land Acquisition Biological Reconnaissance Report, 8; John E. Cely in discussion with the author, October 2011; Mayer and Brisbin, Wild Pigs in the United States, 62.

32. Fisichelli et al., "Climate, Pests, Trees, and Weeds."

Appendix A

1. See Richland County Deed Book F, p. 29 (plat of A. M. Hunt tract); plat of "Hunt's Tract," ca. 1870, Records of the South Carolina Land Commission, SCDAH. The South Carolina Land Commission was established in 1869 to acquire large tracts of former plantation land and redistribute it in small parcels to freed slaves and landless whites. (Few whites, however, chose to acquire land from the commission.) The commission acquired seven tracts in lower Richland between 1869 and 1870. Two of these tracts bordered the future Congaree National Park, and a third ("Hunt's tract") eventually became Parcel 13 of the Beidler Tract. The amount of land purchased by the commission in Richland County (9,402 acres) was the third largest in the state. Only in Charleston and Colleton counties did the commission acquire more land. Nearly 180 freed men and women purchased land in lower Richland, acquiring 6,310 acres of the 9,402 owned by the commission. Of these purchasers, 39 (none in the park) were able to make all payments and receive clear title to their property. The result was that about 1,399 acres, or just over 22 percent of the land originally purchased from the commission, passed in fee to former slaves. With the end of Reconstruction in 1876, land sales were transferred from the Land Commission to the South Carolina Sinking Fund Commission. Most of the remaining land held by the Sinking Fund Commission was sold in large parcels to whites. See Almlie et al., Prized Pieces of Land, 18–21, 24–25.

Bibliography

Historic newspapers and miscellaneous unpublished documents are cited fully in the notes rather than in the bibliography. Materials from the South Carolina Department of Archives and History (SCDAH) that are cited in notes are generally not included in this bibliography as they can be located via the SCDAH Online Index or are cited fully in the notes.

Ackerman, Robert K. *South Carolina Colonial Land Policies*. Columbia: University of South Carolina Press, 1977.

"An Act for Raising and Paying into the Public Treasury of this State, the Tax Therein Mentioned, for the Use and Service Thereof" (enacted 1784). In *Statutes at Large of South Carolina*, vol. 4, *1752–1786*, edited by Thomas Cooper, 627–38. Columbia, S.C.: A. S. Johnston, 1838.

"An Act to Extend the Provisions [Authorizing Alteration] of the Fence Laws . . . to Lower Township, Richland County." In *Acts and Joint Resolutions of the South Carolina General Assembly Passed at the Regular Session of 1879 and Extra Session of 1880*, 305–6. Columbia, S.C.: Calvo and Patton, State Printers, 1880.

Adams, Edward C. L. *Tales of the Congaree*. Edited by Robert G. O'Meally. Chapel Hill: University of North Carolina Press, 1987. Compilation of titles published in 1927 and 1928.

Adams, James Hopkins. *History and Sketches of the Adams Family of Richland County, South Carolina*. N.p., microfilm, South Caroliniana Library, University of South Carolina, Columbia. Compiled approximately 1910.

Allen, Bruce P. "Vegetation Dynamics and Response to Disturbance, in Floodplain Forest Ecosystems with a Focus on Lianas." Ph.D. diss., Ohio State University, 2007.

Allen, Bruce P., P. Charles Goebel, and Rebecca R. Sharitz. *Long-Term Effects of Wind Disturbance on the Old-growth Forests and Lianas of Congaree National Park*. Report for the National Park Service. University of Georgia, Savannah River Ecology Laboratory, 2010.

Allen, R. L. "Letters from the South.—No. 2 [November 26, 1846]." In *American Agriculturalist*, vol. 6, edited by A. B. Allen, 20–21. New York: Harper and Brothers, 1847.

Almlie, Elizabeth, Angi Fuller Wildt, Ashley Bouknight, Amanda Bowman, Lee Durbetaki, Keri Fay, Haley Grant, Benjamin Greene, Nathan Johnson, Amanda Roddy, Sarah Scripps, and Morgen Young. *Prized Pieces of Land: The Impact of Reconstruction on African-American Land Ownership in Lower Richland County, South Carolina*. Columbia: University of South Carolina, Public History Program, 2009.

American Lumbermen: The Personal History and Public and Business Achievements of 100 Eminent Lumbermen of the United States. Second series. Chicago: American Lumberman, 1906.

Anderson, David G. "The Initial Human Occupation of the Southeast." In *Southeast Project Area Historic Context*. Website of the National Park Service, Southeast Archeological

Center, Tallahassee, Fla., n.d. http://www.nps.gov/seac/hnc/outline/02-paleoindian/ se_paleo/04-initial.htm (accessed August 1, 2015).

———. "The Mississippian in South Carolina." In *Studies in South Carolina Archaeology: Studies in Honor of Robert L. Stephenson,* edited by Albert C. Goodyear III and Glen T. Hanson, 101–32. Anthropological Studies 9. Columbia: South Carolina Institute of Archaeology and Anthropology, University of South Carolina, 1989.

———. *The Savannah River Chiefdoms: Political Change in the Late Prehistoric Southeast.* Tuscaloosa: University of Alabama Press, 1994.

———. "Stability and Change in Chiefdom-Level Societies." In *Lamar Archaeology: Mississippian Chiefdoms in the Deep South,* edited by Mark Williams and Gary Shapiro, 187–213. Tuscaloosa: University of Alabama Press, 1990.

Anderson, David G., and Robert C. Mainfort Jr., eds. *The Woodland Southeast.* Tuscaloosa: University of Alabama Press, 2002.

Anderson, Virginia D. "Animals into the Wilderness: The Development of Livestock Husbandry in the Seventeenth-Century Chesapeake." In Sutter and Manganiello, *Environmental History and the American South,* 25–60.

Andreas, Alfred T. *The History of Chicago, from the Earliest Period to the Present Time.* Vol. 3, *From the Fire of 1871 until 1885.* Chicago: A. T. Andreas Company, 1886.

Ayers, Edward L. *The Promise of the New South.* New York: Oxford University Press, 1992.

Bailey, N. Louise, and Elizabeth Ivey Cooper, eds. *Biographical Directory of the South Carolina House of Representatives.* Vol. 3, *1775–1790.* Columbia: University of South Carolina Press, 1981.

Baker, James B., and O. Gordon Langdon. "*Pinus taeda* L., Loblolly Pine." In Burns and Honkala, *Silvics of North America.* Vol. 1, *Conifers,* 497–512.

Ball, Charles. *Slavery in the United States: A Narrative of the Life and Adventures of Charles Ball, a Black Man.* New York: John S. Taylor, 1837. Available online at http://docsouth .unc.edu/neh/ballslavery/menu.html.

Bandera, Juan de la. [The "long" Juan de la Bandera relation, April 1, 1569.] Translated by Paul E. Hoffman. In Hudson, *The Juan Pardo Expeditions,* 205–96.

Banschbach, Mary, Dominic J. Day, Emma Mason, Christopher Lee Curry, Sarah Love, and Daniel P. Bigman. "Long-Term Changes in Landscape Use Patterns at Sampson Island Congaree National Park, South Carolina." Poster presented at the annual conference of the Archaeological Society of South Carolina, Columbia, S.C., February 2015.

Barnes, Burton V., Donald R. Zak, Shirley R. Denton, and Stephen H. Spurr. *Forest Ecology.* 4th ed. New York: John Wiley and Sons, 1998.

Barnes, Mark R. "National Historic Landmark Nomination Form, Charlesfort-Santa Elena Site." Website of the South Carolina Department of Archives and History. n.d. http:// pdfhost.focus.nps.gov/docs/NHLS/text/74001822.pdf (accessed September 13, 2015).

Batson, Wade T. [Eligibility of Congaree Swamp to be designated a national natural landmark.] University of South Carolina report to the Secretary of the Interior's Advisory Board on National Parks, Historic Sites, Buildings, and Monuments, ca. 1970.

Battaglia, Loretta L., Beverly S. Collins, and Rebecca R. Sharitz. "Do Published Tolerance Ratings and Dispersal Factors Predict Species Distributions in Bottomland Hardwoods?" *Forest Ecology and Management* 198, nos. 1–3 (2004): 15–30.

Battaglia, Loretta L., and Rebecca R. Sharitz. "Effects of Natural Disturbance on Bottomland Hardwood Regeneration." In Fredrickson, King, and Kaminski, *Ecology and Management of Bottomland Hardwood Systems,* 121–36.

———. "Responses of Floodplain Forest Species to Spatially Condensed Gradients: A Test of the Flood-Shade Tolerance Tradeoff Hypothesis." *Oecologia* 147, no. 1 (2006.): 108–18.

Battalio, Raymond C., and John Kagel. "The Structure of Antebellum Southern Agriculture: South Carolina, a Case Study." *Agricultural History* 44, no. 1 (1970): 25–37.

Beeson, Kenneth H., Jr. "Indigo Production in the Eighteenth Century." *Hispanic American Historical Review* 44, no. 2 (1964): 214–18.

Bell, Malcolm, Jr. *Major Butler's Legacy: Five Generations of a Slaveholding Family.* Athens: University of Georgia Press, 1987.

Bennett, Frank, and A. M. Griffen. "Soil Survey of the Orangeburg Area, South Carolina." In *Field Operations of the Bureau of Soils, 1904,* 185–205. Sixth Report, United States Department of Agriculture, Bureau of Soils. Washington, D.C.: Government Printing Office, 1905.

Bennett, Frank, G. W. Talby Jr., James L. Burgess, Grove B. Jones, W. J. Latimer, and H. L. Westover. "Soil Survey of Sumter County, South Carolina." In *Field Operations of the Bureau of Soils, 1907,* 299–321. Ninth Report, United States Department of Agriculture, Bureau of Soils. Washington, D.C.: Government Printing Office, 1909.

Bennett, Robert B., Jr. "The Santee Canal, 1785–1939." Master's thesis, University of South Carolina, 1988.

Biedma, Luys Hernández de. "Relation of the Island of Florida." Translated by John E. Worth. In Clayton, Knight, and Moore, *The De Soto Chronicles,* 1:225–46.

"Bits of Telephone News." *Telephone Magazine* 24, no. 159 (1904): 276–81.

Blanding, Abram. "Address of A. Blanding, Esq. to a Meeting at Camden, on the 15th Ultimo. on the Subject of Internal Improvement." *Niles' Weekly Register* 15, no. 9 (1818): 135–38. Originally published in the *South Carolina Gazette* (Columbia).

Blassingame, John W. Introduction. *Slave Testimony: Two Centuries of Letters, Speeches, Interviews, and Autobiographies,* edited by John W. Blassingame, xvii–lxv. Baton Rouge: Louisiana State University Press, 1977.

Bleser, Carol, ed. *Secret and Sacred: The Diaries of James Henry Hammond, a Southern Slaveholder.* New York: Oxford University Press, 1988.

Brantley, Christopher G., and Steven G. Platt. "Canebrake Conservation in the Southeastern United States." *Wildlife Society Bulletin* 29, no. 4 (2001): 1175–81.

Bryant, Ralph C. *Logging: The Principles and General Methods of Operation in the United States.* New York: John Wiley and Sons, 1913.

Brown, Richard M. *The South Carolina Regulators.* Cambridge, Mass.: Belknap Press of Harvard University Press, 1963.

Brunswig, Norman L., and Stephen G. Winton. *The Francis Beidler Forest in Four Holes Swamp: A Self-Guided Tour of the Boardwalk.* New York: National Audubon Society, 1978.

Bull, Kinloch, Jr. *The Oligarchs in Colonial and Revolutionary Charleston: Lieutenant Governor William Bull II and His Family.* Columbia: University of South Carolina Press, 1991.

Bull, William, Jr. Memorial of Lt. Gov. William Bull Jr., March 1784, as supplemented Jan.– Dec. 1788. London: Public Record Office, Audit Office Records—Claims, American Loyalists. Audit Office Series 12, Vol. 52, pp. 85–118, and Series 13, Vol. 97, pp. 22–23, 45–46, 55–56.

Burns, Russell M., and Barbara H. Honkala, technical coordinators. *Silvics of North America.* Vol. 1, *Conifers.* Agriculture Handbook 654. Washington, D.C.: U.S. Department of Agriculture, Forest Service, 1990.

———. *Silvics of North America.* Vol. 2, *Hardwoods.* Agriculture Handbook 654. Washington, D.C.: U.S. Department of Agriculture, Forest Service, 1990.

Calkins, William W. *The History of the One Hundred and Fourth Regiment of Illinois Volunteer Infantry, War of the Great Rebellion, 1862–1865.* Chicago: Donohue and Henneberry, 1895.

Cantey Family Papers. Manuscripts Division, South Caroliniana Library, University of South Carolina, Columbia.

Cantwell, R. C., surveyor. *Plat of the Swamp Lands and Timber Holdings of the Santee River Cypress Lumber Company Lying on the Northern Side of the Congaree River and Situate in Lower Township Richland County, South Carolina. Surveyed Feb'y.–June, 1909.* Scale 1" = 1000'. On file at Congaree National Park.

Carney, Judith. "Landscapes of Technology Transfer: Rice Cultivation and African Continuities." In Sutter and Manganiello, *Environmental History and the American South,* 80–105.

Carroll, Wayne D., Peter R. Kapeluck, Richard A. Harper, and David H. Van Lear. "Historical Overview of the Southern Forest Landscape and Associated Resources." In *Southern Forest Resource Assessment,* edited by David N. Wear and John G. Greis, 583–605. United States Department of Agriculture, Forest Service, Southern Research Station, 2002.

Carruth, Amy, and Deborah Joy. *Archaeological and Architectural Survey Report: US 601 Road Widening and Bridge Replacements, Calhoun and Richland Counties, South Carolina.* Report prepared for Florence & Hutcheson, Inc. on behalf of the South Carolina Department of Transportation, Environmental Unit. PIN 30616/SC, File # 4.224B, 2004.

Catesby, Mark. "An Account of Carolina, and the Bahama Islands." In *Catesby's Birds of Colonial America,* edited by Alan Feduccia, 139–69. Chapel Hill: University of North Carolina Press, 1985. First published in Catesby, *The Natural History of Carolina, Florida and the Bahama Islands,* vol. 2 (1743).

Caughman, H. I. "Agricultural Resources of Lexington District, S.C." *Farmer and Planter* 10, no. 5 (1859): 134–35.

Cecilia [sic]. "Memories of Home Travels." *Southern Literary Messenger* 20, no. 3 (1854): 141–44.

Cely, John E. "Is the Beidler Tract in Congaree Swamp Virgin?" In *Congaree Swamp: Greatest Unprotected Forest on the Continent,* 91–95. Columbia: South Carolina Environmental Coalition, 1975.

———. "Congaree Swamp's Virgin Cypress Trees." *Newsletter: Friends of Congaree Swamp* (March 2000): 4–5.

———. *Map of Original Land Grants, Congaree Swamp National Monument.* Scale not given. 2001. On file at Congaree National Park.

———. "Tree Species, in Order of Abundance, Used as Boundary Markers for Original Land Grants, Congaree Swamp National Monument." Unpublished manuscript, 2003. In possession of the author.

———. *Map of Congaree National Park.* Large-format map, version 3.8, scale 1" = 1500'. Hopkins, S.C.: Eastern National, 2004.

———. "Is the Beidler Tract in Congaree Swamp Virgin? An Update 35 Years Later." Unpublished manuscript, 2010. In possession of the author.

———. *Cowasee Basin: The Green Heart of South Carolina.* Manning, S.C.: Totally Outdoors Publishing, 2011.

———. *Map of Early Land Grants, Congaree National Park, East and Vicinity.* Scale 1" = 30 chains. 2014. On file at Congaree National Park.

Chappell, Buford S. "Names Old, New, and Forgotten along Monticello Road and Little River." *Names in South Carolina* 21 (Winter 1974): 15–19.

Chittenden, Alfred K. *The Red Gum.* United States Department of Agriculture, Bureau of Forestry, Bulletin no. 58. Rev. ed. Washington, D.C.: Government Printing Office, 1906.

Clayton, Lawrence A., Vernon J. Knight Jr., and Edward C. Moore, eds. *The De Soto Chronicles: The Expedition of Hernando de Soto to North America in 1539–1543.* 2 vols. Tuscaloosa: University of Alabama Press, 1993.

Coate, Marmaduke. *Survey of Richland District.* Holograph map, scale not given, 1820. SCDAH, MB 3–7.

Cobb, Charles R., and Michael S. Nassaney. "Domesticating Self and Society in the Woodland Southeast." In Anderson and Mainfort, *The Woodland Southeast,* 525–39.

Cohen, Arthur D., David C. Shelley, H. Thomas Foster II, Christopher Judge, Michelle A. Metzler, and Elizabeth A. Cannon. "Palynology and Paleoecology of Late Pleistocene to Holocene, Organic-Rich, Paleomeander/Rimswamp Deposits in South Carolina and Georgia." *Abstracts with Programs* (Geological Society of America) 38, no. 7 (2006): 235.

Cohen, Arthur D., David C. Shelley, and H. Bartley. "Pollen and Palynofacies of Organic-Rich Wetland Deposits in the Northern Margin of the Congaree River Floodplain, Congaree National Park, SC." *Abstracts with Programs* (Geological Society of America) 36, no.2 (2004): 111.

Cokinos, Christopher. *Hope Is the Thing with Feathers: A Personal Chronicle of Vanished Birds.* New York: Putnam, 2000.

Collins, Beverly S., and Loretta L. Battaglia. "Oak Regeneration in Southeastern Bottomland Hardwood Forest." *Forest Ecology and Management* 255, no. 7 (2008): 3026–34.

Committee on Columbia Trade. "South Carolina—Trade and Manufactures [of Columbia and Vicinity] in 1836." In *The Family Magazine; or Monthly Abstract of General Knowledge,* 206–8. Cincinnati: Eli Taylor, 1839.

Congaree Land Trust. "Adams Conserves Wavering Place." *Congaree Land Trust Outlook* 13, (2007): 3.

Conrad, Dennis M., Roger N. Parks, and Martha J. King. *The Papers of Nathanael Greene.* Vol. 9, *11 July 1781–2 December 1781.* Chapel Hill: University of North Carolina Press, 1997.

Conrads, Paul A., Toby D. Feaster, and Larry G. Harrelson. *The Effects of the Saluda Dam on the Surface-water and Ground-water Hydrology of the Congaree National Park Flood Plain, South Carolina.* United States Geological Survey Scientific Investigations Report 2008–5170, 2008. http://pubs.water.usgs.gov/sir2008-5170.

Cook, Harvey T. *The Life and Legacy of David Rogerson Williams.* New York: n.p., 1916.

"Crescent City News." *American Lumberman,* no. 1762 (February 27, 1909): 80.

Croy, Steve, and Cecil Frost. "Reference Conditions, Potential Natural Vegetation Group—Piedmont Floodplain Forest." In *Draft Fire Regime Condition Class (FRCC) Interagency Handbook,* 2005. http://www.ibrarian.net/navon/paper/Fire_Regime_Condition_Class__FRCC__Interagency_Ha.pdf?paperid=3777792.

Culler, John. "Forest of Champions." *South Carolina Wildlife* 21, no. 6 (1974): 16–21.

———. "Whitetail Time." *South Carolina Wildlife* 23, no. 5 (1976): n.p. Available online at http://www.scwildlife.com/articles/novdec2006/whitetail.html

Culler, Daniel Marchant. *Orangeburgh District, 1768–1868: History and Records.* Spartanburg, S.C.: Reprint Company, 1995.

Davidson, Chalmers G. *The Last Foray: The South Carolina Planters of 1860; A Sociological Study.* Columbia: University of South Carolina Press, 1971.

Davies, F. G. "The Facts of the Trade." In *Year Book 1909, City of Charleston, So. Ca.,* appendix, 42–46. Charleston, S.C.: Walker, Evans and Cogswell, 1910.

De Brahm, William G. "Philosophico-Historico-Hydrogeography of South Carolina, Georgia, and East Florida." In *Documents Connected with the History of South Carolina,* edited by Plowden C. J. Weston, 155–227. Ca. 1772. Reprint, London, 1856.

Delcourt, Paul A., and Hazel R. Delcourt. "Pre-Columbian Native American Use of Fire on Southern Appalachian Landscapes." *Conservation Biology* 11, no. 4 (1997): 1010–14.

———. *Prehistoric Native Americans and Ecological Change: Human Ecosystems in Eastern North America since the Pleistocene.* Cambridge, U.K.: Cambridge University Press, 2004.

Delcourt, Paul A., Hazel R. Delcourt, Dan F. Morse, and Phyllis A. Morse. "History, Evolution, and Organization of Vegetation and Human Culture." In Martin, Boyce, and Echternacht, *Biodiversity of the Southeastern United States,* 47–79.

Dennis, John V. *A Preliminary Report on the Woody Plants, Birds, and Mammals of the Congaree Swamp, South Carolina.* Report for the National Park Service, 1967.

———. *Woody Plants of the Congaree Forest Swamp, South Carolina.* Ecological Studies Leaflet no. 12. Washington, D.C.: Nature Conservancy, 1967.

———. "Big Trees of the Congaree Swamp." *National Parks and Conservation Magazine* 46, no. 10 (1972): 18–22.

DePratter, Chester. "The Chiefdom of Cofitachequi." In *The Forgotten Centuries: Indians and Europeans in the American South 1521–1704,* edited by Charles Hudson and Carmen Chaves Tesser, 197–226. Athens: University of Georgia Press, 1994.

DePratter, Chester B. "Cofitachequi: Ethnohistorical and Archaeological Evidence." In *Studies in South Carolina Archaeology: Studies in Honor of Robert L. Stephenson,* Anthropological Studies 9, edited by Albert C. Goodyear III and Glen T. Hanson, 133–56. Columbia: South Carolina Institute of Archaeology and Anthropology, University of South Carolina, 1989.

DePratter, Chester, and Val Green. "John Lawson and the Great Catawba Trading Path." *Carologue* 16, no. 3 (2000): 16–20.

DePratter, Chester B., and Christopher Judge. "Wateree River [Chronology and Phase Characteristics.]" In *Lamar Archaeology: Mississippian Chiefdoms in the Deep South,* edited by Mark Williams and Gary Shapiro, 30–78. Tuscaloosa: University of Alabama Press, 1990.

Derrick, Samuel M. *Centennial History of South Carolina Railroad.* Columbia, S.C.: The State Company, 1930.

Doolittle, William E. "Agriculture in North America on the Eve of Contact: A Reassessment." *Annals of the Association of American Geographers* 82, no. 3 (1992): 386–401.

———. "Permanent vs. Shifting Cultivation in the Eastern Woodlands of North America Prior to European Contact." *Agriculture and Human Values* 21, nos. 2–3 (2004): 181–89.

Downey, Tom. *Planting a Capitalist South: Masters, Merchants, and Manufacturers in the Southern Interior, 1790–1860.* Baton Rouge: Louisiana State University Press, 2006.

Doyle, Thomas. W. *Modeling Floodplain Hydrology and Forest Productivity of Congaree Swamp, South Carolina.* United States Geological Survey Scientific Investigations Report 2009–5130, 2009. Available online at http://pubs.usgs.gov/sir/2009/5130/.

Draine, Tony, and John Skinner. *Richland District, South Carolina Land Records, 1785–1865.* Columbia, S.C.: Congaree Publications, 1986.

Drayton, John. *A View of South Carolina, as Respects Her Natural and Civil Concerns.* 1802. Reprint, Spartanburg, S.C.: Reprint Company, 1972.

Dubose, Samuel. "Address Delivered at the Seventeenth Anniversary of the Black Oak Agricultural Society on Tuesday, April 27, 1858." In *A Contribution to the History of the Huguenots of South Carolina,* edited by Samuel Dubose and Frederick A. Porcher, 1–33. New York: Knickerbocker Press, 1887.

———. "Reminiscences of St. Stephen's Parish and Notices of Her Old Homesteads." In Dubose and Porcher, *A Contribution to the History of the Huguenots of South Carolina,* 35–85.

Dunbar, Gary S. "Colonial Carolina Cowpens." *Agricultural History* 35, no. 3 (1961): 125–31.

Dusinberre, William. *Them Dark Days: Slavery in the American Rice Swamps.* New York: Oxford University Press, 1996.

Early, Lawrence S. *Looking for Longleaf: The Fall and Rise of an American Forest.* Chapel Hill: University of North Carolina Press, 2004.

Edelson, S. Max. *Plantation Enterprise in Colonial South Carolina.* Cambridge, Mass.: Harvard University Press, 2006.

———. "Clearing Swamps, Harvesting Forests: Trees and the Making of a Plantation Landscape in the Colonial South Carolina Lowcountry." *Agricultural History* 81, no. 3 (2007): 381–406.

Edgar, Walter. *South Carolina: A History.* Columbia: University of South Carolina Press, 1998.

Elliot, Jonathan, ed. *The Debates in the Several State Conventions on the Adoption of the Federal Constitution, as Recommended by the General Convention at Philadelphia, in 1787.* 2nd ed. Vol. 4. Philadelphia: J. B. Lippincott, 1836.

Elliott, William. "Reflections on the State of Our Agriculture, Especially on the Advantage of Cultivating Indigo, &c." *Southern Agriculturist* 1, no. 2 (1828): 61–66.

Eyre, Francis H. *A Survey of Proposed Natural Forest Areas in the Southeast.* Report by the Society of American Foresters, 1960. Available online at http://catalog.hathitrust.org/Record/002009303.

Ferguson, Leland G. "South Appalachian Mississippian." Ph.D. diss., University of North Carolina, Chapel Hill, 1971.

Fetters, Thomas. *Logging Railroads of South Carolina.* Forest Park, Ill.: Heimburger House, 1990.

———. *The Charleston & Hamburg: A South Carolina Railroad and an American Legacy.* Charleston, S.C.: History Press, 2008.

Fishburne, William, Papers. Manuscripts Division, South Caroliniana Library, University of South Carolina, Columbia.

Fisichelli, Nicholas A., Scott R. Abella, Matthew Peters, and Frank J. Krist Jr. "Climate, Pests, Trees, and Weeds: Change, Uncertainty, and Biotic Stressors in Eastern U.S. National Park Forests." *Forest Ecology and Management* 327 (2014): 31–39.

Florschutz, Otto, Jr. *Refuge Land Acquisition Biological Reconnaissance Report, Congaree River Swamp, South Carolina.* United States Fish and Wildlife Service, 1971.

Floyd, Gen. ———. "On the Cultivation and Preparation of Indigo." *Southern Agriculturist* 2 (March 1829): 105–8; 154–62. Reprint of article written some years before (?) by General Floyd of Georgia; submitted to the editor of the *Southern Agriculturist* by Thomas Spalding.

Foner, Eric. *Reconstruction: America's Unfinished Revolution, 1865–1877.* New York: Harper and Row, 1988.

Ford, Lacy K., Jr. "Self-Sufficiency, Cotton, and Economic Development in the South Carolina Upcountry, 1800–1860." *Journal of Economic History* 42, no. 2 (1985): 261–67.

———. *Origins of Southern Radicalism: The South Carolina Upcountry, 1800–1860.* New York: Oxford University Press, 1988.

Foster, H. Thomas, II, Bryan Black, and Marc D. Abrams. "A Witness Tree Analysis of the Effects of Native American Indians on the Pre-European Settlement Forests in East-Central Alabama." *Human Ecology* 32, no. 1 (2004): 27–47.

Foster, H. Thomas, II, and Arthur D. Cohen. "Palynological Evidence of the Effects of the Deerskin Trade on Forest Fires during the Eighteenth Century in Southeastern North America." *American Antiquity* 72, no. 1 (2007): 35–51.

Fredrickson, Leigh H., Sammy L. King, and Richard M. Kaminski, eds. *Ecology and Management of Bottomland Hardwood Systems: The State of Our Understanding.* Gaylord Memorial Laboratory Special Publication no. 10. Puxico: University of Missouri–Columbia, 2005.

Fretz, Abraham J. *A Genealogical Record of the Descendants of Jacob Beidler of Lower Milford Township, Bucks Co., Pa.* N.p., 1903.

Frost, Cecil C., and Stephanie Wilds. *Presettlement Vegetation and Natural Fire Regimes of the Congaree Swamp Uplands.* Report for the National Park Service, 2001.

Gaddy, L. L. *Natural Resources Inventory of Congaree Swamp National Monument and Environs.* Report for National Park Service, with large format maps, 1979.

———. *A Preliminary Biological/Hydrological Evaluation of the Kingville East and Bates Fork Tracts, Richland County, South Carolina.* Report for the Trust for Public Land, 1994.

Gaddy, L. L., with John E. Cely. *The Natural History of Congaree Swamp.* Manning, S.C.: Totally Outdoors Imaging, for Terra Incognita Books, 2012.

Gaddy, L. L., Thomas S. Kohlsaat, Eugene A. Laurent, and Kenneth B. Stansell. *A Vegetation Analysis of Preserve Alternatives Involving the Beidler Tract of the Congaree Swamp.* South Carolina Wildlife and Marine Resources Department, 1975.

Gagnon, Paul R. "Population Biology and Disturbance Ecology of a Native North American Bamboo *(Arundinaria gigantea).*" Ph.D. diss., Louisiana State University, 2006.

———. "Fire in Floodplain Forests in the Southeastern USA: Insights from Disturbance Ecology of Native Bamboo." *Wetlands* 29, no. 2 (2009): 520–26.

Gagnon, Paul R., Heather A. Passmore, and William J. Platt. "Multi-Year Salutary Effects of Windstorm and Fire on River Cane." *Fire Ecology* 9, no. 1 (2013): 55–65.

Gagnon, Paul R., William J. Platt, and E. Barry Moser, "Response of a Native Bamboo in a Wind-Disturbed Forest." *Forest Ecology and Management* 241, nos. 1–3 (2007): 288–94.

Gallagher, Tim. *The Grail Bird.* Boston: Houghton Mifflin, 2005.

Gallman, Robert E. "Self-Sufficiency in the Cotton Economy of the Antebellum South." *Agricultural History* 44, no. 1 (1970): 5–23.

Garcilaso de la Vega, the Inca. "La Florida." Translated by Charmion Shelby. In Clayton, Knight, and Moore, *The De Soto Chronicles,* 2:25–559.

Gentleman from Elvas. "The Account by a Gentleman from Elvas." Translated by James Alexander Robertson. In Clayton, Knight, and Moore, *The De Soto Chronicles,* 1:45–171.

Gibbes, R. W. "Agricultural Survey of the Parish of St. Mathews [sic], (So. Ca.)." *Carolina Planter* 1, no. 19 (1840): 148–50.

———. "Extraordinary Freshet." *Carolina Planter* 1, no. 21 (1840): 161.

Glen, James. "A Description of South Carolina." In *Colonial South Carolina: Two Contemporary Descriptions,* edited by Chapman J. Milling, 3–104. Columbia: University of South Carolina Press, 1951. First published 1761.

Goodyear, Albert C. "Evidence for Pre-Clovis Sites in the Eastern United States." In *Paleoamerican Origins: Beyond Clovis,* edited by Robson Bonnichsen, Bradley T. Lepper, Dennis Stanford, and Michael R. Waters, 103–12. College Station: Texas A&M University Press, 2005.

Goodyear, Albert C., and Joseph E. Wilkinson. "Prehistory at High Creek Plantation: A Black Mingo Chert Source and Quarry in Calhoun County, South Carolina." *South Carolina Antiquities* 46 (2014): 35–43.

Goodyear, N. M., and R. F. Hemingway. "Report of Lumber Operation of the Santee River Cypress Lumber Company, Ferguson, S.C." In *Lumber Reports,* vol. 3, *Southern States,* 110–49 (report paginated 1–39). A collection of typewritten reports by Pennsylvania State college students on lumber camp operations. Pennsylvania State University, ca. 1911. Available online at http://archive.org/stream/lumberreports03snsl#page/n281/mode/2up.

Gray, Lewis C. *History of Agriculture in the Southern United States to 1860.* 2 vols. Washington, D.C.: Carnegie Institution of Washington, 1933.

Green, Edwin L. *A History of Richland County, South Carolina.* Vol. 1, *1732–1805.* 1932. Reprinted with new material, Greenville, S.C.: South Carolina Southern Historical Press, Inc., 1996.

Gregg, E. Stuart, Jr. *A Crane's Foot (or Pedigree) of Branches of the Gregg, Stuart, Robertson, Dobbs and Allied Families.* Columbia, S.C.: R. L. Bryan Company, 1975.

[Grego, John.] "Pottery Shard Early Mississippian." *Newsletter: Friends of Congaree Swamp* (Fall 2004): 5.

Gremillion, Kristen J. "The Development and Dispersal of Agricultural Systems in the Woodland Period Southeast." In Anderson and Mainfort, *The Woodland Southeast,* 483–501.

Groover, Mark D. "The Archaeology of Cattle Raisers in the South Carolina Backcountry." Available online at http://mdgroover.iweb.bsu.edu/GPR%20Cattle%20Raisers.htm (accessed August 1, 2015).

Groover, Mark D., and Richard D. Brooks. "The Catherine Brown Cowpen and the Thomas Howell Site: Material Characteristics of Cattle Raisers in the South Carolina Backcountry." *Southeastern Archeology* 22, no. 1 (2003): 91–110.

Hall, Rosine B. W., and Paul A. Harcombe. "Flooding Alters Apparent Position of Floodplain Saplings on a Light Gradient." *Ecology* 79, no. 3 (1998): 847–55.

———. "Sapling Dynamics in a Southeastern Texas Floodplain Forest." *Journal of Vegetation Science* 12, no. 3 (2001): 427–38.

Hammond, Harry. *South Carolina: Resources and Population, Institutions and Industries.* State Board of Agriculture of South Carolina. Charleston: Walker, Evans and Cogswell, 1883.

Hampton, Harry R. E. *Woods and Waters and Some Asides.* Columbia, S.C.: The State Printing Company, 1979.

Hamrick, Elizabeth McRae. "Some Notes on the Weston Family." *South Carolina Magazine of Ancestral Research* 11, no. 3 (1983): 138–40.

Harcombe, Paul A., Rosine B. W. Hall, Jeff S. Glitzenstein, Edward R. Cook, Paul Krusic, Mark Fulton, and Donna R. Streng. "Sensitivity of Gulf Coast Forests to Climate

Change." In *Vulnerability of Coastal Wetlands in the Southeastern United States: Climate Change Research Results, 1992–97,* edited by Glenn R. Guntenspergen and Beth A. Vairin, 45–66. USGS, National Wetlands Research Center, Biological Science Report USGS/BRD/BSR—1998–0002, 1998. Available online at http://www.nwrc.usgs.gov/wdb/pub/others/BSR1998-0002/chapter5.pdf.

Harcombe, Paul A., Lisa E. Mann Leipzig, and I. Sandra Elsik. "Effects of Hurricane Rita on Three Long-term Forest Study Plots in East Texas, USA." *Wetlands* 29, no. 1 (2009): 88–100.

"Hardwood News." *Hardwood Record* 30, no. 5 (1910): 53.

"Hardwood News, Notes." *Hardwood Record* 34, no. 3 (1912): 48.

Hardy, Meredith D. *Congaree National Park: Archeological Overview and Assessment.* National Park Service, Southeast Archeological Center, SEAC Accession Number 1817, 2008.

———. *Archeological Survey of Sampson Island, Bates Fork Tract, Congaree National Park.* National Park Service, Southeast Archeological Center, SEAC Accession Number 2096, 2009.

———. "A Brief Introduction to the Prehistoric Communities of the Congaree River Floodplain, Congaree National Park." *Newsletter: Friends of Congaree Swamp* (Winter 2009): 1, 7.

Hardy, Meredith D., and Guy Prentice. "Cultural Overview." In *Congaree National Park: Archeological Overview and Assessment,* by Meredith D. Hardy, 35–72. National Park Service, Southeastern Archeological Center, SEAC Accession Number 1817, 2008.

Harris, B. *Year Book and Sixteenth Annual Report of the Commissioner of Agriculture Commerce and Industries of the State of South Carolina, 1919.* Columbia, S.C.: Gonzales and Bryan, 1920.

Haw, James. *John and Edward Rutledge of South Carolina.* Athens: University of Georgia Press, 1997.

Heitmeyer, Mickey E., Robert J. Cooper, James G. Dickson, and Bruce D. Leopold. "Ecological Relationships of Warmblooded Vertebrates in Bottomland Hardwood Ecosystems." In Fredrickson, King, and Kaminski, *Ecology and Management of Bottomland Hardwood Systems,* 281–306.

Hilliard, Sam B. *Hog Meat and Hoecake: Food Supply in the Old South, 1840–1860.* Carbondale: Southern Illinois University Press, 1972.

Hilton, William. *A Relation of a Discovery Lately Made on the Coast of Florida.* London, 1664.

Hirsch, Arthur H. *The Huguenots of Colonial South Carolina.* Durham, N.C.: Duke University Press, 1928.

Hodges, John D. "Development and Ecology of Bottomland Hardwood Sites." *Forest Ecology and Management* 90, nos. 2–3 (1997): 117–25.

Holcomb, Brent H., abstractor. *South Carolina Deed Abstracts 1773–1778, Books F-4–X-4.* Columbia: South Carolina Magazine of Ancestral Research, 1993.

———. *South Carolina Deed Abstracts 1776–1783, Books Y-4–H-5.* Columbia: South Carolina Magazine of Ancestral Research, 1994.

———. *South Carolina Deed Abstracts 1783–1788, Books I-5–Z-5.* Columbia: South Carolina Magazine of Ancestral Research, 1996.

Holladay, C. A., Charles Kwit, and Beverly Collins. "Woody Regeneration in and around Aging Southern Bottomland Hardwood Forest Gaps: Effects of Herbivory and Gap Size." *Forest Ecology and Management* 223, nos. 1–3 (2006): 218–25.

Hopkins, Laura Jervey. *History of St. John's Episcopal Church, 1858–1958, Congaree South Carolina*. N.p., 1958.

———. *Lower Richland Planters: Hopkins, Adams, Weston, and Related Families*. Columbia, S.C.: R. L. Bryan Company, 1976.

Hotchkiss, George W. *Industrial Chicago: The Lumber Interests*. Chicago: Goodspeed Publishing, 1894.

Howe, George. "An Essay on the Antiquities of the Congaree Indians of South Carolina." In *Information Respecting the History, Condition and Prospects of the Indian Tribes of the United States, Part 4*, edited by H. R. Schoolcraft for the Bureau of Indian Affairs, 155–69. Philadelphia: J. B. Lippincott, 1856.

Hudson, Charles H. *The Southeastern Indians*. Knoxville: University of Tennessee Press, 1976.

———. *The Juan Pardo Expeditions: Exploration of the Carolinas and Tennessee, 1566–1568*. Washington, D.C.: Smithsonian Institution Press, 1990.

———. "The Social Context of the Chiefdom of Ichisi." In *Ocmulgee Archeology 1936–1986*, edited by David J. Hally, 175–80. Athens: University of Georgia Press, 1994.

———. *Knights of Spain, Warriors of the Sun: Hernando de Soto and the South's Ancient Chiefdoms*. Athens: University of Georgia Press, 1997.

Hudson, Charles H., Robin A. Beck Jr., Chester B. DePratter, Robbie Ethridge, and John E. Worth. "On Interpreting Cofitachequi." *Ethnohistory* 55, no. 3 (2008): 465–90.

Huneycutt, Dwight J. "The Economics of the Indigo Industry in South Carolina." Master's thesis, University of South Carolina, 1949.

Hunter, Louis C. *Steamboats on the Western Rivers: An Economic and Technological History*. 1949. Reprint, Mineola, N.Y.: Dover Publications, 1993.

"Installed Electric Plant." *Lumber Trade Journal* 66 (August 15, 1914): 28.

"Isolated Plant Digest." *Isolated Plant* 2, no. 9 (1910): 28–29.

Jackson, Jerome A. *In Search of the Ivory-billed Woodpecker*. Washington, D.C.: Smithsonian Books, 2004.

The Jaeger Company. *Survey Report: Lower Richland County, Historical and Architectural Inventory*. Gainesville, Ga., 1993.

Johnson, R. L. "*Nyssa aquatica* L., Water Tupelo." In Burns and Honkala, *Silvics of North America*, vol. 2, *Hardwoods*, 474–78.

Jones, Lewis P. *South Carolina, a Synoptic History for Laymen*. Columbia, S.C.: Sandlapper Press, Inc., 1971.

Jones, Robert H. *Location and Ecology of Champion Trees in Congaree Swamp National Monument*. Report for the National Park Service. Blacksburg: Virginia Polytechnic Institute and State University, 1996.

———. "Status and Habitat of Big Trees in Congaree Swamp National Monument." *Castanea* 62, no. 1 (1997): 22–31.

Keel, Bennie C., John E. Cornelison Jr., and David M. Brewer. *Regionwide Archeological Survey Plan, Southeast Field Area, National Park Service*. National Park Service, Southeast Archeological Center, 1996.

Kellar, Herbert A., ed. *Solon Robinson, Pioneer and Agriculturalist: Selected Writings*. Vol. 2. 1936. Reprint, New York: Da Capo Press, 1968.

Kelsey and Guild. *The Improvement of Columbia, South Carolina: Report to the Civic League, Columbia, South Carolina*. Harrisburg, Pa.: Mount Pleasant Press, 1905.

Kilgo, John C., Mark Vukovich, H. Scott Ray, Christopher E. Shaw, and Charles Ruth.

"Coyote Removal, Understory Cover, and Survival of White-Tailed Deer Neonates." *Journal of Wildlife Management* 78, no. 7 (2014): 1261–71.

King, Adam. *Environmental and Cultural History of the Congaree River Floodplain, Congaree National Park, South Carolina.* Report for the National Park Service. Columbia: South Carolina Institute of Archaeology and Anthropology, University of South Carolina, 2012.

Kinzer, Mark W. *An Annotated Checklist of Floodplain Cultural Features, Congaree National Park, South Carolina.* Report for the National Park Service, 2016.

———. *Chronology: Events Associated with the Establishment of Congaree National Park and the Congaree National Park Wilderness, 1890–2004.* Report for the National Park Service, 2016.

———. *A Partial Chain of Title Covering the Principal Floodplain Tracts within Congaree National Park.* Report for the National Park Service, 2016.

Kirk, F. M. "Belvidere Plantation, Sinkler Family." Rootsweb. N.d. [late 1930s], http://www.rootsweb.com/~scbchs/belvidere.htm (accessed August 1, 2015).

Klein, Rachel N. *Unification of a Slave State: The Rise of the Planter Class in the South Carolina Backcountry, 1760–1808.* Chapel Hill: University of North Carolina Press, 1990.

Knowles, David B., Mark M. Brinson, Richard A. Clark, and Mark D. Flora. *Water Resources Management Plan, Congaree Swamp National Monument.* Plan prepared for the National Park Service, Water Resources Division, 1996.

Kohn, David, and Bess Glenn, eds. *Internal Improvement in South Carolina, 1817–1828.* From the Reports of the Superintendent of Public Works and from Contemporary Pamphlets, Newspaper Clippings, Letters, Petitions, and Maps. Washington, D.C.: Privately printed, 1938.

Kovacik, Charles F., and John J. Winberry. *South Carolina: A Geography.* Boulder, Colo.: Westview Press, 1987.

Kupfer, John A., Kimberly M. Meitzen, and William L. Graf. *Forest Recovery and Hydrologic Modeling on New Park Lands.* Report for the National Park Service, Piedmont-South Atlantic Cooperative Ecosystem Studies Unit. Columbia: University of South Carolina, 2009.

Kupfer, John A., Kimberly M. Meitzen, and Ashley R. Pipkin. "Hydrogeomorphic Controls of Early Post-logging Successional Pathways in a Southern Floodplain Forest." *Forest Ecology and Management* 259, no. 10 (2010): 1880–89.

Landaal, Sally. [Association description of the sweet gum–(laurel oak, water oak)–(loblolly pine)/giant cane/thicket sedge (*Liquidambar styraciflua–Quercus (laurifolia, nigra)–(Pinus taeda)/Arundinaria gigantea/Carex abscondita*) forest]. CEGL007732. Version: May 1, 1998. United States National Vegetation Classification. Federal Geographic Data Committee, Washington, D.C. http://www1.usgs.gov/csas/nvcs/nvcsGetUnitDetails?elementGlobalId=683508.

———. ["Association description of the green ash–American elm/American hornbeam/small-spike false nettle (*Fraxinus pennsylvanica–Ulmus americana/Carpinus caroliniana/Boehmeria cylindrica*) forest]. CEGL007806. Version: January 1, 2013. United States National Vegetation Classification. Federal Geographic Data Committee, Washington, D.C. http://www1.usgs.gov/csas/nvcs/nvcsGetUnitDetails?elementGlobalId=686687.

Landaal, Sally, Alan Weakley, and Jim Drake. *Classification of the Vegetation of Congaree National Park.* Report for the United States Geological Survey-National Park Service

Vegetation Mapping Program. Nature Conservancy, 1999. Available online at http://www1.usgs.gov/vip/cong/congrpt.pdf.

Landmeyer, James. "Determination of the Source(s) of Water Used by Wetland/Floodplain Plants in the Congaree National Park and Implications for Management." Investigator's Annual Report to the National Park Service, reporting year 2009. Available online at https://irma.nps.gov/App/Portal/Home.

Langley, Clara A., abstractor. *South Carolina Deed Abstracts, 1719–1772.* Vol. 3, *1755–1768, Books QQ–H-3.* Easley, S.C.: South Carolina Historical Press, 1983.

———. *South Carolina Deed Abstracts, 1719–1772.* Vol. 4, *1767–1773, Books I–E-4.* Easley, S.C.: South Carolina Historical Press, 1984.

Larson, Lewis H. *Aboriginal Subsistence Technology on the Southeastern Coastal Plain during the Late Prehistoric Period.* Gainesville: University Presses of Florida, 1980.

Lawrence, Carl B. *Soil Survey of Richland County, South Carolina.* United States Department of Agriculture, Soil Conservation Service, 1978.

Lawson, John. *A New Voyage to Carolina.* Edited by Hugh Talmage Lefler. 1709. Reprint, Chapel Hill: University of North Carolina Press, 1967.

Lennon, Gered, William J. Neal, David M. Bush, Orrin H. Pilkey, and Jane Bullock. *Living with the South Carolina Coast.* Durham, N.C.: Duke University Press, 1996.

Leonard, John W., ed. *The Book of Chicagoans: A Biographical Dictionary of Leading Living Men of the City of Chicago.* Chicago: A. N. Marquis, 1905.

Letter to the editor from Sumter District, S.C. *Carolina Planter* 1, no. 50 (1840): 393.

Lieber, Oscar M. "Stray Notes on the Agricultural Capacities of South Carolina." *Farmer and Planter* 10, no. 9 (1859): 265–67.

Lin, Jie, Paul A. Harcombe, Mark R. Fulton, and Rosine W. Hall. "Sapling Growth and Survivorship as Affected by Light and Flooding in a River Floodplain Forest of Southeast Texas." *Oecologia* 139, no. 3 (2004): 399–407.

Lockley, Timothy J., ed. *Maroon Communities in South Carolina: A Documentary Record.* Columbia: University of South Carolina Press, 2009.

Lossing, Benson J. *Pictorial Field Book of the Revolution.* Vol. 2. New York: Harper and Brothers, 1852.

Lowry, Harold D. *The Hooper and Weston Families of Richland County, South Carolina.* Raleigh, N.C.: Lulu Press, 2003.

Lyell, Charles. *A Second Visit to the United States of North America.* 2nd ed. Vol. 1. London: John Murray, 1850.

Martin, William H., Stephen G. Boyce, and Arthur C. Echternacht, eds. *Biodiversity of the Southeastern United States: Lowland Terrestrial Communities.* New York: John Wiley and Sons, 1993.

Martineau, Harriet. *Society in America.* 2nd ed. Vol. 2. London: Saunders and Otley, 1837.

Mathew, William M., ed. *Agriculture, Geology, and Society in Antebellum South Carolina: The Private Diary of Edmund Ruffin, 1843.* Athens: University of Georgia Press, 1992.

Matthews, Marty D. *Forgotten Founder: The Life and Times of Charles Pinckney.* Columbia: University of South Carolina Press, 2004.

Mattoon, Wilbur R. *The Southern Cypress.* United States Department of Agriculture, Bulletin no. 272. Washington, D.C.: Government Printing Office, 1915.

Mayer, John J., and I. Lehr Brisbin Jr. *Wild Pigs in the United States: Their History, Comparative Morphology, and Current Status.* 1991. Reprint, Athens: University of Georgia Press, 2008.

McLendon, Willie E. "Soil Survey of Clarendon County, South Carolina." In *Field Operations of the Bureau of Soils, 1910,* Twelfth Report, 419–51. United States Department of Agriculture, Bureau of Soils. Washington, D.C.: Government Printing Office, 1912.

McWhiney, Grady. *Cracker Culture: Celtic Ways in the Old South.* Tuscaloosa: University of Alabama Press, 1988.

Meadows, James S., and John D. Hodges. "Silviculture of Southern Bottomland Hardwoods: 25 Years of Change." In *Proceedings of the Twenty-Fifth Annual Hardwood Symposium: 25 Years of Hardwood Silviculture; A Look Back and a Look Ahead,* edited by Dan A. Meyer, 1–16. Memphis, Tenn.: National Hardwood Lumber Association, 1997.

Medlin, William F. *Richland County Landmarks.* Vol. 1, *Lower Richland.* Hopkins, S.C.: Ben Franklin Press, 1981.

Meitzen, Kimberly M. "Lateral Channel Migration Effects on Riparian Forest Structure and Composition, Congaree River, South Carolina, USA." *Wetlands* 29, no. 2 (2009): 465–75.

———. "Flood Processes, Forest Dynamics, and Disturbance in the Congaree River Floodplain, South Carolina." Ph.D. diss., University of South Carolina, 2011.

Mendenhall, Marjorie S. "A History of Agriculture in South Carolina, 1790–1860: An Economic and Social Study." Ph.D. diss., University of North Carolina, Chapel Hill, 1940.

Meriwether, Robert Lee. *The Expansion of South Carolina, 1729–1765.* Kingsport, Tenn.: Southern Publishers, 1940.

Meynard, Virginia G. *The Venturers: The Hampton, Harrison and Earle Families of Virginia, South Carolina and Texas.* Easley, S.C.: Southern Historical Press, 1981.

———. *History of Lower Richland County and its Early Planters.* Columbia, S.C.: R. L. Bryan, 2010.

Michie, James L. *An Archeological Survey of Congaree Swamp: Cultural Resources Inventory and Assessment of a Bottomland Environment in Central South Carolina.* Research Manuscript Series 163. Columbia: South Carolina Institute of Archaeology and Anthropology, University of South Carolina, 1980.

———. *The Discovery of Old Fort Congaree.* Research Manuscript Series 208. Columbia: South Carolina Institute of Archaeology and Anthropology, University of South Carolina, 1989.

Miller, Randall M., and John David Smith, eds. *Dictionary of Afro-American Slavery.* Westport, Conn.: Greenwood Press, 1988.

Mills, Robert. *Atlas of the State of South Carolina.* Baltimore: F. Lucas Jr., 1825.

———. *Statistics of South Carolina, Including a View of its Natural, Civil, and Military History, General and Particular.* Charleston, S.C.: Hurlbut and Lloyd, 1826.

Minchin, Peter R., and Rebecca R. Sharitz. *Age Structure and Potential Long-term Dynamics of the Floodplain Forests of Congaree National Park.* Report for the National Park Service. University of Georgia, Savannah River Ecology Laboratory, 2007.

"Miscellaneous Notes." *Hardwood Record* 30, no. 9 (1910): 88.

Mock, Cary J., Douglas O. Mayes, Jan Mojzisek, Michele McWaters, and Michael Chenoweth. "Reconstructing South Carolina Tropical Cyclones Back to the Mid Eighteenth Century." Extended abstract of paper presented to the American Meteorological Society, 26th Conference on Hurricanes and Tropical Meteorology, Miami, Fla., May 2004. Available online at http://ams.confex.com/ams/pdfpapers/75813.pdf.

Moore, John Hammond. *Columbia and Richland County: A South Carolina Community, 1740–1990.* Columbia: University of South Carolina Press, 1993.

Moore, Peter N. *World of Toil and Strife: Community Transformation in Backcountry South Carolina, 1750–1805.* Columbia: University of South Carolina Press, 2007.

Moore, Willis L. *The Work of the Weather Bureau in Connection with the Rivers of the United States.* United States Department of Agriculture, Weather Bureau, Bulletin no. 17. Washington, D.C.: Government Printing Office, 1896.

Morgan, Philip D. *Slave Counterpoint: Black Culture in the Eighteenth-Century Chesapeake and Lowcountry.* Chapel Hill: University of North Carolina Press, 1998.

Morse, Jedidiah, ed. "South Carolina." In *The American Gazetteer, Exhibiting a Full Account of the Civil Divisions, Rivers, Harbours, Indian Tribes, &c. of the American Continent.* 2nd ed. Charlestown, Mass.: Samuel Etheridge, 1804.

National Park Service. *Appendix to Specific Area Report, Proposed Congaree Swamp National Monument.* 1962.

———. *Specific Area Report: Proposed Congaree Swamp National Monument, South Carolina.* 1963.

———. *Assessment of Alternatives for Proposed General Management Plan and Wilderness Suitability Analysis, Congaree Swamp National Monument, South Carolina.* 1979.

———. "Multiple Property Documentation Form Prepared in Support of Addition of Various Sites at Congaree Swamp National Monument to the National Register of Historic Places." Website of the South Carolina Department of Archives and History. 1996. http://www.nationalregister.sc.gov/MPS/MPS029.pdf.

———. *Environmental Assessment: Installation of a 100-foot Fire Weather Station Tower at Congaree Swamp National Monument.* 1997.

———. "Southeastern Prehistory, Late Woodland Period." Website of the National Park Service, Southeast Archeological Center. n.d. http://www.nps.gov/seac/hnc/outline/04 -woodland/index-3.htm (accessed August 1, 2015).

National Park Service, American Rivers, and others. *Final Report and Recommendations of the Saluda/Congaree Ecologically Sustainable Water Management Process.* 2008.

Natural Resources Conservation Service. *An Assessment of the Congaree Subbasin, Hydrologic Unit Code (8 Digit): 03050110.* May 17, 2010. Available online at http://www.congaree riverkeeper.org/files/file/Congaree%5B1%5D.pdf.

Neuffer, Claude H. "Calhoun County Plantations of St. Matthew's Parish near the Congaree-Santee River." *Names in South Carolina* 12 (November 1965): 45–48.

Nix, Lawrence E., and Jon E. Barry. *Investigation of the Impacts of Clearcutting, Feral Hogs, and White-Tailed Deer on the Native Vegetative Resources of the Congaree Swamp National Monument.* Report for the National Park Service. Clemson, S.C.: Department of Forest Resources, Clemson University, 1992.

North American Tourist. New York: A. T. Goodrich, 1839.

North Carolina Agricultural Experiment Station. "On the Temperature of the Soil." In *Tenth Annual Report of the North Carolina Agricultural Experiment Station, for 1887,* 174–95. Raleigh, N.C.: Josephus Daniels, 1888.

Noss, Reed F., Edward T. LaRoe III, and J. Michael Scott. *Endangered Ecosystems of the United States: A Preliminary Assessment of Loss and Degradation.* United States Department of the Interior, National Biological Service, Biological Report 28, 1995. Available online at http://noss.cos.ucf.edu/papers/Noss%20et%20al%201995.pdf.

[Notice of contracting opportunity at Ferguson, S.C.] *American Contractor* 34, no. 11 (1913): 36.

O'Meally, Robert G. Introduction to Adams, *Tales of the Congaree*, xi–lxix.

Ouchley, Keith, Robert B. Hamilton, Wylie C. Barrow, and Kelby Ouchley. "Historic and Present-Day Forest Conditions: Implications for Bottomland Hardwood Forest Restoration." *Ecological Restoration* 18, no. 1 (2000): 21–25.

Patterson, Glenn G., Gary K. Speiran, and Benjamin H. Whetstone. *Hydrology and its Effects on Distribution of Vegetation in Congaree Swamp National Monument, South Carolina.* USGS Water-Resources Investigations Report 85–4256, 1985.

Pederson, Neil A. [Comments on age of Weston Lake loblolly pine.] In [Trip report summary, November 2004 big-tree reconnaissance trip to Congaree National Park] by Will Blozan. Website of the Native Tree Society. 2005. http://www.nativetreesociety.org/.

Pederson, Neil A., Robert H. Jones, and Rebecca R. Sharitz. "Age Structure and Possible Origins of Old *Pinus taeda* Stands in a Floodplain Forest." *Journal of the Torrey Botanical Society* 124, no. 2 (1997): 111–23.

"Personal." *Hardwood* 6, no. 10 (1894): 365.

Peterken, George F. *Natural Woodland: Ecology and Conservation in Northern Temperate Regions.* Cambridge, U.K.: Cambridge University Press, 1996.

Peterkin, Julia M. "Ashes." In *Green Thursday: Stories by Julia Peterkin.* 1924. Reprint, Athens: University of Georgia Press, 1998.

Phillips, Ulrich B. *A History of Transportation in the Eastern Cotton Belt to 1860.* 1908. Reprint, Columbia: University of South Carolina Press, 2011.

Pickens, Thomas J. "Report of the Comptroller-General, to the Legislature of South Carolina, November, 1859." Reprinted in *Charleston Mercury,* December 6, 1859, 4.

———. "Report of the Comptroller General to the Legislature of South Carolina, November, 1861." In *Reports and Resolutions of the General Assembly of the State of South Carolina, Passed at the Annual Session of 1861,* 25–101. Columbia, S.C.: Charles P. Pelham, 1861. Available online at http://cdm.bostonathenaeum.org/cdm/ref/collection/p16057coll14/id/92831.

Pinckney, Charles Cotesworth, Family Papers. Manuscript Division, Library of Congress, Washington, D.C.

Platt, Steven G., and Christopher G. Brantley. "Canebrakes: An Ecological and Historical Perspective." *Castanea* 62, no. 1 (1997): 8–21.

Popovich, Luke. "National Highlights." *Journal of Forestry* 73, no. 9 (1975): 568.

Porcher, Frederick A. *The History of the Santee Canal.* With an Appendix by Alexander S. Salley Jr. 1875. Reprint, Charleston: South Carolina Historical Society, 1903. Available online at http://books.google.com/books?id=MhAsAAAAYAAJ&printsec=frontcover&source=gbs_ge_summary_r&cad=0#v=onepage&q&f=false.

Prentice, Guy. "Ninety Six National Historic Site: Cultural Overview." 2003. Website of National Park Service, Southeast Archeological Center. http://archive.today/pSsH.

"A Prominent Cypress Industry." *St. Louis Lumberman* 34, no. 12 (1904): 54.

Purvis, J. C., W. Tyler, and S. Sidlow. *Hurricanes Affecting South Carolina.* Climate Report no. G26. South Carolina Water Resources Commission, 1989.

Ramsay, David. *History of South Carolina, from its First Settlement in 1670 to the Year 1808.* Vol. 2. Charleston, S.C.: David Longworth, 1809.

Rangel, Rodrigo. "Account of the Northern Conquest and Discovery of Hernando de Soto." Translated by John E. Worth. In Clayton, Knight, and Moore, *The De Soto Chronicles,* 1:251–306.

Reed, Christopher. "You, too, Can Visit a Swamp and Bring Yourself Back Alive." *Harvard Magazine* 84, no. 1 (1981): 55–60.

Rice, Steven K., and Robert K. Peet. *Vegetation of the Lower Roanoke River Floodplain.* Report for the Nature Conservancy. Chapel Hill: University of North Carolina, 1997.

Richardson, Katherine H. *Cultural Resource Survey of Goodwill Plantation, Richland County, South Carolina.* Columbia: Applied History Program, Department of History, University of South Carolina, 1985.

Richland County, S.C. Aerial photography of lower Richland, 1939, 1959, and 2000. Available online at http://www.richlandmaps.com/apps/dataviewer/?lat=34.03730&lon=-81 .02280&zoom=10&base=roadmap&expanded=53759|52088|18518|38669|39665&layers =33844|24029.

———. *Prime Agricultural Soils.* Map, scale not given. 2001. Available online at http://www .richlandmaps.com/sites/default/files/prime_ag_soils.pdf.

Richland County Deed Books. Register of Deeds, Richland County Judicial Center, Columbia, S.C.

Robinson, Solon. "Statistics of Cotton Growing—The Product per Acre and per Hand." In *Transactions of the American Institute, of the City of New York, for the Years 1860–61,* 336–43. Printed in *Documents of the Assembly of the State of New York. Eighty-Fourth Session. 1861.* Vol. 7, no. 138. Albany, N.Y.: C. Van Benthuysen, 1861.

Rogers, Warren O. "Steam Turbine in Sawmill Plant." *Power and the Engineer* 32, no. 34 (1910): 1507.

Romans, Bernard. *A Concise Natural History of East and West Florida.* London: R. Aitken, 1776.

Roosevelt, Theodore. "In the Louisiana Canebrakes." *Scribner's Magazine* 43, no. 1 (1908): 47–60.

Rosengarten, Theodore. *Tombee: Portrait of a Cotton Planter.* New York: McGraw-Hill, 1987.

Ruymbeke, Bertrand Van. "The Huguenots of Proprietary South Carolina: Patterns of Migration and Integration." In *Money, Trade, and Power: The Evolution of Colonial South Carolina's Plantation Society,* edited by Jack P. Greene, Rosemary Brana-Shute, and Randy J. Sparks, 26–48. Columbia: University of South Carolina Press, 2001.

Salley, Alexander S., Jr. "Col. Miles Brewton and Some of his Descendants." *South Carolina Historical and Genealogical Magazine* 2, no. 2 (1901): 128–52.

Santee River Cypress Lumber Co. "Engineering Features of a Large Southern Lumbering Development, Including a Logging Railroad through a Dense Swamp, Heavy Skidding Cableways, and an Industrial Town Improved with Sanitary Works." *Engineering Record* 66, no. 17 (1912): 456–58.

Sargent, Charles S. *Report on the Forests of North America (Exclusive of Mexico).* Vol. 9 of *The Tenth Census of the United States* (1880). Washington, D.C.: Government Printing Office, 1884.

Savage, Henry, Jr., Papers. Manuscripts Division, South Caroliniana Library, University of South Carolina, Columbia.

Schafer, Daniel L. *Governor James Grant's Villa: A British East Florida Indigo Plantation.* St. Augustine, Fla.: St. Augustine Historical Society, 2000.

Scharf, Elizabeth A. "Archeology, Land Use, Pollen and Restoration in the Yazoo Basin (Mississippi USA)." *Vegetation History and Archeobotany* 19, no. 3 (2010): 159–75.

Schoepf, Johann D. *Travels in the Confederation, 1783–1784.* Vol. 2. Translated and edited by A. J. Morrison. 1788. Reprint, Philadelphia: William J. Campbell, 1911.

Schweninger, Loren. "Maroonage and Flight: An Overview." Paper presented at the Fourth Annual International Conference at the Gilder Lerhman Center for the Study of Slavery, Resistance, and Abolition, Yale University, New Haven, Conn., December 2002. Available online at http://glc.yale.edu/sites/default/files/files/maroon/schweninger.pdf.

Scurry, James D., J. Walter Joseph, and Fritz Hamer. *Initial Archeological Investigations at Silver Bluff Plantation Aiken County, South Carolina.* Research Manuscript Series 161. Columbia: South Carolina Institute of Archaeology and Anthropology, University of South Carolina, 1980.

Seabrook, Whitemarsh B. "Reclamation of the Swamps." *Farmer and Planter* 5, no. 9 (1854): 217–21. Excerpted from *An Essay on the Agricultural Capabilities of S. Carolina, and the Best Means of Developing and Improving Them.* Columbia, S.C., 1848.

Seibert, Michael A., Meredith Hardy, and Jessica Frye. *Archeological Investigations of Starling's Mound and Congaree Swamp Woodland Mound Congaree National Park, Richland County, South Carolina.* National Park Service, Southeast Archeological Center, SEAC Accession Number: 2562, 2013.

Sharitz, Rebecca R., and Bruce P. Allen. *Quantify Change in the Old-Growth Forests of Congaree National Park.* Revised final report for the National Park Service. University of Georgia, Savannah River Ecology Laboratory, 2009.

Sharitz, Rebecca R., and William J. Mitsch. "Southern Floodplain Forests." In Martin, Boyce, and Echternacht, *Biodiversity of the Southeastern United States,* 311–72.

Shelley, David C. "Geology, Geomorphology, and Tectonics of the Congaree River Valley, South Carolina." Ph.D. diss., University of South Carolina, 2007.

Shelley, David C., Theresa Thom, William Armstrong, and Doug Dvoracek. "Radiocarbon Controls on Late Quaternary Development of Floodplain Landscapes at Congaree National Park, SC." Poster presented at the Joint Conference of the Southern Appalachian Mountains, the Piedmont-South Atlantic Coast, South Florida-Caribbean, and Gulf Coast Cooperative Ecosystem Studies Units, St. Petersburg, Fla., October 2011.

Shelley, David C., Scott Werts, Doug Dvoracek, and William Armstrong. "Bluff to Bluff: A Field Guide to Floodplain Geology and Geomorphology of the Lower Congaree River Valley, South Carolina." In *From the Blue Ridge to the Coastal Plain: Field Excursions in the Southeastern United States,* Field Guide 29, edited by Martha C. Eppes and Mervin J. Bartholomew, 67–92. Boulder, Colo.: Geological Society of America, 2012.

Sierra Club (Bachman Group). "An Introduction to the Swamp Systems of the Congaree, Wateree, and Santee Rivers in South Carolina." Typescript report, 1974. On file at NPS Planning Division, Southeast Regional Office, Atlanta, Ga.

Silver, James W. "The Hardwood Producers Come of Age." *Journal of Southern History* 23, no. 4 (1957): 427–53.

Simms, William Gilmore. *The Geography of South Carolina.* Charleston, S.C.: Babcock and Company, 1843.

Singleton Family Papers. Manuscripts Division, South Caroliniana Library, University of South Carolina, Columbia.

Sitton, Thad. *Backwoodsmen: Stockmen and Hunters along a Big Thicket River Valley.* Norman: University of Oklahoma Press, 1995.

Smith, Alfred Glaze, Jr. *Economic Readjustment of an Old Cotton State: South Carolina, 1820–1860.* Columbia: University of South Carolina Press, 1958.

Smith, Robert L. *Gone to the Swamp: Raw Materials for the Good Life in the Mobile-Tensaw Delta*. Tuscaloosa: University of Alabama Press, 2008.

Smith, Steven D., James B. Legg, Tamara S. Wilson, and Jonathan Leader. *"Obstinate and Strong": The History and Archaeology of the Siege of Fort Motte*. Columbia: South Carolina Institute of Archaeology and Anthropology, University of South Carolina, 2007.

Soucie, Gary. "Congaree: Great Trees or Coffee Tables?" *Audubon* 77, no. 4 (1975): 60–80.

South Carolina Department of Agriculture, Commerce and Immigration. *Handbook of South Carolina: Resources, Institutions and Industries of the State*. 2nd ed. Columbia, S.C.: The State Company, 1908.

South Carolina Department of Agriculture, Commerce and Industries and Clemson College. *South Carolina: A Handbook*. Columbia, S.C.: Department of Agriculture, Commerce and Industries, 1927.

South Carolina House of Representatives. *Resolution Regarding Congaree Swamp Legislation: Hearing on H 3097, Before the South Carolina House Comm. on Agriculture and Natural Resources*. October 23, 1975. 101st Gen. Assembly, 1975–1976.

South Carolina State Historic Preservation Office. "Native American Time Periods for South Carolina." N.d. http://shpo.sc.gov/res/native/Pages/naperiods.aspx (accessed September 7, 2015).

Southerlin, Bobby, Dawn Reid, Rachel Tibbetts, and Mackensie Cornelius, with Carl Steen and Gordon Watts. *Occupation of Socastee Bluff: Data Recovery at the Singleton Sawmill Site (38HR490), Horry County, South Carolina*. Archeological Consultants of the Carolinas, 2007. Available online at http://palmettohistory.org/archaeology/SingletonSawmill.pdf.

Stalter, Richard. "Age of a Mature Pine *(Pinus taeda)* Stand in South Carolina." *Ecology* 52, no. 3 (1971): 532–33.

Stalter, Richard, and Wade T. Batson. "A Giant Loblolly near Columbia, South Carolina." *Castanea* 34, no. 4 (1969): 438.

Steckel, Richard H., and Jerome C. Rose, eds. *The Backbone of History: Health and Nutrition in the Western Hemisphere*. Cambridge, U.K.: Cambridge University Press, 2002.

Steen, Carl, and Christopher Judge. *Archaeology at the Great Pee Dee Heritage Preserve*. Report for the South Carolina Department of Natural Resources, Heritage Trust Program. Diachronic Research Foundation, 1997.

Steen, Carl, and Sean Taylor. *An Archeological Survey of the Congaree Bluffs Heritage Preserve*. Report for the South Carolina Department of Natural Resources, Heritage Trust Program, 2002.

Steinberg, Michael K. "The Importance of Cultural Ecological Landscapes to the Survival of the Bachman's Warbler *(Vermivora bachmanii)* in the Southeastern United States." *Southeastern Geographer* 50, no. 2 (2010): 272–81.

Stroyer, Jacob. *My Life in the South*. 3rd ed. Salem, Mass.: Salem Observer Book and Job Print, 1885.

Stuckey, J. W. "Remarks on the 1850 Mortality Schedule, Sumter District, South Carolina. Certified on December 23, 1850." Manuscript report by assistant marshal, Sumter District. Transcribed by Steven J. Coker from microfilm copy at South Carolina Department of Archives and History. Available online at http://archiver.rootsweb.ancestry.com/th/read/SCSUMTER/1998-03/0890561413 (accessed August 1, 2015).

"Study of the Red Gum." *New York Lumber Trade Journal* 37, no. 433 (1904): 21.

Sutter, Paul S., and Christopher J. Manganiello, eds. *Environmental History and the American South*. Athens: University of Georgia Press, 2009.

Swails, L. F., W. D. Anderson Jr., and Wade T. Batson. "A Mature Pine Stand in the Congaree Bottom Land." *University of South Carolina Publications Series 3: Biology* 2, no. 2 (1957): 82–89.

Tanner, James T. *The Ivory-Billed Woodpecker*. 1942. Reprint, Mineola, N.Y.: Dover Publications, 2003.

———. "Distribution of Tree Species in Louisiana Bottomland Forests." *Castanea* 51, no. 3 (1986): 168–74.

"A $30,000 Skidder." *Hardwood Record* 37, no. 1 (1913): 41–42.

Thomas, Hugh. *The Slave Trade: The Story of the Atlantic Slave Trade, 1440–1870*. New York: Simon and Schuster, 1997.

Thompson, Andrew J. "An Ecological Inventory and Classification of an Old-growth Floodplain Forest in the Southeastern United States Coastal Plain." Master's thesis, University of South Carolina, 1998.

Thomson, William, and Nathaniel Russell. Affidavit on behalf of William Bull Jr., February 10, 1784. London: Public Record Office, Audit Office Records—Claims, American Loyalists. Audit Office Series 13, Bundle 97, pp. 45–46.

"Tight Stave Firm Incorporates." *Barrel and Box* 16, no. 11 (1912): 30.

Tomlinson Engineering Company. *Plan of Five Thousand One Hundred and Eighty Eight Acres Land on North Side of Congaree River and Owned by James and Robert Adams Esquires, Surveyed in April 1839*. Map, half-size reproduction, showing original land grants, scale 1" = 15 chains, 1936. Reduced-size photocopy on file, Congaree National Park.

Townsend, Philip A. "Relationships between Vegetation Patterns and Hydroperiod on the Roanoke River Floodplain, North Carolina." *Plant Ecology* 156, no. 1 (2001): 43–58.

Trenholm, W. L. "The History and Present Condition of Transportation in South Carolina." In Hammond, *South Carolina: Resources and Population, Institutions and Industries*, 611–40.

Trimble, Stanley W. *Man-Induced Soil Erosion on the Southern Piedmont: 1700–1970*. 2nd ed. Ankeny, Iowa: Soil and Water Conservation Society, 2008.

Trinkley, Michael, and Sarah Fick. *Rice Cultivation, Processing, and Marketing in the Eighteenth Century*. Columbia, S.C.: Chicora Foundation, 2003. Available online at http:// www.chicora.org/pdfs/Rice%20Context.pdf.

Trust for Public Land. "2,395 Acres Protected for Congaree NP (SC)." Press release, November 28, 2005. http://www.tpl.org/news/press-releases/2395-acres-protected-for-congaree.html

United States Army. "Annual Report of the Chief of Engineers, United States Army, to the Secretary of War, for the Year 1885." Part 2, Appendix M. In *United States Congressional Serial Set*, House of Representatives, 49th Cong., 1st sess., 1885, Ex. Doc. 1, pt. 2, vol. 2. Washington, D.C.: Government Printing Office, 1885.

———. *Map of Congaree River, S.C., from its Mouth to Columbia*. Surveyed and mapped in 1884 by S. McBee and D. B. Miller Jr. In multiple sheets. 1886. Copies on file, CNP.

———. "Annual Report of the Chief of Engineers, United States Army, to the Secretary of War, for the Year 1887." Part 2, Appendix M. In *United States Congressional Serial Set*, House of Representatives, 50th Cong., 1st sess., 1887, Ex. Doc. 1, pt. 2, vol. 2. Washington, D.C.: Government Printing Office, 1887.

———. "Annual Report of the Chief of Engineers, United States Army, to the Secretary of War, for the Year 1888." Part 2, Appendix M. In *United States Congressional Serial Set,* House of Representatives, 50th Cong., 2d sess., 1888, Ex. Doc. 1, pt. 2, vol. 2. Washington, D.C.: Government Printing Office, 1888.

———. "Annual Report of the Chief of Engineers, United States Army, to the Secretary of War, for the Year 1889." Part 2, Appendix M. In *United States Congressional Serial Set,* House of Representatives, 51st Cong., 1st sess., 1889, Ex. Doc. 1, pt. 2, vol. 2. Washington, D.C.: Government Printing Office, 1889.

———. "Annual Report of the Chief of Engineers, United States Army, to the Secretary of War, for the Year 1891." Part 2, Appendix M. In *United States Congressional Serial Set,* House of Representatives, 52d Cong., 1st sess., 1891, Ex. Doc. 1, pt. 2, vol. 2. Washington, D.C.: Government Printing Office, 1891.

———. "Annual Report of the Chief of Engineers, United States Army, to the Secretary of War, for the Year 1893." Part 2, Appendix M. In *United States Congressional Serial Set,* House of Representatives, 53d Cong., 2d sess., 1893, Ex. Doc. 1, pt. 2, vol. 2. Washington, D.C.: Government Printing Office, 1893.

———. "Annual Reports of the War Department for the Fiscal Year Ended June 30, 1897, Report of the Chief of Engineers." Part 2, Appendix M. In *United States Congressional Serial Set,* House of Representatives, 55th Cong., 2d sess., 1897, Ex. Doc. 2. Washington, D.C.: Government Printing Office, 1897.

———. "Broad and Congaree Rivers, S.C., Letter from the Secretary of War . . . June 24, 1918." In *United States Congressional Serial Set,* Issue 7349, House of Representatives, 65th Congress, 2d Session, 1918, H. Docs. vol. 19, doc. no. 1191. Washington, D.C.: Government Printing Office, 1918.

United States Census Office. *Seventh Census of the United States: 1850.* Washington, D.C.: Robert Armstrong, 1853.

———. *Agriculture of the United States in 1860; Compiled from the Original Returns of the Eighth Census.* Washington, D.C.: Government Printing Office, 1864.

———. [Manuscript Census Returns:] Original Agriculture, Industry, Social Statistics, and Mortality Schedules for South Carolina, 1850–1880. South Carolina Department of Archives and History. Microfilm. No. M/2.

———. Manuscript Census Returns: Population and Slave Schedules for South Carolina (1800–1860). South Carolina Department of Archives and History. Microfilm. Nos. M/19, M/32, M/33, M/252, M/432, M/653, M/704.

United States Department of Commerce and Labor, Bureau of the Census. *Heads of Families at the First Census of the United States Taken in the Year 1790: South Carolina.* Washington, D.C.: Government Printing Office, 1908.

United States Department of Agriculture. *Report of the Commissioner of Agriculture for the Year 1875.* Washington, D.C.: Government Printing Office, 1876.

United States Fish and Wildlife Service. National Wetlands Inventory Mapper [mapping website]. N.d., http://www.fws.gov/wetlands/data/mapper.HTML (accessed August 1, 2015).

United States Forest Service, United States Department of the Interior, and the Nature Conservancy. "LANDFIRE National Biophysical Setting Model, Gulf and Atlantic Coastal Plain Floodplain, Biophysical Setting 5814730. Model contained at pp. 76–81 of comprehensive description of Zone 58. Last modified March 6, 2008. Available online at http://www.landfire.gov/national_veg_models_op2.php.

United States Geological Survey and National Park Service. *Vegetation Map of Congaree National Park.* June 2009, scale 1.5 cm = 1.5 km. Available online at http://www1.usgs .gov/vip/cong/congvegmap.pdf.

United States Geological Survey. *Gadsden, SC Quadrangle* [topographic map]. Scale 1:24,000. 1972. Revised from aerial photos taken 1971.

United States House of Representatives. "Acquiring Land for the Protection of Watersheds for the Conservation of Navigable Streams" [report to accompany S. 4825], H. Rep. 2027. 60th Congress, 2d sess. 1909. In *Acquisition of Forest and Other Lands for the Protection of Watersheds and Conservation of the Navigability of Navigable Streams, Hearings Before the Committee on Agriculture* [with related papers], 119–42 . Washington, D.C.: Government Printing Office, 1909.

———. *Congaree Swamp National Preserve, South Carolina: Hearing on H.R. 11891 and H.R. 12111, Before the House Committee on Interior and Insular Affairs, Subcommittee on National Parks and Recreation.* 94th Cong., 2d sess. 1976.

United States National Archives and Records Administration. Records from Civil Action File nos. 77–652, 77–653, 77–654, 77–2046, styled *United States v. 14,770.65 Acres of Land.* General Case Files, United States District Court for the District of South Carolina (Columbia), Records of the District Courts of the United States.

United States Senate, Committee on Commerce. "Making Appropriations for the Construction, Repair, and Preservation of Certain Public Works on Rivers and Harbors (report to accompany H.R 10419)," S. Rep. 1884. 49th Congress, Second Sess. 1887. In *Reports of Committees of the Senate of the United States for the Second Session of the Forty-Ninth Congress, 1886–'87.* Vol. 2. Washington, D.C.: Government Printing Office, 1887.

United States Senate. *Congaree Swamp National Preserve, South Carolina: Hearing on S. 3497, S. 3498, and S.J. Res. 181, Before the Senate Committee on Interior and Insular Affairs.* 94th Cong., 2d sess. 1976.

Van Duyne, Cornelius, W. E. McLendon, and Thomas D. Rice. *Soil Survey of Richland County, South Carolina.* United States Department of Agriculture, Bureau of Soils, Advance Sheets (with Map). Washington, D.C.: Government Printing Office, 1918.

Vanier, Jeremy A. "A Ceramic Vessel Function Analysis and Foodways Approach to the Late Woodland/Mississippian Interface in Kershaw County, South Carolina." Master's thesis, University of South Carolina, 2010.

Vincent, Preston. "Landowners Speak Out [on the Congaree issue]." *South Carolina Magazine* 39, no. 3 (1975): 20–21, 30–33.

Waddell, Gene. "Cofitachequi: A Distinctive Culture, Its Identity, and Its Location." *Ethnohistory* 52, no.2 (2005): 333–69.

Wagner, Gail E. "National Register of Historic Places Registration Form, Belmont Neck Site (38KE06), Kershaw County, South Carolina." Website of the South Carolina Department of Archives and History. 2005. http://www.nationalregister.sc.gov/kershaw/ S10817728019/S10817728019.pdf.

———. "Mississippian Landscape Managers." Paper presented at the 63rd Annual Meeting of the Southeastern Archaeological Conference, Little Rock, Ark., November 2006.

Walker, Laurence C. *The Southern Forest: A Chronicle.* Austin: University of Texas Press, 1991.

Wallace, David Duncan. *South Carolina: A Short History, 1520–1948.* Chapel Hill: University of North Carolina Press, 1951.

Walsh, Lorena. "Work and the Slave Economy." In *The Routledge History of Slavery*, edited by Gad Heuman and Trevor Burnard, 101–18. New York: Routledge, 2011.

Watson, Geraldine E. *Reflections on the Neches: A Naturalist's Odyssey along the Big Thicket's Snow River*. Denton: Big Thicket Association/University of North Texas Press, 2003.

Weakley, Alan S., and Michael P. Schafale. [Association description of the laurel oak–swamp chestnut oak–sweet gum/American hornbeam *(Quercus laurifolia-Quercus michauxii-Liquidambar styraciflua/Carpinus caroliniana)* forest]. CEGL004678. Version: July 1, 1997. United States National Vegetation Classification. Federal Geographic Data Committee, Washington, D.C. http://www1.usgs.gov/csas/nvcs/nvcsGetUnitDetails?elementGlobalId=683670.

Webber, Mabel L., ed. "Revolutionary Letters." *South Carolina Historical and Genealogical Magazine* 38, no. 3 (July 1937): 75–80.

Webster, Fletcher, ed. *The Private Correspondence of Daniel Webster*. Vol. 2. Boston: Little, Brown, 1857.

Wharton, Charles H., Wiley M. Kitchens, Edward C. Pendleton, and Timothy W. Sipe. *The Ecology of Bottomland Hardwood Swamps of the Southeast: A Community Profile*. United States Fish and Wildlife Service, Biological Services Program, FWS/OBS-81/37, 1982.

"Where Tank Stock Is Made." *Packages* 8, no. 1 (1905): 55.

Wicks, George T. "Culture of Upland Rice as a Staple of South Carolina." Essay read at the spring meeting of the State Agricultural and Mechanical Society, April 29, 1873. Printed in *Columbia (S.C.) Daily Phoenix*, May 1, 1873, 3.

Wilhite, L. P., and J. R. Toliver. "*Taxodium distichum* (L.) Rich., Baldcypress." In Burns and Honkala, *Silvics of North America*, vol. 1, *Conifers*, 563–72.

Williams, Frances L. *A Founding Family: The Pinckneys of South Carolina*. New York: Harcourt Brace Jovanovich, 1978.

Williams, Mark, and Don Evans. *Archaeological Excavations at the Bullard Landing Site (9TW1)*. LAMAR Institute Publication 24. Watkinsville, Ga.: LAMAR Institute, 1993.

Williams, Michael. *Americans and Their Forests: A Historical Geography*. New York: Cambridge University Press, 1989.

Williams, Susan M. *A Devil and a Good Woman Too: The Lives of Julia Peterkin*. Athens: University of Georgia Press, 1997.

Williamson, Joel. *After Slavery: The Negro in South Carolina During Reconstruction, 1861–1877*. 1965. Reprint, New York: W. W. Norton, 1975.

Winberry, John J. "Indigo in South Carolina: A Historical Geography." *Southeastern Geographer* 19, no. 2 (1979): 91–102.

Wolfe, Stanley L. *Wood-using Industries of South Carolina*. South Carolina Department of Agriculture, Commerce and Industries, in Cooperation with the U.S. Forest Service. Columbia, S.C.: R. L. Bryan Company, 1913.

[Woodmason, Charles.] "The Different Species of the Indigo Plant Described [and] the Art of Manufacturing Indigo in Carolina." *Gentleman's Magazine* 25 (1755): 201–3; 256–58.

Woodward, C. Vann, ed. *Mary Chesnut's Civil War*. New Haven, Conn.: Yale University Press, 1981.

Woodward, Karl W. *The Valuation of American Timberlands*. New York: John Wiley and Sons, 1921.

Worcester, Joseph E. *A Geographical Dictionary, or Universal Gazetteer, Ancient and Modern*. 2nd ed. Vol. 1. Boston: Cummings and Hilliard, 1823.

Wright, Gavin, and Howard Kunreuther. "Cotton, Corn, and Risk in the Nineteenth Century: A Reply." *Explorations in Economic History* 14 (1977): 183–95.

Zahniser, Marvin R. *Charles Cotesworth Pinckney, Founding Father.* Chapel Hill: University of North Carolina Press, 1967.

Zhao, Dehai, Bruce P. Allen, and Rebecca R. Sharitz. "Twelve Year Response of Old-Growth Southeastern Bottomland Hardwood Forests to Disturbance from Hurricane Hugo." *Canadian Journal of Forest Research* 36, no. 12 (2006): 3136–47.

Index

Page references followed by *fig.* indicate illustrations or material contained in their captions. Page references followed by *t.* indicate tables.

abiotic disturbances, 182–83

"Account of Carolina, and the Bahama Islands, An" (Catesby), 28

Account of the Northern Conquest and Discovery of Hernando de Soto (Rangel), 7

Act to Promote the Draining and Improvement of Inland Swamps (1856), 100

Adams, Edward Clarkson Leverett, 96

Adams, Harry W., 137 *t. 7*

Adams, James Hopkins, 98, 202, 206, 218, 245n42

Adams, James, Sr.: biographical sketch, 205; death of, 95; floodplain reclamation efforts of, 92–96, 196, 242–43n27; landholdings of, 249n41; land regranted to, 242n19; will of, 92, 95

Adams, James U., 64 *t. 2*, 95, 108, 116, 205–6, 226n19, 247n23, 248n29

Adams, Joel, Jr., 59, 92, 108, 196, 205, 242n19, 243n30

Adams, Joel R., 92

Adams, Joel, Sr., 33 *fig. 2*; biographical sketch, 205; cattle raised by, 40; children of, 205, 216; Congaree flooding and, 85–86; corn grown by, 63–64; as cotton planter, 77; fishery access of, 196; Homestead plantation of, 73; land acquisitions of, 67, 197, 210, 218, 233n48, 240n44; land clearing by, 52; logging by, 32–33; as Martin estate executor, 44; mills operated by, 226n19; as plantation overseer, 73–74, 74–75 *t. 4*, 77; slaveholdings of, 74, 240n44; swamp plantation of, 65 *fig. 7*

Adams, Mary G., 64 *t. 2*, 108

Adams, Robert, 92, 196, 205, 242n19

Adams, Sarah H. ("Sallie"), 206, 216

Adams family, 31, 40, 68, 101, 105, 108, 113, 244n34, 248n29

Adams Pond Dike, 59, 92–96, 196–97

Adams' Quarter, 64, 197

adze, 82

African Americans: Adams (E. C. L.) literary portrayals of, 96; freedmen, 115, 249n49, 266n1; land purchases of, 200; land redistributions to, 266n1; as loggers, 135–36; as sharecroppers, 115

agriculture: cotton, 88–89; of early settlers, 47, 48; historic, 197; Mississippian Period (900–1520 C.E.), 12–13, 12 *fig. 1*, 17–18, 22, 224n57; post-Civil War, 115; post-contact, 23–27; pre-maize, 10–11; scientific, 90; slash-and-burn, 13. *See also* Beidler Tract—historic clearing of; plantation agriculture

air seasoning, 257n76

Alcolu (SC), 171, 172

Allen, Bruce P., 188, 219–20n5

Allen, R. L., 67, 91

American Gazetteer, 74

American Revolution: Congaree planters involved in, 72, 73, 96, 209–10, 211, 213, 215, 216, 217; economic hardships following, 87; indigo production following, 54; Loyalists, 84; McCord's Ferry during, 202, 204; *South Carolina* involved in, 210; transportation improvements following, 81

Anglo-Cherokee War (1761), 30, 47, 215, 231n16
Antley, Mrs. M. E., 144 *t. 8*
aquifers, 190–91
Archaic Period (8000–1000 B.C.E.), 7, 9
Arundinaria gigantea, 24
Arundinaria tecta, 24
ash, 120; agricultural abandonment and, 114; floodplain microtopography and, 12 *fig. 1*; logging of, 174; old tree, in Beidler Tract, 246n6; phase, 105–7, 246–247nn17–18; profitability of, 34, 119, 154 154 *t. 10;* Santee timber rights to, 139, 179, 181; as shade-intolerant species, 186–87
"Ashes" (short story; J. M. Peterkin), 116–17
Ashley Hall Plantation, 207
Ashley River, 207
Assessment of [Management] Alternatives (NPS), 178, 261–62n75
Atlantic Coast Lumber Company, 135
Augusta (GA), 228n39
Auten, Philip L., 209

Back Swamp Plantation, 58
Bahamas, 210
Ball, Charles, 41, 60–61, 112
Barber's Cutoff, 32, 196
Barbour, Mordecai, 196
Barnwell County (SC), 128
Bates, John, 206, 247n23
Bates, John M.: biographical sketch, 206; on hardwood availability, 153; logging by, 138 *t. 7,* 141 *t. 8,* 143 *t. 8,* 144–45 *t. 8,* 146–47, 172, 198; as proponent of bridge over Congaree River, 204; as Santee employee, 146, 150, 198, 206
Bates, Joseph, 127, 174, 176, 213, 247n23
Bates Camp, 146, 254n43
Bates' Ferry, 119, 204
Bates Fork tract, 174–76, 258–59n8
Bates Mill Creek, 92, 94, 208
Bates Old River, 9, 17, 88, 99, 127, 160, 172, 173–74
beavers, 183
Beckham Meadow Mound, 228–29n53
beech, American, 190
Beidler, Elizabeth, 140 *t. 8*

Beidler, Francis, 3, 133 *fig. 16;* biographical sketch, 133–34, 207; as conservationist, 125, 134, 159, 162; death of, 157; goals of, 135; heirs of, 159; local SC opinion of, 136; management decisions of, 155–56, 255n60; Santee Beidler Tract holdings and, 156–57, 174, 252n24. *See also* Santee River Cypress Lumber Company
Beidler, Francis, II, 125, 134, 162, 163
Beidler, Francis, III, 159, 163, 258–59n8
Beidler, Jacob, 133, 209
Beidler and Robinson Lumber Company, 207
Beidler family, 139, 161, 174–75, 176, 179, 258–59n8
Beidler Tract, 3–6; antebellum owners in, 33, 44, 108, 205; burning in, 46; canebrakes in, 46, 158–59; corn plantations in, 61–62, 63–66, 64 *t. 2;* cotton plantations in, 67; cypress dominance reduced in, 157–58; early European settlement of, 29; fire suppression in, 158–59; floodplain reclamation in, 92–100; hardwood forests in, 154; hunt club lease on, 210; indigo plantations in, 56–57; land grants in, 42, 49–50, 54; land purchases in, 233n48; land valuations in, 119; logging east of, 168–76; logging impact in, 157–58; logging in, 33–34, 37, 45, 147–48, 151, 162–66, 181; logging north of, 166–68; logging south of, 176–81; map, xiv; as national monument, 163–64 (*see also* Congaree Swamp National Monument); NPS studies in, 151; NPS title to, 179; "old fields" in, 26–27, 42, 80, 103–4; preservation campaign, 125, 159, 210; pre-settlement cultivation in, 26–27; rice plantations in, 59–61; second- vs. old-growth forests in, 102, 161; timber holdings in, 129, 133, 136–39, 137–38 *t. 7,* 140–45 *t. 8,* 156–57; uneven-aged hardwoods in, 245–46n6; use of term, 22; Weston family holdings in, 96–97
Beidler Tract—historic clearing of: agricultural abandonment, 101, 113–24; cultural features and, 107–8, 108 map 9; limiting factors, 108–12; locations/extent of,

102–7; Singer Tract clearing compared to, 101–2; telltale signs of, 184–85; vegetation associations and, 105–7, 106 map 8

Beidler Tract—Parcel numbers: map, xv map 2; Parcel 1, 64 *t. 2*, 137 *t. 7*, 164, 246n6; Parcel 2, 64 *t. 2*, 137 *t. 7*, 248n32; Parcel 3, 64 *t. 2*, 137 *t. 7*, 253n36; Parcel 4, 64 *t. 2*, 137 *t. 7*, 246n6, 248n32; Parcel 5, 64 *t. 2*, 137 *t. 7*, 248n32; Parcel 6, 64 *t. 2*, 137 *t. 7*; Parcel 7, 137 *t. 7*; Parcel 8, 64 *t. 2*, 137 *t. 7*, 199, 208, 253n37; Parcel 9, 64 *t. 2*, 137 *t. 7*, 208; Parcel 10, 64 *t. 2*, 136, 137 *t. 7*, 140 *t. 8*, 246n6; Parcel 11, 26, 136, 137 *t. 7*, 140 *t. 8*; Parcel 12, 136, 137 *t. 7*, 140 *t. 8*; Parcel 13, 45, 64 *t. 2*, 129, 136, 138 *t. 7*, 140 *t. 8*, 144 *t. 8*, 200–201, 207, 211, 243–44n34, 266n1; Parcel 14, 64 *t. 2*, 89 *fig. 8*, 127, 136, 138 *t. 7*, 140 *t. 8*, 200, 201, 242n17; Parcel 15, 26, 64 *t. 2*, 129, 136, 138 *t. 7*, 141–42 *t. 8*, 146–47, 217, 218; Parcel 16, 138 *t. 7*, 253n36; Parcel 17, 138 *t. 7*, 253n36; Parcel 18, 64 *t. 2*, 136, 138 *t. 7*, 142 *t. 8*, 170; Parcel 19, 26, 64 *t. 2*, 83, 138 *t. 7*, 142 *t. 8*, 172, 202, 203, 211–12

Belleville Plantation, 215

Belmont Neck phase pottery, 16

Belmont Neck site, 11, 13–14

Berkeley County (SC), 235n67

Big Snake Slough, 42, 104

Big Thicket National Preserve (TX), 186, 188–89

biotic disturbances, 182, 183

Black Branch (SC), 259n23

Blanding, Abram, 48–49

Boggy Gut, 197, 205

Bonneau (SC), 259n23

Bostick, John, 238n30, 239n37

bottomland tree species, profitability of, 154, 154 *t. 10*

Braddy's Cattle Mound, 41, 198

Braddy's fields, 198

Brady (Braddy), Jack, 59, 177

Brady/Braddy family 198, 246n14

Brady, Larry, 177

Brady, Leo, 177–78

Brady tract (101–42), 176–78, 197, 209, 237n21, 262–63n75

Brailsford, Samuel, 84

Branchville (SC), 92, 203, 242n19

Brewton, Miles, 70, 72, 208, 212–13

bridges, 107, 151, 155, 204

Brite Savannah Plantation, 96, 216, 243n27

Broad River, 8, 18, 190

Brooklyn Cooperage Company, 157

Brown, Catherine, 42

Brown, Thomas R., 247n23

Bruner (A. P.) tract (101–34), 178, 181

Bruner, A. P., 144 *t. 8*, 178

Buckhead Island, 206, 227n26

Buckhead Neck, 88, 98–99, 203–4, 227n26

Bull, Stephen, 239–40nn38–39

Bull, William, Jr., 70, 72, 84, 207, 212, 239–40nn38–40

Bullard Landing site (GA), 222n31

Bulls Hill, 207

burial sites, 221n6

burial urns, 221n6

burning, 184

Burnside, Marion T., Jr., 137 *t. 7*

Butler, George, 237n20

Butler, Pierce, 48, 77

Butler's Island, 237n20

butt rot, 46

Buxton, Julian T., 162

Buyck (Russell L.) tract (101–36), 179–80

Buyck (W. Peter Sr.) tract (101–35), 178, 180–81

Buyck, Augustine, 199, 207, 241n16

Buyck, Celia Kennerly, 208

Buyck, David D., 33, 138 *t. 7*, 144 *t. 8*, 207–8

Buyck, Elizabeth B. Wise, 129, 140 *t. 8*, 207, 208

Buyck, Peter A., 33

Buyck, Pieter, 207

Buyck, Russell L., 179–80, 208, 263n86

Buyck, William L., 129, 137 *t. 7*, 143 *t. 8*, 208, 253n37

Buyck, W. Peter, Jr., 180

Buyck, W. Peter, Sr., 91–92, 97, 178, 179, 180–81, 208, 263n86, 266n29

Buyck Cotton Company, 208

Buyck family, 199, 241n16, 246n14

Buycks Bluff, 15

Buyck's Ring, 199

Calhoun County (SC), 246n14, 254n50, 263n86, 266n29

Calkins, William, 25–26

Camden (SC), 14, 16

Camden rail line, 38–39, 225–26n18, 242n19

Camp, J. Beidler, 163

campsites, 9

cane, 24, 80, 189; pollen, in archaeological studies, 14

canebrakes, 24–26, 27, 28, 46, 120, 121 fig. 11, 158–59, 189–90

cane fires, 24–25, 189–90

Cantwell, R. C., 196, 198–99

Cape Fear River, 13

Carolina Planter, 99

Carolina Veneer Company, 159–60, 168, 172

Carpenter, Joy Buyck, 33–34, 104, 208

Catawba River, 13, 14

Catawba tribe, 23–24, 211, 223n46

Catesby, Mark, 24, 28, 192–93

Cat Island, 239n35

cattle: agricultural abandonment and, 113–14; colonial-era/antebellum raising of, 40–46; feral, 225n10; free-ranging, 30–31, 40–41, 45–46, 109; grazing and, 45–46, 113–14, 192

"cattle mounds," 10, 40–41, 101, 104, 107, 198, 199, 200

Cedar Creek, 70, 74, 96, 102–3, 146, 147, 200, 218, 233n48, 238n24

Cedar Creek Hunt Club, 192

Cely, John, 27, 46, 71 map 6, 80, 105–7, 171, 184

censuses: 1790, 69; 1810, 77, 244n39; 1820, 77; 1850, 59, 109, 208, 213, 218, 247–48n25; 1860, 64 t. 2, 109; 1880, 36; slaves listed in, 244n39

ceramics, 41

champion trees, 179, 180–81

Charleston (SC), 127–28, 236n13

Charleston, Siege of (1780), 211, 216

Charleston City Gazette, 83, 85, 87

Charleston Daily News, 38

Charleston Mercury, 92, 100

Charleston News and Courier, 255n61

Chastain silty clay loam (soil type), 111, 111 fig. 9

Chenopodium (chenopod), 11

Cheraws District (SC), 70

Cherokee Indians, 30, 47, 215, 231n16

Cherokee Path, 29

Chesnut, Mary Boykin, 101

Chewacla loam (soil type), 111

Chicago Mill and Lumber Company, 2

chiefdoms, 11–12

Chittenden, Alfred K., 45, 119–23, 120–23 figs. 10–15, 152 fig. 17, 153–55, 154 fig. 18, 256n74

Civil War: agricultural abandonment and, 115; Bates' Ferry skirmish during (1865), 204; canebrakes during, 25–26; Congaree landowners serving in, 215, 217; economic devastation caused by, 100; floodplain burning discontinued following, 46; livestock decline following, 44; Sherman's Carolina Campaign destruction during, 203, 243n30

Clarendon County (SC), 128

Clarkson, Thomas B., 52

Clarkson, W., 89

clear-cutting, 106, 157, 164–66, 167, 172, 178, 181

climate change, 158

Clinton, Henry, 213

Coate, Marmaduke, 65 fig. 7, 94, 197–98, 214, 226n19, 243n33

Cofitachequi (Mississippian polity), 13–15, 18, 19 map 4, 21 map 5, 23, 27

"Cofitachequi: Ethnohistorical and Archaeological Evidence" (DePratter), 19 map 4

Columbia (SC), 119, 153, 159, 215, 236n13, 256n67

Columbia Board of Trade, 118–19, 128

Columbia Civic League, 125

Columbia Furniture and Manufacturing Company, 174

Columbia rail line, 38–39, 92, 203, 225–26n18, 242n19

Columbia Register, 41, 116

Colvin, Martin C., 259n23

Colvin, William J., 259n23

common law, 40

condemnation actions, 259n10

Confederate Army, 217

Congaree Bluffs, 15

Congaree Bluffs Heritage Preserve, 17, 84, 207

"Congaree Boat," 37, 227n33

Congaree loam (soil type), 111, 111 *fig. 9*

Congaree Lumber and Veneer Company, 129–31, 130 *t. 5*, 168, 172, 251n12

Congaree National Park: archaeological investigations in, 8; Beidler Tract in, xiv map 1; boardwalk/trail system in, xvi map 3, 56, 98; chronology, xiii; cultural features of, 107–8, 108 map 9, 195–204, 195 map 11; designation as national park, 1–3, 36, 125, 159; dominant tree species in, 184–88; expansion of, 258–59n8; floodplain soil in, 111–12, 111 *fig. 9*; loblolly pine clusters in, 102–3; logging in, 181; old-growth bottomland hardwood forest in, 1, 2, 4–6; parcel/tract numbers, xv map 2; resource management challenges in, 193; Santee landholdings in, 253n34; tree growth rates in, 219–20n5; use of term, 22; vegetation map of, 105–7, 106 map 8, 246–47n17; visitor center at, 98; as window onto the past, 192–93. *See also* Beidler Tract

Congaree National Park—human disturbance impact: difficulties involved in calculating, 182–83; ecological change and, 188–93; non-human disturbance vs., 183–88

Congaree River, 8; agricultural patterns along, 101–2; canebrakes along, 25–26, 28; early European settlement along, 29–31; early land plats along, 26; embanking of, 89, 90–92; farming economy along, 48; ferries on, 81–82, 84, 206, 218; flooding on, 87–88, 117–18, 231n18; logging near, 34; runaway slaves hidden near, 112; snag clearing on, 39, 128–29, 196; soil quality near, 48–49; steamboat traffic on, 32, 37–38, 39, 118–19; timber holdings along, 136; timber shipments on, 132, 132 *t. 6*, 253n40

Congaree River plantations (early): Bull plantation, 84; flooding impact on, 85–86; Gillon plantation ("Gillon's Retreat"),

77, 197, 209, 210, 237–38n21; Huger plantation, 81–84; land acquisition for, 69–70; Lightwood plantation, 79–81, 238n27, 238n30; maps, 71, 93; Mazyck tract, 78–79, 238n24; Middleton plantation, 72–73, 236n7; Mitchell tract, 77–78; Pinckney/Rutledge plantation ("Precipice"), 73–77, 74–75 *t. 4*, 214, 236n13; proliferation of, 84–85; Wise plantation, 70–72

Congaree Swamp, 34, 38–39

Congaree Swamp National Monument: establishment of (1976), 4, 163–64, 178, 210; expansion of, 166–67, 170–71; logging in, 178; opposition to formation of, 259n23; SC citizen-action campaign in support of, 3–4

Congaree Swamp National Natural Landmark, 260n38

Congaree Swamp Woodland Mound (38RD327), 10

Congaree tribe, 23, 223n46

conquistadors, 5. *See also* De Soto, Hernando; Pardo, Juan

conservationism, 125–26, 134, 159, 162, 258n8

Constitutional Convention (1787), 213–14

Continental Army, 211, 215

Continental Congresses, 214

contract system, 115

Cook, John, 50, 231n16

Cooks Lake, 39, 94–95

Cooner, Frederick, 92, 100, 198, 201, 208, 241–42n17

Cooner family, 246n14

Cooner's Cut, 201

Cooner's Dam, 92, 242n17

Cooner's Mound, 41, 104, 113, 198, 208

cordwood, 36–39

corn: abandoned cultivation of, 114–15; colonial-era/antebellum cultivation of, 48, 60, 61–66, 64 *t. 2*, 80, 207; cotton grown along with, 61–62; cotton-to-corn ratio, 234n56; dikes built for, 91–92; flooding and, 67, 86; floodplain cultivation of, 100; growing season of, 62. *See also* maize

cotton: bottomland soils and, 62, 66–67, 86; colonial-era/antebellum cultivation of, 61–62, 66–68, 216; corn grown cotton: corn grown along with (*continued*) along with, 61–62; flooding and, 67, 86; growing season of, 62; Peterkin variety, 129, 213; political advocacy for, 206; price booms, 63, 88–89, 244n40; price drops, 243n27; production decline, 109–10; short-staple, 76–77; in Singer Tract (LA), 102; -to-corn ratio, 234n56

cotton gin, 66

"Cotton Is King" speech (J. H. Hammond), 206

cotton plantations, 66–68, 108–10, 248n29

cottonwood, 12 *fig. 1*, 120, 122 *fig. 14*, 129, 139, 152, 153–54, 154 *t. 10*, 180–81

Council Brothers, Inc., 165, 177, 261n75

Council Lumber Company, 179

Cowpen Gut, 198

cowpens, 41–44, 104, 118, 198

coyotes, 192

Creech, F. B., 137 *t. 7*

Creighton, William, 50, 231n12

Cross, M. B., 156, 252n31

"cutoffs," 107

cypress, bald, 78, 83, 120, 122 *fig. 13*; demand for, 139; drying methods for, 257n76; false rings of, 256n63; floodplain microtopography and, 12 *fig. 1*; logging of, 34, 36, 129, 136, 151–52, 157, 203; nationwide overproduction of, 155–56; northern timber industry interest in, 126–27; old-growth stands of, 136, 151–52; profitability of, 3, 32, 154 *t. 10*, 155–56; qualities of, as wood, 34, 127; rapid thinning out of, on Congaree River, 139; regeneration of, 157–58, 184, 191, 265n25; Santee rights to, 3, 139, 140–45 *t. 8*, 181, 256n63

dams, 91–92, 190

Darby, Annie M., 254n50

Darlington District (SC), 90

Davidson, Chalmers, 108–9

Davis, Grace W. Adams, 64 *t. 2*

Dawson, Francis, 198

Dead River Gut, 227n29

Declaration of Independence, 214

deer, 191–92, 266n29

De la Vega, Gacilaso, 20, 223n36

Denmark (SC), 259n23

DePratter, Chester B., 19 map 4

De Soto, Hernando, 16–17, 18–20, 19 map 4, 23, 222n31

Dibble, Samuel, 254–55n50

dikes, 59, 67–68, 85, 90–92, 101, 107, 113, 114, 201, 202, 235n67. *See also* Adams Pond Dike; Northwest Boundary Dike; Old Dead River Dike system

disease, 23, 111, 135, 136, 155

Dolsen, Robert B., 134

Douglas, Marjory Stoneman, 1

Doyle, Tom, 185–86

draft animals, 147–48

drainage ditches, 104, 107, 197

Drayton, John, 58–59, 62, 64

drought, 27, 63

"Dr. Weston's Quarter," 98, 201–2

Dry Branch, 96

Dubose, Samuel, 85

Duffie, W. J., 137 *t. 7*, 140 *t. 8*

Duffie, W. K., 137 *t. 7*, 140 *t. 8*

Duffies Pond, 32, 233n48, 243n27

Earl, James, 43 *fig. 3*

Eastern Lumber Company (Tonawanda, NY), 134, 207, 209

ecological change, 188–93

Edisto River, 226n25

Ehrlich, L. S., 128

Elder, Jim, 3, 105, 107

Elliott (barge), 159

Elliott, Barnard, 70, 208

Elliott, John E., Jr., 168

Elliott, Susannah Smith, 208

Elliott, William, 68

Elliott family, 168

Elliott Tract (101–33), 168

elm, 12 *fig. 1*, 114, 120, 186

Elm Savannah Plantation, 243n30

EmaE Orata (Hymahi cacique), 20–21

endangered species, 24

English explorers, 23, 223n46

English settlers, 47

epidemics, 23

European exploration period (1520–1670 C.E.), 220n1

European settlement: early, 28–31; hide trade during, 191–92; land disturbances caused during, 183–84; logging activities during, 31–36, 225n14

Eutaw Springs (SC), 134–35

Evans, Joshua, 47

Everglades National Park, 1

Everleigh, Thomas, 211

Fagus grandifolia, 190

Farrar, Benjamin, 31, 50, 208, 231n16

Faulkner, James E., 137 *t. 7,* 140 *t. 8,* 253n38

Federalist Party, 214

fence rows, 104, 197

feral stock, 192, 225n10

Ferguson (SC), 34, 135, 150, 155, 156, 159, 161, 252n31, 255n61

Ferguson, B. F., 3, 134, 136, 156, 209, 252n24

ferries, 81–82, 84, 107, 119, 199, 202, 203–4, 206, 218, 236n10

fields, 107

fires, 24–25, 26, 27, 103, 120, 156, 158–59, 183, 189–90

First South Carolina Regiment (Infantry), 211

Fishburne, Ann, 209

Fishburne, Richard H., 49, 86

Fishburne, William H., Jr., 49, 85–86, 209, 210

Fishburne, William, Sr., 209

Fishburne family, 73

Fisher, Tucker H., 137 *t. 7*

fishery, 196

Flint River, 14

float roads, 146–47, 149

flooding: 1796 ("Great Yazoo Freshet"), 87, 88, 95; 1840, 88, 95; 1852, 88, 227n26; 1886, 116, 199; 1928, 228–29n53; as abiotic disturbance, 182, 183; agricultural abandonment and, 117–18; cattle mounds and, 228–29n53; during colonial/antebellum eras, 50, 85–86, 88; cotton production and, 68; damages from, 199; dikes built for, 68; European settlement patterns and, 30, 231n18; floodplain cultivation and, 110–11; Mississippian period agriculture and, 17; plantation agriculture and,

69; pulses, 241n4; reclamation efforts and, 87–89, 95; southern bottomland hardwood forest and, 187; timber industry and, 131–32

floodplain environment, 12–13, 12 *fig. 1,* 17–18

floodplain reclamation: advocacy for, 99–100; within Congaree National Park boundaries, 92–100, 242–43n27; cost/risks of, 100; early efforts, 89–92; flooding and, 87–89, 95

floodplain soil, 111–12

flood scouring, 4, 26

flood signal service, 40, 150

foot adze, 82

forest: even-aged, 45, 102–7, 108, 114, 120, 184–85, 188, 198; shade-tolerance in, 186–90; uneven-aged, 103, 164, 245–46n6. *See also* southern bottomland hardwood forest

forest management, 164–65, 173

forestry, 134, 163, 180–81

"Forks of the River" area, 23

Fork Swamp area, 9, 22, 127, 129, 174–76, 247n23

Fort Motte, 70, 112, 204, 207, 240n40

Fort Motte Lumber and Shingle Company, 131–32, 168, 172, 203

Fort Watson Mound, 14, 16, 18

Four Holes Swamp, 258n8

4th South Carolina Regiment (Artillery), 208

Francis Beidler and Company (Chicago, IL), 133, 207, 252n31

Francis Beidler Forest, 258n8

Fraser, Charles, 131

Frazier's Farm, Battle of (1862), 217

freedmen, 115, 249n49, 266n1

free-ranging stock, 30–31, 40–41, 45–46, 109

French and Indian War, 54, 70

French Huguenots, 210, 231n15

Frenchman's Pond, 209, 231n12

Frentz, John, 198, 209, 231n12

Frost, Frank R., 137 *t. 7*

Frost, W. B., 137 *t. 7*

furniture factories, 153

Gaddy, L. L., 103–4, 105, 165–66, 245–46n6

Gagnon, Paul, 24

Gaillard, Elizabeth, 208
Gaillard, Peter, 85
Gaillard, Tacitus, 208
Georgetown (SC), 128, 135
Georgetown Board of Trade, 128
Georgia, 222n31
Georgia-Pacific Corporation, 165, 167, 170–72, 173–74, 261n45
Germany: early settlers from, 29, 47; immigrants from, 115, 213; POWs from, 3
Gibbes, James G., 251n9
Gibbes, J. Heyward, 228–29n53
Gibbes and Thomas (real estate firm), 127–28, 249n34
Gillon, Alexander, 70, 77, 197, 207, 209–10, 214, 237–38n21
Gills Creek, 29
girdle farming, 118
Glen, James, 26, 53
Goodson, Aesop, 200
Goodwill Plantation, 58, 90
Goodwyn, Boswell, 210
Goodwyn, Francis, 49, 197, 209, 210, 214, 237n21
Goodwyn, Jesse, 210
Goodwyn, Martha, 50
Goodwyn, Martha Epps, 210, 233n48
Goodwyn, Robert, 210
Goodwyn family, 31, 216
"Goose Pond" (short story; E.C.L. Adams), 96
Graham, Benjamin, 137 t. 7
Granby (SC), 87
grazing, 45–46, 113–14, 184, 192
Great Cane Brake, Battle of (1775), 215
Great Lakes states, 126
Great Pee Dee (snag boat), 39
Great Pee Dee River, 15, 90, 98
"Great Yazoo Freshet" (1796), 87, 88, 95
Green, Edwin L., 56, 96
Greene, Nathanael, 81, 204, 215
Green Hill, 29
Green Hill Mound (38RD4), 15, 221n6
grist mills, 226n19
Grovewood Plantation, 96, 217, 243n27
Guilford Courthouse, Battle of (1781), 81, 211
Guiomae. See Hymahi (Mississippian village)

Gum Tree Plantation, 96, 97, 98, 205–6, 216–17. See also Pine Bluff Plantation
"guts," 40, 57

hackberry, 120
Hahn, T. Michael, 171
Hammond, Harry, 31, 88, 114–15
Hammond, James Henry, 31, 88, 94, 206, 225n14, 226n21, 228n39
Hampton, Harry R. E., 2, 36, 125, 200, 210, 245n4
Hampton, Wade, I: biographical sketch, 210; Congaree landholdings of, 48, 51, 205, 233n48; cotton grown by, 66, 76–77; political influence of, 215; SC capital location debate and, 236n13; slaveholdings of, 60
Hampton, Wade, II, 68, 90–91, 95
Hampton family, 101
Harcombe, Paul, 186, 188–89
hardwoods: logging of, 152–55, 152 fig. 17; southern bottomland hardwood forest, 4–5, 182–83, 186–87; uneven-aged, 245–46n6; veneer production and, 129. See also specific species
Hardy, Meredith, 41
Harmon, Belton, 169–70
Harvey (LA), 135
Harvey, Brantley, 165–66
"headright" system, 29–30
hemorrhagic fever, 135
hemp, 78, 80
Heritage Trust Program (SC Natural Resources Dept.), 172–73
Herlong, Mrs. H. A. D., 140 t. 8
hickory, 12 fig. 1, 114, 179, 230n6
hide trade, 191–92
High Creek Plantation, 15
Hildebrand, J. S., 137 t. 7, 143 t. 8
Hilton, William, 13
Hoffman Lumber Company, 145 t. 8, 167
hogs, 30–31, 192, 225n10
Holly Hill Lumber Company, 167, 169–70, 172–73, 178, 259n23
Holly Hill Tract (101–32), 167
home sites, 107
Hoofman, Phillipina, 78

Hooker's Old Field, 26
Hopewellian tradition, 9–10
Hopkins, John, 58
Hopkins, Laura Jervey, 249n41
"Horsepen Gut," 40
horses, feral, 225n10
House, Reuben, 239n37
Howe, Robert, 217
Howell, Martha, 42, 50
Howell, Thomas, 42
Howell, William, 42, 54
Howell family, 31
Hudson, Charles, 18–19, 19 map 4
Huger, Daniel, 90, 210
Huger, Daniel, II, 58
Huger, Isaac, 55 *fig. 5*, 77; biographical
    sketch, 210–11; Cat Island plantation of,
    239n35; Congaree River plantation of,
    70, 81–84; Congaree slaveholdings of, 55;
    ferry of, 202; land acquisitions of, 211; as
    lowcountry planter, 55; Revolutionary
    War military service of, 81; on Sumter's
    plundering, 240n40
Huger's Ferry, 202, 236n10, 238n27
Huguenots, 210, 231n15
Hunt, Alfred M., 64 *t. 2*, 97, 200–201, 211
hunting, 28, 46, 184, 192
hurricanes: 1822, 185; canebrake disappear-
    ance and, 159; Congaree diversity and,
    4; Congaree forest composition and,
    103, 107, 184, 185; Gracie (1959), 161–62;
    Hugo (1989), 103, 107, 114, 120–23, 159,
    180, 181, 184, 185, 187–88; salvage logging
    following, 161–62, 180, 181; Sea Islands
    Hurricane (1893), 185; southern bottom-
    land hardwood forest and, 182–83
hydrology: altered, 158, 190–91; floodplain,
    187
hydropower, 190
Hymahi (Mississippian village), 15, 17, 19–22,
    19 map 4, 21 map 5

Immigration Society of Richland Fork, 115
Indians, 23; declining populations of, 24,
    27; intertribal conflicts, 223n46; land
    disturbances caused by, 22, 183–84;
    post-contact land use of, 23–27; settlers

attacked by, 29; Spanish contact with,
    18–22, 19 map 4, 21 map 5; travel routes
    of, 204. *See also* Mississippian Period
    (900–1520 C.E.); Woodland Period (1000
    B.C.E.–900 C.E.)
Indian traders, 28
indigo, 78; colonial-era/antebellum cultiva-
    tion of, 48, 52–58; cultivation of, within
    park boundaries, 56–57, 96–97; dikes
    built for, 91–92; flooding and, 67; free-
    range cattle and, 28; post-Revolution
    market collapse of, 66, 86, 87; production
    process, 57–58; vats for, 53, 56–57, 58, 73,
    112, 202–3. *See also* indigo plantations
Indigo Branch, 56
indigo plantations, 28, 52–58, 60, 70, 72–73,
    80, 207, 216
"Indigo Vat Gut," 57
indigo vats, 202–3
insects, 183
invasive species, 192
Irish immigrants, 115

Jackson, Miles, 203
Jacob (slave), 225n14
James Adams (pole boat), 226n20
James Adams (steamer), 32, 226n20
James Island (SC), 211
Japanese stilt grass, 192
Jaudon, Elias, 238n27
Jeffers, H. L., 249n49
Jefferson, Thomas, 214
J. H. Rathborne and Company, 134
Joe (runaway slave), 112
Jones, Robert, 104–5, 184
Joyner, Robert, 247n23
Joyner's Ferry, 203–4
Junction Mining Company (Springfield,
    IL), 207

Kaminer, John J., 143 *t. 8*
Kearse, Chester M., Jr., 180
Kearse Manufacturing Company (Olar, SC),
    165
Kelsey and Guild (landscape architecture
    firm), 125–26
Kennedy, James, 239n37

Kershaw, Joseph B., 215
kiln drying, 257n76
Kingsnake Trail, 42, 113
Kingville (SC), 38, 59, 132, 148, 214, 228n38, 242n19, 259n23
Kingville East tract (101–73), 172–74
Kingville West tracts (101–44/101–45/101–46), 168–72
Kinzer, Mark, 71 map 6
Kirkland, Moses, 231n16
Knights of Spain, Warriors of the Sun (Hudson), 19 map 4
Knoth, R. F., 164, 182
Kochaline (stern wheeler), 159

Lake Marion Dam, 235n67
Lamar Mounds and Village site, 222n31
Lamar period pottery (1350–1600 C.E.), 15–16
land grants, 29–30, 42, 49–50, 54, 101, 231n12, 231n14
land speculation, 50
land valuations, 119, 230nn6–7
Lang Syne Plantation, 116–17, 129, 213, 251n9
Laurelwood Mansion, 214
Lawson, John, 23, 223n46
Lee, Henry ("Light-Horse Harry"), 204, 240n40
levees, 90–91. *See also* dikes
levees, natural, 12–13, 12 *fig. 1*, 17, 22
levee zone, 104, 111, 123, 185, 241n4
Lexington County (SC), 29, 32, 255n56
Lieber, Oscar M., 62–63
lightning, 26
Lightwood, Edward, 79–81, 202, 211, 238n27, 238n30, 239n37
Lightwood's Old Field, 26, 79, 80, 211
Ligustrum spp., 192
Limerick Plantation, 210
Liquidambar styraciflua, 34
Live Oak Plantation, 206, 243n30
livestock, 40–46, 69, 109, 225n10, 228–29n53
Log Castle tract, 234n66
log fords, 147–48
logging, 5–6, 45, 203; animal-powered, 147–48; colonial-era/antebellum, 31–36, 225n14; early regulations, 226n25; environmental impacts of, 157–58, 185;

historic, 197; land disturbances caused by, 184; national park campaign begun as result of, 3–4; post-1920, 104; railroad, 148–51, 254–55n50, 255n56, 255n61; salvage operations, 161–62, 180, 181; selective, 178; steam-powered, 148–50, 157; telltale signs of, 184; vegetation associations and, 106
logging, industrial (1870–1918): agricultural abandonment and, 119, 123–24; cost of, 148, 148 *t. 9;* decline of, 159–60, 161, 168, 172; early conservation efforts and, 125–26; northern timber industry and, 126–32, 130 *t. 5,* 132 *t. 6;* river vs. railroad transport in, 254–55n50; transportation costs, 127–28. *See also* Santee River Cypress Lumber Company
logging, post-1920: in Beidler Tract (1969–1976), 162–66, 166 map 10; east of Beidler Tract, 168–76; north of Beidler Tract, 166–68; south of Beidler Tract, 176–81
logging camps, 107, 139–46, 198–99, 254n43
logging roads, 107, 179, 261–62n75
logging trams, 148–51
log skidders, 254n49
Lord, Andrew, 238n22
Lord, John, 238n22
Lord Lake, 238n22
Lords Proprietors, 53
Lossing, Benjamin, 99
Louisiana, 2, 25, 101–2, 135, 183
Louisville, Cincinnati, and Charleston Railroad (LC&CRR), 228n38
Loyalists, 84, 207, 215, 239–40nn38–40
Lucas, Eliza, 53–54
Lumbermen's Mutual Insurance Company (Chicago, IL), 207

Madison, James, 214
Madison Parish (LA), 102
Magnolia Plantation, 243n30
maize, 11, 12–13, 17–18, 22, 224n57. *See also* corn
malaria, 111, 135, 136, 155
maples, 120
Map of Early Land Grants, Congaree National Park (Cely), 71 map 6

Map of Original Land Grants, Congaree Swamp National Monument (Cely), 71 map 6
Marion, Francis, 204, 209, 213, 240n40
Marion, Lake, 167, 235n67
Martin, Joseph, 42, 44, 49, 73, 198, 199–200, 214
Martineau, Harriet, 90–91
Mattoon, Wilbur, 149, 157
maygrass, 11
Mazyck, Isaac, 50, 79, 238n26
Mazyck, Mary, 238n24
Mazyck, Peter, 78–79, 201, 212, 238n24
Mazyck, William, 50, 79, 212, 238n26
Mazyck, William, Jr., 79
Mazyck family, 201, 231n15, 238n24
Mazyck's Cut, 79, 201, 212, 238n24
McCord, David, 204, 213
McCord, John, 204, 211
McCord, Louisa Cheves, 213
McCord, Sophianisba Russell, 85, 204, 211
McCord's Ferry, 34, 81, 119, 202, 204, 236n10
McDaniel, Robert, 168, 171
McJacob's Old Field, 26
McKelvie, James, 50, 78
McKenzie, Daniel, 64 *t. 2*, 211–12
McKenzie, Laura J., 145 *t. 8*
McKenzie, Marion, 179, 263n86
McKenzie, Ross S., 138 *t. 7*, 142 *t. 8*
McKenzie, Sultan W., Jr., 138 *t. 7*, 142 *t. 8*
McKinley, William, 155
McKnight, J. Sid, 161, 164–65
McLeod Plantation Historic Site (Charleston County, SC), 211
McMaster, Monteith and Roath, 127, 172, 174, 176, 203
Medlin, William F., 26
Meitzen, Kimberly, 246n12
Melrose (FL), 217
"Memories of Home Travels" (anon.), 38
Mercier, Elizabeth, 26, 50
Meriwether, Robert, 23
Mexico Plantation, 51–52, 67, 90, 114, 235n67
Michie, James, 15, 63
Microstegium vimineum, 192
Middleton, Henry, 72–73, 76, 214, 236n7

Middleton family, 76
Mill Creek, 23, 29, 30, 31, 42, 48, 60
Miller, D. G., 97, 114
Miller, Lawrence E., 259n23
Milliken, William, 151
Milliken Forestry Company, 180
millponds, 32
Mills, Robert, 32, 48, 50–51, 52, 62, 66, 109
Minchin, Peter, 105
Mississippian Period (900–1520 C.E.): cultural development during, 11–15; intertribal conflict during, 18; land use during (pre-contact), 7–8, 15–22, 224n57; time spans assigned to, 220n1
Mitchell, Eliza, 203, 247n23
Mitchell, Ephraim, 212
Mitchell, John, 45, 50, 77–79, 212
Mitchell, John A., 203, 212, 247n23
Mitchell, Washington, 212
Mitchell, William A., 212, 247n23
Mitchell's Mound, 41, 203
Mitchell's Quarter, 106–7, 203
Mock, Cary, 185
Moderator movement, 231n16
Monteith, Walter S., 127, 174
Moore, Peter, 231n14
Morris, Lewis, 240n40
Morton, Rogers, 260n38
Motte, Elizabeth, 213
Motte, Frances, 213
Motte, Jacob, Jr., 208, 212, 213
Motte, Mary Brewton, 212, 213
Motte, Rebecca Brewton, 70, 72, 85, 208, 212–13, 215, 240n40
Moultrie, William, 208
mounds, 10, 15, 18, 107, 198, 199, 228–29n53
Mount Joseph Plantation, 212, 213
Muckenfuss, Michael, 50
mulberries, 16, 20
Mullers Barn Ridge (38CL18), 15
Murphy, John D. A., 243n33
Murray, W. J., 36
Muskegon (Mich.) Chronicle, 139–46
Myers, David, 202, 218
Myers Creek, 58

National Audubon Society, 2, 171, 258n8

National Park Service: Beidler Tract purchases of, 159, 161, 163–64, 166, 167, 171,
175–76, 177–78, 254n43, 258–59n8; Congaree Swamp research studies of, 2, 45,
151, 162; publications of, 178, 261–62n75;
resource management challenges of, 193;
Tract 101–21, 248n32; Tract 101–24, 141 t.
8; Tract 101–25, 141 t. 8; Tract 101–32, 141
t. 8, 143 t. 8, 145 t. 8, 167, 218; Tract 101–33,
168, 206, 245n42; Tract 101–34, 144 t. 8,
181; Tract 101–35, 89 fig. 8, 92, 180–81,
201, 208, 215, 242n17, 263n86; Tract
101–36, 144 t. 8, 179–80, 208, 263n86;
Tract 101–37, 143 t. 8, 178–79, 208; Tract
101–41, 143 t. 8, 178, 208; Tract 101–42,
176–78, 197–98, 205, 209, 210, 214,
237n21, 262n75; Tract 101–44, 144–45 t.
8, 168–72, 203; Tract 101–45, 168–72, 203;
Tract 101–46, 26, 168–72; Tract 101–73,
172; Tract 101–74, 174–76; Tract 101–75,
174–76; tract numbers, xv map 2
National Park Service Southeast Archaeo-
logical Center, 221n6
National Park System, 1–2, 163
Native Americans. See Indians
Natural Resources Conservation Service,
247n25
Nature Conservancy, 2, 258n8
"Negro cabin," 200–201
Neuffer, Charles, 213
New Oxford (Pa.) Item, 251n12
New Road, 107, 179, 261–62n75
Nicotiana sp. (tobacco), 11
Ninety Six, Battle of (1775), 215
North Carolina, 29, 190
North-Eastern Railroad, 127–28
Northwest Boundary Dike, 92–96, 114, 196
Nyssa aquatica, 157

oak, 120, 128; agricultural abandonment and,
114; cherrybark, 105, 184, 219n5, 246nn6,
13; floodplain microtopography and, 12
fig. 1; growth rate of, 219–20n5; land valuations and, 230n6; logging of, 34, 172–74;
old trees, in Beidler Tract, 246n6; pollen,
in archaeological studies, 14; profitability
of, 32, 119, 154, 154 t. 10; Santee timber

leases and, 139; shade-intolerant and
intermediately intolerant species, 184–87;
vegetation associations and, 105–7,
246n15, 247nn17, 19
Oaks Plantation, 217, 218
oats, 67
Ocmulgee National Monument, 222n31
Ocmulgee River, 14, 222n31
Oconee River, 14
Ocute (Mississippian chiefdom), 18
O'Hanlon, James, 67, 234n66
Ohio River Valley, 10
Old Dead River, 200, 216, 237n20, 243n33
Old Dead River Cattle Mound, 200
Old Dead River Dike system, 59, 63, 98, 99,
200, 201, 227n29
"old fields," 26–27, 42, 80, 103–4
Orangeburg County (SC), 134, 199
Orangeburg County Court of Common
Pleas, 199
Orangeburgh District (SC), 55, 79
Orangeburg Times and Democrat, 40–41
orchards, 16
oxbow lakes, 39, 88

Paleoindian Period (12,000–8000 B.C.E.), 7
Palmetto Lumber Company, 129, 141–43 t. 8,
146–47, 174, 253n34
Panic of 1837, 63, 243n27
Pardo, Juan, 16, 20–22, 21 map 5, 23, 204
Partial Chain of Title Covering The Principal
Floodplain Tracts within Congaree Na-
tional Park (Kinzer), 71 map 6
pastures, 107, 114
Pauling family, 246n14
Pearce, S. A., 128
Pea Ridge Plantation, 113, 205, 206, 249n41
Pee Dee phase pottery (1200–1550 C.E.), 16
Pee Dee River, 14, 87
Perkins, Francis M., 138 t. 7
persimmon, 180, 184, 263n91
Peterken, George, 114
Peterkin, James A., 129, 130–31, 160, 168, 172,
213, 251n9, 253n34
Peterkin, John A., 129, 203
Peterkin, Julia Mood, 116–17
Peterkin's mill, 130–31

Phalaris caroliniana (maygrass), 11

Pinckney, Charles, 48, 51, 76–77, 212

Pinckney, Charles Cotesworth, 43 *fig. 3;*
    biographical sketch, 213–14; Congaree
    River plantation of ("Precipice"), 63, 70,
    73–77, 74–75 *t. 4*, 214, 236n13, 237n20;
    corn grown by, 63, 76; cotton grown
    by, 76–77; death of, 237n20; financial
    difficulties of, 73; as indigo planter, 53, 55,
    76; land leased by, 199; land purchases
    of, 42, 44; law practice of, 73; ledgerbook
    of, 74, 74–75 *t. 4;* Revolutionary War
    military service of, 209; Rutledge and, 73;
    SC capital location debate and, 236n13;
    slaveholdings of, 77; as slavery supporter,
    69, 213–14

Pinckney, Elizabeth Motte, 213

Pinckney, Harriott, 237n20

Pinckney, Maria Henrietta, 237n20

Pinckney, Thomas, 213

Pinckney's Neck, 237n20

pine, 78; agricultural abandonment and,
    114; as cordwood, 39; in fence rows, 197;
    floodplain microtopography and, 12 *fig.*
    1; loblolly, 14, 27, 45, 46, 56, 59–60, 82,
    95, 98, 102–3, 113–14, 184, 245n4, 246n6,
    257n76; longleaf, 13, 35, 126, 226n19,
    246n6; old tree, in Beidler Tract, 246n6;
    old-growth, as evidence of abandon-
    ment, 27, 45, 49, 56, 60, 82, 95, 98, 102–3,
    105, 108, 113–14; pollen, in archaeological
    studies, 14; profitability of, 119; Santee
    timber leases and, 139, 181; white, 126;
    yellow, 37, 129

Pine Bluff Plantation, 110, 116, 217, 249n34.
    See also Gum Tree Plantation

Pinus palustris, 13

Pinus strobus, 126

Pinus taeda, 27

plantation agriculture: corn, 61–66; cotton,
    66–68; indigo, 52–58; rice, 58–61; rise of,
    47–52, 69–70. *See also specific crop*

plant communities, floodplain, 12 *fig. 1*

planter, use of term, 225n11

Pleistocene Era, 5

Pond Bluff mill site (Eutaw Springs, SC),
    134–35

Populus deltoides, 129

Populus heterophylla, 129, 181

Porcher, Philip, 238n24

Porcher, Samuel, 51–52, 67, 90, 99, 235n67

potatoes, 60

Pough, Richard H., 2

"Precipice" (Pinckney/Rutledge plantation),
    73–77, 74–75 *t. 4*, 214, 236n13

predators, elimination of, 191–92

Pregnall (SC), 259n23

Prince Georges Parish, 239n35

Pringle, Robert, 239–40n38

prisoners of war, 3

privet, 192

provision crops, 48, 52, 61, 62, 70, 80, 86

Quercus pagoda, 105

rafts, 35, 227n29

railroad logging, 148–51, 254–55n50, 255n56,
    255n61

railroads: during Civil War, 203; cordwood
    as fuel for, 36; logging and access to,
    127–28, 151; river transport vs., 127–28,
    254–55n50; Santee Canal and, 225–26n18;
    SC line construction, 228nn38–39; slaves
    hired out to build, 92, 242n19; in swamp-
    land, 38–39, 155

Ramsay, David, 27, 85

Rangel, Roderigo, 7, 20

Rathborne, Joseph, 134, 135

Rawls, Benjamin A., 203

Rawls, Mary D., 144–45 *t. 8*

Rebel Lumber Company, 175

Reconstruction Era, 115–17, 266n1

Red Gum, The (Chittenden), 119–23, 120–23
    figs. 10–15, 152 *fig. 17,* 154 *fig. 18,* 256n74

Red Shirts, 215

Regulator movement, 231n16

Republican Party, 215

Revolutionary War. *See* American Revolu-
    tion

rice plantations, 28, 53, 58–61

Richland County (SC), 263n86; agriculture
    in, 69; corn plantations in, 62, 63, 234n56;
    cotton plantations in, 77, 108–10, 234n56;
    early logging in, 32, 35–36; farmland in,

Richland County (SC), farmland in
(*continued*)
247–48n25; first European settlement in,
29; floodplain soils in, 69–70; founding
of, 215; population decline in (1850s), 109;
population increase in, 47–48; post-Civil
War economy of, 115–16; railroad con-
nections to, 228n38; Red Shirt movement
in, 215; rice plantations in, 58–59, 63; SC
Land Commission acquisitions in, 266n1;
slaveowners in, 54–55, 66 *t. 3*, 69, 108;
stock law in, 44–45
Richland County Register of Deeds, 159,
253n34
Ricker, Elizabeth, 237n21
R. L. Moore Lumber Company (Bowyer,
SC), 259n23
road beds, 104
roads, 81–82, 107, 146–47, 149–51, 179,
261–62n75
Roanoke River, 190
Robinson, Solon, 109
Roosevelt, Theodore, 25
Royal Council, 208
Ruffin, Edmund, 51–52, 67, 88, 91, 99, 104,
112, 113–14, 235n67
Running Gut, 200
Running Lake Slough, 57, 170, 173–74, 202
Russell, Eugenia, 211
Russell, Sophianisba, 211
Rutledge, Edward, 43 *fig. 4*; biographical
sketch, 214; Congaree River plantation
of ("Precipice"), 63, 73–77, 74–75 *t. 4*,
214, 236n13, 237n20; corn grown by, 63,
76; cotton grown by, 76–77; as indigo
planter, 53, 55, 76; land purchases of, 42,
44; Pinckney and, 73; SC capital location
debate and, 236n13; slaveholdings of, 55

St. Helena Island, 207
St. John's Episcopal Church (Congaree, SC),
216
St. Matthews (SC), 29, 207, 210–11, 212
Saluda Dam, 190–91
Saluda River, 18, 190
Sampson Island, 9, 17
sand ridges, as burial sites, 221n6

Santa Elena (Spanish settlement), 22, 28
Santee Canal, 112, 225–26n18
Santee Canal Company, 226n18
Santee Cooper, 162, 167
Santee River, 14, 16, 20, 86; bridges over, 151,
155; canebrakes along, 25–26; flooding
on, 87; floodplain reclamation on, 87;
snag clearing on, 128; timber holdings
along, 136; timberland acquisitions on,
131
Santee River Cypress Lumber Company:
animal-powered logging by, 147–48;
Bates (John M.) as employee of, 146,
150, 198, 206; Beidler Tract assembled
by, 3; bottomland logging costs, 148, 148
t. 9; environmental impacts of, 157–58;
establishment of, 134; Ferguson mill
site of, 135, 150, 155, 156, 252n31, 255n61;
Ferguson operations ceased, 148, 150, 156,
159, 161; financial difficulties of, 155–56;
fire suppression policies of, 158–59; land
acquisitions for, 45, 131, 132–33, 136–39,
137–38 *t. 7*, 140–45 *t. 8*, 155, 174, 176, 178,
181, 207–8, 217, 252n24, 252–53nn33–34,
254n50, 255n56; leadership of, 207, 209;
liquidation/dissolution of, 162–63; logging labor for, 135–36; logging methods
of, 139–46, 198–99, 201; Pond Bluff mill
site of, 134–35; reorganization of, 252n31,
255n60; steam-powered equipment used
by, 148–50, 157, 255n61; as sweet gum
research study site, 119–23, 120–23 *figs.*
10–15, 153–55, 187, 256–57n74; trusteeship
of, 163
Santee Swamp, 85, 151, 157, 253n40
Santee tribe, 23
Satilla River, 207
Savannah, Siege of (1779), 211, 217
Savannah River, 14, 42, 88, 94, 104, 219–20n5,
225n14
saw, circular, 34
sawmills, 31–32, 35–36, 107, 110, 132, 203,
225n14, 226n19
Saxe Gotha Township, 23, 29, 31, 50, 61, 208
Scott, Samuel, 197
Scott, William, Jr., 67, 197–98, 210, 214
Scott, William, Sr., 214

Scott family, 31
Scott's Quarter, 197–98
Seabrook, Whitemarsh, 67–68, 87
Seay, James H., 59, 64 *t. 2*, 109, 214, 247n23
Seay, Thomas, 109, 206, 214
secession movement, 211
2nd South Carolina Regiment (Infantry), 208
sediment deposition, 4, 12–13, 12 *fig. 1*, 158, 191, 220n6
Seeley, Fred, 135–36, 149, 155, 252n31, 256n74
Seminole Wars, 226n20
Sewee Indians, 25
shade tolerance, 186–90
shad fishery, 196
sharecropping, 115
Sharitz, Rebecca, 105, 188
Sherman, William T., 203, 243n30
shingle mills, 36, 131–32
Silver Bluff Plantation, 88, 225n14, 226n21
Silver Lake Stock Farm, 45, 144–45 *t. 8*, 203
Sims Trail, 103
Singer Tract (LA), 2, 101–2, 183
Singleton, John, 90, 95
Singleton, Matthew, 52
Singleton tract, 234n66
Sinkler, James, 85
Sinkler, Peter, 85
Sitton, Thad, 40
6th South Carolina Regiment (CSA), 217
slave quarters, 107, 198
slavery, inland spread of, 53
slaves, 34; during American Revolution, 240n40; as "cattle hunters," 40; in censuses, 244n39; floodplain reclamation by, 97–98; hiring out of, 242n19, 244n40; on indigo plantations, 54–55, 57–58; land clearing by, 89, 183–84; narratives of, 101; "planters" as owners of, 225n11; post-Revolution escapes/killings of, 87; on rice plantations, 60–61; Richland County ownership of, 54–55, 66 *t. 3*; runaway, 112; taxes on, 230n7
slave trade, 70, 206, 212
Smith, L. Russell, 176
Smith, Nellie G., 176
Smith, Susannah, 208

snag clearing, 39, 196
soil erosion/pollution, 4, 157
soil exhaustion, 109
soils, floodplain, 111–12
Soucie, Gary, 1
South Atlantic Coastal Plain, 17
South Branch Lumber Company, 133, 134, 207, 209
South Carolina: capital location debate in, 236n13; colonial-era land-grant policy of, 29–30; colonial-era racial imbalance in, 29; Constitution ratified by, 213–14; cotton booms in, 63, 88–89; cotton exports of, 77; early settlement of, 28–31; floodplain reclamation in, 90; frontier, cowpens in, 42; human occupation in, 7–8, 8 *t. 1*; indigo as commercial staple in, 56, 58; logging in, 31–36; Mississippian culture in, 13–15; mound-building era in, 15; post-Revolution economy in, 87; railroad system in, 203; rice as commercial staple in, 56; transporation infrastructure of, 81; wood products market in, 31
South Carolina (frigate), 207, 210
South Carolina & Georgia Railroad, 147
South Carolina Agriculture Department, 117
South Carolina Bar, 208
South Carolina Court of Appeals in Law, 201
South Carolina Gazette and Country Journal, 31
South Carolina General Assembly, 100, 202, 210, 211, 214, 225–26n18, 226n25, 236n10
South Carolina House of Representatives, 91–92, 161, 177, 206, 216
South Carolina Immigration Commission, 36
South Carolina Land Commission, 200, 266n1
South Carolina Natural Resources Department, 172–73, 180, 210
South Carolina Ordinance of Secession, 206
South Carolina Public Service Authority. *See* Santee Cooper
South Carolina Rail Road Company, 131, 228n38
South Carolina Sinking Fund Commission, 129, 266n1

South Carolina State Historic Preservation
Office (SHPO), 220n1
South Carolina Wildlife and Marine Re-
sources Department, 210
South Carolina Wildlife Federation, 171
southern bottomland hardwood forest:
as disturbance-mediated ecosystem,
4–5, 182–83; old-growth, in Congaree
National Park, 1, 2, 4–6; 119–24; research
studies of, 119–23, 120–23 figs. 10–15;
sweet gum reproduction in, 186–87
Southern Literary Messenger, 38
Southwest Boundary Dike, 59, 196–97
Spanish conquistadors, 5. See also De Soto,
Hernando; Pardo, Juan
Spigener, Paul, 64 t. 2, 88, 97, 201, 208, 215,
241–42n17, 244n34, 244n40
Spigener family, 246n14
Spigener Regrant, 88, 89 fig. 8
Stanley, Charles D., 142 t. 8
Starling, Wesley D., 41, 197, 199, 215
Starling's Mound, 10, 41, 146, 199, 221n6
Starling's Quarter, 199
Starling's Upper Stock Farm, 197
State (newspaper), 119, 126, 131, 139, 150,
152–53, 160, 210, 242n26
Statistics of South Carolina (Mills), 50–51
steamboats, 32, 36, 37–38, 118–19
steam skidders, 148–50, 157, 255n61
stilt grass, 192
stock law, 44–45
stockmen, 28
stone tools, 13
Stoney Hill Plantation, 98, 202, 245n42,
249n49
Stono Ferry, Battle of (1779), 81, 211
storms, 103, 120, 182–83
stream migration, 4
Stroyer, Jacob, 52, 89
stumps, 197
sugarberry, 12 fig. 1, 35, 105–7, 165, 186, 246n6
Sullivan, Michael, 50, 78, 231n12
Sullivan's Island, Battle of (1776), 215, 217
Sumter, Thomas, 84, 215, 236n13, 240n40
Sumter Stave Company, 159
Survey of Richland District (Coate), 65 fig. 7,
94, 197–98, 214, 226n19, 243n33

Sus scrofa, 192
Swansea Lumber Company, 165, 178,
261–62n75
sweet gum: agricultural abandonment and,
102, 105–8, 114, 184; as champion trees,
179; commercial importance of, 119,
152–53, 165, 256n67; drying methods for,
257n76; early unprofitability of, 34–35;
even-age, 103, 114, 184–85; floodplain
microtopography and, 12 fig. 1; old tree,
in Beidler Tract, 246n6; old-growth, 46,
185; pasture abandonment and, 45; phase,
105–7, 246–47n17; profitability of, 154 t.
10; regeneration of, 184, 186–87; research
studies of, 119–23, 120–23 figs. 10–15,
153–55, 187; veneer production and, 129
Switzerland, 29
sycamore, 120, 165

Tanner, James T., 1, 2, 102, 183
Tarleton, Banastre, 204
Tawcaw silty clay loam (soil type), 111, 111
fig. 9
Taxodium distichum, 3
Taylor, Edward B., 138 t. 7, 142 t. 8
Taylor, Guy, 59, 64, 97, 196–97, 221n6,
227n29, 254n49
Taylor, Thomas, 48, 215
Taylor, Vassar H., 138 t. 7, 142 t. 8
Taylor family, 101
Tennessee Gut, 57
Tensas Bayou, 25
Tensas River, 2, 102
Texas, 186
Third South Carolina Regiment (Rangers),
215, 216, 217
Thomson, Eugenia Russell, 211
Thomson, William, 56 fig. 6; biographical
sketch, 215–16; Congaree River planta-
tion of, 85; cotton grown by, 76; family
of, 57; as plantation overseer, 72–73, 84,
207; Revolutionary War military service
of, 217; slaveholdings of, 55
Thomson, William Russell, 57, 72–73, 112,
202–3, 216
Thomson family, 246n14
Thurmond, Strom, 167

timber industry, 126–32, 155–56

timber leases, 127, 132, 136–39, 137–38 *t. 7,* 140–45 *t. 8,* 173

tip-up mounds, 4

tobacco, 11, 66

Toccoa loam (soil type), 111

toll bridges, 206

Tomlinson Engineering, 65 *fig. 7*

Toms Creek, 81, 98, 99, 112, 221n5

trade, 9–10, 11

tram roads, 149–51

tree growth rates, 219–20n5

tree-ring studies/counts, 4, 6, 95, 101, 113–14, 118, 185–86, 245n4, 246n6

Trumble, James, 213, 247n23

Trust for Public Land, 175

Tucker, Christian Grace, 216, 244n34

Tucker, Isaac, 44

Tucker, Isaac Raiford, 97, 216

Tucker, William, 216

Tucker family, 31, 244n34

tupelo, water, 12 *fig. 1,* 120, 121 *fig. 12,* 154 *t. 10,* 157–58, 184

United States Agriculture Department, 35–36

United States Army Corps of Engineers, 36, 128, 198, 201, 203, 246n12, 253n40

United States Congress, 39, 166–67, 178

United States Forestry Bureau, 34, 114, 119–23, 134, 139, 153

United States Forest Service, 149, 154, 154 *t. 10,* 164, 186–87

United States Hotel (Columbia, SC), 211

United States House of Representatives, 210

United States Senate, 206

United States Weather Bureau, 40, 117

Upper Santee Swamp Natural Area, 167

U.S. Plywood Corporation, 138 *t. 7,* 174–75

Vawser, Bartholomew, 237n21

veneer, 129, 160, 165, 256n67

Vermivora bachmanii, 24

Vestal Lumber and Manufacturing Company, 175

Virginia, 29

Wagner, Gail E., 220n1

walnuts, 16

Walterboro (SC), 259n23

warbler, Bachman's, 24

War of 1812, 86, 210

Washington, George, 73, 213

Washington, William, 81

Wateree Embankment Company, 100

Wateree River, 8, 11, 13, 14, 15, 16, 18, 20; early land plats along, 26; embanking of, 89–90; flooding on, 87, 89; floodplain reclamation on, 87; plantation land acquisition along, 69; rice plantations along, 58; snag clearing on, 39, 128; timber holdings along, 136

Wateree tribe, 23

Watkins, James, 131

Webb, David, 50

Webster, Daniel, 68

Weston, Grace, 73, 205

Weston, Isaac Tucker, 46, 64 *t. 2,* 98, 103, 108, 116, 217, 248n32, 249n34

Weston, Malachi, 96–97, 216

Weston, Robert, 96

Weston, Thomas, 216

Weston, Thomas Philip, 46, 116

Weston, William, I, 96, 205, 216

Weston, William, II, 96, 216

Weston, William, III: biographical sketch, 216; Congaree River plantation of, 96–98, 110, 217; death of, 248n31; dike construction of, 97–98, 243–44n34, 244n34; family background of, 96; as hunter, 46; loblolly pine stands on land of, 103; logging by, 33; slaveholdings of, 97–98

Weston, William, IV, 98, 115, 201–2, 216, 217, 218, 243n30

Weston, William W., 116, 129, 137 *t. 7,* 140 *t. 8,* 217

Weston family, 31, 40, 68, 108, 244n34, 248n29

Weston Lake, 96, 103, 216

Weston's Quarter, 201–2

wheat, 66

Whitehall Plantation, 214

Wilderness Act (1964), 181

Wilderness of Ocute, 18–19
wild hogs, 192
Williams, David Rogerson, 90, 98
Williams, James B., 138 *t. 7,* 140 *t. 8*
Williams, James R., 200
Williams, Jerry, 200
Williams, John G., 200
Williams Furniture Company (Sumter, SC),
    162, 165, 171, 261n45
wills, 101
wind disturbance, 4, 26, 27, 107, 182–83, 185.
    See also hurricanes
Wise (Frank W.) tract (101–37), 178–79
Wise, Frank W., 137 *t. 7,* 143 *t. 8*
Wise, Frank W., Jr., 179
Wise, Jane Ann, 218
Wise, Moses Felder, 144 *t. 8*
Wise, Samuel, 70–72, 209, 217–18
Wise family, 178, 179, 246n14, 263n86
Wise Lake, 70, 218
Woodland Period (1000 B.C.E.–900 C.E.):
    Early (1000 B.C.E.–500 B.C.E.), 9; land use

during, 7, 8–11, 221nn5–6; Late (500–
    900 C.E.), 10–11, 221n6; Middle (500
    B.C.E.–500 C.E.), 9–10, 13, 17, 221nn5–6;
    time spans assigned to, 220n1
Woodmason, Charles, 55, 57
woodpecker, ivory-billed, 1–2
Woods and Waters and Some Asides (H.
    Hampton), 200
Woodward, Caroline E., 218
Woodward, Isom, 217, 218
Woodward, Lieuellan, 59, 64 *t. 2,* 108, 211–12,
    217, 218, 248n29
Woodward family, 68, 108

Yamassee War (1715–1718), 223n46

Zea mays (maize), 11, 224n57
Zeigler, Daniel, 64 *t. 2,* 199, 218
Zeigler family, 116, 246n14
Zeigler's Ferry, 199

About the Author

Mark Kinzer is an environmental protection specialist in the Southeast Regional Office of the National Park Service in Atlanta, Georgia. Before joining the National Park Service in 2003, Kinzer was an environmental lawyer in private practice in Atlanta. He is a graduate of Davidson College and the University of Georgia School of Law.